D0214504

Peace and Freedom

POLITICS AND CULTURE IN MODERN AMERICA

Series Editors: Michael Kazin, Glenda Gilmore, Thomas J. Sugrue

Books in the series narrate and analyze political and social change in the broadest dimensions from 1865 to the present, including ideas about the ways people have sought and wielded power in the public sphere and the language and institutions of politics at all levels— national, regional, and local. The series is motivated by a desire to reverse the fragmentation of modern U.S. history and to encourage synthetic perspectives on social movements and the state, on gender, race, and labor, on consumption, and on intellectual history and popular culture.

Peace and Freedom

The Civil Rights and Antiwar Movements in the 1960s

SIMON HALL

PENN

University of Pennsylvania Press

Philadelphia

10 9 8 7 6 5 4 3 2 1

Published by
University of Pennsylvania Press
Philadelphia, Pennsylvania 19104–4011

Library of Congress Cataloging-in-Publication Data

Hall, Simon, 1976–
    Peace and freedom : the civil rights and antiwar movements in the 1960s / Simon Hall.
        p.   cm. (Politics and culture in modern America)
    ISBN 0-8122-3839-7 (cloth : alk. paper)
    Includes bibliographical references (p.) and index.
    1. African Americans—Civil rights—History—20th century. 2. Civil rights
movements—United States—History—20th century. 3. African Americans—Politics and
government—20th century. 4. Vietnamese Conflict, 1961–1975—Protest movements.
5. Peace movements—United States—History—20th century. 6. United States—Race
relations. 7. United States—Social conditions—1960–1980. 8. United States—Politics
and government—1963–1969. I. Title. II. Series
E185.615 .H274   2004
959.704´3´8996073—dc22   2004055478

For Olive, a friend and mentor

Contents

Introduction

In February 1966, world heavyweight champion Muhammad Ali was in Miami, training for his title defense against Eric "the Octopus" Terrell. One afternoon a television reporter sought Ali's reaction to the news that the Louisville Draft Board had upgraded his draft status from 1-Y to 1-A, thereby making him eligible for immediate induction into the United States Army. Ali's retort, "I ain't got no quarrel with the Viet Cong," helped define an era. Fourteen months later Ali refused induction, explaining "I am not going ten thousand miles from here to help murder and kill and burn another poor people simply to help continue the domination of white America."[1] Ali's response to the war in Vietnam seemed to many to epitomize a new militancy within Black America. The October 1966 platform of the Black Panther Party demanded that all African Americans be exempted from military service—"Black people should not be forced to fight . . . to defend a racist government that does not protect us." The Panthers refused to "fight and kill other people of color who, like black people, are being victimized by the white racist government in America."[2] Stokely Carmichael and the Student Nonviolent Coordinating Committee (SNCC) attacked the war too. Speaking at one antiwar march, Carmichael defined the draft as "white people sending black people to make war on yellow people to defend land they stole from red people."[3]

It was not just black militants who were critical of America's actions in Vietnam. The Rev. Dr. Martin Luther King, Jr., the nation's most important and most respected civil rights leader, also condemned the war in the strongest possible way. In the spring of 1967, King bitterly denounced the "madness of Vietnam" and called on his government to take the initiative in halting the conflict.[4] Indeed, by the time that the Paris Peace Accords were signed in January 1973, every major civil rights leader had spoken out against the war.

The years between 1960 and 1972 saw the emergence of two of the most significant social movements in American history—the African American freedom struggle and the movement to end the war in

Vietnam. This book sets out to offer a detailed analysis of the relationship between them, by exploring two key themes.

First, the response of the various civil rights groups to the war is documented and explained. Although a large number of civil rights groups opposed the war early on—including SNCC, the Congress of Racial Equality (CORE), and Martin Luther King's Southern Christian Leadership Conference (SCLC), the civil rights movement was far from united in its reaction. Important organizations like the National Association for the Advancement of Colored People (NAACP) and the National Urban League did not initially support civil rights groups speaking out against the war and did not adopt antiwar positions until the end of the 1960s.

Second, the nature of the relationship between antiwar civil rights organizations and the mainstream peace movement is analyzed. On the surface there were good reasons why they should have cooperated closely: many early white opponents of the war were veterans of the civil rights movement; African Americans had powerful reasons to oppose the war in Vietnam; and the two movements shared a similar critique of American society. For a variety of reasons, though, a meaningful coalition was never constructed. Nothing better illustrates this than the fact that at both the 1967 March on the Pentagon and the demonstrations at the 1968 Democratic Convention in Chicago, two protests that have come to symbolize the peace movement in the popular imagination, African Americans were conspicuous by their absence.

Any account of the relationship between the peace and freedom movements must acknowledge the historical background to this story. From the abandonment of the freed people by Republicans during Reconstruction through to the present, the relationship between Afro-America and white radicals has rarely been straightforward. With regard to the modern black freedom struggle, the 1930s saw widespread cooperation between white leftists and the nascent civil rights movement. The U.S. Communist Party (CPUSA) took the lead, becoming a fierce opponent of racism and a champion of civil rights. This commitment was epitomized by their vigorous defense of the Scottsboro Boys—nine blacks who were falsely accused of raping two white women on a freight train in Alabama in 1931. But despite their courageous stands on civil rights and bold advocacy of racial justice, Communists proved to be less than reliable allies—often because of their propensity to switch policy dramatically at the request of the Kremlin. Even their involvement in Scottsboro was controversial. The NAACP, for example, believed that the CPUSA was more interested in discrediting the American legal system and recruiting new members than in actually securing the release of the black plaintiffs. The Communists, meanwhile, condemned the NAACP as "bourgeois misleaders."

During the Popular Front period (1934–1939), when the CPUSA made common cause with the non-Communist left, tensions between black activists and Communists continued. The National Negro Congress (NNC), a coalition of almost every important black group in America, represented a "coming together of left-wing radicalism, labor militancy, and heightened racial consciousness," according to Adam Fairclough. Set up in 1936, it was headed by Asa Philip Randolph, founder of the Brotherhood of Sleeping Car Porters, the first all-black union. But he resigned in 1940 in protest at Communist manipulation of the NNC and their efforts to secure its opposition to U.S. entry into World War II. Indeed, the CPUSA's U-turns on the war following the Nazi-Soviet Pact and then the launch of Operation Barbarossa caused many former allies, white and black, to view Communists as little more than incorrigible cynics. Nevertheless, there had been signs of black-white tension within the Congress before Communist manipulation came to the fore. In his inaugural address Randolph had welcomed white support, but noted that "in the final analysis, the salvation of the Negro . . . must come from within." This was a theme that he returned to when organizing his March on Washington in January 1941 to oppose racial discrimination in the armed services and defense industries. Believing that "all oppressed people must assume the responsibility and take the initiative to free themselves" he restricted the effort to blacks only. Another reason for excluding whites was to reduce the chance of Communist manipulation.[5]

There were other leftists and non-communist socialists who appealed for black support and responded to black needs during the New Deal era. In 1932 Myles Horton, a graduate of New York's Union Theological Seminary, founded the Highlander Folk School in Tennessee. Dedicated to promoting the tenets of grassroots, interracial democracy, Highlander produced two generations of civil rights and labor activists and symbolized the best about relations between black activists and white leftists. Organized labor also became increasingly responsive to black concerns during this period and made big efforts at unionizing black workers—for pragmatic as well as ideological reasons (white employers frequently used blacks as strike breakers). The militant trades unions of the Congress of Industrial Organizations—especially the United Auto Workers, led by Walter Reuther, and John L. Lewis's United Mine Workers, which organized workers without respect to race—were particularly appealing to blacks. The civil rights movement's increasing orientation toward the labor movement was most clearly indicated in 1941, when NAACP executive secretary Walter White traveled to Detroit to rally black support for a UAW strike against the Ford Motor Company. Nevertheless, white working-class racism remained a significant obstacle to interracial unionism, and many of the CIO's southern leadership were reluctant to attack Jim Crow—due both to personal prejudice and a desire not to alienate white workers.[6]

Despite McCarthyism's decimation of the legacy of the interracial leftist activism of the 1930s and 1940s, this prehistory is important. While the experiences of the New Deal era showed that interracial cooperation on the American left was both possible and potentially fruitful, it also revealed the problems and obstacles that existed. These problems—black fears of cooptation by white leftists; concern that whites sought black support merely to legitimate their own radicalism; and the sense of whites as potentially unreliable allies—would all characterize the relationship between the peace and freedom movements during the sixties.

The civil rights movement's response to the Vietnam War and its relationship with the peace movement was also shaped by the historic links between the black movement and American pacifism. Although not all black critics of the war were pacifists, some of the earliest and most prominent were—or else held a deep commitment to the philosophy of nonviolence. Though a product of a number of factors the antiwar positions of people like James Farmer (CORE), Bob Moses and John Lewis (SNCC), and Martin Luther King were shaped by pacifism and Gandhianism. While historians such as Tim Tyson have shown that perceptions of "the civil rights movement" as wholly nonviolent are simplistic, the black freedom movement of the 1950s and early 1960s tended to use nonviolent direct action as its weapon of choice, and did so to great effect. Moreover, there were a number of important organizational and personal links between the black movement and American pacifism. Activists with the Fellowship of Reconciliation (FOR), for example, founded the Congress of Racial Equality in 1942. FOR, a nondenominational body that rejected violence and war, was headed by Abraham J. Muste—a six-foot tall, gaunt, thin, one-time Communist turned dedicated Christian pacifist. Muste became a key figure in the 1960s peace movement. CORE's leader in the early 1960s, James Farmer, had helped found the organization while race relations secretary with FOR. A man of "robust physique" who "spoke with the resonant tones of a Shakespearean actor," Farmer refused to fight in World War II (he was granted a draft deferment). He also helped pioneer the application of Gandhian tactics to the civil rights struggle—launching a number of sit-in protests in Chicago during 1942, for example. Farmer himself represents the intersection of the pacifistic and leftist traditions within black America, and also offers a link with the New Left of the 1960s. As well as opposing World War II, Farmer briefly worked for the League for Social Democracy—a non-communist, pro-union social democratic organization. During his tenure as student field secretary, he worked for the

Student League for Industrial Democracy, the forerunner of Students for a Democratic Society (SDS), the most influential radical student organization of the 1960s.[7]

SNCC was one of the most militant civil rights groups of the 1960s. Founded at Shaw University in April 1960, it engaged in grassroots organizing in an attempt to nurture indigenous black leadership and build community institutions. Its young organizers, fired by a faith in the ability of ordinary people to make their own decisions and committed to interracial cooperation, sought to build the "Beloved Community" in some of the most inhospitable areas of the Deep South. Like CORE, SNCC had strong links with the pacifist movement. James Lawson, who helped draw up the organization's founding statement—a searing advocacy of Christian love and redemptive nonviolence—had chosen prison rather than military service during the Korean War. He subsequently became FOR's first southern field secretary. In the late 1950s he played a vital role in stimulating nonviolent civil rights activism in Nashville. Bob Moses, an icon of the civil rights movement and leading SNCC activist was another who had moved in pacifist circles. At the end of his junior year at New York City's Hamilton College he had worked at a European summer camp sponsored by the pacifist American Friends Service Committee. Moses was also influenced profoundly by existentialism—particularly Albert Camus' emphasis on the need to cease being a victim without becoming an executioner.[8]

Although his political odyssey during the 1960s took him toward the right, in the 1950s Bayard Rustin, like Farmer, represented the intersection of the leftist and nonviolent traditions within the black movement. Rustin, a man of athletic build (he had been a high school track and football star) with a deeply moving tenor voice, had been raised by his maternal grandparents in West Chester, Pennsylvania, where he was heavily influenced by his grandmother's Quaker beliefs. Rustin, who became a sincere pacifist himself, had been a member of the Communist Party in the 1930s, remained a disciple of black labor leader A. Philip Randolph, and at various times worked for FOR and the War Resisters League. His pacifism led to his resignation from the Communist Party in 1941 when it supported World War II, and also resulted in him serving time in prison as a conscientious objector.

Rustin, an intellectual, raconteur, and keen collector of antiques, became an important force within the civil rights movement. Although his conviction on a "morals charge" (he was caught having sex with two men in a car in Pasadena) meant that he was excluded from public leadership, Rustin exerted considerable influence behind the scenes. For example, during the Montgomery Bus Boycott he helped tutor Martin Luther King in nonviolent philosophy, and he was the organizational mastermind behind the awesome 1963 March on Washington, at which King delivered his "I have a dream" oration.[9] Moreover, through his friendship with Tom Kahn, one of the few white undergraduates at Howard University and a member of its Nonviolent Action Group, Rustin acted as mentor to a number of activists who would play important roles in SNCC. These included Stokely Carmichael, Charles Cobb, Courtland Cox, Ruth Howard, and Mike Thelwell. Carmichael in particular was impressed by Rustin's ability to link social democratic politics with the struggle for black rights.[10]

Other important links between pacifism and the black movement included *Liberation Magazine*, a journal edited by David Dellinger, a pacifist and future anti-Vietnam War movement leader (Rustin was a coeditor). In the 1950s *Liberation* offered its support to the civil rights movement, publishing the first piece of political journalism to carry Martin Luther King's byline. Moreover, many of the civil rights movement's earliest white supporters came from pacifist circles. A number of white participants in the Freedom Rides of May 1961, for example, were veterans of the pacifist movement.[11] Attempting to build links between the 1960s peace movement and the civil rights movement, then, at one level represented a return to the movement's pacifist roots, and provided at least some common ground on which to construct a coalition.

Frequently portrayed as excessively patriotic in its support for American foreign policy, black opposition to the war in Vietnam has often been viewed as representing a major break with the past. W. E. B. Du Bois's 1918 exhortation calling on blacks to forget their "special grievances" and "close ranks" with white Americans and the allied nations in support of World War I has been seen as representative of black attitudes toward U.S. foreign policy. But this represents at least a partial misreading of history.[12] Indeed, the twentieth century witnessed frequent fierce black criticism of American foreign policy. Gerald Horne, for example, has argued that African Americans "have been among the vanguard of anti-imperialism and militant political activity."[13] Far from representing a break with the past, black leaders' responses to Vietnam were part of a long tradition of critical engagement with U.S. foreign policy.

Between 1915 and 1920, for instance, the NAACP opposed American military involvement in Haiti—the world's first black republic. Following a detailed investigation by the Association's executive secretary, James Weldon Johnson, the NAACP demanded a withdrawal of American troops, and suggested that American policy toward Haiti was racist.[14] In the 1920s, Garveyism linked black American progress with a strong and independent Africa, and Garvey himself urged African Americans to fight for Africa, not America.[15]

The 1930s and 1940s saw much criticism of colonialism by black organizations and leaders. Mussolini's invasion of Ethiopia in 1935 generated particular condemnation. On August 3, 1935 approximately 25,000 blacks attended a rally in Harlem organized by the Provisional Committee for the Defense of Ethiopia, a popular front group. The rally's sponsors included A. Philip Randolph, Lester Granger of the Urban League, and the NAACP's Roy Wilkins.[16] Many blacks were also active in popular front activities in support of the Republicans in Spain. In Harlem, the American League Against War and Fascism organized a number of peace marches and conferences in the spring of 1937. Once again Roy Wilkins joined a host of other black activists in supporting popular front actions, believing that African Americans had much to gain by working in anti-fascist organizations that were sensitive to civil rights.[17] By the mid-1940s, the NAACP's opposition to colonialism was strong. Along with the National Negro Congress it had signed the "Declaration by Negro Voters," calling for an end to imperialism and colonial exploitation.[18] In March 1946, NAACP executive secretary Walter White warned that blacks were "determined once and for all to end white exploitation and imperialism."[19] Moreover, throughout the 1940s and early 1950s the pages of the Association's magazine, *The Crisis*, often contained articles attacking Western colonialism and empathizing with liberation struggles throughout the Third World.[20]

Although black America exuded patriotism during the Second World War, attempts were made to use war abroad to gain racial progress at home—the so-called "Double-V" campaign.[21] While the NAACP supported the war against Nazism it, along with A. Philip Randolph's March on Washington Movement also pushed for reforms such as fair employment practices and the desegregation of the military.[22] This tactic of placing demands for civil rights within a wider framework of patriotism and national service—a tactic that had been used by blacks since the founding of the nation—would remain an important model for the civil rights movement, particularly during the early Cold War.

Though the Cold War was originally seen as a total disaster for the civil rights movement, in recent years a rich scholarship has emerged that reconsiders its impact on black America. Historians such as Thomas Borstelmann, Mary Dudziak, Azza Salama Layton, and Penny Von Eschen have shown how the Cold War offered new opportunities to civil rights activists as well as presenting them with new problems.[23] It is clear that McCarthyism generated powerful pressures on black organizations to embrace anticommunism or perish. The NAACP therefore quickly softened its stand on anticolonialism and became a firm supporter of anticommunist measures, domestic and foreign. Those civil rights organizations and activists that did not take such steps, such as the Civil Rights Congress, the Southern Conference Educational Fund, W. E. B. Du Bois, and Paul Robeson were either destroyed or incapacitated as a result.[24]

Nevertheless, at a time when America was championing the cause of world freedom and attempting to win the hearts and minds of recently decolonized third world peoples, the Cold War offered black leaders new opportunities to press for racial progress at home. Civil rights leaders were well aware that domestic racism was an international embarrassment that threatened to undermine America's Cold War mission, and they attempted to use this situation to their advantage by pressing for change at home in order to better fight Communism abroad. America's leaders responded by granting some important concessions.[25]

Some black leaders, however, went beyond this to make broad criticisms of what they viewed as American imperialism. Malcolm X, for example, repeatedly urged African Americans to internationalize the struggle by taking their grievances to the United Nations. It is not surprising, then, that Malcolm was a fierce critic of the war in Vietnam. He believed that the war and domestic racism were related, and he linked the oppression of African Americans with the use of military force against people of color in Asia. Malcolm declared that "this society is controlled primarily by racists and segregationists . . . who are in Washington, D.C., in positions of power. And from Washington, D.C., they exercise the same forms of brutal oppression against dark-skinned people in . . . Vietnam."[26]

Malcolm's views on the war echoed those of Paul Robeson, who in 1954 had condemned American policy toward Vietnam as racist. For Robeson, whose support for the Communist Party line on most issues was well known, Ho Chi Minh was the Toussaint L'Ouverture of Indo-China, and he wondered aloud whether "Negro sharecroppers from Mississippi" would be sent to "shoot down brown-skinned peasants in Vietnam—to serve the interests of those who oppose Negro liberation at home and colonial freedom abroad?"[27] Speaking shortly before his assassination, Malcolm declared that Vietnam, Mississippi, Alabama, and Rochester, New York, were all victims of racism.[28] It was a view that would increasingly be accepted by both the white New Left and the radical black movement.

While Martin Luther King was in many ways less radical than either Malcolm X or Paul Robeson, and tended to engage with the Cold War simply to gain concessions for blacks at home, there is some evidence of the radicalism that characterized his later opposition to Vietnam. In May 1961, King was asked for his reaction to the Bay of Pigs debacle in Cuba. He declared that "For some reason, we just don't understand the meaning of the revolution taking place in the world. There is a revolt all over the world against colonialism, reactionary dictatorship, and systems of exploitation." King continued, "unless we as a nation . . . go back to the revolutionary spirit that characterized the birth of our nation, I am afraid that we will be relegated to a second-class power in the world with no real moral voice to speak to the conscience of humanity."[29] King went on to state that he was as concerned about international relations as he was about the domestic civil rights movement.[30]

In early 1965, as the climactic battle of the civil rights movement was unfolding in Selma, a Cold War conflict came to the fore that would have profound consequences for America. The United States had been sending military advisors to South Vietnam since 1959, having previously supported France's attempt to regain control of her colony. But American involvement increased rapidly after Lyndon Johnson's election in November 1964. The bombing of North Vietnam, which began in February 1965, was followed by the deployment of American ground forces. In early March, two battalions of marines were placed near Danang to defend an air base, and by the middle of June there were approximately 50,000 U.S. troops in Vietnam. The number would more than double by the end of the year.[31] By then, important civil rights groups and leaders, including SNCC, CORE, and King, would either have opposed the war, or signaled extreme unease over it.

African Americans certainly had good reasons to oppose the war in Vietnam. With their racial consciousness raised by the civil rights movement, many blacks wondered why they should fight abroad for a nation that still denied them first class citizenship. As Martin Luther King explained, "we have been repeatedly faced with the cruel irony of watching Negro and white boys on TV screens as they kill and die together for a nation that has been unable to seat them together in the same schools."[32] SNCC chairman Stokely Carmichael urged blacks not to fight since they were denied freedom at home, and went so far as to term black soldiers mercenaries. He explained that a "mercenary will go to Vietnam to fight for free elections . . . but doesn't have free elections in Alabama. . . . A mercenary goes to Vietnam and gets shot . . . and they won't even bury him in his own home town." Carmichael concluded, "we must . . . when they start grabbing us to fight their war . . . say, 'Hell no'."[33] Many civil rights activists argued that, rather than fight in Vietnam, African Americans should instead be focusing their energies on the struggle for change in America.[34]

A second objection to the war derived from the discriminatory nature of the draft. It was not unknown for the Selective Service System to give black militants and civil rights organizers "special attention." In January 1966, for example, the Selective Service announced it was reviewing the Conscientious Objector (CO) status of SNCC's John Lewis because of his recent antiwar and antidraft statements.[35] Mississippi native James Jolliff, an epileptic, found his classification upgraded from 4-F to 1-A after he became president of his local NAACP chapter.[36] The Selective Service also drafted blacks in disproportionate numbers. In the early years of the war African Americans accounted for more than 20 percent of all draftees, despite making up just 10 percent of the U.S. population.[37] A mentally qualified white inductee was 50 percent more likely than a mentally qualified African American to fail his pre-induction physical in 1966, and the following year 64 percent of eligible blacks were drafted compared with 31 percent of eligible whites.[38]

At the same time, there were almost no African Americans serving on draft boards. In 1966 blacks made up just 1.3 percent of total draft board membership. Some board members were staunch racists. Jack Helms, head of the largest draft board in Louisiana, was a Grand Dragon in the Ku Klux Klan.[39] In 1968 the chairman of Atlanta's draft board referred publicly to former SNCC activist Julian Bond as a "nigger" and expressed regret that he had not been drafted.[40] This was not lost on black activists as they formulated their response to the war. SNCC's Walter Collins, for example, denounced the draft as a "totalitarian instrument used to practice genocide against black people."[41]

The fact that America was waging war on a non-white people also caused a good deal of concern among many black Americans. Increasingly, black activists took the position that the war was itself racist. In a posthumously published essay Martin Luther King declared that America's "disastrous experiences in Vietnam . . . have been, in one sense, a result of racist decision-making. Men of the white West, whether or not they like it, have grown up in a racist culture, and their thinking is colored by that fact. . . . They don't really respect anyone who is not white."[42] Carmichael also linked the war to a version of white paternalism that was remarkably similar to King's analysis. He explained that "we are going to kill for freedom, democracy, and peace. These little Chinese, Vietnamese yellow people haven't got sense enough to know they want their democracy, but we are going to fight for them. We'll give it to them because Santa Claus is still alive."[43] Many black Americans developed a sense of racial solidarity with the Vietnamese, as illustrated by the comments of one SNCC fieldworker who stated "you know, I just saw one of those Vietcong guerrillas on TV. He was dark-skinned, ragged, poor and angry. I swear, he looked just like one of us."[44]

Other reasons for African Americans and the civil rights movement to oppose the war in Vietnam included the commitment to the philosophy of nonviolence. Martin Luther King explained that it was becoming impossible for him to speak out against violence in the ghettos whilst refusing to condemn America's use of military force in Vietnam.[45] A more practical reason for opposing the war was its negative effect on Lyndon Johnson's efforts to build a Great Society in the United States. Being disproportionately poor, black Americans stood to gain most from domestic liberal-reform policies like the war on poverty.[46] However, the war in Vietnam helped to undermine the Great Society—both by diverting political attention from the domestic to the foreign sphere and by siphoning off billions of dollars in federal funding that might have otherwise have been spent on welfare programs.[47] King referred to the war as "an enemy of the poor" in April 1967.[48]

Throughout 1965–1972, African Americans appear to have been more opposed than white Americans to the Vietnam War. Opinion polls repeatedly showed that blacks were the "most dovish" social group.[49] In April 1967 the *Chicago Defender* surveyed black opinion regarding the war. The poll showed that 57.3 percent of blacks favored the United States pulling its troops out of Vietnam, always the least popular sentiment among opponents of the war.[50] But black hostility to the war did not translate into active support for the peace movement. Despite widespread opposition to the war within the civil rights movement, and the peace movement's consistent attempts to attract black support, the mostly white antiwar leadership was discussing the lack of black participation in 1972, just as it had been in 1965.[51]

Initially, the civil rights movement responded to the Vietnam War by stressing the discrepancies between America's claims to be fighting for freedom in Southeast Asia while denying millions of blacks basic democratic rights at home. The legitimacy of the war itself was left unquestioned. African American leaders simply tried to use the conflict to increase the pressure on the federal government to meet the movement's demands. For example, shortly before being taken to the hospital for treatment to injuries received on Bloody Sunday, 7 March 1965, during the Selma voting rights campaign, SNCC chairman John Lewis told reporters that he did not understand how President Johnson could send troops to Vietnam but not to Selma, Alabama.[52] On 8 March the NAACP executive committee discussed the violence at Selma, and passed a resolution noting the irony that "the report of these carefully planned attacks on the Negro citizens" shared the "spotlight with the landing of U.S. Marines on Vietnam, sent to protect the Vietnamese against Communist aggression."[53] An editorial in the March edition of the *Crisis* declared that "the entire nation—the leader of the free world—has been compromised by the defiance of law, morality and humanity at Selma. American pleas for the 'free and unfettered ballot' in distant lands has been made an international mockery by Selma's arrant flouting of basic democratic principles."[54]

While attending the Mississippi Freedom Democratic Party (MFDP)

Washington Conference on 25 April 1965, John Lewis again attempted to use the war to advance the black cause. He told the delegates at the Metropolitan AME church that "if we can call for free elections in . . . Saigon, we can call for free elections in Greenwood and Jackson, Mississippi."[55] It would not be long, though, before the radical wing of the civil rights movement abandoned this uncritical approach to the Vietnam conflict and confronted the war head-on.

Chapter 1

The Organizing Tradition

Our criticism of Vietnam policy does not come from what we know of Vietnam, but from what we know of America.

—Bob Moses, 1965

Toward the end of the summer of 1964, civil rights workers from all over Mississippi traveled to Neshoba County to attend a memorial service for James Chaney, Michael Schwerner, and Andrew Goodman. These three civil rights activists, who had been working in the Magnolia State as part of the "Freedom Summer" project, had been abducted and brutally murdered on June 21 after traveling to Longdale, near Philadelphia, to investigate a Ku Klux Klan church-burning. Standing in the quiet sunny glen, amid the blackened rubble of the Mount Zion Baptist Church that had also functioned as a Freedom School, Bob Moses addressed the mourners. Radical historian and activist Howard Zinn recalled that the SNCC leader spoke "with a bitterness we were not accustomed to seeing in him."[1] Moses condemned the federal government for showing great willingness to send troops thousands of miles to Vietnam to defend "freedom" while consistently refusing to provide civil rights workers protection from white violence.[2] Referring to the headline of the morning newspaper, which read "President Johnson Says 'Shoot to Kill' in Gulf of Tonkin," Moses said, "that is what we're trying to do away with—the idea that whoever disagrees with us must be killed."[3] During the early 1960s, as civil rights workers strove to mobilize African Americans at the grass-roots level, they became radicalized by their experiences. This, in turn, helped shape their response to the war in Vietnam.

Between June and August 1964, the SNCC-dominated Council of Federated Organizations (COFO) launched a major civil rights organizing drive in Mississippi. Known as "Freedom Summer," it brought hundreds of white, middle-class northern college students to the Magnolia State to work with veteran black civil rights activists, in a bold and creative attempt to focus national attention on the problems facing Mississippi blacks and compel the federal government to intervene. The project's major strategies were voter registration drives (in Mississippi only 6.4 percent of eligible blacks were registered to vote); the promotion of black dignity and self-respect through the use of Freedom Schools that also taught African Americans vital skills; and the organization of the Mississippi Freedom Democratic Party (MFDP). In organizing the MFDP, black activists were responding to the fact that the regular state party practiced systematic discrimination in order to exclude blacks from the political process. The civil rights movement hoped that the MFDP would undermine the state's lily-white Democrats and help reshape the national party into a more effective force for social change. This would be achieved by pressing for MFDP delegates to be recognized as the official state delegation at the 1964 Democratic Convention, in Atlantic City.[4]

The level of violence encountered by Freedom Summer volunteers and those they worked with in Mississippi was horrifying. Four people were killed, 80 were beaten, 1,000 were arrested, and over 60 churches, homes, and businesses were burned or bombed.[5] Civil rights workers constantly asked the federal government to provide them with protection and were consistently told that it did not have the power to do so. Indeed, the failure of the government to protect activists was an open sore in the movement. As civil rights workers in the early 1960s quickly discovered, the federal government was extremely reluctant to intervene to protect them even when local law enforcement was clearly inadequate. When SNCC activists intensified their voter registration efforts in Mississippi in 1962, for example, they believed that the Justice Department had promised protection—but none was forthcoming. This fact contributed significantly to SNCC's growing disenchantment with the federal government even before Freedom Summer. In his speech at the 1963 March on Washington, for example, SNCC chairman John Lewis addressed the lack of federal protection for civil rights workers when he asked, "what did the federal government do when Albany's deputy sheriff beat attorney C. B. King and left him half-dead? What did the federal government do when local police officials kicked and assaulted the pregnant wife of Slater King, and she lost her baby?"[6]

The answer to those questions was, at best, "very little." The government took the position that law enforcement was the responsibility of the states and that the constitutional "balance of powers" prevented it from taking decisive action where local law enforcement was nonexistent or, as was often the case, part of the problem. At the Oxford, Ohio, orientation sessions for the Freedom Summer volunteers, for example, the Justice Department's John Doar explained that the government was unable to offer protection to the civil rights workers because there was no federal police force and it was unwilling to create one.[7] SNCC activists, in contrast, held a much broader view of federal authority. Supported by numerous legal experts, they argued that the federal government was obliged to guarantee first amendment rights that were protected by the fourteenth amendment. Furthermore, they insisted that the government could use the powers assigned to it under Section 242, Title 18 and Section 3052, Title 18 of the U.S. code. These provisions provided for the punishment of those who denied citizens their constitutional rights and allowed the FBI to make arrests, without warrants, "for any offense against the United States committed in their presence."[8] SNCC activists, along with others in the civil rights movement, considered it the duty of the president, as the ultimate defender of the Constitution, to enforce the laws in every part of the Republic, including the South.

The federal government, however, often gave the impression that it was more concerned with placating southern Democrats, mollifying the potential "white backlash," and constraining dissent than with upholding or enforcing the constitutional rights of African Americans. President Johnson refused to meet Freedom Summer leaders to discuss the issue of protection before the project began, and when a group representing the parents of volunteers requested a meeting, Johnson again declined. Presidential assistant Lee White told LBJ that "it is nearly incredible that those people who are voluntarily sticking their head into the lion's mouth would ask for somebody to come down and shoot the lion."[9] It should be noted, however, that this attitude was not new. Dwight Eisenhower, a gradualist on civil rights, was reluctant to use the power of the federal government on behalf of black rights. This reflected both his personal empathy with white southerners and his strong belief in federalism. John Kennedy's approach, at least until 1963, was similar. He shied away from deploying federal force or taking a proactive stance on civil rights for fear of alienating powerful southern Democrats and undermining his efforts to fight the Cold War and revive the economy.[10]

One effect of this policy of nonintervention was to increase civil rights activists' disillusionment with the Democratic Party in particular and American democracy more generally. While many historians view Johnson as a courageous president who did much to advance the cause of black rights, movement activists had less reason to feel grateful to him. This was because they had "suffered years of jailings and beatings, and visited morgues to identify the bodies of victims, all the time waiting for the federal government to act" to protect them from racist violence.[11] SNCC's disillusionment with the federal government could be seen in a sign that was often hung on the walls of its Freedom Houses, which stated:

There's a street in Itta Bena called FREEDOM
There's a town in Mississippi called LIBERTY
There's a department in Washington called JUSTICE[12]

With less residual loyalty toward the Johnson administration, it would be easier for these civil rights activists to oppose its policies in Vietnam.

Black Mississippians and seasoned civil rights workers had long understood the violence that underpinned race relations and institutionalized white supremacy in the Magnolia State, and they also expected the federal government's stubborn response. However, for the hundreds of white volunteers who traveled to Mississippi in the summer of 1964 the lesson was both new and sobering. One volunteer, Michael Kenney, wrote that Mississippi was the only state where "you can drag a river any time and find bodies you were not expecting. . . . Negroes disappear down here every week and are never heard about." Kenney explained that "things are really much better for the rabbits here. There is a closed season on rabbits when they may not be killed. Negroes are killed all year round. So are rabbits. The difference is that arrests are made for killing rabbits out of season. . . . Jesus Christ, this is supposed to be America in 1964."[13] While the depth of poverty and racism in Mississippi helped to radicalize many of the volunteers, what shocked them most of all, as Doug McAdam has shown, was the extent of federal complicity in maintaining Mississippi's segregationist system.

If SNCC field secretaries had already begun to doubt Washington's commitment to civil rights, most of the volunteers who arrived in June generally held positive views of the federal government, and many had been inspired by John F. Kennedy's call to service. Initially, many of the volunteers went to Mississippi under the impression that the "redneck farmer, Southern sheriff, and Dixiecrat politician" were the enemy.[14] They soon discovered that the situation was far more complex, as volunteer Brian Peterson explained: "the Klansman-assassin at the local gas station has close connections with the local sheriff, who in turn has connections with the legislature and governor, who in turn have connections with Congress and the President."[15] Karen Duncanwood, a freshman at San Francisco State College, traveled to the Magnolia State a self-described "patriotic American," but quickly became disillusioned by her experiences. She had low expectations of the local law enforcement agencies, but she had anticipated more from the federal government. Duncanwood recalled that "people's lives were in danger, people were getting fire-bombed and shot up and beat up, and the FBI knew exactly who was doing it. It was a real shock to realize that the federal government didn't give a hoot if you lived or died."[16]

Indeed, many of the volunteers' fiercest criticisms were leveled at the FBI, whose agents were frequently disobliging or hostile when called upon to investigate violence against Freedom Summer projects or staff. Often, the most the FBI would do was take notes. Doug McAdam has argued persuasively that, to an overwhelming degree, the volunteers left

Mississippi with a much more pessimistic opinion of the federal government—which, in their eyes, had shown itself to be cowardly and
amoral.[17]

The traumatic events at the Democratic Party National Convention, held
in Atlantic City at the end of August, seemed to confirm radicals' claims
that the federal government was part of the problem. The MFDP
demanded recognition as the legitimate Mississippi delegation on the
grounds that the state regulars prevented blacks from participating in
precinct, county, and state elections. They believed they had enough liberal support on the credentials committee to force a debate and "roll
call" vote on the convention floor. Once it became clear, however, that
any seating of the MFDP would precipitate a Southern walk-out, Lyndon
Johnson ensured that they would not be seated. Johnson, dangling the
vice-presidency before Minnesota Senator Hubert Humphrey, arranged
for the doyens of American liberalism—including the UAW's Walter
Reuther—to urge the MFDP to accept a compromise in which they
would accept two at-large seats and a promise of future reform. At the
same time, supporters of the Freedom Democrats on the credentials
committee came under intense pressure not to force the issue onto the
convention floor. The MFDP ultimately voted to reject the compromise,
Mississippi sharecropper and FDP spokesperson Fannie Lou Hamer
explaining that they had not traveled all the way to Atlantic City for "no
two seats" because "all of us is tired."[18]

Numerous historians have joined movement veterans in seeing
Atlantic City as a decisive moment in the relationship between the
Democratic Party and the activist civil rights movement.[19] SNCC's Joyce
Ladner described the convention as the "end of innocence," while Bob
Moses stated that "Atlantic City was a watershed in the movement
because up until then the idea had been that you were working more or
less within the Democratic Party. . . . With Atlantic City, a lot of movement people became disillusioned. . . . You turned around and your support was puddle-deep."[20] The Democratic Party's refusal to recognize
the Freedom Democrats helped destroy SNCC members' remaining faith
in American liberals. Former SNCC activist Courtland Cox recalled
that the liberal power structure's machinations against the FDP at Atlantic City were particularly radicalizing. He explained that SNCC activists "went there feeling that if you played by the rules, that is to say
even if it was dangerous you played by the rules, you got the votes, you
did all the things that people said you should do, then the rules would
work." Not only was it clear that playing by the rules did not work, but
"the coalescing of the power structure against us," particularly the use
of Hubert Humphrey and Walter Reuther, was a radicalizing influence

for SNCC members. "From that day on," Cox recalled, "we felt that playing by the rules was not enough, that the power was aligned to maintain itself and that in fact the sense . . . that if you did everything right they would be on your side, people said no. Just not going to happen."[21]

The Democratic Party's liberal establishment was prepared to sacrifice principle and morality on the altar of political expediency. Fears about the white backlash or a Barry Goldwater victory in the November election may have had a degree of legitimacy, but for people who had risked death for the cause of equality, such arguments were irrelevant. Courtland Cox has explained how the arguments about the "wider picture," such as the need to avoid harming Johnson's chances for election, were received unsympathetically by SNCC activists and FDP delegates. According to Cox, "nobody cared about that. The reality was, our view was that these people were suffering, they had suffered all this time, that they were going to go back to a hostile environment, their lives were on the line that summer. You know . . . people got killed and nobody cared. So our agenda was the primary agenda, we were not going to view that their agenda was the primary agenda and ours secondary, no."

When black Representative William L. Dawson attempted to persuade the FDP delegates that they had to support Lyndon Johnson, Annie Devine replied that "we have been treated like beasts in Mississippi. They shot us down like animals. We risk our lives coming up here . . . politics must be corrupt if it don't care none about the people down there."[22] Although many FDP members continued to believe that the Democratic Party could become a worthy ally, and the party campaigned for Johnson in the November election, most SNCC members now dismissed the Democrats as part of the problem.[23]

SNCC executive director James Forman explained how Atlantic City brought home to grass-roots civil rights activists the realization that the federal government, and in particular the national Democratic Party, was not the savior of black people, that in fact the federal government was an opponent rather than an ally. Forman, who was at least ten years older than most of his SNCC comrades (he had been born in Chicago in 1928) had been a reporter and school teacher before becoming involved in the civil rights movement at the end of the 1950s. According to Forman, who had joined SNCC in the fall of 1961, "Atlantic City was a powerful lesson. . . . No longer was there any hope, among those who still had it, that the federal government would change the situation in the Deep South." Forman stated that five years of struggle had radically changed many people, "changed them from idealistic reformers to full-time revolutionaries. And *the change had come through direct experience.*"[24]

SNCC's radicalization continued in the aftermath of Atlantic City when eleven activists traveled to the West African state of Guinea. This experience encouraged them to view the black struggle in America in a global context, and the sight of blacks running their own country left a lasting impression. Although most returned to the U.S. on October 4, John Lewis and Donald Harris stayed for another month, visiting Egypt, Liberia, Ghana, and other countries. A chance encounter with Malcolm X in Nairobi led to the former Nation of Islam spokesman seeking to forge links with SNCC during the remaining months of his life.[25]

Despite historians' emphasis on the progressivism of Lyndon Johnson's presidency, many civil rights workers remained unconvinced about the administration's commitment to the cause of black equality.[26] Black activists' direct experience of the Democratic Party was often a negative one. South of the Mason-Dixon line the party was the enemy of the freedom movement, which was denounced, red-baited, and opposed by the likes of James Eastland, George Wallace, and Paul Johnson—all important Democrats. Despite the liberal reputation of the national administration, events after Atlantic City further undermined the confidence of civil rights workers in the party. James Coleman's nomination to the U.S. Fifth Circuit of Appeals in June 1965 was one such instance.[27]

Coleman, a former governor of Mississippi (1956–1960), was a staunch segregationist who had played a leading role in Mississippi's response to desegregation. As governor he had opposed school desegregation, black voting, and "race-mixing," and he had helped create the Mississippi State Sovereignty Commission—a secret police force tied to the white supremacist Citizens' Councils. The Commission's official role was to "prevent encroachment upon the rights of this and other states by the Federal Government." Described by one journalist as "something akin to the NKVD among the cotton patches," it wiretapped phones, infiltrated civil rights organizations, and influenced local press coverage.[28] Running for governor again in 1964, Coleman's platform had included continued support for segregation.[29] To make matters worse, at the time of his nomination Coleman was acting as an attorney for four of the five Mississippi representatives whose seating was being challenged in Congress by SNCC and the MFDP on the basis that blacks had been "systematically and deliberately excluded from the electoral process."[30] Coleman's nomination was, unsurprisingly, condemned by civil rights groups. The MFDP's Victoria Gray stated that "it is with unbelieving and indescribable shock and fear that we learned . . . of the tragic nomination." She pointed out that Coleman had "spent almost all of his adult life advising and planning in one way or another how to continue the suppression and dehumanization of the Negro people in Mississippi."[31]

The NAACP leadership had initially asked Johnson simply to reconsider the nomination, but grass-roots pressure at the 1965 annual convention forced a stronger line—the Association's leaders were instructed to put pressure on senators to oppose the nomination.[32] There can be little doubt that the nomination of Coleman damaged Johnson's claims to be a friend of the civil rights movement, especially in the eyes of activists working at the local level. Referring to the president's March 15 speech advocating voting rights legislation, an editorial in *The Movement* questioned the national government's commitment to black America when it asked LBJ, "when you said, We Shall Overcome—who did you mean by 'we'?"[33]

Civil rights workers understood that passage of civil rights legislation, while welcome, would mean nothing without vigorous enforcement backed by the federal government. For many SNCC and MFDP activists, the Johnson administration failed to do this adequately. Writing in the summer of 1965, SNCC's Jack Minnis was critical of the "shoddy" enforcement of the 1964 Civil Rights Act with respect to the desegregation of schools and hospitals. He was also pessimistic about the impact of the proposed voting rights legislation—"the law won't be worth a damn if Lyndon won't enforce it—and we have no reason to think he will."[34] The Voting Rights Act, which became law in August 1965, did result in hundreds of thousands of blacks being registered to vote, but widespread violations of the law occurred. Howard Zinn declared that, "while the nation congratulates itself over the voting bill, intimidation and violence continue in the rural counties of the Deep South, mostly unreported in the newspapers, and lost in the glow of legislative accomplishment."[35]

The government was reluctant to use its new powers to send federal voting registrars to the South, preferring this only as a last resort while relying on "voluntary compliance." Initially, Attorney General Nicholas Katzenbach sent officials to just eight Mississippi counties, for example.[36] In May 1966, only 40 of 600 Southern counties had federal officials observing voter registration.[37] In Mississippi, as late as March 1966, 30 counties where black registration was below 25 percent had yet to be visited by federal registrars. One of these, Sunflower County, was the home of influential Democratic senator James Eastland.[38] After Katzenbach stated that new laws might be needed to prevent the problem of all-white juries finding racists innocent of crimes against blacks, Jack Minnis pointed out that laws already existed that prevented keeping blacks off juries because of their color. The problem was that such laws were not enforced. Why not enforce them? he asked—"but no. That's not how the Great Society works. It doesn't enforce civil rights laws. It passes them. And passes them. And passes them."[39] Even Roy Wilkins conceded that "it is a justifiable criticism to state that civil rights legislation has been enforced spottily," although he made sure to exempt President Johnson from his comments.[40]

The "on the ground" experience of civil rights activists shaped their attitudes toward the federal government, the Democratic Party, and America itself. The government's failure to protect civil rights workers from white violence; the refusal to seat the MFDP at Atlantic City; and problems involving the enforcement of civil rights laws all contributed to a loss of faith in the "American System" among the radical wing of the civil rights movement. In the spring of 1966, veteran leftist and civil rights activist Anne Braden explained how SNCC's turn toward "Black Power" was not a sudden change in direction but part of a long-term trend and a product of its experiences. SNCC's disillusionment with the government, Braden asserted, had started when "civil rights workers' calls for help brought much talk but little action; when FBI agents kept taking endless notes but people kept getting shot and beaten and killed; when new laws were passed but scantily enforced and nothing really changed in the South."[41] Many activists, who had started out as reformers with a faith in the underlying goodness of the United States, became revolutionaries demanding fundamental structural changes to America's socioeconomic and political system. As SNCC's Mike Thelwell explained, "there was a naïve notion in the beginning that as long as we open [racism] up and expose it to the light of day the high-flown principles of American democracy and constitutional promises will come into play and the system will correct itself. It would never happen." Indeed, "it turned out the system was absolutely complicit in the oppression that was going on, the exploitation. And they weren't doing anything to keep the promises they had made to the movement . . . [and] the government itself and the system was proving itself to be bankrupt and corrupt. And that's very disillusioning."[42]

George Vlasits, a community organizer in North Carolina, articulated the psychological, emotional, and intellectual journey that many activists made during the 1960s. In September 1968, prior to being sentenced to five years imprisonment for refusing induction into the armed services, Vlasits explained that, after "discovering" poverty, racism, and injustice in late 1950s America, his reaction had been to "work to reform this society. After all, the basic institutions are good—justice, freedom, equality—they are not just empty sounding words—they are what America really stands for." However, Vlasits's experience as an activist had taught him that he had been naïve—"racism is not a problem of a few individuals like Bull Connor and George Wallace. It is a basic institution of American society." Vlasits concluded his courtroom remarks by declaring that "the man makes the rules and he don't make them for us—he don't make them for poor folk, he don't make them for dissenters, he don't make them for blacks—he makes them for the man."[43] Carl Davidson, a Freedom Summer volunteer and student leader, put it more succinctly—"I learned it from the Ku Klux Klan and the Mississippi Highway Patrol, that you needed revolution, and that there wasn't any other way."[44]

The radicalizing experience of civil rights work at the grass-roots level would help shape responses to the Vietnam War within organizations such as SNCC, CORE and the MFDP. Writing in the *Student Voice* in August 1965, Howard Zinn—one of SNCC's "adult advisors"—encouraged the organization to oppose the war in Vietnam. Movement people, he said, were in the best position to understand America's immoral actions in Southeast Asia, not from any expert knowledge of foreign policy, but because they knew so much about America. Zinn explained that "they understand just how much hypocrisy is wrapped up in our claim to stand for 'the free world.' . . . Events in Vietnam become easier to understand in the light of recent experience in the South."[45] In late 1965, Zinn eloquently argued that opposition to the Vietnam War among black civil rights activists in the American South did not result from a simple application of leftist ideology. Rather, it came "from the cotton fields, the country roads, the jails of the Deep South, where these young people have spent much of their time." In other words, antiwar sentiment flowed, at least in part, from the organizing experience itself. As Bob Moses put it, "our criticism of Vietnam policy does not come from what we know of Vietnam, but from what we know of America."[46] When SNCC publicly opposed the war in January 1966, it placed its policy within the context of its own experience of America during the previous five years—"our work, particularly in the South, taught us that the United States government has never guaranteed the freedom of oppressed citizens."[47]

Although the U.S. military commitment in Vietnam began in May 1959, the war did not emerge as an important national issue until 1965. At the end of Johnson's first year in office, America's military commitment to Vietnam accounted for just 23,000 troops, but within twelve months it had risen to 181,000. Operation Rolling Thunder, a massive bombing campaign against the Democratic Republic of Vietnam, was launched in February 1965; this made the war a major political issue, and it also energized a domestic peace movement that had been declining in strength since the 1963 signing of the nuclear test ban treaty. In the same month that the bombing began, the first teach-in on the war was held at the University of Michigan. Within two months hundreds more had occurred, including one at Berkeley that involved 30,000 people and lasted for 36 hours. The teach-ins consisted of lectures, debates, and discussion groups on the war, and served to legitimize dissent. As Charles DeBenedetti has stated, "the vacuum of understanding which they exposed created a market for information," and this need was met by a cadre of academic experts who challenged national policy and established an alternative source of information.[48]

Any story of the antiwar movement of the 1960s must give some consideration to the emergence and development of the New Left. Not only was it a key participant in the emergent antiwar sentiment of the 1960s, but it also played an important role in forging links between the various social movements of the decade. Always an assorted coalition of different groups, and thus difficult to define, the New Left's major characteristics were its campus base, its rejection of anticommunism, its high degree of decentralization, its advocacy of participatory democracy, and its emphasis on a politics of authenticity. As the decade progressed, the New Left changed—morphing from a reformist movement inspired by John Kennedy's call to service into an association of various radical groups that embraced elements of an anti-American worldview and often espoused competing versions of Marxist-Leninism. By the mid-1960s the New Left had been involved in a number of progressive causes—including civil rights, anti-poverty, and campus reform (for example, the Free Speech movement had erupted on the campus of the University of California, Berkeley in the fall of 1964). Increasingly, though, student activism would center on efforts to end American involvement in the Vietnam War.[49]

The most important New Left organization was Students for a Democratic Society (SDS). Formed in 1960 as the renamed Student League for Industrial Democracy, in 1962 it published the Port Huron Statement, a widely influential and much read manifesto for the generation of 1960s student activists. It emphasized participatory democracy and "values," especially the need for spiritual meaning in modern society, as well as more traditional demands for civil rights, social justice, and an end to militarism. During its early years, SDS focused on the struggle for black rights and also attempted to organize an "interracial movement of the poor" through a program of community organization modeled on SNCC-style activism, known as the Economic and Research Action Project (ERAP). As Vietnam began to emerge as a national issue, however, SDS turned its attention to events in Southeast Asia.[50]

In December 1964, SDS decided to hold an antiwar march in Washington, D.C., the following April.[51] The escalation of the war during early 1965 fueled interest in the prospective action, and SDS responded by hiring more staff to deal with the administrative burdens of staging what would be the first significant national antiwar demonstration. Endorsements were received from James Farmer, Staughton Lynd, Harvard historian and SANE leader H. Stuart Hughes, Berkeley Free Speech icon Mario Savio, veteran pacifist A. J. Muste, and Howard Zinn, among others.[52] The SDS decision to adopt a nonexclusionary approach to antiwar activity, however, produced controversy and dissent. The official call stated that "we urge the participation of all those who agree with us that the war in Vietnam injures both Vietnamese and Americans and should be stopped."

Antiwar liberals did not take kindly to the idea that they might be marching alongside communists.[53] In New York, a few days before the march, Stuart Hughes, A. J. Muste, socialist Norman Thomas, and Bayard Rustin warned people away from the event because of its alleged communist taint. The group declared that they were concerned about Vietnam, but believed in "the need for an independent peace movement, not committed to any form of totalitarianism or drawing inspiration from the foreign policy of any government."[54] A *New York Post* editorial added fuel to the fire when it claimed that "on the eve of this weekend's 'peace march' . . . several leaders of the peace movement have taken clear note of attempts to convert the event into a pro-Communist production."[55] Hughes and Thomas subsequently apologized to SDS for their involvement in this unsavory episode, although the issue of nonexclusion (or anti-anticommunism) would continue to be debated furiously within the peace movement.[56]

April 17, 1965 was "one of those flawless Washington spring days," and it augured a successful march. Perhaps as many as 25,000 people attended, and they came from all over the country. African Americans were particularly well represented—partly the result of "conscious effort" by the SDS to get a black turnout.[57] SNCC's Bob Moses was a featured speaker, and he compared the killing in Vietnam to the killing in Mississippi. He told the crowd to ask themselves and their government whether they had the "right to plot and kill and murder in defense of the society you value?"[58] Moses was perhaps the SNCC member most active in the early antiwar movement, and he frequently linked his opposition to the war with his own experiences in the Deep South. For example, he had told the audience at a Berkeley teach-in that "the South has got to be a looking glass, not a lightning rod. You've got to learn from the South if you're going to do anything about this country in relation to Vietnam."[59] The influence of the civil rights movement on the anti-Vietnam War movement, and its desire to generate black support for peace actions, were evident from the start.

SDS president Paul Potter closed the rally with a fiery speech that placed the Vietnam War firmly within a wider context, and called for the building of a multi-issue movement for progressive change in the United States. Potter asked, "what kind of system is it that justifies the United States . . . seizing the destinies of the Vietnamese people and using them callously for its own purpose?" He continued, "what kind of system is it that disenfranchises people in the South, leaves millions upon millions of people . . . excluded from the . . . promise of American society . . . and still persists in calling itself free and still persists in finding itself fit to police the world?" In a memorable peroration Potter declared, "we must name that system, we must name it, describe it, analyze it and change it. For it is only when that system is changed and brought under control that there can be any hope for stopping the forces that create a war in Vietnam today or a murder in the South tomorrow." Potter then called for the creation of a massive social movement that understood "Vietnam in all its horror as but a symptom of a deeper malaise." After applauding Potter's speech enthusiastically, the large crowd marched from the Washington Monument down the mall toward the Capitol, singing "We Shall Overcome," the anthem of the civil rights movement. About 150 yards from the Capitol the crowd stopped and a small contingent handed a peace petition to a congressional aide.[60]

In terms of linking Vietnam with the civil rights movement, the march appeared to be a success. The SDS action had been supported by CORE's James Farmer as well as senior SNCC representatives. Indeed, SNCC's Executive Committee had decided "with little discussion and no dissent" to support the April march. On the eve of the action, SNCC members meeting in Holly Springs, Mississippi, had discussed both Vietnam and the SDS march. Silas Norman argued that the war was a logical extension of American imperialism, and stated that a consensus existed within the organization over supporting the march. In addition— "we have people taking an active part in the march and we have helped people get students (from the South) for it." SNCC chairman John Lewis also spoke in favor of taking an antiwar position, arguing that the U.S. should withdraw from Vietnam.[61]

A group of black high school students from Mississippi were among those participating in the Washington protest. Signaling the continuity between the peace and freedom movements was the fact that all the students were veterans of the Freedom Schools that had been established during Freedom Summer. Otis Brown, a sixteen-year-old student leader from Indianola, explained that they had come to Washington "because we have to look beyond just Negro freedom. We don't want to grow up 'free' at home in a country which supports this kind of war abroad."[62]

The civil rights and antiwar movements were also linked by a common spirit, one SDS leader explained that the "breadth and urgency of the march could never have been achieved without the life instilled in the student movement by the Southern civil rights struggle."[63] Many of the antiwar student radicals were veterans of the black freedom struggle, and a significant proportion of the peace marchers, perhaps 10 percent, were African American. This seemed to represent the beginning of a new working alliance between the peace and freedom movements. As one reporter commented, "the most important new liaison was that between the young, vibrant freedom workers of the South and the peace-oriented students of the North."[64]

The growing opposition to the war within the civil rights movement seemed to suggest that the black movement might provide an important source of strength to the peace forces. Indeed, when Martin Luther King, his Christian conscience troubled by events in Vietnam, began to express hostility to the war, it seemed that the antiwar movement might have found a potential leader with huge crossover appeal. King first voiced opposition to the war on March 2, 1965. Speaking to an audience at Howard University, he called for a negotiated settlement and declared that the war was "accomplishing nothing."[65] However, the road from civil rights to antiwar activism would not be an easy one for black leaders to tread.

CORE's national director James Farmer had endorsed the April march and had also linked the struggles for peace and freedom. On CBS's *Face the Nation*, on April 25, he had stated "I think as American citizens, persons who participate in the civil rights movement have not only a right, but a duty to be interested in all activities of our government—domestic policies outside of the civil rights area and foreign policy."[66] In early June, Farmer had been one of many sponsors of an "Emergency Rally on Vietnam," held at New York's Madison Square Garden. The rally, called by SANE and supported by SDS, had significant black support. SNCC and the Northeastern Regional Office of CORE gave their endorsement, black entertainer Ossie Davis was a co-chairman of the rally, and Martin Luther King's wife Coretta gave a speech. Bayard Rustin, a featured speaker, talked about the "common ground" shared by the peace and freedom movements.[67]

At a news conference in Durham, North Carolina, on the eve of CORE's 1965 national convention, a reporter asked Farmer whether the civil rights and peace movements were synonymous. He explained that the civil rights movement was an autonomous movement, but that it was proper for civil rights people "as concerned citizens" to be interested in such issues as peace.[68] As well as the involvement of civil rights leaders and organizations in anti-Vietnam activities, there was also growing opposition to the war within CORE itself. On April 10 the organization's principal policy-making body, the National Action Council, decided to endorse "efforts across the country to gain peace in Vietnam and wage war on discrimination."[69] However, events at its 23rd annual convention would reveal that the organization was deeply split over the nature of its relationship with the antiwar movement.

During June, the membership of Brooklyn CORE had passed an antiwar resolution which had subsequently been unanimously endorsed at the

Eastern Region CORE conference in New York City. The resolution declared that "to fight for human freedom at home and seek to destroy it abroad is the height of immorality"; described the U.S. bombing of North Vietnam as "utterly incomprehensible"; and called for the withdrawal of American troops.[70] Historians August Meier and Elliot Rudwick have argued that by the summer of 1965 CORE was split on a number of issues, one of which was Vietnam. One faction within the organization believed that, for tactical reasons, CORE should refrain from publicly opposing the Vietnam War. This put them in conflict with those who believed that the organization should move in a more radical direction.[71]

On July 5, meeting in closed session, the convention debated an antiwar resolution. Although a majority of the 1,000 delegates opposed the war, many were wary of committing the organization to such a controversial stand. After a lengthy and heated discussion, a resolution calling for an "immediate withdrawal of American troops" from Vietnam, and condemning the Johnson administration's foreign policy as racist, was passed by just ten votes.[72] Farmer had not been present during this debate, and he quickly attempted to reverse the decision. At first sight his actions seem surprising—Farmer had personally made many antiwar statements and had taken an active role in peace demonstrations. In addition, his annual report to the convention had stated that "it is impossible for the Government to mount a decisive war on poverty and bigotry in the United States while it is pouring billions down the drain in a war against people in Vietnam."[73] However, the national director urged the delegates to table the motion on Vietnam because it was not an issue on which CORE could get the unanimous support of the ghetto community, and opposing the war might also jeopardize public support for the civil rights movement.[74] Farmer argued that although individuals should support the peace movement, CORE as an organization should not "get out of step" with the community.[75]

The resolution was duly withdrawn, over the furious objections of chapter heads Ollie Leeds and Lincoln Lynch, and for the time being the organization refrained from taking an antiwar position.[76] Farmer subsequently explained that he believed that protesting Vietnam would "provide too easy a cop-out for some of our chapters who were trying to tackle complex Northern issues"; would confuse two issues which he felt should be separate; and would open up CORE to possible communist infiltration—which had been a problem in the past.[77] Although the organization had pulled back from opposing the Vietnam War, many of its members would become increasingly active in the antiwar movement. Indeed, the organization would continue to travel in a radical direction—moving from nonviolence to self-defense, and from integration to Black Power.

The MFDP also found the Vietnam issue problematic. In July 1965 John D. Shaw joined the growing list of black American GIs who had been killed in Vietnam. Shaw, a twenty-three-year-old native of McComb, Mississippi, had been active in the local civil rights movement, having been involved in SNCC's first direct action campaign in the state. McComb activists Clint Hopson and Joe Martin responded to Shaw's death by writing and circulating a radical antiwar leaflet in the local community, which counseled draft resistance:

> No Mississippi Negroes should be fighting in Vietnam for the white man's freedom, until all the Negro people are free in Mississippi.
> Negro boys should not honor the draft here in Mississippi. Mothers should encourage their sons not to go.
> We will gain respect and dignity as a race only by forcing the United States Government and the Mississippi government to come with guns, dogs and trucks to take our sons away to fight and be killed protecting Mississippi, Alabama, Georgia and Louisiana.
> No one has a right to ask us to risk our lives and kill other colored people in Santo Domingo and Vietnam, so that the white American can get richer. We will be looked upon as traitors by all the colored people in the world if the Negro people continue to fight and die without a cause.[78]

The leaflet suggested hunger strikes as a possible protest tactic. The July 28 issue of the Mississippi Freedom Democratic *Newsletter* reprinted this leaflet, without comment, just as it had done previously with letters that expressed opposition to the war. However, this action set off a storm of controversy that threatened to engulf the organization.

Opponents of the MFDP seized on the chance to undermine it by portraying its members as unpatriotic, communistic traitors. Writing in the *Delta Democrat*, liberal journalist Hodding Carter III argued that the leaflet was "close to treason," while Claude Ramsey of the AFL-CIO compared the MFDP to the Ku Klux Klan.[79] Rather than defending the right to free speech, many liberals joined in the assault on the Freedom Democrats. Black Representative Charles Diggs, for example, called the draft statement "ridiculous and completely irresponsible."[80] In his syndicated newspaper column, NAACP executive director Roy Wilkins condemned the "smart-alecks" and "young squirts" who had played into the hands of Mississippi racists.[81]

The leadership of the MFDP sought desperately to deflect the criticisms that were being leveled against them. On July 31, Lawrence Guyot, chairman of the MFDP executive committee, and the Rev. Edwin King, white chaplain at Jackson's Tougaloo College and a leading MFDP figure, made a statement. They explained how television and newspaper reports had been claiming that the party had been circulating material urging blacks to resist the draft or, if they were already in the army, to stage hunger strikes. Guyot and King stated that "the news media are totally inaccurate in saying that this is an MFDP position or policy. At no time has the State Convention, the State Executive Committee, or any county MFDP Executive Board voted on such a position." Furthermore, "a group of McComb citizens, many of whom are active in the FDP, circulated a petition as a result of [John D. Shaw's] untimely death. This activity was reported as a news story in the MFDP Newsletter—a report on current activity within the state—not as an editorial or official policy of the MFDP." As part of the story, they had reprinted the antiwar leaflet that had been distributed. After distancing themselves from the leaflet, Guyot and King went on to express a degree of sympathy with the sentiments behind it, when they linked hostility to the war with local experience:

It is very easy to understand why Negro citizens of McComb, themselves the victims of bombings, Klan-inspired terrorism, and harassment arrests, should resent the death of a citizen of McComb while fighting in Viet Nam for "freedom" not enjoyed by the Negro community of McComb. However, the Mississippi Freedom Democratic Party does not have such a position.

As the Negroes of Mississippi continue our struggle for the freedom to participate totally in the decisions which govern our lives, it is inevitable and desirable that a growing interest and awareness in local and national issues such as war and peace must follow. The MFDP encourages and welcomes discussion and debate of these issues among its members. We reaffirm the right of our members to take public positions and actions on any issue. As we understand democracy, this is what it means . . . .

[We] are proud to have been part of the movement in Mississippi which has liberated people to the point where they feel free to express their feelings on issues which affect them.[82]

Although Guyot later told the *New York Times* that he would serve in the armed forces if drafted, the damage to the party had already been done. The MFDP lost the support of moderates in Mississippi and the congressional challenge suffered.[83] Indeed, Guyot voiced the suspicion that the fierce criticism leveled against the MFDP over the Vietnam leaflet was "quite possibly an attempt to project as unpatriotic and irresponsible the Freedom Democratic Party because of the political and moral ramifications of our challenge now before Congress."[84]

Edwin King later recalled that the MFDP was grappling with the Vietnam issue during the summer of 1965, but that the "evil" attacks by people like Carter tried to force the organization into a position that it was reluctant to assume. He explained that "the FDP's questioning of the war early on was turned . . . into a kind of absolutist position against the war, which we didn't really take for another year." While the party was "obviously . . . headed that way," they "wouldn't let us play the kind of nuances." Even though the majority of MFDP executive committee members opposed the war, they did not want to come out against it because "it wasn't that much of an issue to the local people. We would not go too far beyond the local people or take a stand and impose it on them. But we would support them as we could. Nobody liked that. They wanted to push us."[85] This desire to not get ahead of "the people" illustrates nicely a point made by Charles Payne, who has argued that community organizers had to "confront the complexities and contradictions of flesh-and-blood people," who were "in many respects culturally conservative, deeply religious, patriotic Americans."[86]

The MFDP leaders may have wished to distance themselves from the McComb anti-draft leaflet, but many in the party and the wider community were sympathetic to its radical message. Freedom School teacher Rainer Seeling claimed that his class had written statements on their feelings about the war—"they all say they don't want anything to do with [it]." Clint Hopson, the black law student who had helped write the controversial pamphlet, told journalists that MFDP leaders had seen the McComb leaflet, and praised it, prior to its publication. Hopson described Guyot's statement as an effort to keep the party "off the line." Hopson declared that the opposition to the war "came from the people . . . this is how they feel, we just put their feelings into words after talking with them, singing with them and living with them."[87]

Although it is hard to generalize about the extent to which black Mississippians agreed with the antiwar sentiments expressed in McComb in the summer of 1965, such support certainly existed. On July 28 Daniel J. Wacker, a civil rights volunteer working with the Delta Ministry, talked with a black Korean War veteran in a chicken shack—"news of the increased draft brought the comment: why should we fight in some other country when we are not free here."[88] An African American mother in Natchez told Dick Gillian of KZSU radio that "it's not our war cuz we don't have no right and we don't have no freedom."[89] Stewart Meacham and Paul Lauter of the American Friends Service Committee spent a month in Mississippi and Louisiana talking about peace and the Vietnam War. They were convinced that antiwar sentiment was widespread— "everything we saw and heard led us to the inescapable conclusion that there is a strong, grassroots, anti-war sentiment building in the Negro community in the Deep South."[90] The national peace movement would hope to build both on this grassroots black opposition to the war, and the growing antiwar sentiment within national civil rights organizations.

In August 1965, the black freedom struggle and the anti-Vietnam War movement briefly intersected in a formal way, through the Assembly of Unrepresented People. The AUP was conceived by Staughton Lynd—

Yale historian, pacifist, and civil rights supporter (he had been heavily involved in the organization of the Freedom Schools)—who advocated convening a new Continental Congress to help launch a new form of politics in America, one that would be founded on participatory democracy.[91] A central tenet of New Left political ideology, participatory democracy exerted great influence within both SDS and SNCC. At its core was the notion of a "democracy of individual participation, governed by two central aims: that the individual share in those . . . decisions determining the quality and direction of his life; that society be organized to encourage independence in men and provide the media for their common participation."[92]

From its inception, the AUP was designed as a multi-issue organizing project that would attract support from the peace and civil rights movements, as well as from assorted radical, new left, anti-poverty, and reformist groups. The AUP's official call stated that it intended to bring together opponents of the Cold War, civil rights activists, and those who were opposed to "inquisition by Congressional committees, inequities in labor legislation, the mishandling of anti-poverty and welfare funds, and the absence of democratic process on the local level."[93] In July several SNCC field secretaries, including Bob Moses and Courtland Cox, had argued that it was necessary for SNCC people to address themselves to the "broader implications" of their work in the South, "such as in relation to foreign policy. " They went on to explain that the idea for the AUP had come out of a number of "exploratory meetings" involving civil rights, peace, church, community groups, and interested individuals.

SNCC was hoping to build support for the MFDP congressional challenge, but recognized that "a large amount of activity" during the summer would be "concerned with protesting the war in Vietnam." SNCC wanted to channel some of that energy into support for the Freedom Democrats, but acknowledged that peace activists would be more likely to support the challenge if they were convinced that it would "foster a growing concern among civil rights people about the question of peace." The SNCC activists pointed out that "people active in various protest movements in the country have always talked from time to time about the need for communication between movements . . . sharing ideas . . . manpower, and generally strengthening each other," and they viewed the summer as an "opportunity to begin the long-awaited dialogue between activists in various political struggles."[94]

The link between the civil rights and antiwar movements was made explicit by the AUP—"in Mississippi and Washington the few make the decisions for the many. Mississippi Negroes are denied the vote; the voice of the thirty per cent of Americans now opposed to the undeclared war in Vietnam is not heeded and all Americans are denied access to facts concerning the true military and political situation."[95] This argument was echoed in the fall by Ray Robinson, Jr., an African American antiwar activist and former Golden Gloves boxer. Robinson declared that "the same people who won't let the people of Vietnam decide what's best for them are the same people that won't let the Negroes of the South decide who should represent them."[96] The AUP's program included demonstrations against the war and workshops designed to facilitate dialogue between people active in various "progressive" movements. Approximately 2,000 people attended the AUP, and on August 6 the twentieth anniversary of Hiroshima was marked with a silent vigil outside the White House. Three days later, on the anniversary of Nagasaki, the AUP concluded its activities with an antiwar march of 800 people from the Washington Monument to the Capitol.[97] A total of about 350 activists were arrested for engaging in acts of civil disobedience over the weekend.[98]

Despite the involvement of civil rights figures such as Moses and Cox at the leadership level of the AUP, most SNCC workers were less interested in antiwar protest, preferring to focus their attentions on organizing around civil rights in the black community. Only a handful of southern civil rights workers were actively involved in the AUP, and black movement activists were a "distinct minority" at the Assembly.[99] The NAACP, anxious to dissociate the civil rights movement from Vietnam dissent, had attacked the AUP as an attempt to hoodwink civil rights groups into supporting protests against U.S. policy in Vietnam. Roy Wilkins accepted that the AUP's official call mentioned civil rights, but he argued that the "main emphasis" was on Vietnam, and that "Mississippi" was just a "come-on word". The NAACP executive director thus warned Branch and Youth Council presidents against becoming involved in the AUP.[100]

Although Wilkins was being unfair in claiming that the AUP was designed to co-opt the civil rights movement, its goal of generating productive dialogue between various progressive movements remained largely unfulfilled. In part this was because so few civil rights people attended—there was a "busload from Mississippi, two delegates from New Orleans, small groups from other Southern communities, and a few staff members of civil rights organizations," but that was all. A second reason was that for many of the participants Vietnam was *the* overriding issue, and many peace activists were prepared to sacrifice the success of the workshops in order to protest against the war. As Anne Braden explained, for opponents of the war, "sitting down in the gates of the White House seemed more urgent" than trying to build constructive working relationships with various groups around a broad range of issues. Consequently, there was a tendency for peace and civil rights activists to meet separately. However, on the occasions when they did get together, there were problems with "intellectuals using big words and dominating conversations." Only once during the weekend, at the "community people's workshop," was productive cooperation achieved—and this was because the people from Mississippi talked and requested that the "intellectuals" just listen.[101]

Jack Newfield's report on the AUP was even less positive than Braden's—he claimed that "all the contradictions and polarities within the new radical movement crystallized during the four picnic-like days of the assembly." Newfield described an incestuous gathering of movement people that seethed with tensions. There were tensions between black and white, between radical and moderate, and between those who wanted to bear religious witness against Vietnam and those who wished to organize a radical political movement that focused on the war.[102]

Newfield documented one clash that offers an interesting insight into the tension that existed between the civil rights and peace activists. On the final morning of the Assembly, Clint Hopson, the black activist from McComb whose anti-draft work had recently landed the MFDP in hot water, read a statement urging Mississippi blacks to refuse to register for the draft. He also accused the MFDP of employing "expediency" in its refusal to support the call for draft resistance. Bob Moses, angered by the enthusiastic response of the 800-strong, mostly white crowd, took the floor. He defended the party and criticized what one might term the *rhetorical radicalism* of many of the delegates. Moses explained that he had "watched MFDP people risk their lives and I've heard you folks debate for the last three days about going to jail for a few hours. . . . Mississippi people have paid a terrible price and I don't see anybody here doing that. You people should be supporting the Congressional challenge, not attacking the MFDP."

In many ways the AUP augured the shape of things to come regarding attempts to bring about closer cooperation between the peace and freedom movements. Arguments about emphasis and multi-issuism, the cultural and "intellectual" barriers between white student antiwar activists and black civil rights workers, and interracial tensions would, throughout the decade, plague efforts to build a broad, radical, multiracial, multi-issue antiwar coalition.

The fissures within the antiwar coalition over race, multi-issuism, and exclusionism and the tensions between radicals and liberals came to the fore once again during antiwar activities in the nation's capital over the 1965 Thanksgiving holiday. Two important events coincided—the first national convention of the National Coordinating Committee to End the War in Vietnam (NCC) which had been founded at the AUP, and a National Committee for a SANE Nuclear Policy (SANE)-sponsored peace march.

Sanford Gottlieb, coordinator of the SANE march, had announced that one of his objectives was to keep "kooks, communists or draft-dodgers" out of the demonstration in an attempt to appeal to moderates.[103] But despite SANE's policy of rejecting civil disobedience and discouraging communist support, radicals were not completely alienated from proceedings. Although signs calling for immediate withdrawal were strongly discouraged, for example, they were not banned, and the radicals' commitment to inclusiveness obliged them to give at least grudging support.[104] The NCC decided to support the SANE march for a number of reasons. It was considered important to try to maintain the unity of the peace movement, and there was also a belief that SANE was moving in a radical direction—it was, for example, being less exclusionary than normal. Indeed, during the mid-1960s SANE, which had been founded by radical pacifists and peace liberals in 1957, was wracked by internal divisions between radicals and moderates who disagreed over policy and tactics. As well as seeing the chance to "connect" with the radical segments of SANE's middle-class constituency, the NCC also saw an opportunity to link the peace and freedom movements. It was rumored that SANE was trying to persuade Martin Luther King to speak at the antiwar rally, and the radicals noted that

Negroes from the South are being mobilized for a demonstration in Washington. If we hope to involve civil rights as a component in a broad struggle for human rights, we can do it only if we have a conference in Washington after a rally at which King speaks of peace. There may never again be such an opportunity . . . to hear the Southern part of the dialogue.[105]

However, it is worth noting that, although a number of African Americans attended the NCC convention, only about 5 percent of those participating in the SANE march were black, and, contrary to the King rumor, no important civil rights leader spoke.[106]

Indeed, the late summer of 1965 had seen a blow to efforts to unite the civil rights and peace movements, as Martin Luther King retreated from his initial opposition to the war in Vietnam. He had first spoken out in March, before making an important speech at an SCLC rally in Petersburg, Virginia, on July 2. Before a cheering crowd of 2,000 at a local football stadium, King declared that "the United States should spare no effort in pursuing" a negotiated settlement to the conflict, even if that meant talking to the Viet Cong. Moreover, King suggested that Americans should hold peace rallies, "just like we have freedom rallies."[107] However, several members of the SCLC board were uneasy over King's Vietnam comments. While his right to express dissent was confirmed, the board also made it clear that the SCLC did not have enough resources to work for peace as well as civil rights. This did not prevent

King from announcing, in early August, a plan to write letters to LBJ and the leaders of the USSR, China, North and South Vietnam, and the National Liberation Front (NLF), calling on them to begin negotiations. He also urged Johnson to consider a bombing pause and to indicate willingness to negotiate with the Viet Cong.

King, though, quickly came under pressure to retreat from his antiwar stance. Johnson chided him for his antiwar comments, and at the beginning of September UN Ambassador Arthur Goldberg met with King to bring him "on-side." The next day, Connecticut Senator Thomas Dodd, a close Johnson ally, publicly attacked King for his antiwar remarks and pointed out that it was illegal for private citizens to engage in independent foreign policy ventures. The message was clear—LBJ would brook no dissent over Vietnam. If King persisted with his antiwar activism he could expect a barrage of stinging criticism and frosty relations with the Johnson White House. King confessed to aides that he did not have the strength to take on the power structure over the war while fighting for civil rights. Furthermore, he was reluctant to break with the president at a time when the Voting Rights Act and war on poverty seemed to offer huge opportunities for black advancement. Consequently, the letter writing idea was quietly dropped and King refrained from public condemnation of the war for eighteen months.[108]

Despite its growing aversion to mass marches and its critique of SANE-style liberalism, SDS, like the NCC, decided on a policy of cooperation. As new SDS president Carl Oglesby explained, they could either have sat on the sidelines and seen the march fail or "go in there and try to make it work."[109] After tense negotiations it was agreed that, in return for participating, SDS could issue its own call to the march and would be allowed to appoint a speaker.[110] In contrast to SANE's demands for a cease-fire and negotiations, and its strategy of staging a "responsible" single-issue protest that was designed to generate broad support, SDS called for a withdrawal of American troops and articulated an antiwar strategy based on a multi-issue perspective. SDS's official "call" to support the November march stated that "the only way to stop this and future wars is to organize a domestic social movement which challenges the very legitimacy of our foreign policy." Such a movement "must also fight to end racism, to end the paternalism of our welfare system, to guarantee decent incomes for all, and to supplant the authoritarian control of our universities with a community of scholars."[111] Seeing an opportunity to proselytize to a largely liberal audience, Oglesby readily agreed to be the SDS spokesman.

On a chilly overcast Saturday, November 27, 1965, around 30,000 people surrounded the White House before marching to the Washington Monument to hear protest songs and antiwar speeches.[112] With the sun setting, Carl Oglesby rose to make a searing indictment of America. The SDS president, a thirty-two-year-old father of three with working class roots, attacked corporate liberalism, with its imperialistic tendencies that he argued had caused the war in Vietnam. Oglesby, an intellectual and some-time playwright, also linked Vietnam and the black freedom struggle—"this country, with its thirty-some years of liberalism, can send 200,000 young men to Vietnam to kill and die in the most dubious of wars, but it cannot get 100 voter registrars to go into Mississippi." He called on "humanist liberals" to support the broad, multi-issue movement for real democracy that SDS and its allies was trying to construct. The applause was deafening, and Oglesby received a standing ovation.[113]

The NCC convention held November 25–28 was far from successful, particularly in its attempts to bring the peace and freedom movements closer together. The NCC had, from its inception in August, linked the civil rights and antiwar movements. At a September meeting of the steering committee, for instance, NCC leader Frank Emspak, a resident of Madison, Wisconsin who had been raised by left wing trade union parents in New York, "read a letter from Mississippi, stressing the consensus of people in McComb that Vietnam and civil rights were only two aspects of what they understand as human rights. Frank asked that this be the organizing focus of the meeting; although the South was not represented, he said, we 'are not talking just to ourselves.'"[114] A number of civil rights activists from groups like SNCC and MFDP attended the NCC convention, which brought together 1,500 participants from about 100 local and national antiwar organizations.[115] Unfortunately for most of these "ordinary people," the convention quickly descended into internecine factional warfare. On one side of the ideological divide were the Communist Party and Du Bois Clubs, who favored creating a broad multi-issue organization concerned with civil rights, poverty, and university reform as well as Vietnam. They were opposed by the Socialist Workers Party and the Young Socialist Alliance, who wanted a single-issue coalition based on the demand for immediate American withdrawal from Vietnam. It was a split that would become a depressing characteristic of the peace movement. One participant recalled that "factions, maneuvers, caucuses, deals, parliamentary procedure and parliamentary disruption flew about like bats in a dark cave," and this "fighting about trivia" alienated the vast majority of delegates.[116] Berkeley's Marilyn Mulligan remembered how the experience was "demoralizing to the whole antiwar movement. Anybody who came to that convention who was just an ordinary person . . . and not a member of one of those political groups was totally demoralized . . . these people closeted themselves out of reach."[117]

The African American delegates were especially alienated by the proceedings. At a meeting of black southerners this resentment was expressed freely. Ray Robinson explained how black people had failed to relate to the white peace movement at the April and August actions as well as at the NCC convention—"people from Mississippi have traveled here 3 or 4 times. Each time they came here they've felt unrepresented. In April they just marched. In August they just sat on the grass. Today they watched all this shit. They came here with the idea of finding out how people can help each other. But that isn't what these people seemed to want to talk about."[118] Another announced that "it's fine for these people to come from Chicago and want to manipulate the power structure, to play politics," but "where is people making sense to themselves and each other?" Clarence Senior addressed the problems that many of the civil rights workers had in communicating with the white "intellectuals"—"we need to find a way to get our feelings made known to the body in our own language. We want to be part of the whole movement, not caught up in parliamentary procedure and factionalism. If some of the speakers get up in the clouds, we need to have someone to get him to break it down."

The "tedious debate" over the structure of the NCC, which dominated the convention, antagonized the southern civil rights delegates—many of whom were so repelled by the factionalism that they left early.[119] The NCC's Frank Emspak recalled how the political maneuverings of leftist factions often resulted in African Americans feeling estranged from the antiwar movement. He explained that "some of the maneuvering was carried on in such a way . . . that turned off black people deliberately—you would have black people speaking and disrupted." In addition,

the black organizations that came actually had a mass base. You talk about the Methodist Student Movement, or you talk about SCLC, or . . . the NAACP to the extent that some people came from those chapters—who were these people, these kids raising hell all the time and disrupting things and making it impossible to function, who do they represent, you know, ten people? Then they go back to some town someplace and they have a chapter of several hundred people, and they say "what happened up there?" you know, so it was that kind of . . . disconnect because, for the black organizations . . . they saw the war as important, but . . . that wasn't their crucial thing, they had another agenda. So then to be insulted on top of everything else, you know they don't need it.[120]

The year 1965 saw the first stirrings of antiwar dissent within the civil rights movement. Often, black activists' opposition to Vietnam was shaped by their experience of civil rights organizing itself. As the war in Southeast Asia intensified, it fueled the growth of a domestic peace movement. This movement, many of whose leaders had been involved in the struggle for racial justice, sought to forge links with their black counterparts almost immediately. However, the problems of white politicking and intellectualism, and the failure to link the antiwar cause with the civil rights struggle in anything more than a rhetorical way, undermined black involvement in the predominantly white antiwar movement. These problems, evident from the very moment that civil rights and antiwar groups began trying to work together, remained largely unresolved and would continue to hamper the peace movement's efforts to attract substantial African American support.

Chapter 2

Black Power

The relationship between the genocide in Vietnam and the smiles of the white man toward black Americans is a direct relationship.

—*Eldridge Cleaver*

The embarrassing thing about the peace movement . . . is that it's white.

—*a peace activist*

Following a six-week pause instigated by LBJ, the American bombing of North Vietnam resumed on January 31, 1966, and the following months saw an intensification of the military campaign. Between January and July more than 50,000 people were killed, 2,691 of them Americans.[1] At the end of December 1965, 180,000 U.S. troops were stationed in Vietnam; within two years the number would exceed 500,000. The $5 billion spent on the war during 1965 would become $10 billion the following year and, despite impressive Pentagon statistics, it soon became clear to the American people that the war would not be over quickly. Indeed, by the spring of 1966 the phrase "credibility gap" was widely used to describe LBJ's tendency to mislead the public, and the president's approval rating was falling.[2] The pollster Louis Harris reported that "a sense of 'travail without end' " was "straining both the patience and normal optimism of the American people."[3] Dissent from within South Vietnam itself by Buddhists, students, and even factions within the South Vietnamese military compounded the situation, and increasing numbers of Americans wondered whether their presence in South Vietnam was even wanted. As the military effort in Vietnam bogged down, domestic disquiet over the war increased.

Toward the end of 1965, the Student Nonviolent Coordinating Committee began to consider adopting an official position on the Vietnam War. The organization had already begun to develop links with the nascent peace movement. During the April 1965 antiwar demonstration in Washington, for example, it had shared its office with Students for a Democratic Society. SNCC chairman John Lewis had signed the

Declaration of Conscience Against the War in Vietnam, in which signatories affirmed their noncooperation with the war effort and offered support to draft resisters. And during August, Bob Moses had helped organize the AUP. As Clayborne Carson has asserted, the overwhelming majority of SNCC activists "opposed U.S. involvement in Vietnam as soon as they became aware of it." There was a reservoir of pacifist sentiment within the organization, which helped shape its response to Vietnam; while for others opposition to the war was rooted in a general distrust of the federal government, or in a sense of solidarity with the worldwide struggle against white imperialism.[4] Despite this antiwar feeling, the organization had not taken a formal position against the war. James Forman recalled that most SNCC members had considered Vietnam "not irrelevant, but simply remote. Its importance to black people had not come home to us."[5]

Some within the group began to push for an official antiwar pronouncement during the summer of 1965. The August 30, 1965, issue of SNCC's newspaper, the *Student Voice,* ran an article by the radical white historian and civil rights activist Howard Zinn, along with Miss Ella Baker, one of SNCC's "adult advisors." After asking, "should civil rights workers take a stand on Vietnam?" Zinn gave three reasons why civil rights groups and SNCC in particular should oppose the war. First, the black movement had a duty to offer support to its allies. Zinn pointed out that if peace groups were asked to support civil rights initiatives and "said they supported them, but could not come out publicly because it would harm their peace work, movement people would be rightly indignant."[6] Second, he explained that opposing the war would not mean giving up on civil rights to focus on peace—SNCC could simply offer a feasible level of support to the antiwar movement. Third, Zinn placed opposition to the war in the context of civil rights activists' experiences. He explained that "movement people' were in an ideal position to understand America's actions in Vietnam—"they understand just how much hypocrisy is wrapped up in our claim to stand for 'the free world.' . . . Events in Vietnam become easier to understand in the light of recent experience in the South."[7]

Bob Moses also argued in favor of adopting an official antiwar position and, like Zinn, he believed that the experiences of civil rights activists made them more likely to be skeptical of the noble claims that America was making about Vietnam. Moses declared that there was a "sickness in America" regarding the way that it viewed the world, and that it was "possible that those who have been part of the agonies of the South in recent years" were better able to understand this than others. The SNCC leader went beyond this, though, to place opposition to the war within a broader conceptual framework of participatory democracy.

Moses attacked those who argued that civil rights groups had no business commenting on foreign policy issues. He explained that one of the fundamental rights that the civil rights movement had been fighting for was the "right to participate fully in the discussions of the great issues that face the country." This included foreign policy which, as Moses noted, was generally left in the hands of the president. But the civil rights movement, or at least the portion that Moses represented and inspired, believed that "people should be involved in all the major decisions that affect them."

Moses also thought that Vietnam cut to the nature of the movement itself. The SNCC veteran did not believe that it was possible for the civil rights movement to simply "join" the peace movement. Instead, the "question we must ask ourselves is what kind of a movement are we going to be . . . are we going to address ourselves to the broader problems of society? Can we build a wider base for a movement in this country; and actually can the freedom movement as it has existed survive and achieve its goals unless it does this?"[8]

Not all SNCC members agreed that it made sense to attack the Vietnam War. Mitchell Zimmerman, a white activist with SNCC's Arkansas project, wrote to the *Student Voice* criticizing Zinn's call for an antiwar stance. Zimmerman acknowledged that there was a "certain level of agreement within SNCC" about the war, but that this did not "settle the question as to whether SNCC as an organization should take a stand." He argued that civil rights work was more acceptable to the wider American public than peace work, and that while peace groups would gain from associating with the black movement, civil rights groups would suffer. Indeed, Zimmerman asserted that SNCC ran the risk of being "seriously injured by being identified with dissent on Vietnam." Opposing the war would, he argued, hand the movement's enemies an effective means of red-baiting them, compromise the organization's fundraising capability, and curtail any further cooperation with the federal government. Moreover, Zimmerman felt that the peace movement was doomed to fail, and that "left wing dissent on Vietnam will have no significant impact on either our foreign policy, or on public opinion." The young activist concluded that "while we care a great deal about both Vietnam and civil rights, we can't do anything to help the Vietnam situation, and we can hurt ourselves by trying."[9]

SNCC finally debated Vietnam at a staff meeting held at Gammon Theological Seminary in Atlanta at the end of November. The discussion, which took place on the evening of November 29, was generally supportive of taking an antiwar position. Marion Barry—a former graduate student at Fisk who had played a leading role in the Nashville student movement—and his allies, who feared that opposing the war would damage the organization, were in the minority.[10] Gwendolyn Patton, for example, urged that SNCC "talk to the people about how rotten the country is that we live in. The MONSTER we live in." James Forman recognized the importance of the draft to an organization in which 80 percent of the staff were eligible, but also cautioned against shifting their focus. Forman explained that the peace movement did not have grassroots work going on, that SNCC could "relate things to people where we work," and urged that any action on Vietnam be made relevant to current work with black people.[11] Cleveland Sellers recalled Courtland Cox's role in persuading SNCC to adopt an antiwar policy. According to Sellers, Cox took the floor and "waxed eloquently" on the parallels between Vietnam and black America—"Mississippi and Vietnam; they are very much alike. Think about Vietnam's Ky and Senator James O. Eastland. . . . Think about the problems of Mississippi's poor, disenfranchised blacks and the problems of Vietnam's poor, disenfranchised peasants . . . consider the similarities between Vietnam's National Liberation Front and SNCC. They ought to be very much alike!'"[12] The discussion, which apparently involved much "debate and hassle," concluded with a decision to authorize the Executive Committee to draft an antiwar statement that would subsequently be released to the press.[13]

It is tempting to try to link the position on the war to the developing factionalism within SNCC. Clayborne Carson has argued that during 1965 the organization was torn by a dispute between "floaters" such as Bob Moses, who opposed centralizing and bureaucratizing trends within the group, and "hardliners" like Cleveland Sellers and James Forman, who favored greater discipline to make the organization more effective.[14] There are indications that the "Freedom High" or "floater" faction within SNCC was keener than "hardliners" on antiwar activism. Bob Moses, for example, had been the black staff member most active in antiwar activities, while at the November staff meeting Marion Barry spoke out against opposing the war on the grounds that it would harm the organization's health. James Forman also warned against SNCC shifting its attention away from black concerns. Ultimately, however, there is insufficient evidence for such a convenient dichotomy. Both "hardliners" and "floaters" opposed the war, most came to support SNCC's adoption of an official antiwar stance, and, ultimately, very few black SNCC field secretaries involved themselves in efforts to build an interracial antiwar movement.

The racist murder of a black SNCC worker, Sammy Younge, Jr., in Alabama, provided the catalyst for the release of a militantly antiwar statement by the organization.[15] Younge, a U.S. navy veteran enrolled at Tuskegee Institute, was shot to death by Marvin Segrest, a white gas station

employee, on January 3, after he tried to use a restroom that was for
"whites only." Cleveland Sellers recalled that "the absolute absurdity of a
man having to die for attempting to [use] a toilet filled us with rage,"
and the contradiction between "the freedom that Americans were killing
and dying for in Vietnam and the race hatred that motivated Sammy's
murder" was evident to all.[16] For SNCC communications director Julian
Bond, Younge's death provided him with an epiphany on Vietnam. He
recalled that it "crystallized everything. Everything became so stark." The
fact that Younge was a veteran made his murder even more powerful.[17]

On Thursday January 6, 1966, the day after Younge's funeral, SNCC
issued its antiwar statement.[18] The organization asserted its "right and
responsibility" to dissent with American foreign policy when it saw fit;
accused the U.S. government of being "deceptive in its claims of concern for the freedom of the Vietnamese people"; and it drew a parallel
between America's democratic claims in Southeast Asia and its alleged
inaction and indifference to murder and law-breaking in the South.
SNCC also questioned America's leadership in the Cold War struggle
against communism. The group suggested that the "cry of 'preserve
freedom in the world'" was "a hypocritical mask behind which [Amer-
ica] squashes liberation movements which are not bound, and refuse to
be bound, by the expediencies of United States cold war policies." SNCC
noted the disproportionate drafting of African Americans, expressed
solidarity with draft-resisters in America, asked "where is the draft for
the freedom fight in the United States?" and called on those who preferred to "use their energy to build democratic forms in this country" to
work with civil rights and human rights organizations as a "valid alternative" to the draft.[19] Indeed, concern over the inequities of the Selective Service System played an important role in SNCC's opposition to
the war. The disproportionate drafting of black Americans was an understandable cause of concern for the organization, and a good deal
of the discussion at the November 1965 staff meeting had been centered
around this.[20]

SNCC's antiwar pronouncement came during a period of great turmoil for the organization, which was increasingly turning away from
its nonviolent, interracial roots and embracing black separatism and
armed self-defense. Evidence of increasing radicalization was not hard
to find. In the summer of 1965, for example, SNCC workers founded
the Lowndes County Freedom Organization in Alabama, designed to win
political power for local blacks. The all-black party took a black panther
as its symbol. The year 1966 saw SNCC's Atlanta Project, located in the
Vine City neighborhood, take an anti-white, racially separatist line. In
May 1966 John Lewis would be replaced as SNCC chairman by the
twenty-four-year-old Stokely Carmichael—and by the end of the year the

remaining white members of the organization would be expelled. Julius Lester, who joined SNCC after Carmichael's election, wrote that the "angry children of Malcolm X" were replacing the idealistic activists of the early 1960s.[21]

As well as earning SNCC the wrath of the establishment, the ire of liberals, and the condemnation of former allies in the civil rights struggle, the war also had serious repercussions for Julian Bond, who had recently won election to the Georgia state legislature.[22] He was preparing to take his seat, representing the 136th district in Atlanta, when the antiwar statement was released—a statement that he endorsed. Amid accusations of "treason," Bond was denied his seat on January 10; his struggle to regain it occupied much of the next twelve months and was finally resolved by the U.S. Supreme Court in December.[23] Bond recalled that James Forman told him he was naïve, but "who would think that you would win the election, and then have the election declared null and void . . . I couldn't believe that when it happened. . . . of course I woke up fast, quickly. But . . . I had no idea that would happen."[24]

Support for Bond's right to be seated came from a wide variety of sources. John Lindsay, Republican mayor of New York, said that he wished that he still practiced law so that he could represent him.[25] Martin Luther King led a march in support of Bond and declared that "our nation is approaching a dangerous totalitarian periphery when dissent becomes synonymous with disloyalty."[26] The would-be legislator also received overwhelming backing from his Atlanta constituents—"there was almost unanimity in support of my right to be seated, and my right to have this opinion." But while local African Americans backed Bond's bid to claim his seat, there was less support for SNCC's attack on the Vietnam War. Bond recalled that "lots of people were against the antiwar statement but didn't say." Many constituents were "fairly conservative, and had a conservative world view, and this is a fight against communism, and the communists are bad, we have to fight them, they're exploiting these people, and so on. So there wasn't an embrace, by any means, of the statement. But there wasn't real hostility to it or pulling back from it."[27] This reflected the findings of a Harris poll commissioned by *Newsweek*, which showed that only 18 percent of African Americans favored a unilateral American withdrawal from Vietnam; 37 percent apparently supported LBJ's policies in Southeast Asia, with the same number unsure. While this survey indicated that a relatively large segment of black America was either opposed to, or hesitant about, Vietnam, it also revealed that the type of radical antiwar stance adopted by SNCC at the beginning of 1966 did not yet command widespread support among ordinary blacks.[28]

An editorial in the *Movement* claimed that the denial of Bond's seat validated SNCC's criticisms of America. The organization's antiwar statement had declared that "We know for the most part, elections in this country . . . are not free." As the *Movement* noted, "this month, in a revealing display of attitudes in the "New South," the Georgia legislature proved this point."[29] The editorial placed Bond's exclusion within a wider indictment of the Johnson administration. It argued that the government's failure to protect black lives in the South, James Coleman's nomination to the federal bench, and the "pitiful number" of federal registrars dispatched to the South "all fly in the face of the government's pious pleas that the movement work through 'acceptable' channels."

The episode propelled Bond into both the national limelight and the peace movement. According to John Lewis, Bond became seduced by the "flush of celebrity. He was a star, and he liked it."[30] At times, however, Bond seemed a little resentful that Georgia reactionaries had pushed him into the leadership of the antiwar struggle. In February 1967 he told one journalist that he had "begun to receive honors based on my ability to represent at once youth, peace and civil rights, and wanted only to represent the 136th District of Georgia."[31] He later recalled, "it seemed to me that . . . being elected to the legislature was a real accomplishment of which I was quite proud. Being involved in the antiwar movement in this way, was something other people had done to me." While he was proud of his role in the peace movement and "believed in it strongly," his election was "the thing I was most proud of, and most wanted to do."[32]

The Bond incident was one example of how the Vietnam War could affect the civil rights movement at the local level. Another came from Arkansas, where from late 1965 through 1966 the war intruded into the SNCC-related civil rights project there. SNCC's Arkansas Project was established in the autumn of 1962, after a formal request from the Arkansas Council on Human Relations. The project's headquarters was in Little Rock, but other movement centers included Gould, Pine Bluff, and Helena. The Arkansas movement helped desegregate lunch counters, hotels and theaters by early 1963, and in the summer of 1965, a "Summer Project" was initiated in order to register voters.[33] Beginning in the autumn of 1965, the Vietnam War began to emerge as an issue within Arkansas SNCC.

In September 1965, Mitchell Zimmerman, a SNCC worker with the Arkansas Project, had penned a rebuff to Howard Zinn's call for the organization to oppose the war in Vietnam, which was later published in the *Student Voice*. Zimmerman, a native of the Bronx who had first been inspired to activism by the Cuban Missile Crisis, had spent the summer of 1964 working in SNCC's Atlanta office. He arrived in Arkansas in August 1965 and served as communications officer for the project. In addition, Zimmerman was also involved in organizing around school board elections in the delta.[34]

Some thirty-five years later, Zimmerman disagreed with his warning against taking an antiwar position. It was, he said, "cowardly," "timid," and "wrong."[35] Zimmerman's caution in the autumn of 1965, however, was not borne of personal doubts about the immorality of the war. As early as December 1965, activists in the Arkansas project, including Zimmerman, were attacking America's involvement in Southeast Asia. William Hansen, a white field secretary from Cincinnati who had been active in SNCC since 1961, and who had arrived in Arkansas in the fall of 1962, wrote to the *Arkansas Gazette* condemning American foreign policy. In a letter that was published on December 1, Hansen denounced America's policies in Rhodesia, the Dominican Republic, and Vietnam. The civil rights leader charged that U.S. foreign policy was predicated on race and that America defined its "sphere of influence" on the basis of skin color.[36] A few days later Zimmerman attacked the Vietnam War and linked the conflict to the black freedom struggle. He complained that those who had the power to change things in the South were concentrating their efforts elsewhere—"like protecting the 'freedom' of the Vietnamese peasants to have their villages destroyed by napalm. No price is too high for us to inflict it upon the Vietnamese to prevent them from rejecting the American Way of Life—nor is any opportunity sufficiently costless for us to protect the rights of Negro Americans."[37]

Following the controversy generated by SNCC's antiwar statement, Hansen offered an explanation to the *Arkansas Democrat*. He asserted that the antiwar pronouncement was "general" and "not intended to dictate a position for all [SNCC] members." But he went on to say that African Americans were beginning to realize the effect of the war on them, which led to questions and protests. The newspaper article noted that three Arkansas SNCC members had registered as conscientious objectors.[38]

One of the COs was Vincent O'Connor, a devout Catholic and committed pacifist from San Francisco. Although he initially registered with the Selective Service as a CO, O'Connor later withdrew from cooperation with the system.[39] After leaving SNCC in the summer of 1966, he became active in local efforts to mobilize Vietnam dissent and worked with Arkansans for Peace in Vietnam.[40] In January 1966, though, O'Connor was opposed to SNCC using its limited resources to aid the peace movement—especially a peace movement that could be too easily tarred with the twin evils of leftist sectarianism and counterculturalism.

On January 12, 1966, the *Pine Bluff Commercial* carried a story about a planned antiwar demonstration, to be held in Pine Bluff on February 12. The action had been called by the National Coordinating Committee to End the War in Vietnam (NCC) during a conference in Milwaukee, Wisconsin. The date, Abraham Lincoln's birthday, was chosen to "symbolize the freedom movement." Jon Jacobs, director of the Southern Coordinating Committee to End the War in Vietnam (SCC) explained that Pine Bluff had been chosen because of the SNCC presence there— "SNCC's activities lead us to believe that the people of Pine Bluff are open to such a movement."[41] O'Connor fired off a response to Jacobs in which he stated that while he might participate in an antiwar demonstration he would not engage in organizing activity around the war— "I am not in Pine Bluff to organize peace demonstrations."

O'Connor explained that as a pacifist he was opposed to *all* wars, and that he did not care for "leftist revolutionary factions" (at a press conference Jacobs had worn a Du Bois Club badge). He also pointed out that, in the South, association with countercultural forms of expression would serve only to hinder the forces of progress. O'Connor explained that "many people who've come South to work for freedom have shaved off beards & done other things to make it less easy for people to reject them—not what they say—as "Beat" or "Red" or whatever." He expressed hope that "in future those who work for peace . . . would refrain, knowing the mind of the South, from wearing buttons that might tend to turn people off." O'Connor suggested Little Rock as a more appropriate location for an antiwar demonstration and implied that there would be little support in Pine Bluff for peace activity. O'Connor again emphasized that SNCC's purpose was not to organize peace demonstrations, which, he said, would be a full-time task.[42]

Despite such objections, there were a small number of antiwar activities in Arkansas during February 1966 in which SNCC had a visible presence. A teach-in on the war was held at Little Rock University, at which Mitchell Zimmerman joined with Chris Hobson of SDS to present the antiwar case.[43] The SNCC activist recalled that a crowd of around 800, a quarter black, had been supportive.[44] Then, in Little Rock on February 12, a tiny crowd of 19 protesters demonstrated against the war. The action was supported by six people with links to SNCC, including William Hansen and Jim Jones (a black student at the University of Arkansas and former SNCC activist).[45]

During late 1965 and early 1966 civil rights workers with SNCC's Arkansas Project were struggling with how to deal with the war in Vietnam. It is clear that, at the very least, the activists felt discomfort over it. However, antiwar sentiment was tempered by concerns about harming the local civil rights movement—as evinced by the comments made both by Hansen during the furor caused by SNCC's January statement and by O'Connor over the planned NCC action in Pine Bluff. This is a good example of how the "national" affected the "local." In January

1966, not all SNCC activists were enthusiastically embracing radical positions or emphasizing internationalism. Those in Arkansas, for example, were trying to focus on local grassroots organizing. The story of the Virginia Students' Civil Rights Committee (VSCRC) also reveals how local and national concerns often conflicted.

The VSCRC's founding in December 1964 illustrates the inter-related nature of much of the progressive activism of the 1960s. Howard Romaine, a veteran of SNCC's Mississippi Freedom Summer, enrolled at the University of Virginia in the fall of 1964, where he met David Nolan, who was active in the University Young Democratic Club. At one YDC meeting, Archie Allen, campus traveler with the Southern Students Organizing Committee (a Nashville-based student group founded in 1964 that sought to bring progressive change to the South) spoke.[46] He persuaded some of the students to attend an organizing conference in Atlanta. When the delegates returned, they gave a talk to the Virginia Council on Human Relations (VCHR), during the time when the Free Speech Movement at Berkeley was headline news. Howard Romaine, who had met Mario Savio during Mississippi Freedom Summer, urged that a sympathy demonstration be staged at the University of Virginia campus. The consensus within the VCHR was that a new group would be needed for non-civil rights movement activities, and the Students for Social Action (SSA) was formed, with Romaine as its chair. At a subsequent SSA meeting it was announced that a civil rights conference, sponsored by SNCC, was being held at Hampton Institute in December 1964.

Several people who would play important roles in the VSCRC (including Nan Grogan, Bill Towe, Betty Cummings, and Nolan) attended the conference, where they heard a number of SNCC activists recall their experiences as civil rights workers and pass on some of their expertise. Indeed, although many scholars have emphasized SNCC's retreat from the laborious and exhausting work of nurturing local projects in the aftermath of Freedom Summer and Atlantic City, it is clear that the group did not simply give up on organizing. According to David Nolan, "there was a missionary zeal in the air, and the rather clear desire to bring the Mississippi experience to bear on the Virginia Black Belt." James Forman told the conference that "you don't have to go to Mississippi to find these conditions."[47] At an evening party during the conference hosted by Virginius Thornton, a history teacher at Hampton, "people kept talking about the need to have a summer project in Virginia." On the final morning of the conference, a continuations committee was set up to carry out research on race relations in the Virginia black belt and to plan future conferences. The committee chose the name Virginia Students' Civil Rights Committee.

The organization's purpose was to attack "the roots . . . of poverty, deprivation, and segregation" in the Old Dominion. The group's former chairman, Ben Montgomery, recalled that they "decided we didn't need to go to Mississippi to find work that needed doing. We had problems right here." Drawing on the example of SNCC's 1964 Summer Project, the young black and white activists, drawn from a dozen Virginia colleges, made plans for a summer of civil rights work during 1965. Their activity would be focused on Virginia's Southside, a bloc of agricultural counties stretching from Norfolk to Lynchburg, which made up the fourth and fifth congressional districts. The area's African American residents lived in poverty under a strictly segregated system, and were denied political power by local whites.[48]

William Faulkner wrote that the whole land of the South is "indubitably, of and by itself, cursed," and that "all of us who derive from it, whom it ever suckled, white and black both, lie under the curse."[49] Certainly the "bleak country of red clay and scrub pine" that was the Virginia Southside was plagued by the "race problem . . . as no other section" of the state. Indeed, for more than two centuries the "cursed" land of the black belt, soaked in the blood of slaves and Confederates alike, was inextricably bound up with what James Baldwin termed America's racial nightmare. Slaves had outnumbered whites in the antebellum period, which made Nat Turner's bloody insurrection in Southampton County during 1831 particularly terrifying. In 1865, the war to free the slaves had left the region desolate and the plantations plundered—facts which "the lowland [white] South has never forgotten."[50] During Reconstruction the area provided the heart of black political power in the state, electing John M. Langston to the House of Representatives in 1888. He was the only African American to represent the Old Dominion in the hallowed halls of Congress until the election of Bobby Scott in 1994. By the mid-twentieth century a rigid caste system, relying on custom and law rather than Klansmen and rope, kept the black population of the Southside firmly "in their place." African Americans earned about three-fifths the income of whites, and averaged just five years of schooling.[51]

In the years following the Second World War, the region witnessed the rise of the modern black freedom struggle. A long and painful campaign to desegregate Prince Edward County's public schools eventually made it all the way to Washington, DC, where, in 1954, the U.S. Supreme Court considered the case as part of *Brown* v. *Board of Education*.[52] In 1960, in the wake of the Greensboro sit-ins, protests were held in Richmond, Norfolk, Newport News, Hampton and Suffolk.[53] Three years later, the tobacco and textile city of Danville saw mass protests against Jim Crow segregation, which were met by a response violent enough to inspire a SNCC freedom song.[54]

The Southside counties targeted by the VSCRC proved that no activist needed to travel to Mississippi to find serious problems that needed addressing. Lucius "Duke" Edwards explained that many people believed that "Virginia Negroes are free just because nobody is shooting at them every few nights." But Edwards, a black activist and student at Virginia State College, pointed out that the Old Dominion was actually a "controlled society" in which African Americans were denied basic civil, economic and political rights.[55] The fourth congressional district was impoverished, and its black residents lacked political power. The median annual income of the district in the mid-1960s was $3,532, which gave it a ranking of 405 out of the nation's 435 congressional districts. In most Southside counties, between a quarter and a third of African American families earned less than $1,000 a year, and 86 percent of the adult black population of the Southside had not completed high school.[56] Most of those who managed to find employment worked as unskilled laborers, and many lived on tenant farms.[57]

Like countless communities across the South, economic deprivation went hand-in-hand with political impotence. While African Americans made up 47.9 percent of the fourth congressional district's population, only 18.6 percent of eligible blacks were registered to vote.[58] As W. Lester Banks, executive secretary of the Virginia State Conference of the NAACP noted, though Virginia did not use violence to the same extent as Mississippi or Alabama to prevent blacks from voting, "registrars in the Black Belt Counties of Virginia do effectively discourage registration by Negro citizens." They did so by being uncooperative about opening hours and by requiring blacks to answer questions not required under the state constitution.[59]

The VSCRC, though an independent organization, was heavily influenced and aided by SNCC. Stanley Wise, a native of North Carolina who had been active in Howard University's Nonviolent Action Group and the Cambridge civil rights movement, was pivotal in the group's founding and attempted to pass on the lessons learned by SNCC activists.[60] On the eve of the summer project, SNCC field secretaries Stokely Carmichael, Charles Cobb, and Chuck Neblett spent three days in Virginia "giving pointers" to the VSCRC activists.[61] The young Virginians' declaration that their "primary function" was to "meet the needs of the people as *they* see them," owed much to SNCC's belief in participatory democracy and group-centered leadership. Indeed, one activist recalled that "VSCRC workers were thoroughly imbued with what is known . . . as the 'SNCC philosophy.'"[62]

"It's very much like the 1964 Mississippi Summer Project in miniature—except that the accents of most of the workers are Southern," began the *Southern Patriot*'s September 1965 article on the VSCRC.[63]

Anne Braden, a white southerner and civil rights stalwart, declared that "no civil rights project in the South has been more carefully prepared for than this one."[64] Twenty students, mostly Southerners, from seven Virginia colleges moved in to work in six Southside counties (Amelia, Brunswick, Dinwiddie, Lunenburg, Nottoway, and Powhatan).[65] VSCRC headquarters were established in an old pool hall in Blackstone, Nottoway County, which had a population of 3,659.[66]

Believing, as Howard Romaine put it, that their job was "to find out what people want and need and help them organize themselves," the VSCRC activists spent "a lot of time just listening."[67] Programs "varied sharply from county to county," and depended largely on what local blacks requested or supported.[68] Activities included voter registration, organizing black farmers, establishing selective buying campaigns, carrying out research, and publishing a newsletter. The VSCRC also worked at building up the local infrastructure by establishing community centers and forming sports teams.

At the end of the summer project, six students remained to continue working with the local black population. The activists' decision to engage in full-time organizing reflected the fact that short-term commitment was of limited use. As Nolan explained, "with students in summer projects [there] is barely time to start a baseball team."[69] Instead the young activists would have to immerse themselves in the communities where they worked, and become what Bob Moses called "deep-sea divers."[70]

Over the next six months or so, VSCRC continued much of the work that it had begun during the summer. In cooperation with the SCLC's Summer Community Organization and Political Education (SCOPE) project, more than 1,200 people were registered to vote. The largest increase took place in Lunenburg County, where the number of registered African American voters doubled. The VSCRC also helped to organize marches and rallies, which resulted in the electoral boards in Lunenburg and Dinwiddie Counties granting additional registration days. Crop allotments were a major local issue, with African Americans often suffering from discrimination. The group attempted to educate black farmers about relevant federal farm programs, and organized mass meetings. VSCRC reported that "in each of the magisterial districts of three counties farmers nominated and had placed on the ballot candidates for the county Agricultural Stabilization and Conservation committees." This was the "first time, in counties where Negroes comprise a majority or near-majority of farmers, that Negroes have been represented on the farm ballot."[71] VSCRC activists also organized local blacks to take advantage of the war on poverty programs, and worked to improve local schools.[72]

During late 1965 and early 1966 the war in Vietnam began to have an impact on the VSCRC. At a January 1966 staff meeting, the Georgia leg-islature's refusal to seat Julian Bond because of his stand against the war was discussed. The following month, the VSCRC staff agreed that "dis-cussion of peace" should form part of the program for a planned state-wide student conference. At a staff meeting in March, David Nolan expressed his opposition to the war and the draft.[73] Indeed, Nolan was particularly enthusiastic about opposing the war. In July, for example, he argued that Vietnam and the black freedom struggle were inextricably linked. Nolan believed that the war presented a "moral test of the civil rights movement. It forces us to examine all the ideals we have claimed to be fighting for. Are we indeed working for everybody's freedom, or are we merely out for our own selfish ends." Nolan considered it "incon-ceivable that one who supports the ideals of the civil rights movement could also support what is being done by the United States to the people of Vietnam."[74]

The activists' opposition to the war could sometimes have a personal dimension. Rives Foster was classified 1-A for almost a year, and con-fessed that he did not know what he would have done if he had been drafted.[75] At a staff meeting on July 18, the VSCRC decided to sponsor a peace demonstration on August 6. Reflecting his mounting interest in the war, Nolan was "delegated to make further plans . . . and to report back."[76]

Opposition to the war, though, was not always an issue that com-manded broad support among the local black population. As David Nolan explained, the white workers tended to have views "on such subjects as . . . Vietnam that don't jibe with those of local people." Nolan recognized that most blacks "had a single interest in civil rights and proclaimed themselves '100% with LBJ.'"[77] The potential of Vietnam to divide move-ment activists from those whom they were trying to organize had paral-lels within SDS. By 1965 its attempt to mobilize the poor through ERAP (Economic Research and Action Project) was already struggling but, as James Miller has argued, Vietnam was the "last straw." The escalation of the war, and the desire of many SDSers to oppose it, introduced a volatile and destabilizing element into the relationship between com-munity organizer and community. Many poor people, believing that America fought only just wars, were hostile to the growing antiwar move-ment.[78] VSCRC activist Rives Foster acknowledged that Vietnam helped to push the Virginia civil rights movement off course—"at first anti-war efforts . . . seemed to be hurting the movement," and "the result of the war was the drifting along of projects and problems."[79]

Venturing outside the field of civil rights also threatened to damage re-lations with the group's white supporters, some of whom were offended by its tentative opposition to Vietnam. After the VSCRC decided to sponsor an antiwar demonstration, a Charlottesville doctor who had contributed money to the group wrote to ask "how much time we were going to spend on Vietnam, so he could reduce his contributions accordingly." Another financial supporter wrote that "we were not really civil rights workers, but rather draft-card burners, anarchists and subversives, and he wanted his money back."[80]

Antiwar activity in Virginia's Southside seems to have generated very little enthusiasm. Fewer than fifty people, described as a "disgustingly low turn-out," attended a daylong peace seminar on April 23.[81] Moreover, the peace demonstration planned for 6 August had to be canceled because of a lack of support.[82] As David Nolan explained, "at the last staff meeting we voted not to have the demonstration, after people began finking out right and left, getting county fever, deciding that one day of voter registration work was worth more than trying to do something about the war."[83] It is interesting to note Nolan's implication that Vietnam *was* more important than civil rights.

The VSCRC's increasing interest in Vietnam, which coincided with the rise of separatist tendencies within the freedom movement as a whole, pushed the white volunteers away from their organizing work among Virginia's black population and onto the college campuses. Black Power had always been a factor within the VSCRC. John "Coolie" Washington "came on the project a black nationalist," and believed that "if there was a war between all the whites and Negroes . . . the Negroes would win," while the group's black chairman, Ben Montgomery, was "influenced by SNCC workers who came through singing the praises of Malcolm X."[84]

The VSCRC's white activists increasingly accepted that organizing African Americans was a job best done by blacks themselves. Within the grass-roots civil rights movement, whites were increasingly seen by their black counterparts as perpetuating a culture of dependency among poor African Americans and reinforcing racial stereotypes. In 1965, for example, CORE's Bill Bradley outlined some of the problems caused by white activists—"the general experience expressed by project leaders . . . was that white workers generally found it difficult to accept Black leadership." There were also cultural differences, such as when white workers decided not to bathe "until practically forced to." Perhaps more important, though, was the realization that the relationship between white activist and black community could be a potentially damaging one. Bradley explained that "too often the white worker becomes a crutch for members of the black community. . . . Case after case of Black dependency (upon) whites could be cited. The reasons are clear, we are used to depending upon white folks (good or bad) for practically everything. We are taught from birth that the white man is the greatest and a 'nigger ain't shit.'" The CORE leader concluded, "the very independence we are trying to encourage is discouraged by the presence and activity of whites."[85]

David Nolan explained that white VSCRC activists "were given preferential treatment to the Negro workers. This is . . . understandable . . . since the white workers were something new . . . but it grated on the Negro staff members." He continued, "Negroes in the community had a hard time breaking their own stereotypes about whites. When Mr. Claiborne came over . . . to get me for church he was hesitant about coming in, hesitant about sitting down, always calling me Mr. or sir."[86]

Nolan had raised the problem of whites organizing blacks as early as September 1965. Somewhat patronizingly, he explained that "I think you get non-ordinary whites (social revolutionaries) working with ordinary Negroes (peoples). "[87] Rives Foster, who was white, believed that "black-white hangups in community organizing was always a problem. Many times I talked to groups of Negroes instead of with them . . . Black nationalism was and is the answer."[88] In November 1966, as the VSCRC considered abandoning its work among black Virginians, the staff agreed that any future civil rights organizing "should not be geared toward participation by white students." Instead, local black students should be recruited.[89]

In late 1966, the VSCRC staff decided to withdraw from the Southside, and focus on organizing "Virginia students" rather than local African Americans. One explained that the VSCRC "had a dual constituency—Virginia Negroes and Virginia college students, the former by the nature of our commitment and the latter because of our origin. We had a responsibility to both of them, a responsibility to change." Many of the organization's activists felt, as David Nolan noted, that they "were not living up to that responsibility by continuing to work only in Southside" because it was not "the most effective place to work to change the condition of the Negro in Virginia and it was not the most effective place to work to change American policy in Vietnam."[90] With the war in Vietnam escalating, student protest against the war continued to build. Nolan wrote that "we were . . . derelict in our obligations to Virginia students. Increasingly, their main concerns were the Vietnam War and the draft." In a July 1966 memorandum, Nolan argued that "the problems of organizing" African Americans was "best done by" African Americans, and he urged the white VSCRC activists to switch their focus to Virginia students and the war in Vietnam. He believed that they "should focus Virginia students on their own problems . . . rather than drain off their efforts by working in southside." Nolan felt that there was a "need for more peace work in Virginia which would more logically be located in the college communities than in southside. . . . I think there is work to be done on the question of the draft." Nolan thought that "people in

VSCRC are probably the best qualified in the state to do something about these things, and I think that this is where they should train their efforts."[91]

It would appear that, within the VSCRC, Black Nationalism to some extent provided white activists with the excuse they were looking for to leave the civil rights movement in order to concentrate their efforts on protesting against the war in Vietnam. By 1966 many were coming to agree with Michael Ferber, founder of the anti-draft *Resistance* movement, that Vietnam was a more "urgent national issue" than civil rights.[92]

The white activists' increasing focus on, and interest in, protesting against the war in Vietnam blended with Black Power ideology to derail the VSCRC and its civil rights organizing work. Evidence from Virginia shows how the war in Vietnam increasingly replaced civil rights as "the issue" in the consciousness of politically aware progressive white activists as Black Power ideology simultaneously nudged them out of the struggle for black liberation.

While many black SNCC activists—Bob Moses, Cleveland Sellers, Ivanhoe Donaldson, Gwendolyn Patton, and John Wilson, to name just a few—passionately opposed the war in Vietnam and were active in the movement to end it, the majority of those featured in the previous discussion—Zinn, Zimmerman, Nolan, Hansen, and O'Connor—were white. Although white activists retained their commitment to the cause of black freedom, the Vietnam War increasingly occupied their attention and, as noted, the developing ideology of Black Power encouraged this. Indeed, SNCC chairman Stokely Carmichael appeared to countenance such a development. Writing in the *New York Review of Books*, he explained that one of the "most disturbing things about almost all white supporters of the movement has been that they are afraid to go into their own communities—which is where the racism exists—and work to get rid of it. They want to run from Berkeley to tell us what to do in Mississippi; let them look instead at Berkeley." Carmichael continued, "they admonish blacks to be nonviolent; let them preach nonviolence in the white community. . . . *Let them work to stop America's racist foreign policy.*"[93]

The emergence of Black Power was, as many scholars have recognized, a tremendously important development in the history of the African American freedom struggle. Robert Cook and David Burner, for example, both cite Black Power as one of the principal reasons for the collapse of the civil rights movement.[94] Black Power first came to public attention in the summer of 1966. In Greenwood on June 17, SNCC activists Stokely Carmichael and Willie Ricks popularized the controversial slogan. John Dittmer has described how an angry Carmichael, out on bail, told an agitated crowd of 600 mostly local people that "this is the

27th time I have been arrested—I ain't going to jail no more, I ain't going to jail no more." Then, as the crowd became increasingly enthusiastic, he repeatedly yelled "We want black power!" The SNCC leader continued, "Every courthouse in Mississippi ought to be burned tomorrow to get rid of the dirt . . . from now on when they ask what you want, you know what to tell 'em. What do you want?" The crowd thundered back, "Black Power."[95] The powerful cry was no spontaneous eruption, though. Willie Ricks had tested it on crowds during the previous week and urged Carmichael to use it. Moreover, SNCC as an organization had been moving toward Black Nationalism since the cataclysmic summer of 1964.

Black Power's meanings have always been fiercely contested and, despite the efforts of scholars, it remains a notoriously hard concept to define. The Black Power label can encompass such diverse philosophies as cultural nationalism, black capitalism and black separatism, but some generalizations can be made. Black Power ideology drew on the example and rhetoric of Malcolm X, emphasized racial pride and solidarity with nonwhite peoples, identified Afro-America with the worldwide struggle against white "imperialism," advocated the support and development of black-controlled institutions, and endorsed self-defense. Carmichael and Charles Hamilton, a political scientist, provided one of the best intellectual definitions of Black Power in their 1967 book, *Black Power: The Politics of Liberation in America*. They attacked integration as a middle-class obsession, called on African Americans to abandon the tactic of coalition with white liberals, and encouraged the formation of locally based community organizations and political parties. Ultimately, though, Carmichael and Hamilton did not promote black separatism; instead, they placed African American development within the pluralist tradition of American politics. They wrote, in an oft-quoted passage, that "the concept of Black Power rests on a fundamental premise . . . before a group can enter the open society, it must first close ranks."[96]

Most of white America, however, cared little for the subtleties and distinctions of the ideology, and focused instead on its alleged racism and violence. This misunderstanding was aided not only by "media misperception and manipulation," but also by mainstream civil rights leaders and their white liberal allies.[97] The NAACP's Roy Wilkins, never a friend of the radicals, defined Black Power as "the father of hatred and the mother of violence. It is a reverse Mississippi, a reverse Hitler, a reverse Ku Klux Klan." The Association simultaneously viewed the development of Black Nationalism within SNCC and CORE as an opportunity to recruit "mature and balanced young people" from the "defections in their ranks."[98] Vice President Hubert Humphrey declared that "racism is racism—and there is no room in America for racism of any color."[99] Of course some black power militants were also to blame, especially when they went out of their way to shock whites by using provocative language. CORE leader Floyd McKissick's comment to reporters, for instance, that "the greatest hypocrisy we have is the Statue of Liberty. We ought to break the young lady's legs and point her to Mississippi" was never likely to help secure a favorable reception for Black Power.[100]

Although historians have followed contemporaries in highlighting the discontinuities between the Black Power movement of the late 1960s and the nonviolent direct action protests of the first half of the decade, a new historiography is emerging that challenges such assumptions. In his study of the Monroe, North Carolina civil rights leader Robert F. Williams, for example, Timothy B. Tyson has skillfully demonstrated that the conventional dichotomy is simplistic, and that it often obscures rather than enlightens the scholarly discussion. According to Tyson the civil rights and Black Power movements "grew out of the same soil, confronted the same predicaments, and reflected the same quest for African American freedom." He has shown that "virtually all of the elements that we associate with Black Power were already present in the small towns and rural communities of the South where the civil rights movement was born."[101] Both Black Power and nonviolent direct action, then, were deeply embedded in the history of the black freedom struggle.

Indeed, the historical roots of Black Power, and the traditions from which it drew strength and inspiration are striking. Armed self-defense was nothing new—it had an established tradition in the rural South. During the 1950s, legendary NAACP lawyer Thurgood Marshall relied on armed guards and even machine guns for protection when he argued controversial cases in the Deep South, while black activists like Fred Shuttlesworth in Birmingham and Medgar Evers in Mississippi used guns to defend themselves.[102] It was not just Malcolm X and Stokely Carmichael who promoted international solidarity among people of color. In *A Rising Wind* (1945), the NAACP's Walter White had written that the Second World War had given American blacks a sense of kinship with other non-white peoples—"he senses that the struggle of the Negro in the United States is part and parcel of the struggle against imperialism in India, China, Burma, Africa. "[103] Roy Wilkins had marched in support of Ethiopian freedom during the 1930s.

In the build-up to Freedom Summer, SNCC members had engaged in an emotional debate about whether white volunteers should be restricted from leadership roles in the movement, and whether their presence was welcome at all. They may have been aware that, in the 1940s, A. Philip Randolph had insisted that his March on Washington Movement be all black.[104] Moreover, the white activist Anne Braden, who had recruited SNCC's first white field secretary in 1961, had long believed that "the job of white people who believe in freedom is to confront white

America."[105] The professed ideals of the Beloved Community had always existed alongside an instinctive caution, if not hostility, among many black activists about white participation in the freedom movement. When SNCC expelled its few remaining white members in December 1966, and when Black Power militants called on whites to organize whites and blacks to organize blacks, many liberals were indignant. But it is illuminating to recall Bayard Rustin's speech to a 1964 SNCC conference. The veteran nonviolent activist declared that "the time has come for the white students who want to aid the civil rights movement to stop putting on blue jeans and going to Mississippi to organize Negroes." "Instead," he advised, "do something that is harder and much less glamorous: stay home, go into white communities, work as hard as any black SNCC worker to convince the white people to support this movement."[106] The exhortation of Rustin, a leading exponent of liberal coalitionism, bears an uncanny resemblance to the sentiments expressed by Carmichael, a Black Nationalist. It clearly indicates that the relationship between the Black Power and nonviolent wings of the civil rights movement need further examination.

In addition to SNCC's embrace of Black Power in 1966, the Congress of Racial Equality was also adopting a more radical orientation. As Robert Cook has shown, the organization's increasing focus on organizing in black urban neighborhoods resulted in it recruiting more African American activists, thereby changing its racial composition. By 1964, 80 percent of CORE's National Action Committee were black and the group's overall white majority was quickly disappearing. Moreover, contact with ghetto blacks also increased CORE's receptivity to the black separatist outlook of groups like the Nation of Islam, which exerted a powerful influence in the northern cities. By the mid-1960s, CORE's attachment to the principles of Gandhian nonviolence was fading, and in July 1967 the term "multi-racial" was expunged from the organization's constitution.[107]

New Black Power groups also emerged. The most (in)famous was the Black Panther Party (BPP), founded in Oakland, California by Huey Newton and Bobby Seale in October 1966. Inspired by the SNCC-organized Black Panther party in Lowndes County, Alabama, the Panthers opposed police brutality, called for black economic and political power, and advocated the formation of black self-help organizations to take control of ghetto neighborhoods. Imbued with the ideas of Malcolm X and Frantz Fanon, the sociologist whose writings on the "cleansing" power of revolutionary violence exerted great influence on black militants, they also embraced armed self-defense. On 2 May 1967, thirty gun-carrying Panthers marched into the California state capitol in Sacramento to protest a bill barring the carrying of firearms in public. The

Panthers, with their anti-capitalist rhetoric and fierce opposition to the war in Vietnam, quickly became folk heroes to a generation of white radicals. But while the BPP did engage in serious community organizing, it also had a sinister, criminal side.[108]

Black Power cannot be divorced from the context of the urban riots in which it developed. Five days after the passage of the Voting Rights Act, rioting erupted in the Watts district of Los Angeles. Lasting for four days, it cost 34 lives (most of them black), injured 1,000, and destroyed an estimated $45 million of property. It marked the start of three years of "long, hot summers." In 1966, 43 "instances of urban turmoil" occurred—the most serious a four-day riot in Cleveland. In the summer of 1967, Tampa, Cincinnati, Atlanta, Newark, and Detroit all suffered serious urban unrest. The six days of rioting in Newark cost 23 lives; the disorder in Detroit killed 43. In 1968, the murder of Martin Luther King led to riots in more than 100 cities, at the cost of 46 lives and $100 million in property damage. The riots were caused by a number of factors—not least police brutality and the conditions of extreme poverty in which ghetto blacks lived. They were also a testament to the failure of both liberals and the civil rights movement to deal adequately with the problems that affected urban blacks in the North.

The riots, or "urban rebellions" as they were known in radical circles, had an important political impact too. Combined with the rising frustration with the ongoing war in Vietnam, they helped create a sense of despair and disillusionment that fueled the radicalization of the New Left and Black Power movements. They also helped deepen the divide between the black freedom struggle and white liberals. Many whites reacted with shock, bewilderment, and anger to the fact that such events took place when historic progress on race relations had occurred, and while the Great Society was attempting to deal with the problems of urban poverty and racism. But although Johnson's Great Society vision was noble, its rhetoric created raised expectations that were not met by a war on poverty that suffered from organizational confusion as well as budgetary constraints imposed by the rising cost of war in Vietnam. In 1966, for instance, Congress slashed the budget of the Office for Economic Opportunity (the major war on poverty agency) by $500,000,000.[109] The riots also discredited liberalism. Conservative critics called for a law-and-order crackdown, an end to federal handouts that they claimed rewarded rioters, and a slowdown on civil rights.[110] The 1966 mid-term elections, which saw widespread gains for the Republicans, augured a resurgence of American conservatism.[111]

Peace movement historian Charles DeBenedetti has claimed that Black Power "precluded cooperation with whites" over the question of the war in Vietnam, while David Burner has accused Black Power militants of "repelling . . . as much of the antiwar movement as possible."[112] However, the relationship between Black Power, the Vietnam War, and the American peace movement, is more complex than this. Black Power acted as a double-edged sword—while black radicals shared both the New Left's critique of liberalism, and its radical analysis of the war in Vietnam, Black Nationalism made the task of constructing an interracial antiwar movement more difficult.

As we have already seen, Black Power bolstered the peace movement by encouraging white activists, who had previously given their energies to the civil rights struggle, to turn their attention instead to ending the war in Vietnam. The antiwar forces were strengthened further by the Black Power movement's forceful opposition to Vietnam. At a speech at Morgan State University in January 1967, Stokely Carmichael emphasized the economic imperialism that he believed drove American policy in Southeast Asia.[113] Other radical blacks adopted uncompromising stances. The pages of the Black Panther's newspaper, the *Black Panther*, frequently contained fierce condemnation of the "Yankee Imperialist" war of "aggression" in Vietnam.[114] According to the Panthers, the war was "a struggle for liberation; [a] revolutionary war against the largest and most repressive monopoly system in the world—the United States."[115] Panther leader Eldridge Cleaver, a convicted rapist turned Black Nationalist writer and activist, declared that "the black man's interest lies in seeing a free and independent Vietnam, a strong Vietnam which is not the puppet of international white supremacy."[116]

For militant black leader Robert Williams, Black Nationalism was, by definition, antiwar. On August 8, 1966, the third anniversary of Chairman Mao Zedong's statement in support of American blacks, the North Carolinian exile gave a speech in the Great Hall of the People, Beijing. He told a 10,000-strong audience, including Chinese premier Zhou EnLai, that "Black Power is a dissident force challenging the racist white power structure that is so heinously exterminating the people of Vietnam."[117] Williams vehemently condemned the "racist white man's war of imperialism" in Southeast Asia and opposed America's "vicious crusade to dehumanize, emasculate, and enslave the great Vietnamese people."[118] Militant black opposition to the war thus constituted both a potential source of strength for the white antiwar movement, and a common interest around which cooperation between the peace and freedom movements might be built.

However, sharing what Clayborne Carson has described as a "common radical vocabulary and anti-imperialistic perspective," obscured the emerging chasm that separated black and white radicals during the late 1960s.[119] The white student left quickly understood that Black Power posed problems as well as providing opportunities. In June 1966, SDS's National Council approved a resolution that endorsed SNCC's Black Power position. The organization also welcomed SNCC's opposition to the war in Vietnam—"we applaud SNCC for recognizing that the enemies of deep-seated social change at home are the enemies of revolution abroad."[120] Just two months later, when planning its forthcoming national convention, the SDS newspaper *New Left Notes* examined the potential difficulties that Black Power might cause the peace movement. An article in August explained that many radicals viewed the Black Power movement as a natural antiwar constituency. But the paper wondered whether white antiwar activists could "fruitfully join with them in antiwar activities? Will any cooperation be possible between those engaging in black electoral politics and those participating in the developing peace and third party politics?" They also wondered whether "the violence that voices itself in the anti-war rhetoric of SNCC" would "be a possible basis for white peaceniks to relate to" or whether it would "undermine much of the moral basis of middle-class anti-war ferment." Concern was also expressed that "tactics which blacks may identify with may leave most white people (including our constituencies) feeling uncomfortable."[121]

Throughout 1966 the peace movement made attempts to broaden its appeal to African Americans and, specifically, to involve civil rights groups and black activists in the antiwar coalition. One way in which the peace movement tried to do this was to tie domestic issues, especially racism, to the struggle against the war. For example, over April 23–24, the Southern Coordinating Committee to End the War in Vietnam (SCC) held an antiwar conference in Nashville to focus on the problems of organizing the peace movement in the South. There were few blacks among the 100 or so delegates, and this caused some concern. A peace activist from Gainesville, Florida, declared that "the embarrassing thing about the peace movement in the South is that it's white." One SNCC worker suggested that "[black] people don't understand the war . . . it's very far away and the trouble they see is right there in the courthouse." Additionally, for many black southerners, economic dependence on whites made it particularly risky to take an antiwar stance.[122]

Racial division was also a factor that kept the peace movement white. One black representative from Mississippi said that he knew many people who took the attitude that the war "is the white man's problem. He started it, let him figure a way to stop it." Ed Hamlett, a white activist, echoed similar sentiments in the May 1966 edition of *New Left Notes*, when he wrote that "the blacks who say that the war in Vietnam is a racist, white man's war assert that whites must end it. A corollary of this is that they will admit of no responsibility for participation in the Peace Movement as such."[123]

The fact that there was already a movement (civil rights) in the South that occupied the energy and attention of progressive activists certainly helps explain the relative weakness of the peace movement below the Mason and Dixon line. However, the delegates at Nashville concluded that the peace movement could be made more attractive to African Americans if blacks felt that they would gain something from it. A consensus emerged that antiwar activity had to be tied to the struggle for black freedom. SCC chairman Dwain Wilder declared that the peace movement "should become involved in civil rights and other social and political matters."[124]

There was some cooperation between black and white radicals over Vietnam. For example, SNCC's Stokely Carmichael and SDS's Carl Oglesby made a joint statement opposing the draft before the House Committee on the Armed Services in July. But the relationship became increasingly strained.[125] Black Power brought with it heightened racial sensitivities; and cultural differences between black civil rights workers and white student peace activists often hampered the process of coalition. There were signs as early as March 1966 that Black Power could undermine attempts to build a multiracial antiwar movement. In an article for *New Left Notes*, Bob Ross analyzed the radical movement in Chicago—which was centered on the Committee for Independent Political Action (CIPA). Ross explained how "CIPA, at a city-wide level, is 'factioned' along civil rights vs. peace interests. Often this appears to be a Negro vs. white conflict, tainting discussions with rancorous and frightening tones."[126]

Another example of the tensions between black and white radicals comes from the founding convention of the Student Mobilization Committee to End the War in Vietnam (SMC). Between December 28 and 30, 1966, some 200 young opponents of the war attended a meeting at the University of Chicago, called by Communist Party student leader Bettina Aptheker, who was attempting to organize a student strike.[127] SNCC sent two of its field secretaries, Charles Cobb and Gwendolyn Patton, and their experiences are revealing. The SNCC activists were disappointed that what they perceived as the racist nature of the Vietnam War was not discussed, and they were also repelled by the incessant political factionalism of white leftists. Charles Cobb apparently "felt stupid" at the meeting, while Patton reported that many of the black delegates were "amazed at the white naïve intellectualism and the deep-seated factionalism."[128]

The Chicago experience was evidently important to both Cobb and Patton. Cobb's future reluctance about working with white radicals had its origins in Chicago, while Patton referred to the December gathering a year later when discussing the black movement's relationship with the predominantly white antiwar movement. Patton recalled that black people found it "very difficult" to relate to the Chicago meeting. She continued, "Black people were talking about self-determination and liberation and white people were talking about 'end the war' and 'peace.'" In addition, black delegates were unable to deal with "white radical factionalism." Patton explained that "Black people were only in a position to react to the white radicals; it was the question of accepting or rejecting the white program, and as an alternative for not having their own program black people walked out of the Chicago meeting."[129] This inability or unwillingness to deal with racism, and the debilitating effects of white political factionalism, continually plagued the peace movement's attempts to win black support.

The spring of 1966 saw a number of "peace campaigns" across America, in which activists on the left of the political spectrum ran in the midterm congressional elections, normally against liberal Democrats, on the issue of Vietnam. These campaigns also constituted an example of tentative coalition between the peace and freedom movements. Although the war was the primary motivating force, many of the candidates also addressed black concerns, which they often linked to the war. There were a number of high-profile challengers, such as Howard Morgan in Oregon, and Robert Cook in Connecticut; and many of the electoral insurgencies were encouraged by the National Conference for New Politics (NCNP).

The NCNP evolved out of a series of meetings involving peace, civil rights, and student leaders, held over the summer and fall of 1965.[130] The organization's purpose was to bridge the gap between radicals and antiwar liberals, which it hoped to accomplish by bringing about a coalition among New Left and antiwar groups, the civil rights movement, and reform Democrats. It was envisaged that this alliance would be centered on the common goals of ending poverty, racism, and the war in Vietnam.[131] The make-up of the NCNP executive committee reflected the desire for inclusiveness, covering as it did the left-of-center political spectrum. SDS's Paul Booth and SNCC's Julian Bond were joined by reform Democrat Simon Casady; Arthur Waskow of the Center for the Study of Democratic Institutions; and SANE's Benjamin Spock. Antiwar liberals Anne and Martin Peretz provided a sizeable amount of funding.

Designed to coordinate "new politics" activity, the NCNP aimed to provide communication links through literature, newsletters, and meetings, to "help coalesce the many peace, poverty, and militant civil rights groups with student demonstration groups, disaffected intellectuals, social welfare, labor and religious organizations."[132] The organization announced that New Politics was an "organized effort to return decision-making to the people by providing a democratic way to take effective political action at a time when the conventional American politics of party labels and personalities has become sterile." New Politics encouraged the "coalition of the many different groups and constituencies into a dynamic movement whose combined resources can have impact on the future politics of the nation."[133] This coalition was based around four broad objectives—ending the Cold War and U.S. military intervention abroad, establishing racial equality, encouraging world disarmament and constructive relations with Third World revolutionaries, and using America's growing productive capacity to meet the needs of her inner cities and depressed rural areas.[134]

During 1966, believing that left-wing dissent needed to be transformed into political power, the NCNP called on Americans to support "new politics" candidates against the "old politics" of military intervention abroad and racial and economic injustice at home."[135] The NCNP backed candidates who spoke clearly for "peace and a full scale assault on the root causes of poverty." The organization was not simply against the conflict in Vietnam, it was also for a genuine war on poverty, which would particularly help African Americans. It believed that this could not happen while America continued to wage war in Asia, "it is now abundantly clear that the cost of the war has doomed hopes of any meaningful attack on our slums and ghettos."[136]

The energetic and innovative primary campaign waged by Robert Scheer against Jeffrey Cohelan in California's seventh congressional district came to embody the "new politics" of 1966. Helped by the peculiar circumstances of the constituency, which encompassed both the radical Berkeley campus and part of the Oakland ghetto, Scheer, the thirty-year-old foreign editor of *Ramparts*, took on the liberal incumbent under the slogan "Withdraw the Troops. End Poverty."[137] Scheer's campaign constituted a massive effort, with billboards, leaflets, precinct work, and 1,000 volunteer workers operating from six headquarters.[138] Campaign expenses eventually ran to some $69,000.[139] Scheer received the endorsement of some liberal groups, such as the International Longshoremen's and Warehouseman's Union, and many of his supporters were middle aged or older.[140] Although Scheer was supported by some of the radicals involved with the Vietnam Day Committee (a militant antiwar organization located in the Bay Area) and SDS, he was opposed by many who rejected the tactic of working within the Democratic Party. As historian Kirkpatrick Sale noted, "SDS had never gone on record in support of the NCNP and Berkeley SDSers, in general, soured on electoral politics . . . had not lifted a finger for Scheer." Indeed, when SDS national secretary Paul Booth gave the impression that his organization was solidly behind the NCNP and the peace campaigns, he was attacked by some of his more radical colleagues. Berkeley New Leftist Buddy Stein called for his resignation, and the SDS leadership prohibited Booth from attending a May 1966 NCNP meeting.[141]

Though motivated by opposition to the war, the Scheer campaign was multi-issue in nature. Part of the plan was to build a local political movement that would survive the expected election defeat.[142] Scheer thus concerned himself with a whole range of issues that the traditional community leaders had allegedly denied or ignored—"the plight of Oakland's notorious ghettoes, failure of the poverty program, school desegregation, civil liberties, urban renewal, job discrimination, and police brutality."[143] The attempt to build a multi-issue radical insurgency required the support of African Americans, and Scheer was reasonably successful in achieving this. He had announced his candidacy in January 1966 at a press conference in Oakland, accompanied by the NAACP's Carlton Goodlett and Casandra Davis, and Elijah Turner of CORE. Goodlett, a former president of the San Francisco NAACP, was an internationally active peace advocate; he had served as chairman of the Committee for International Peace Action, and supported the World Council of Peace, and in 1966 he was running in the Democratic gubernatorial primary as a peace candidate.[144] Dr. Thomas Burbridge, another past president of the San Francisco NAACP, also endorsed Scheer, declaring that "the issues of civil rights at home and the war in Vietnam are inseparably linked."[145]

Ultimately, Cohelan managed a victory over Scheer by winning 55 percent of the vote to Scheer's 45 percent.[146] Interestingly, the NCNP gave only limited backing to Scheer, furnishing him somewhat reluctantly with $1,000 in the final weeks of the campaign.[147] In fact, the NCNP's strategy for the 1966 elections was muddled and it had entered the electoral arena "haphazardly."[148] In the late summer of 1966, Simon Casady complained to the NCNP board that the organization had made hasty decisions about the primaries. He expressed his fear that "somehow no one quite finished the job of designing NCNP and thinking through its purpose and objectives before they decided to launch her and sail her to the moon."[149] In many ways this lack of direction, which manifested itself in the continuing debate over whether to run third party candidates, work within the two party system or focus on "local organizing" would torment the organization throughout its existence.[150]

Antiwar candidates who were committed to the cause of black freedom could not always count on the support of those national civil rights organizations that were opposed to the Vietnam War. Although James Farmer had resisted attempts to adopt an official antiwar position for CORE during the summer of 1965, he soon relented. In January 1966 CORE's leadership had declared that "the escalation of that war [Vietnam] is wrong . . . the war which must be escalated is the war against poverty and discrimination."[151] In April, CORE's Northeast Regional Council voted by 43 to 9 to denounce the war as a racist and diversionary effort to stifle civil rights policy.[152] This position would be endorsed by the annual CORE convention in July, which adopted a militantly antiwar resolution.[153] In March 1966, however, James Farmer was reluctant to become involved in acts of high profile opposition toward the Johnson administration.

Jim Williams, chairman of Philadelphia CORE, had written to Farmer asking him to speak at a rally for William Akers, a CORE attorney who was running for election to Congress on an antiwar and pro-civil rights platform. Williams explained that Philadelphia CORE was supporting Akers, and that he was a member of his program and policy board. Williams described the strong civil rights plank in Akers's election platform, pointing out that the campaign was "being directly geared to the need of black voters." He also mentioned that the antiwar plank was supported by local liberal peace groups, such as SANE. Williams concluded, "Mr. Akers has consulted with me at every stage of his campaign and sought my advice on issues and how they should be stated, to avoid conflict or lose our support. I certainly hope you will lend your prestige to his effort."[154]

Farmer replied on March 24, explaining that while he was "enormously impressed" with Akers's qualifications, and hoped that he would succeed, he thought it "unlikely" that he would become active in his campaign. Farmer was waiting for news about the funding of a literacy program that he hoped to run under the auspices of the Office of Economic Opportunity (OEO), and thought it unwise to attract more flak at a time when the program was stalled in a "political storm of sorts." Farmer did, however, say that "in the event the program is interminably delayed, or finally rejected, I will then jump with both feet into many campaigns, including Mr. Akers.'" Farmer asked to be kept in touch with developments in Philadelphia, and suggested that Floyd McKissick might be prepared to lend his support.[155] It is interesting to note that Farmer, though personally opposed to the war and leading figure in an organization increasingly outspoken on it, felt the need to maintain a low profile over Vietnam rather than risk further alienation with the Johnson White House.

The case of William Akers is illustrative of both the close links between the peace and black movements (local CORE leaders were heavily involved in the mechanics of his campaign), and the difficult balance that national civil rights leaders sometimes had to strike between principle and pragmatism. As CORE moved in the direction of militant Black Power, though, it effectively cut off ties with the Democratic administration. Floyd McKissick, who replaced Farmer as director in March, and other CORE delegates, for example, attempted to raise the issue of Vietnam during the June White House Conference on Civil Rights.[156]

Promised during Lyndon Johnson's historic Howard University commencement address of June 1965, the White House Conference on Civil Rights, "To Fulfil These Rights," was originally scheduled for November 1965. Envisaged as a forum in which black leaders, academics, and government officials could discuss eliminating the remaining obstacles to black equality, the conference was postponed in the aftermath of the Watts riot. The November gathering became a planning conference, with the main event moved to June 1966.[157]

According to Robert Weisbrot, LBJ "orchestrated" the White House Conference on Civil Rights to "show black support for both his domestic and his foreign policies."[158] Johnson had even tried to keep Martin Luther King away from the gathering, but had to settle for marginalizing him instead. But not all the delegates were prepared to cooperate in the charade. On the afternoon of June 1, in a session dedicated to "Housing," Ruth Turner (CORE's national secretary) scolded the committee chairman. To applause from other delegates, she declared that "I don't know that this country will spend the kind of money . . . that the recommendations of this Conference . . . propose and at the same time fight an expanding war in Vietnam. I am very sure that we will not do it." Turner believed that the Conference should demand guarantees that Vietnam would not interfere with domestic spending—"unless we are going to answer this question . . . I think much of the discussion here is unreal.[159] The following day Patricia Darien of Jackson, Mississippi, wondered about the lack of black representation on draft boards; and Samuel Cornelius, from Omaha, Nebraska, complained about the way the Conference had been set up. In remarks that were also met with approval, Cornelius went on record as "being against the way the mechanics of the conference has been organized, to squash any kind of controversial comment."[160] Opposition to the Vietnam War was raised in a number of other sessions, principally by CORE delegates, but, enjoying only limited support, it was effectively contained.

There were other civil rights groups, besides SNCC and CORE, that opposed the war during 1966. The Southern Conference Educational Fund (SCEF) was a relic of the 1930s liberal left. During the late 1950s and 1960s, this southern-based organization, led by Louisville radicals Anne and Carl Braden, offered vital support to the civil rights movement. It had strong links with SNCC, and helped fund their first white field secretaries—Bob Zellner and Sam Shirah—to try and increase support for black rights among southern whites.[161] In April, it adopted an official antiwar position. The organization's board passed a resolution stating that the black freedom movement could not remain indifferent to the war. It also declared that "we believe there is a close relationship between the use of violence and repression in Vietnam and the use of violence and repression in our own country, and particularly in the South, to maintain things as they are."[162] These developments were accompanied by an increasing amount of antiwar activity among African Americans, although the numbers involved remained relatively modest.

On March 25 there was an antiwar march in New York City as part of the Second International Days of Protest (nominally organized by the National Coordinating Committee to End the War in Vietnam). There was a high degree of militancy, with black protesters among the 50,000 protesters carrying placards with "Bring Our Black GIs Home" and "The VC Never Called Me Nigger" on them. The parade had been preceded by a march of 1,200 people from Harlem. Students from Columbia and City College, together with 500 high school students, had walked through the black ghetto to drum up African American support.[163] Eight hundred people also marched against the war in Newark, New Jersey. They heard twenty-five-year-old Betty Moss, a black community organizer, attack the war for exploiting poor Americans. Moss declared that "this country only thinks about the big man and how it can make itself bigger . . . it don't care whether the poor man live or die; that's the reason the poor man shouldn't be in Vietnam today . . . [and] have to come back and live with rats and roaches."[164]

Antiwar sentiment also manifested itself in Mississippi, where the MFDP had become embroiled in a controversy over Vietnam in the summer of 1965. In March, for example, the first peace march in Jackson was held, instigated by 35 Tougaloo students who marched from the Freedom Democratic Party offices through downtown. SNCC's *News of the Field* reported that "FDP workers say that people are asking, 'why are we fighting?'"[165] That same month there was some antiwar activity in the small rural community of Sidon. The party sponsored a prayer meeting on the war, to be held in the local Newton Chapel Church on Saturday March 26, as part of the International Days of Protest. Some local antiwar activists made up a leaflet on the war:

Negroes in Mississippi know
That just a few getting together
Can't stop the war in Viet Nam
We know that talk can't stop the War
But we know that if we can't speak about the War
Getting that vote wasn't much good
We looked at what happened to Julian Bond
They told him his election didn't mean anything
Because he said the War should stop
We know there will be no one to work the land we want
Or to build the houses we want

Or to live in them
Or to learn in better schools
If all our sons go off to Viet Nam.
We know that only prayer
Can do the things we need
So we are getting together for a prayer meeting
To see if all the prayers
Help stop the War in Viet Nam.[166]

About thirty local people attended the meeting, which lasted four hours, and heard local civil rights activist Rev. Clifton Whitney speak. Whitney, who was the MFDP candidate for the U.S. Senate, "spoke on the war in Vietnam and its relationship to the Civil Rights Movement."[167] After the meeting, late on the Saturday night, the church was burned to the ground.[168]

The Freedom Democratic Party was involved in other antiwar activities. The party fought the 1966 mid-term elections, for instance, on a "varied program for social and economic justice" that included a call for an end to the Vietnam War, and the demand that poor people be given control of local antipoverty programs.[169] There is evidence that the growing opposition to the war may have enjoyed quite broad support among the black population of the Magnolia State. Writing in May to Herb Callender, NCNP member and leader of Bronx CORE, on behalf of the Rev. Clint Collier, MFDP candidate for the 4th congressional district, George Raymond stated that "feeling is high among Mississippi Negroes against the war in Vietnam, but they have had no opportunity to vote against the war." He explained that Collier had spoken against the war in all of his campaign speeches, reminding the people of the blacks "dying every day who have no voice in determining U.S. policy in Vietnam." Collier believed that "Mississippi's treatment of Negroes is no isolated case: that it is a mirror of U.S. policy all over the world." Raymond pointed out that "when two buses went to Washington, D.C., last November for an anti-Vietnam demonstration, the state MFDP office was besieged with calls after the buses were filled from people asking to go."[170] In July the party attempted to sue the Selective Service Commission because its Mississippi draft boards were all white. The suit was filed on behalf of twenty-year-old Ulysses Z. Nunnally of Holly Springs, an active civil rights worker and MFDP member, who had been due to be inducted into the army.[171]

There was black opposition to the war elsewhere in the South. In May, Simuel Schutz, a twenty-year-old SNCC field secretary, reported to his Alabama draft board one day late for a pre-induction physical. He had only received the notice on the day of the appointment, May 4, because he had been working in the Lowndes County (Alabama) primary "getting people to the polls to vote." On arrival at the Center, Schutz "said that he had come to report as ordered but wasn't going to be inducted because he had been discriminated against in his selection and because his draft board was segregated." The young civil rights activist was charged with "1 day's tardiness in reporting for induction" and on October 21 was sentenced to three years in the federal penitentiary by Judge Virgil Pittman. The irony of Schutz being sentenced in the same Opelika courthouse where Marvin Segrest, killer of Sammy Younge, had been acquitted was not lost on civil rights activists. James Forman claimed that Schutz's heavy sentence resulted from his active involvement in the drive for free elections in Alabama, and his participation in SNCC's antiwar activity.[172]

During August, the Atlanta Induction Center became the site of heated antiwar protest by African Americans. On August 16, eleven black demonstrators gathered at 699 Ponce de Leon, which served as the headquarters of the 12th Army Corps as well as the induction facility for the Atlanta area. The demonstrators, led by SNCC's Michael Simmons, had "gathered to protest the drafting of Black men to fight in the racist illegal war in Vietnam," and they handed out leaflets. Some carried placards with the slogan "The Vietcong never called me Nigger." Army personnel responded by spitting at the demonstrators and dropping lighted cigarettes and liquid on them. By August 18 the number of protesters had grown to thirty. When Simmons attempted to obey a draft notice by reporting to the Center, military officials turned him away four times. On the fifth attempt he was arrested along with ten other demonstrators. All were found guilty of various charges and imprisoned, where they remained for two months while the judge, who had a son fighting in Vietnam, refused to accept bail (which he had set at $37,000). Protests from civil liberties and peace groups poured into Atlanta, and SNCC workers threatened to sue Mayor Ivan Allen. On October 14 the judge finally signed the release papers.[173]

The year 1966 saw an increase in black opposition to America's war in Vietnam, a result both of discomfort about events in Southeast Asia and a growing awareness among blacks of the ways the war affected them. SNCC and CORE adopted militant antiwar positions, while the Black Panthers made their hostility toward the conflict abundantly clear. There were also signs of an embryonic "peace and freedom" coalition, particularly in the New Politics campaigns, and the radical antiwar movement stepped up its attempts to attract black support by striving to build a multi-issue peace movement.[174]

The growth of Black Power posed a stern test to the white peace movement and would help restrict black involvement in antiwar protests.

Despite their uncompromising opposition to the Vietnam War, Black Power activists remained wary of the white-dominated antiwar movement. Examples of integrated peace protests were rare and, increasingly, black and white opposition to the war diverged as militant African American critics of Vietnam built their own separate antiwar groups. Nationally, the peace movement remained overwhelmingly white, as a *New York Times* report of an April antiwar protest illustrates—"the vast majority [of the marchers] were white. There were a few delegations of civil rights workers from the South, but most of these, too, were white."[175]

In the South, where the black freedom movement still dominated the consciousness of most activists at the progressive end of the political spectrum, the antiwar movement sometimes seemed barely visible. As one sympathetic commentator wrote in the spring of 1966, "the Southern peace movement is still a minuscule, though growing, minority in a hostile or indifferent land."[176] While Southern protest against the war grew, it did so from a tiny base and seldom managed to tap into the modest residual antiwar sentiment that appears to have existed among local blacks.

Roy Wilkins believed that the civil rights movement should not take a position on the Vietnam War. Library of Congress, photo April 5, 1963.

Bayard Rustin, architect of the coalition politics strategy, retreated from his early antiwar activism. Library of Congress, photo August 27, 1963.

Although James Farmer opposed the conflict, in July 1965 he sought to prevent CORE from taking an antiwar stance. Library of Congress, photo April 15, 1964.

Martin Luther King, Jr., delivering his antiwar speech, "A Time to Break Silence," Riverside Church, New York, April 4, 1967. Copyright © John C. Goodwin.

King delivering his antiwar speech. Copyright © John C. Goodwin.

Demonstrators gather in Sheep Meadow, Central Park, New York, for the Spring Mobilization, April 15, 1967. Records of *WIN* magazine, Swarthmore College Peace Collection, photograph by Diana Davies.

Two African American protestors at the Spring Mobilization in New York, April 15, 1967. Copyright © John C. Goodwin.

Martin Luther King and Benjamin Spock leading the march to the United Nations, April 15, 1967. Copyright © John C. Goodwin.

Chapter 3

Black Moderates

*Johnson needs a consensus . . . if we are not with him on Vietnam, then he
is not going to be with us on civil rights.*
—*Whitney M. Young, Jr., 1966*

On Tuesday April 4, 1967, Martin Luther King, Jr., launched a powerful
attack on America's military involvement in Southeast Asia. Speaking
from New York City's historic Riverside Church, the nation's most
prominent civil rights leader condemned the Vietnam War for undermining the war on poverty and for disproportionately taking African
Americans to die in Vietnam for freedoms that they did not yet enjoy at
home. The Southern Christian Leadership Conference (SCLC) president lambasted the American government as the "greatest purveyor of
violence in the world today" and called upon the Johnson administration to take the initiative in ending the war by halting the bombing and
negotiating with the NLF. King argued that the Vietnam War was, in
essence, a civil war and that America was betraying her own revolutionary heritage by pursuing a reactionary foreign policy. Asserting that the
war was "but a symptom of a far deeper malady within the American
spirit," King stated that "if we are to get on the right side of the world revolution, we as a nation must undergo a radical revolution of values. We
must rapidly begin the shift from a 'thing-oriented' society to a 'person-
oriented' society."[1] Although King had spoken out against the war as
early as March 1965, he had tempered his criticisms and been unwilling
to break completely with the Johnson Administration.[2] But by the spring
of 1967, with the war abroad escalating while the domestic war on poverty was being cut back, King felt that he could no longer remain silent.

Although King was pleased with his speech, the response to it was far
from favorable. Unsurprisingly, the federal government reacted badly.
Presidential aide John Roche told Lyndon Johnson that King had "thrown
in with the commies."[3] Opinion polls indicated that around 50 percent
of African Americans disagreed with King's antiwar stance, and the SCLC
leader was attacked in the pages of many of the nation's newspapers.[4]

The *New York Times* censured King for trying to combine the peace and civil rights movements, while *Life* magazine called his speech "a demagogic slander that sounded like a script for Radio Hanoi" and accused him of betraying the civil rights cause.[5]

Criticism also came from the "moderate" wing of the civil rights movement. Although consisting of numerous groups and leaders, at its center stood the National Association for the Advancement of Colored People (NAACP). America's largest and oldest civil rights organization had grown increasingly conservative in the years following the Second World War. During the 1940s and 1950s the Association had attempted to dissociate itself from more radical civil rights groups such as CORE, and it had accepted the domestic and foreign tenets of anticommunism. Although the NAACP supported many of the civil rights demonstrations of the 1960s, frequently supplying bail money and legal help, it remained lukewarm to the tactics of protest. Robert Cook, for example, has argued that the Association "failed to embrace wholeheartedly the concept of nonviolent direct action."[6] The organization preferred to concentrate its efforts in Washington, D.C., in an attempt to win support for progressive legislation by lobbying congressmen, and by using litigation to strike down segregation laws.[7]

The NAACP's executive director, Roy Wilkins, was a prominent civil rights moderate. After an early career in journalism, Wilkins had been appointed assistant secretary of the NAACP in 1931. Three years later he replaced W. E. B. Du Bois as editor of the *Crisis*, the Association's magazine, before succeeding Walter White as head of the organization in 1955. According to Robert Cook, Wilkins was "temperamentally unprepared" to commit the Association to a strategy of civil disobedience and protest. He was also equivocal about the efforts of groups like SNCC to build a civil rights movement from the bottom up by fostering indigenous black leadership and empowering local African Americans.[8]

The moderate wing also included the National Urban League (NUL) and its leader, Whitney M. Young, Jr. Young, a native of Kentucky and former dean of the School of Social Work at Atlanta University, was appointed executive director of the Urban League in 1960. Six feet two inches tall and weighing around two hundred pounds, he cut an imposing figure. Young's biographer, Nancy J. Weiss, has written that "everyone who knew him remarked on his style: frank, without pretense; exuberant, eager to take on the challenges and pleasures of life; aggressive, indefatigable, a study in perpetual motion." Though traditionally a black social service agency rather than a protest organization, Young helped to make the Urban League a part of the civil rights movement. While he "led no demonstrations and changed no laws," his work, out of the public eye, in selling civil rights to powerful whites and trying to secure greater job opportunities for black Americans was vitally important. He was also able to act as an effective mediator within the civil rights movement, helping to keep the peace and smooth over tensions. Bayard Rustin described him as an essential part of "the concrete that kept the bricks from falling apart."[9]

Rustin himself is something of an enigmatic figure within the civil rights movement. Initially no moderate, the chain smoking, guitar playing, folk singing Quaker became less radical as the 1960s progressed. Rustin, a former field secretary with the pacifist Fellowship of Reconciliation (FOR), had helped tutor Martin Luther King in Gandhian nonviolence during the Montgomery Bus Boycott. He also played a critical role in the founding of the SCLC in 1957 and was largely responsible for organizing the August 1963 March on Washington.[10] By the mid-1960s, however, Rustin—along with his mentor A. Philip Randolph—was urging the civil rights movement to move from the streets into legislative halls and courtrooms. This position contrasted with that of civil rights activists from the radical wing of the movement who were becoming increasingly critical of mainstream American institutions and values.[11]

Unlike the militants of SNCC and CORE, the Black Panther revolutionaries, or the increasingly radical King, the moderate wing of the movement, which had always been somewhat ambivalent about direct action and street protest, continued to believe in working within the American political system to bring about change. It also retained its faith in the ability of the federal government to solve the race problem through legislation and antipoverty programs. Between 1965 and 1969, the moderates refused to take a position on the war in Southeast Asia, believing that to do so would only harm the struggle for black equality. They adopted what Manfred Berg has termed the "separate issues doctrine," which held that the war and civil rights were entirely distinct issues that should not be mixed.[12] A detailed analysis of the moderates' response helps us expand our understanding of the civil rights movement. Indeed, while we know a good deal about the African American groups that opposed the war, those who did not take a stand have tended to be dismissed as conservative sell-outs. Many historians of the civil rights movement appear to have shared, at least implicitly, the view of one contemporary critic who believed that the NAACP had become "little more than an Administration houseboy."[13] The time for a more nuanced explanation is long overdue.

Responding to King's Riverside speech in the pages of the *Amsterdam News*, on April 22, 1967, Bayard Rustin defended King's right as an individual to speak out against the war and argued that, as a Nobel Peace Prize winner, he had a moral obligation to work for peace. However, the article was implicitly critical of the SCLC president's stance, suggesting that an honest debate about King's proposals "may encourage Dr. King to embark upon a reexamination of his position . . . [and may] be as illuminating for Dr. King as for the rest of us."[14] Rustin went on to state that he considered "the involvement of the civil rights organizations . . . in peace activities distinctly unprofitable and perhaps even suicidal."[15]

Rustin's attitude appears odd given his history as a pacifist and his previous opposition to the war in Vietnam (he had spoken at antiwar demonstrations in 1965). In part it reflected his belief that future black gains could only be achieved through coalition with the progressive wing of the Democratic Party, but it also derived from his uneasiness with the antiwar movement itself. Rustin viewed the radical antiwar movement as being more anti-American than anti-war and he was especially concerned by its romantic view of the Viet Cong. Despite the growing strength of the peace movement, the war in Vietnam continued to escalate. This helped forge a sense of despair and desperation within the antiwar movement. Radical critics of the war began to adopt more militant tactics to oppose it—including draft resistance, burning the American flag, and adopting pro-NLF banners and flags. While only ever constituting a minority among antiwar activists, such developments attracted prominent publicity and gave the peace movement an anti-American flavor.[16] In a 1967 letter to the *New York Times*, Rustin explained that no "effective" and "enduring" peace movement could be built, or win influence with the American people, if it became publicly identified with groups that desired a victory for the Viet Cong.[17]

Rustin's criticisms of the peace movement and his general move away from the political left have been placed within the context of his homosexuality by John D'Emilio. Indeed, he goes so far as to claim that Rustin's political odyssey is a "tale of gay oppression."[18] D'Emilio argues that being stigmatized as a "sex pervert" had helped Rustin lose any attachment to "left-wing romanticism." He was thus critical of the peace movement's tendency toward radical posturing and third world romanticism and "grasped the bankruptcy of radical marginality in a way that few of his peers did." Rustin's homosexuality also resulted in him lacking an institutional base. Martin Luther King, for example, had decided against bringing him onto the SCLC staff because of concerns over his sexuality. This lack of organizational roots made Rustin vulnerable to overtures from conservative organizations. In 1965 Rustin eventually agreed to head the A. Philip Randolph Institute, which, being funded by the AFL-CIO, greatly restricted his room for dissent.[19] However, while D'Emilio's thesis is intriguing, it does not deal with the fact that many heterosexual radicals suffered similar political conversions.

NAACP executive director Roy Wilkins had stated as early as July 1965 that if the civil rights movement went "off on a foreign policy kick" it would "weaken its effectiveness in discharging its major responsibility" at home, and he consistently resisted attempts to link the peace and freedom movements, which he claimed would dilute the "civil rights drive."[20] A few days after King's Riverside speech, the NAACP National Board of Directors unanimously endorsed a resolution stating that any attempt to merge the peace and civil rights movement was "a serious tactical mistake." They also pledged that the NAACP would "stick to the job for which it was organized."[21] Although Dr. King was not mentioned by name there was no doubting that he was the intended target of the attack.[22] In his syndicated newspaper column on April 15, 1967, Roy Wilkins wrote that, while King had the right to express his views, he did not speak for the whole civil rights movement. Wilkins again stated that civil rights should remain the focus of the movement.[23] Wilkins and John Morsell, assistant executive director of the NAACP, also condemned King for lending respectability to an antiwar coalition that included communists, after he endorsed the radical Spring Mobilization.[24] These attacks on King were criticized by some of the Association's members, and protest letters outnumbered supportive statements by 2 to 1. Esther S. Frankel, for example, resigned from both the national NAACP and the executive board of the Paterson, New Jersey, branch, citing the national board's attacks on King and others who opposed the war.[25] While it is impossible to gauge accurately the level of support for King's antiwar stance within the NAACP, or to estimate the proportion of the Association's membership that regretted the thinly veiled attacks on him, it is clear that the organization's membership was divided on the issue. Sidney L. Jackson, of the Kent, Ohio, NAACP Branch wrote that the active membership was split on the peace question, with half likely to support King and half the national board.[26]

The NAACP had been concerned about the war from very early on, and during the period 1965–1969 its official policy concerning Vietnam was, in effect, to have no policy. The Association's leadership argued that civil rights and Vietnam were entirely separate issues that should not be mixed, and Roy Wilkins insisted that diverting attention to Vietnam would weaken the fight for black progress. In August 1967, for example, Wilkins accused black leaders who were "moaning about" the war of neglecting the fight for civil rights at home and giving too much attention to "Asia, Africa, and the islands of the sea."[27] Moreover, as John Morsell explained, the organization's membership comprised a "wide range of party loyalties and . . . opinions on a variety of issues," there was unanimity only on the concern for racial justice.[28] Wilkins asserted that the NAACP had no right to assume that members who had signed up for the civil rights fight would "want their civil rights organization to commit them to a stand on the Vietnamese War."[29]

The Association's policy was shaped by a number of important factors. Manfred Berg has argued that the NAACP's reaction to the war was molded by concepts of loyalty and patriotism, and rested upon the notion that a moderate, integrationist civil rights organization could not afford to oppose a war that was being fought in the name of democracy.[30] This chapter emphasizes two factors that Berg has discussed in his work on the NAACP, though applying them to the moderates as a whole—the personal and political closeness of the NAACP leadership to the Johnson administration and the Association's anticommunism. More important, however, the moderates' response to Vietnam will be placed in a context of "organizing experience."

The "on the ground" experience of civil rights workers, who were active at the grass-roots level with groups like SNCC and CORE during the early 1960s, led to many of them becoming frustrated and disillusioned with the federal government, the Democratic Party, and white liberals. Speaking in Detroit in January 1967, for example, SNCC leader Stokely Carmichael described the Democratic Party as the "most treacherous enemy the Negro people have."[31] Behind the hyperbole lay genuine feelings of bitterness and betrayal. The radicalizing effect of "organizing experience," in turn, increased cynicism about the war in Vietnam or outright opposition to it among the activist wing of the civil rights movement. However, the experience of the moderate wing of the black movement was markedly different. The passage of landmark civil rights legislation in 1964 and 1965, with the support of a liberal president and a progressive congress, accompanied by the Great Society's promise of combating poverty, convinced them that the future for progressive change lay within the Democratic Party. The moderates' position on Vietnam was, in many ways then, a logical product of their own experiences in the civil rights movement.

The fundamental objective of the NAACP had always been the full participation of African Americans in all phases of American life.[32] The leaders were determined that nothing would deflect them from this goal. Herbert Hill, a former labor secretary of the NAACP who possessed what one journalist described as a "deep, voice-of-doom delivery that can bounce of walls in a Senate committee hearing room or hold a private audience of one in shell-shocked thrall," recalled Roy Wilkins's philosophy. Wilkins believed that the NAACP's "sacred mission" was to deal with the struggle for black rights: "we must never compromise, we must be undeterred, we must never let anything get in our way. He used to say 'Steady as she goes.'"[33] Clearly, opposing the Vietnam War would have made the ship very unsteady.

Unlike the militants of SNCC or Students for a Democratic Society, the NAACP did not advocate a revolutionary overhaul of the American social, economic, and political system. The Brooklyn-born Hill, a music buff who was stimulated by the "dramatic struggles of labor and eventually Negro labor," was one of the national NAACP's most radical officials. During the 1940s and 1950s he had embarked on an uncompromising crusade against racism in the labor movement. Roy Wilkins recalled that Hill, who was Jewish, "grabbed hold of Jim Crow in the AFL-CIO and squeezed so hard you could hear George Meany's splutters all the way to New York."[34] Hill explained that the leaders of the NAACP during the 1960s were not revolutionaries. "I think for the most part we accepted the assumptions about American society, with the reservation that we ought to get rid of racial discrimination." He continued, "[we] were radicals on the subject of race, [we] were revolutionaries on the subject of race, but [we] identified with this society."[35]

Now, for the first time in American history, the national government also seemed to be committed to the goal of eradicating racial discrimination and opening up opportunities for African Americans. Speaking in 1969, Roy Wilkins explained that Lyndon Johnson "committed the White House and the Administration to the involvement of government in getting rid of the inequalities between people solely on the basis of race. And he did this to a greater extent than any other President in our history." Wilkins continued, "when the chips were down he used the great powers of the presidency on the side of the people who were deprived."[36] In his autobiography, the NAACP executive director articulated his positive experience of working closely with the Johnson government. Wilkins stated that he often came away from conversations with LBJ "feeling that he was not only with us but often ahead of us."[37] For the national leadership of the NAACP, the Democratic Party was, overwhelmingly, viewed as friend, not foe.

In February 1965, *Commentary* magazine carried Bayard Rustin's "From Protest to Politics: The Future of the Civil Rights Movement." In it Rustin, one of the foremost strategists of the civil rights movement, outlined his hopes and tactical approach for the rest of the decade.[38] Rustin claimed that the civil rights movement was evolving from a protest movement into a full-fledged social movement and that the future of the black freedom struggle lay in a realignment of the Democratic Party.[39] Believing that the Johnson administration was determined to fulfill the promise of the New Deal, Rustin argued that direct action be replaced with politics. He declared that "the future of the Negro struggle depends on whether the contradictions of this society can be resolved by a coalition of progressive forces which becomes the *effective* political majority in the United States." This progressive coalition, which had "staged the March on Washington, passed the Civil Rights Act, and laid the basis for the Johnson landslide," was made up of "Negroes, trade unionists, liberals, and religious groups."[40] The idea that the civil rights movement should seek further gains in alliance with the progressive wing of the Democratic Party was shared by Roy Wilkins, A. Philip Randolph, and the National Urban League's Whitney Young. They all believed that Vietnam did not necessarily mean that domestic progress would have to go on hold, and argued that it was possible to have both guns *and* butter.[41] Such a strategy actually made forthright criticism of the Vietnam War impossible. The moderates understood that breaking with, or merely offending the president over Vietnam would have repercussions for the Great Society programs. This was recognized by Whitney Young when he told Martin Luther King that "Johnson needs a consensus. . . . If we are not with him on Vietnam, then he is not going to be with us on civil rights."[42] Antiwar critics like Staughton Lynd believed that Rustin's strategy of working with the Democratic Party required the implicit acceptance of the government's war policy.[43] Lynd, for example, infamously accused Rustin of advocating coalition with the marines.[44]

Asa Philip Randolph, the veteran civil rights leader and founder of the first all-black labor union—the Brotherhood of Sleeping Car Porters —also agreed with Rustin's strategy of coalition politics. His own position on the Vietnam War was, however, somewhat ambiguous. Randolph, whose militant anticommunism was rooted in the ideological battles that took place within the Socialist Party shortly after the Bolshevik Revolution, was a pragmatic pacifist who had opposed the First World War and, through his March on Washington Movement, had threatened massive civil disobedience during the war against Nazism.[45] Randolph was an early critic of Vietnam. At a December 1964 demonstration in New York, for example, he had "pilloried America's foreign policy." Randolph had also signed the Declaration of Conscience against the war in Vietnam, and at the December 1965 AFL-CIO convention in San Francisco he warned that America's poor were bearing the burden of the war and that the conflict was being used as an excuse to stall on civil rights.[46]

Randolph had been prepared to rock the boat in 1941 and, given his early opposition to Vietnam, he might have been expected to do the same in the late 1960s. But instead he sided with the "no position" adherents, and adopted the same line as the NAACP—an organization with which he had often had a fraught relationship (the result of both his own radicalism and the Association's jealous regard for all potential rivals).[47] The veteran black leader agreed with Rustin that cooperation with white allies and the federal government was the "only feasible way of delivering power to an essentially powerless people."[48] This commitment to the strategy of coalition politics would prevent him from becoming an outspoken critic of the Vietnam War.

Randolph, described by Roy Wilkins as the "spiritual and historical father" of the Vietnam era draft resisters, downplayed his personal opposition to America's use of military force in Southeast Asia. Indeed, he argued that it was "tactically unsound" for a "civil rights leader or a leader of the peace movement to attempt to assume a position of leadership in both . . . at the same time."[49] Randolph also disagreed with attempts to involve the civil rights movement in antiwar actions. He explained this position in some detail in the fall of 1966. He believed that "it would be unfair to the Negro masses for the civil rights leaders to abandon the Mississippi-Alabama front and leave it exposed to the racists of the George Wallace stripe, and turn the Negro's attention and plunge him into participation in demonstrations to end the war in Vietnam." He continued, "having long experience in the field of mass movements, I am aware that you cannot fight on two fronts at the same time."[50] While he was personally committed to seeing the war end "at the earliest possible moment," Randolph argued that the leadership of the civil rights movement had "no mandate from the Negro masses . . . to carry on any broad, massive movement to end the war in Vietnam." Moreover Randolph, like Rustin, was uneasy with the radical elements of the peace movement—he was, for example, "unequivocally opposed to burning of draft cards and especially to . . . burning the flag of our country."[51]

On occasion Randolph appears to have indicated a measure of support for the war. In the spring of 1965 he wired LBJ, expressing approval of the president's April 7 Johns Hopkins address at which, in addition to reaffirming America's commitment to an independent South Vietnam, he had also stated his willingness to participate in "unconditional discussions" with any government to try and end the war, and had outlined an ambitious $1 billion development program for the Mekong River Valley. Johnson expressed gratitude for this "most welcome" support.[52] However, Randolph continued to harbor private doubts. On May 20 veteran socialist Norman Thomas wrote, expressing his opposition to America's recent military interference in the Dominican Republic. He declared that he was "thoroughly convinced that what the U.S. is doing in the Dominican Republic and, I may add, Vietnam is doing more for communism than communism could do for itself." Randolph replied the next day with a telegram in which he stated "I agree with you," though he referred explicitly only to Thomas's" comments about the Dominican

Republic.[53] But while Randolph wanted to "see the United States stop the bombing . . . and disengage its military forces from involvement in South East Asia at the earliest possible date" he did not support a unilateral withdrawal, nor did he "place all the blame for the continuance of the war on the United States." Indeed, Randolph evidently believed that President Johnson was attempting to secure a just peace in Vietnam.[54]

By the decade's end, Randolph applied a selective reading of his own position when he told Jervis Anderson that he had "always been opposed" to wars in principle, and that Vietnam represented "no defense of our vital national interest." He continued, "as for Dr. King's decision to oppose the war, I cannot say I regard it as any great moral contradiction. He was, after all, one of the moral leaders of the country. Opposing wars and fighting for civil rights have natural and complementary motivations. And long before Dr. King came along, the *Messenger*, which I edited in World War I, was fighting for civil rights and opposing the war at the same time."[55]

In fact, during the mid-1960s Randolph believed that opposing the war was not a vital concern to the black freedom struggle and feared that the peace movement would divert energy from the civil rights movement. Randolph had also argued that the freedom movement had much to lose and little to gain by breaking with the Johnson administration in order to criticize the war in Vietnam.[56] One does, though, get a strong sense of the private horror with which Randolph, along with Wilkins and Rustin, viewed developments in Southeast Asia. Just as the forces of progressivism seemed poised to triumph, the war in Vietnam threatened everything. Randolph encapsulated the tragedy of 1960s liberalism when he wrote that "the Vietnam War . . . has practically pushed the civil rights movement off the center of the stage of American history." While the "white liberals and students" were "still for civil rights," they were now "asking for peace in Vietnam, not for civil rights in Alabama and Mississippi."[57]

The National Urban League's policy on Vietnam in many ways mirrored that of the NAACP, Randolph, and Rustin: it insisted that foreign policy and civil rights remain separate. As early as August 1965 the League's Delegate Assembly had approved a resolution that recommended that the organization stay out of the burgeoning Vietnam controversy. The resolution called on the NUL to "not divide nor divert its energies and resources by seeking to merge domestic and international issues where armed conflict is involved."[58] The League, which attempted to increase black economic opportunities by using persuasion and negotiation in the boardrooms of American corporations to sell civil rights to powerful whites, had a somewhat restrained and cautious agenda. The League had joined the civil rights movement thanks to the efforts of its executive director, Whitney M. Young, Jr., and, of all the civil rights groups, it was perhaps the one least influenced by grass-roots pressure and most easily controlled by its national leadership. Young himself traveled to Vietnam in July 1966 on an independent fact-finding mission financed by the League, where he investigated the welfare of black troops fighting there. The NUL leader expressed pride in efforts of the black soldiers and emphasized interracial cooperation in the U.S. armed forces, although he also drew attention to the lack of African American officers. Still, Young was careful to explain that he was not making any judgment on the conflict itself.[59] It was a point he made again in August. Speaking on *Meet the Press* he stated that "the Urban League takes no position on Vietnam. We know this, that we had a race problem in this country before Vietnam; we will have a race problem after it is gone."[60] The Urban League head insisted that the civil rights movement focus on "rats tonight and jobs tomorrow." Indeed, Whitney Young disagreed vehemently with Martin Luther King's opposition to the war, and the two famously traded personal insults in March 1967.

The coalition strategy was cemented by the close personal relationship Roy Wilkins and Whitney Young enjoyed with Lyndon Johnson. James Farmer recalled that LBJ "adored" Whitney Young, and he became, along with Wilkins, a major adviser on White House civil rights initiatives.[61] Young biographer Dennis C. Dickerson has claimed that Young had "insider status" during the Johnson years and that he was consulted extensively about the war on poverty and other Great Society programs.[62] Young's role as the "inside man" of the black revolution, a figure who "served as a bridge and interpreter between black America and the businessmen, foundation executives, and public officials who comprised the white power structure," and his relationship with LBJ, helped shape his response to the Vietnam War.[63]

As well as sharing a political philosophy with the liberal leadership of the Democratic Party during the early 1960s, Roy Wilkins also enjoyed an extraordinarily close relationship with the 36th president of the United States. Interviewed in 1969, Wilkins confessed that he had great affection and admiration for Johnson.[64] In his autobiography, Wilkins vividly recalled his reaction to Johnson's message to Congress in support of voting rights legislation in March 1965. Wilkins "had waited all my life to hear a President of the United States talk that way. There was a great roar of applause. I looked to my left and I looked to my right and I saw men and women with their eyes full of tears. And at that moment, I confess, I loved L.B.J."[65]

Lyndon Johnson certainly appears to have valued Roy Wilkins's friendship, and he shamelessly flattered the civil rights leader, frequently "buttering up" Wilkins in his official correspondence. In February 1966 he wrote to Wilkins, stating that he had "always been a man on whom I could depend, regardless of the winds of change."[66] In September 1968 the president, whose capacity to flatter knew no bounds, told the NAACP head that he could call him any time he needed to—"I am always proud and grateful to have you by my side."[67] In the final days of his presidency, Johnson wrote Wilkins, once again conveying great affection—"[your name] will live . . . in my memory, where I will be grateful forever for the wise counsel, the unfailing generosity, and the selfless friendship you gave me throughout my Presidency. I hope we see each other often in the years ahead, Roy. God bless you."[68]

To a certain degree, the federal government appears to have actively courted the civil rights movement's more moderate leaders after 1965. Indeed, an autumn 1965 memorandum from George Reedy, Johnson's press secretary declared that moderate civil rights leaders would be the most effective at consolidating the civil rights gains already made. It recommended that the federal government "make a public point of consulting Randolph, Wilkins, and Young (*particularly Wilkins*) in the period immediately ahead." Reedy suggested that "frequent invitations to the White House would be in order and anything that could be done to increase [Wilkins's] prestige would help to shift the focus from demonstrations in the streets to the type of constructive work that now is so badly needed."[69]

The federal government certainly cultivated Wilkins's support, but there can be little doubt that Wilkins and Johnson, besides sharing many of the same political goals, also developed a close personal relationship. The NAACP executive director constantly received phone calls from Johnson, and Wilkins and his wife were regular guests for barbecue at Johnson's Texas ranch.[70] NAACP labor secretary Herbert Hill recalled "I don't think in the entire history of the NAACP the president of the United States had evolved such a close personal relationship with the head of the [Association]."[71] This clearly was yet another reason why the NAACP refused to take a stand against the Vietnam War, especially considering the very personal attacks that many antiwar movement participants made on Lyndon Johnson.

The combination of the coalition strategy and personal affection for LBJ made criticism of the war in Vietnam a virtual impossibility. The only way the NAACP and the NUL officially interacted with the war was in using the conflict to advance the Great Society. For example, early in 1967 Whitney Young claimed that white liberals were using Vietnam as an excuse for their failure to support the civil rights movement, because the black struggle had hit them too close to home. In a reference to northern housing drives he stated that "when we began to talk about issues that involved them next door in their communities they suddenly decided there was a more important issue"—Vietnam. Young concluded, "we are insisting that this country fight a war on poverty, and had better fight a war on poverty, with the same tenacity as in Vietnam."[72] At the end of June 1967, after the House of Representatives had rejected a $10 million appropriation to extend a rent supplement program, Young commented that "it is tragic that when the front pages are filled with pictures and stories of the courage of Negro soldiers dying in Viet Nam in disproportionate numbers that the Congress should see fit to reward their impoverished loved ones back home in the ghetto by cruelly cutting out any additional funds for rent supplements."[73]

Using the war to advance a progressive domestic agenda had been adopted as official policy by the Council of United Civil Rights Leadership (a coordinating body set up in 1963 to raise money and encourage cooperation among civil rights groups) in March 1966.[74] Believing that the Republic could afford both guns and butter, moderate civil rights leaders sought to apply pressure on an often recalcitrant Congress by using African American service in a foreign war as a bargaining chip. This was in the tradition of the Double-V strategy that had been employed so successfully during the Second World War, and it reflected the traditional way black America had attempted to use service for one's country as leverage for domestic progress. The flaw in the strategy by the late 1960s, however, was that there was virtually no leverage left—legal equality had recently been assured, the Great Society was already under serious political assault, and conservatives were preparing to reap the harvest of the white backlash. Some civil rights leaders understood this, even as they held firm to the strategy. In February 1968 Gloster Current, NAACP director of branches, explained that because of America's growing involvement in Vietnam, "a wave of reaction has swept the land and it is not as easy to get progressive legislation passed."[75]

The close relationship between moderate civil rights leaders and the federal government was certainly a cause of concern among some of the rank-and-file. One report of the 1965 NAACP convention in Denver claimed that "opposition that flared from the floor . . . mirrored objections that the leadership was too closely tied with the Johnson Administration."[76] While the NAACP was able to contain dissent over Vietnam in Denver, it was forced to take a stronger position against the nomination of James Coleman to a federal judgeship. The initial, mild resolution prompted claims that a deal had been struck with Johnson, and Wilkins was forced to deny that he had been offered a cabinet position. It was an incident that the NAACP's Herbert Hill remembered clearly some thirty-five years later. He recalled that "there was a rumor that Wilkins was selling out the NAACP and Johnson was going to . . .

give him some high . . . post. Roy had to get up at the Convention and deny that, and say that . . . no matter what Johnson offered him, he would not take it." Hill considered it outrageous, given Wilkins's tireless work for the Association, that this was even regarded as a possibility, and he explained that Wilkins had been hurt and angered by the accusations.[77] Nevertheless, the episode suggests that among ordinary NAACP members there was concern about the nature of the relationship between the organization and the government.

Henry Wallace, an NAACP member from Kentucky, also accused the organization of being too intimate with the Johnson administration. After the NAACP condemned SNCC's antiwar statement of January 1966, Wallace wrote that "the NAACP is fast becoming the leading Uncle Tom of the civil rights movement. You are jumping through President Johnson's hoop so regularly and humiliatingly that you have become little more than an Administration houseboy."[78] A few days later he wrote to John Morsell, claiming that the NAACP stood "with the Johnson crowd in the current Vietnam policy."[79] In May 1967, Current attended a meeting with a number of New York branches that opposed many NAACP national policies. While one of their major grievances was the Association's refusal to oppose the war in Vietnam, there was also a "concentrated attack upon the organization for its 'support of the Johnson Administration.'" Current came away so concerned that he suggested the NAACP consider supporting Muhammad Ali's fight against the draft, since he seemed "genuinely to be a pacifist." In addition, such a move "might confuse some who believe we are growing conservative."[80] Eugene T. Reed, a Brooklyn-born dentist and staunch Catholic, and national board member Jack E. Tanner, perennial critics of Roy Wilkins's leadership, also alleged that the Association was too attached to Lyndon Johnson. Reed claimed that the NAACP was "in the pocket" of LBJ, while Tanner charged that the 1966 annual convention had been "LBJ controlled."[81]

Scholars might dismiss these criticisms as the bleating of a radical fringe, whose members often had personal axes to grind. It is therefore extremely significant that senior figures in the Association's national staff appear to have shared some of the concern over the organization's relationship with the Johnson administration. In the spring of 1966, during an NAACP staff meeting, Current accused Wilkins of being too close to LBJ. Wilkins, unsurprisingly, took great offense, describing the charge as "gratuitously insulting, with no substantive basis."[82] The executive director denied any closeness to the administration, stated that no such claim had ever been made before in a staff meeting, and demanded that Current either provide evidence to support his accusation or offer an apology. Remarkably, Current's apology appears to have fallen short of a full retraction. The director of branches stated that he was sure that because the staff members knew him so well, they would not believe that he would be "deliberately insulting to one who is doing so much for our common cause." Current admitted that his remarks had been "tactless" and gave an impression that "would be difficult to substantiate." Nevertheless, one is left with the distinct impression that there was considerable concern that the NAACP was tying itself too tightly to the Johnson administration.

A further reason for the moderate wing of the civil rights movement's refusal to condemn the Vietnam War was anticommunism. During the late 1940s and early 1950s, the NAACP had embraced Cold War liberalism. It had tempered its criticisms of colonialism, adopted policies designed to exclude communists or "fellow travelers," and equated criticism of American foreign policy with pro-communism. The NAACP's hostile and suspicious attitude toward the domestic peace movement of the Korean War era was replicated during the 1960s. In the summer of 1950 the NAACP board had passed a resolution supporting American efforts to "halt Communist aggression" in Korea.[83] The following year the organization turned its attention to the peace movement. It warned against "so-called 'peace' organizations that . . . are . . . urging a policy desired by the communist bloc of nations."[84] The NAACP's reaction to the Vietnam War and the 1960s peace movement would be shaped by and reflect the anticommunist liberalism the organization had adopted during the early Cold War. The NAACP leadership, along with the majority of America's liberal establishment, proved incapable of conceiving that the anti-Vietnam War movement could be anything other than communist-influenced. The Association's genuine opposition to communism was also, in part, a reflection of its bruising encounters with the American Communist Party during the 1930s. While anticommunism was not restricted to the NAACP, it was the civil rights group most at ease with it, and least comfortable with radicalism.[85]

In April 1965 the Flint, Michigan, branch of the NAACP became the first to engage with the Vietnam War when it passed a resolution urging a withdrawal of American troops.[86] John Morsell responded by informing the renegade branch that their resolution did not reflect national NAACP policy, and that they could not use the NAACP name in connection with individual positions. He also ordered them not to release the resolution to the press.[87] The NAACP's national leadership interpreted such signs of dissent as the product of an organized left-wing insurgency. Gloster Current wrote that the "left-wing in America is having a field day! Its most recent project is to create problems over our country's Vietnam policy." He cited Flint as a case in point and warned that the Association had to take decisive action to prevent local branches getting involved in "left-wing shenanigans."[88] Current, who had been active in the Detroit branch of the NAACP before being promoted to the national office in 1946, presided over the functioning of the organization's 1,400 branches. The Methodist and former jazz musician was, according to colleague Herbert Hill, "the bureaucrat incarnate" (he had received a master's degree in public administration from Wayne State University) and he guarded his NAACP turf resiliently. James Farmer, who served briefly as the Association's "activities co-ordinator," recalled Current telling him that "I coordinate the activities of our branches, and *I* am the director of their programs."[89]

The director of branches was a committed anticommunist who remained suspicious of the more radical wing of the freedom struggle. In February 1968, for example, he referred to SNCC militants Stokely Carmichael and H. Rap Brown as "nuts" and declared that "it would really be worth our while if we could squelch these do-nothing negativists . . . because they are standing in the way of progress."[90] Herbert Hill believes that Current's zealous anticommunism was largely the result of his bureaucratic mindset. Current, whom Hill describes as a "wonderful human being" but "not very politically sophisticated," viewed the communists as a threat to the organization—they were an alien force who were not loyal to the NAACP. The director of branches merely responded to protect the Association. Hill claims that Current would have done the same if the "Episcopalian Church were coming in"—"his job was to protect the internal integrity of the NAACP. He wasn't going to let anybody gain control of the branches . . . he did what he thought he had to do."[91]

The NAACP leadership was worried that attempts would be made at the 1965 annual convention to get the organization involved with antiwar protests. Such attempts were viewed as the work of a left-wing conspiracy. Current explained that "we certainly will have left-wingers raising issues in the Resolutions Committee," though he also recognized that "there are many others who are not left-wingers, but who have genuine reservations about Vietnam and the Dominican Republic." Current suggested that key staff members should take advance action to strengthen control over convention proceedings.[92] The following year the NAACP leadership also worried about what they viewed as an organized left-wing insurgency designed to cause problems at the Los Angeles convention over the Vietnam issue. Current explained that "there is evidence that the left wing is at work to influence our resolutions to be adopted in Los Angeles." He cited efforts to place known militants on important convention committees and the Greenwich Village branch's efforts to promote discussion of an antiwar resolution. Current concluded, "the left wing is coming out of the woodwork, and the Vietnam issue could well be the biggest problem we will be confronted with in Los Angeles."[93]

Current's obsession with communism also colored his interpretation of the Spring Mobilization in April 1967. He attended the massive demonstration in New York City, where he heard black leaders including Stokely Carmichael, Floyd McKissick, and Martin Luther King attack the Vietnam War. Reflecting the legacy of the Association's negative experience of communists in the New Deal era, Current concluded that "the entire performance was reminiscent of the 30s when the commies harangued a crowd with certain well-chosen speakers." Current warned the NAACP national staff that "we have a resurgence of the left such as we have not had since World War II. NAACP branches are going to be invaded and urged to get aboard the peace movement. . . . We need to mount an offensive to give the American people the facts and to urge youth and Negroes in the communities to pay no attention to the fools."[94]

Fears that Vietnam might wreak havoc within the Association persisted. Current added a new set of miscreants to his traditional cast of villains when he informed the national staff that they should be prepared for the efforts of "peace-niks, militants and . . . odd balls," as well as leftists, to ruin the 1967 convention.[95] He warned branch officials to keep their eyes open for people stirring dissent and to report them to national staff. Current also asked them to "urge delegates not to be taken in by those who would seek to turn the NAACP into another extremist organization."

Anticommunism also affected the way in which the NAACP viewed the domestic peace movement, and the Association was not afraid to share its views. Indeed, from the earliest opportunity the organization red-baited the antiwar movement. Writing in the *New York Post* in July 1965, Roy Wilkins referred to the role of Martin Luther King's "aides" in his decision to urge a negotiated peace in Vietnam. He went on to explain that, while in a broad sense all men were brothers, Chinese Premier Zhou EnLai was "no close relative. At least, he and his are not close enough for me to ease my fight here against racial bigotry in order to enter into *a foreign policy matter that seems to be of more than passing interest to Communist China.*"[96] After SNCC released its antiwar statement in January 1966, Wilkins responded with a newspaper column emphasizing that SNCC's view reflected the "official leftist line" rather than the thinking of the civil rights movement as a whole.[97] Wilkins was also prepared to red-bait Martin Luther King to the president of the United States. In a telephone call with Lyndon Johnson in August 1964 the two men discussed the problem that the MFDP posed at the Democratic Party national convention. Johnson told Wilkins that Martin Luther King was not being very supportive—"maybe I'm not the one for him." Wilkins then made a clear reference to the alleged communist influences on King—"the motivation of King, of course, is known to yourself. You know some of the forces behind it." Johnson replied "yes, yes I do."[98]

Support for the Cold War also resulted in much of the NAACP leadership privately viewing the war in Vietnam as a just cause. Anticommunism blended with patriotism, and although the Association took no official policy on the conflict, its leaders were less inclined to agree with the antiwar movement's claims that the United States was intervening in a civil war in order to perpetuate imperialism, under the guise of defending Vietnamese "freedom" from Communist "aggression." Herbert Hill acknowledged that most of the Association's leadership adhered to the traditional Cold War arguments—stopping communism, the Domino Theory, and so on—"I think with very few exceptions they bought all of that, yeah. They were Cold Warriors."[99]

Until the spring of 1967, as Manfred Berg has documented, there was little organized opposition within the NAACP toward the "no position" stance on Vietnam.[100] However, this does not mean that the Association's policy went unchallenged. While it is difficult to gauge the extent of opposition to the war within the Association, it is clear that there were many NAACP members who both opposed the war and worked to generate opposition to it within their local branches and the organization as a whole. Although opposition to the war within the NAACP appears to have been quite limited, its very existence helps to counter the notion of a single, monolithic organization. Often local branches could be more radical, and more flexible, than the national office in New York City. The opposition to the war within the NAACP during this period also helps to explain its later decision to take a stand against the war.

As Berg has shown, the first sign of organized antiwar dissent within the Association came from the Flint, Michigan, branch in the spring of 1965.[101] On April 10 the branch's executive board adopted a resolution urging Lyndon Johnson to use his influence to mediate the "civil war" in Vietnam and arrange negotiations between South Vietnam's government and the NLF. The resolution also called for American troops to be withdrawn immediately.[102] At the 1965 NAACP annual convention an attempt was made to force the Vietnam War issue onto the agenda, and delegates from Flint played a role in the effort to persuade the Resolutions Committee to consider an antiwar resolution. The political and organizational machinations of the NAACP bureaucracy ultimately stymied this radical threat. Herbert Hill candidly explained that the NAACP staff "understood" that the antiwar resolutions which invariably came up at conventions would not be allowed to get to the floor, since the Resolutions Committee was "easy to manipulate." Hill went on—"the

NAACP was a very democratic institution . . . it was, in terms of structure and forms. The conventions were very democratic. On the other hand . . . like all democratic institutions there is bureaucratic control."[103]

The antiwar resolution had been introduced on the grounds that the convention was discussing the "freedom of peoples." But the Resolutions Committee refused to approve the statement for consideration by the convention on the grounds that the civil rights and the peace movement should be separate, and "that such a resolution was entering the sphere of foreign affairs, 'outside the NAACP bailiwick.'"[104] One report of the convention explained that "the closed operation of the Resolutions Committee was likened to that of a 'Star Chamber'; delegates complained that they could not tell what was going on." One delegate claimed that "if the membership had not been so restricted by organization they might have been more progressive."[105] Hill is less sure that the delegates would have voted in favor of the NAACP taking an antiwar position during this period. While he believes that a majority might have opposed the war he thinks that there would still have been a majority favoring the "no position" approach. According to Hill, "most of the rank and file delegates were interested in stopping the war, getting out of the war, because black people were disproportionately paying a very high price." However, there was less agreement on whether it was in the best interests of the NAACP to adopt an antiwar position.[106]

A number of NAACP people were active in various peace campaigns during the mid-1960s. Robert Scheer, who ran against Jeffrey Cohelan in California in 1966, was supported by Carlton Goodlett and Dr. Thomas Burbridge—both former presidents of the San Francisco NAACP.[107] In New York's 26th Congressional District, Leslie Roberts was campaigning for election. The forty-four-year-old Roberts, who had been a delegate to the June White House Conference on Civil Rights, had moved to America from Jamaica at twenty-five. A resident of New Rochelle, he was the first black to seek congressional nomination in Westchester County.[108] Roberts, who was active in his local NAACP branch, opposed the war in Vietnam and argued for negotiations with the NLF. His campaign literature emphasized the negative effects that Vietnam had on the war on poverty—"you can drive through the streets of Westchester any day of the week and see casualties of the Vietnam War. Those families living in the peeling old houses with no toilets or hot water, they're Vietnam casualties. Those men standing on street corners with no jobs, no training, no hope—they're Vietnam casualties." Roberts stated that "the only victory we are assured of in Vietnam is that the Vietnam War has defeated the War on Poverty."

There was also antiwar activity in some NAACP branches, and often opposition to the war was linked to concerns about the Great Society.

Indeed, by 1966, despite Lyndon Johnson's protestations, it was becoming increasingly clear that the war was diverting both political and financial capital from the War on Poverty.[109] In the spring of 1966, for example, members of the Lunenburg County (Virginia) branch were "disturbed about the expanding war in Vietnam and the consequence it might have on the Federal government's domestic program." They urged "that no cuts be made in the domestic programs, including civil rights and anti-poverty projects."[110] The leading opponent of the war within the NAACP was the Greenwich Village (New York) branch. In February 1966 the branch had elected to hold a forum to discuss the links between the peace and civil rights movements, but the NAACP national office had requested that this event be cancelled.[111] In the May edition of *Advance*, the branch newsletter, president Ed Preets attacked the war. He complained that African Americans were yet again being asked to fight abroad for a democracy that they did not enjoy at home. Preets asked, "shall we question and protest this war, or shall we willingly go, bringing to distant lands the democracy we have not known at home?"[112] In April, at the branch's regular membership meeting, a resolution was approved for submission to the national convention. It called on the convention to acknowledge the negative effect of the war on the Great Society programs and to encourage local branches to debate this issue. The attempt to get this resolution adopted failed.[113]

During 1967 there were further rumblings of antiwar feeling within the NAACP. In February a twenty-one-year old African American, Raymond DuVernay, was sentenced to five years imprisonment for resisting the draft. DuVernay had been active in the civil rights movement, and was vice-president of the New Orleans NAACP Youth Council. He believed that America should not be in Vietnam, and articulated an opposition to the war that was distinctly racial. DuVernay declared that he was refusing to be a "black mercenary for white imperialism."[114] Elsewhere, the Rev. Loma St. Clair was seeking election to the post of presiding supervisor in the town of Hempstead and Nassau County, New York. St. Clair, vice-president of the Hempstead branch of the NAACP, was running as part of the United for Peace slate of candidates. Their election program emphasized ending poverty, but also attacked the "inane" war in Vietnam.[115]

The Greenwich Village branch continued its opposition to the war. Toward the end of May, Gloster Current wrote to NAACP officials in New York state, explaining that an effort was being made by the Greenwich Village and the Astoria, Long Island branches to "press for passage" of an antiwar resolution at the annual convention. Current was bringing this matter to their attention because he believed that they "would want to support the unanimous position taken by the Board and not permit the branches . . . to . . . inject the peace issue into the Annual Convention at a time when we are trying to focus all attention on civil rights."[116] The attempt to head off militancy was successful, and the 1967 annual convention loyally reaffirmed the position taken by the board of directors in April. A resolution was passed urging LBJ to pursue all avenues that would lead to a just and honorable peace and complained about the disproportionately high number of blacks serving in Vietnam. However, the main emphasis was on "guns and butter"—the resolution insisted that America could afford to fund the War on Poverty while simultaneously fighting a war in Vietnam.[117] Former board member John Henry Hammond, Jr., resigned as a vice-president of the NAACP in protest at its refusal to take a stand against the war. He believed that Roy Wilkins had "moved steadfastly in the wrong direction."[118]

Evidence of serious dissent with the Association's Vietnam policy did not surface until the fall of 1967. In October the Michigan State Conference of the NAACP adopted an antiwar resolution that had been introduced by the leadership of the Ann Arbor Chapter. The resolution noted the detrimental effect of the war on the antipoverty programs; the high numbers of black casualties; and the reluctance of the South Vietnamese Army to fight. It urged President Johnson to implement an unconditional bombing halt and called for a gradual yet honorable deescalation of the war.[119] Later that month the New York State NAACP adopted an antiwar resolution during a stormy session at the state convention, largely due to the efforts of younger activists. Often there was a generational element to antiwar feeling within the Association. In New Orleans, the local NAACP Youth Council had supported King's Riverside Speech, and the group's twenty-one-year-old vice-president, Raymond DuVernay, had been jailed that February for draft resistance.[120] Furthermore, in early 1967 the NAACP's Youth and College Division had called for a system of voluntary national service as an alternative to the "unjust" draft.[121]

In 1968 the Mississippi NAACP expressed strong antiwar sentiments. Local field secretary Charles Evers was running for Congress in the state's third district. The brother of the martyred Medgar was both courageous and opportunistic; he had been a bootlegger and petty criminal in Chicago before heading to the Magnolia State to become the Association's first self-appointed field secretary, and he remained a divisive and controversial figure.[122] Opposition to Vietnam formed part of Evers's election platform. He stated "I am against the war. I will not have our people fight for someone else's freedom when they are going to have to come home and have to fight in this country for their own freedom." Evers was also opposed to "lily-white draft boards."[123] Evers's concern with the selective service system was reflected in a class action suit that he filed in April.[124]

There is also some evidence that members of the national staff were reevaluating their personal feelings about the war. In January 1966 John Morsell had been "thoroughly convinced of the righteousness" of the war. But in an April 1967 letter to a peace activist he wrote, "I will tell you, candidly, that my own opinions about the war in Vietnam are mixed and . . . I am still unable to advocate a hard and fast line one way or the other."[125] It should not be surprising to discover that, with the war in Asia dragging on and the War on Poverty suffering as a consequence, opposition to or discomfort with the war within the moderate wing of the civil rights movement increased between 1965 and 1968.

It is important to note, however, that dissent and radicalism within the NAACP did not automatically mean support for an antiwar position. In July 1966, for example, Jack E. Tanner, a national director of the NAACP, gave the keynote address at the 63rd annual convention of the Prince Hall Grand Lodge of Washington. Tanner offered support for the "Black Power" slogan and criticized Hubert Humphrey and Roy Wilkins for interpreting it as a form of reverse racism. He also expressed concern about the closeness of the relationship between the NAACP leadership and the Johnson White House. But Tanner also expressed his personal support for America's stand in Vietnam.[126]

Although the policy of treating civil rights and Vietnam as distinct and unconnected issues was upheld until 1969, it was weakened by a number of factors. First, the claim that foreign policy issues lay outside the NAACP's gamut was in fact incongruous with the Association's history. Throughout its existence the NAACP had engaged with international affairs and debated the nature of America's role in the world. Early leaders of the Association, such as Moorfield Storey and Oswald Garrison Villard, had frequently spoken out against American foreign policy, and the organization had sometimes adopted critical positions.[127] For example, in 1915 it had condemned the American occupation of Haiti. The NAACP also spoke out against the Italian invasion of Ethiopia in 1935, and for most of the 1940s it had consistently passed anticolonial and anti-imperialist resolutions. As one history teacher at Michigan State University explained in a letter to the *New York Times*, "it has been forgotten that the precedent of a civil-rights organization . . . criticizing American foreign policy, was not set by Stokely Carmichael . . . but by the NAACP."[128] After the organization's shift to anticommunism at the end of the 1940s, foreign policy still remained an area of concern— the NAACP passed a resolution supporting American actions in Korea at its 1951 annual convention, for example.[129] While Wilkins and other

NAACP leaders stated that foreign policy and civil rights should not be mixed, they cannot but have been aware of the history of their own organization. It was a history that suggested exactly the opposite.

The policy was further undermined by the fact that, on occasion, the NAACP came close to full public support for the war.[130] Responding to the McComb controversy in the summer of 1965, for instance, Wilkins wrote that the young militants who had advocated draft resistance should have been told not to "tinker with patriotism at a time when their country is engaged in armed conflict."[131] Gloster Current and the NAACP national office also encouraged the Mississippi State NAACP to issue a patriotic statement attacking the McComb antidraft sentiment. Charles Evers and Aaron Henry told reporters that they strongly urged "all citizens, Negroes and whites, to support our country in this major crisis [Vietnam]. It is the duty of every American to give unstinted support to the fight for freedom abroad and step up the pace in the fight for democracy at home."[132] In December 1965, responding to a critic of the NAACP's stance on the war, John Morsell explained that many liberals believed that "a free and stable world" was "incompatible with Communist aggression."[133]

In January 1966 Roy Wilkins expressed support for the Johnson administration's principal foreign policy when he sent a telegram to the president praising his Sate of the Union Address—"your call for carrying on domestic crusade for the Great Society projects including all aspects of anti-poverty program *along with fulfilling our nation's commitment in Vietnam* is the right call and is a challenge to every American."[134] In the spring of 1967 the NAACP leader attacked Martin Luther King for putting peace above civil rights. Wilkins then proceeded to offer a partial endorsement of the war effort—"I don't speak as a hawk or a dove. . . . But, is it wrong for people to be patriotic? Is it wrong for us to back up our boys in the field. . . . They're dying while we're knifing them in the back at home." He continued, "maybe I'm a bit old fashioned . . . maybe we are wrong, maybe we shouldn't be in Vietnam. But when you're out there in the trenches being fired at, you have to fight back."[135]

Moreover, by taking stands on other foreign policy issues, black moderates undermined their own arguments about not mixing civil rights and international affairs. During the June 1967 Arab-Israeli war, for example, Whitney Young participated in a Washington demonstration in support of Israel.[136] The NAACP, meanwhile, paid a $200 registration fee to allow Gloster Current to attend the spring 1968 Foreign Policy Association Convocation. The conference's theme was "futurism" and the challenges confronting U.S. foreign policy in the next 50 years.[137]

Some critics believed that, in traveling to Vietnam in July 1966, Whitney Young had given implicit endorsement to the war, while others accused him of being a tool of the Johnson administration.[138] Cecil B. Moore, militant head of the Philadelphia NAACP, for example, denounced Young bitterly and claimed that he had been used to "whitewash" racial discrimination in Vietnam.[139] But the following year the Urban League executive director flouted the policy of keeping civil rights and Vietnam separate explicitly. During the "long hot summer" of 1967, Young appears to have experienced a "wobble" over his support of the guns and butter policy—he began to realize that "rats and jobs" were linked to the Vietnam War. At the NUL national conference in Portland, Oregon, at the end of August, Young explained that he was no longer sure that it was possible to have both guns and butter. If it came to a choice, Young declared that "the first priority ought to be peace and justice here at home."[140]

It was after this "wobble" that President Johnson telephoned Young to tell him that he wanted him to be part of the American delegation to observe the elections in South Vietnam. Young was reluctant to go but was faced with little choice after LBJ applied some of his infamous "treatment"—"Whitney, you wanted a Negro on the Supreme Court and I put on one. . . . Now I want a Negro on this group going to Vietnam. . . . Well Whitney, I'm going to announce you as one of the team, and if you feel you can't serve your country, you explain it to the press."[141] Andrew Young believed that Young had been tricked into supporting the administration and, confirming the "wobble" theory, suggested that the NUL executive director had been experiencing "inner conflict" over the Vietnam War.[142] It is likely that Marcia Young's opposition to the Vietnam War contributed to this inner turmoil. Young's eldest daughter, a student at Bryn Mawr College, engaged in a hunger fast as part of her antiwar protests.[143]

In accepting this mission, albeit reluctantly, Young became a "significant participant in a major foreign policy matter," and seriously compromised his position of neutrality on the war itself. The 22-man U.S. delegation, which included three senators, three governors, mayors, churchmen, businessmen and labor leaders, arrived in Saigon on Wednesday, August 30. Young made the journey aboard Air Force One carrying serious concerns about the war—the lives being lost, and the resources being diverted.[144] However, he returned impressed with the election effort in South Vietnam, which had taken place under unusual and difficult circumstances. Young had been particularly struck by the enthusiasm for the elections—in which South Vietnam's military leaders Nguyen Cao Ky and Nguyen Van Thieu claimed victory with 35 percent of the vote. The election observers, including Young, ignored charges that major opponents of the Thieu-Ky regime had been prevented from running or had been jailed, as well as reports of voter intimidation and fraud, to declare that the elections had been "reasonably efficient, free, and honest."[145] At an hour-long debriefing with the president in September, Young declared that he was "completely satisfied that these were free elections as well as could be expected under the conditions." The Urban League head also stated that America might learn some lessons from South Vietnam's version of democracy—such as allowing eighteen-year-olds to vote.[146] But perhaps it was another U.S. "observer," John Knight of *Knight Newspapers*, who best exemplified the U.S. government's attitude toward "democracy" in South Vietnam. Addressing concerns about the possible repression of political opponents during the elections, he told Johnson that he had "sought out dissidents such as the suspended editors and the candidates who were not permitted to run and he heard them out thoroughly and fully and at the close he had the opinion that he would not want them running his country."[147]

In joining the American delegation to observe the South Vietnamese elections Whitney Young had stretched the policy of treating civil rights and Vietnam as unconnected issues to the breaking point.[148] Young had moved beyond using Vietnam for the purposes of gleaning domestic political concessions to become a reluctant supporter of the Johnson Administration's foreign policy. SNCC's John Wilson described the Urban League leader as a "puppet" of the American government, and claimed that he "was used by the US government to make those [South Vietnamese] elections appear legitimate in the eyes of black people."[149] With LBJ out of office a year later, Whitney Young's doubts over the war, feelings he had suppressed in 1967, would reemerge and move him to extend support to the peace movement.

During the mid-1960s, with the federal government seemingly committed to eradicating racial discrimination and poverty, civil rights moderates had little to gain by joining with the peace movement in condemning American military intervention in Southeast Asia. The political and personal links between moderate black leaders and the Johnson administration were so strong that they were never going to risk losing all that they had worked so hard for, especially when there was relatively little pressure from below to oppose the war. Moreover, anticommunism would prevent many moderates from viewing the peace movement as anything other than a communist-driven conspiracy. After 1968, with a Republican in the White House and a newly invigorated "respectable" peace movement, the moderate civil rights movement would come to oppose the war and give qualified support to the movement to end it.

Chapter 4

Racial Tensions

Black people are in no mood for marching to [the Pentagon] and listening to folk singing.
—*Omar Ahmed, 1967*

The rain that fell intermittently on the morning of Saturday April 15, 1967 did not deter tens of thousands of Americans from taking to the streets of San Francisco to protest against America's ongoing involvement in Vietnam. About 30,000 gathered at the foot of Market Street, and walked four miles through the heart of the city to Kezar Stadium, at the edge of Golden Gate Park. As the sun came out, the crowd at the afternoon rally swelled to 75,000—a record turnout for a West Coast antiwar protest. The main speakers in the packed stadium included civil rights leaders Coretta Scott King and Julian Bond, as well as Robert Vaughn (star of television's *Man from Uncle*). One journalist noted that the civil rights movement was "represented more conspicuously than before." Coretta King told the crowd that "freedom and justice in America" were "bound together with freedom and justice in Vietnam," while Georgia legislator Julian Bond attacked the "growing cancer" of American militarism. He urged that the "screams of the children in Harlem and Haiphong" be replaced with "cheerful, loving laughter." TV star Vaughn asked, "Haven't enough men been killed, enough women slaughtered, enough babies burned?" The *National Guardian* commented on the demonstration's countercultural flavor, explaining that participants left the stands to hand out daffodils and paper flowers, while artists including Country Joe and the Fish provided musical entertainment.[1]

In a show of solidarity it also rained in New York, where tens of thousands of Americans filtered into Central Park. At Sheep Meadow, at 11 a.m., a group of around 100 people gathered to burn their draft cards. By the time the twenty-block march to the UN plaza began shortly after noon, some observers estimated that about 400,000 Americans had turned out. The demonstrators came from all walks of life—there were blacks, whites, and native Americans; children and grandparents; hippies and church members; military veterans and Viet Cong sympathizers; businessmen and students; housewives and teachers; priests and doctors. Many were protesting against the war for the first time.[2]

Martin Luther King, James Bevel, pediatrician Benjamin Spock, and black entertainer Harry Belafonte led the swarming mass of protesters in the procession from Central Park to the UN, where King, Stokely Carmichael, and Floyd McKissick were among the featured speakers. Although a heavy downpour ended the rally at 5 p.m., marchers continued to arrive at the UN for another hour. The massive demonstrations in New York and San Francisco were organized by the Spring Mobilization Committee, an antiwar coordinating coalition that had been founded in November 1966 and which later became the National Mobilization Committee (Mobe). The actions were, according to university professor and veteran leftist Sidney Peck, "successful beyond all expectations." Historian Tom Wells has explained that the April protests "showed the Johnson administration and public that the antiwar movement had carved out a large political base in the United States."[3]

The 1967 protests occurred within a context of deepening crisis at home and drift abroad. Growing antiwar activism combined with urban riots and the ongoing war in Vietnam to undermine Lyndon Johnson's presidency. Public approval of the president had fallen from 67 percent in 1965 to 47 percent two years later. However you looked at it, Johnson was in trouble politically, and it was becoming increasingly difficult for the president to leave the White House without encountering fierce demonstrations. In the spring of 1967 only 40 percent of Americans supported the administration's Vietnam policy, and by the end of the year McGeorge Bundy, Johnson's national security advisor, told the president that "public discontent with the war is now wide and deep." The increasing unpopularity of the war led Johnson to choose what he viewed as a "middle course"—neither unleashing the full might of America's military power nor withdrawing, but engaging in limited escalation. Thus, while Johnson announced plans to send a further 50,000 troops to Vietnam in August, this fell short of General Westmoreland's request for 200,000. But however "limited" the escalation, the effect on the antiwar movement was to increase despair and militancy. With traditional tactics seemingly ineffective, more radical methods, such as draft resistance, began to flourish. Indeed, the growing anguish and rage within the New Left over the ongoing war would lead to the emergence of terrorist revolutionary groups like the Weathermen at the end of the decade.[4]

The Spring Mobilization to End the War in Vietnam marked the first significant attempt at coalition between the peace and freedom movements, on a national level, since the Assembly of Unrepresented People in Washington of August 1965. The prominence of black leaders and civil rights groups at the April protests seemed encouraging for those seeking to forge closer links between black and white critics of the war. However, by the end of the year, the two movements seemed as far apart as ever.

The Spring Mobe hoped to unite a broad coalition of forces against the war, and encourage cooperation between the peace and civil rights movements. At the November 1966 conference that established the Spring Mobe, a resolution was adopted calling for the organization to widen peace activities and reach out to civil rights groups.[5] One official mailing explained that while the Spring Mobe sought close cooperation between civil rights and other groups, organizations would be given the freedom to "determine the extent and manner of their activity." The aim was not to replace existing organizations but to "stimulate increased activity everywhere."[6] An expansion of antiwar activity within the African American community was a major goal.[7]

The time seemed ripe for such a development. Not only were important black leaders like Martin Luther King openly condemning the war, but antiwar feeling among ordinary African Americans was also growing. Always the "most dovish" social group, a poll in the *Chicago Defender* at the beginning of April showed that almost half of black Chicagoans wanted America to withdraw from Vietnam. A national poll conducted in May, meanwhile, showed that while 73 percent of white Americans opposed King's stance on the war, only 48 percent of blacks disagreed with him.[8]

On an organizational level the civil rights movement was integrated into the structure of the Spring Mobilization Committee. In January 1967, James Bevel, a close aide of Martin Luther King, was appointed national director of the organization, and he expressed a desire to involve much of the black community in "not just a march, but a total movement to end the war."[9] Bevel's hiring was seen as a significant move toward attracting substantial black participation in the peace movement.[10] Indeed, the *New York Times* reported that the thirty-year-old Baptist minister had been recruited because the Spring Mobe wanted "greater participation of civil rights organizations than has been the case."[11] Bevel bitterly opposed the war, on once occasion stating that "each passing day makes more and more plain to millions of Americans the hollowness and wickedness of this war of oppression against a foreign colored people, which parallels in military terms what has been done to . . . the colored people of America for centuries." Bevel, a native of Leflore County, Mississippi, explained that the black community was beginning to view the Vietnam War as a racist conflict, and that they also understood the negative implications of the war for the Great Society.[12]

The involvement of civil rights leaders in an organizational capacity was not restricted to Bevel. Cleveland Robinson, president of the Negro American Labor Council, and SCLC vice-president Ralph Abernathy were made vice-chairmen of the Spring Mobe. In addition, many prominent black activists sponsored the organization—including Julian Bond, Stokely Carmichael, and Ivanhoe Donaldson of SNCC; James Farmer, Floyd McKissick and Ruth Turner of CORE; the SCLC's Fred Shuttlesworth and Wyatt T. Walker; and individuals such as the black entertainer Harry Belafonte and former SNCC chairman John Lewis.[13] An unstated aim of the Spring Mobe was to attract the support of Martin Luther King, who had been cautious in his opposition to the war since the summer of 1965.[14] In the aftermath of his Riverside Speech, King agreed to appear at the New York demonstration. The decision, though, was somewhat controversial since most of his close advisors (with the exception of Bevel) were opposed. Stanley Levison, for example, repeatedly urged King not to undermine his position by aligning himself with fringe elements—the "squabbling, pacifist, socialist, hippy collection."[15]

At the New York demonstration, the vast crowd at the United Nations heard Martin Luther King counsel against a "mechanical fusion" of the peace and civil rights movement and Stokely Carmichael define the draft as "white people sending black people to make war on yellow people to defend land they stole from red people."[16] The SNCC chairman also had a specific message for white antiwar activists. Carmichael believed that it was "crystal clear" that "white people, in their turn, must begin to deal with the fundamental problems of this country: racism and exploitation." He told the whites to "go into the white community, where racism originates . . . go into the white community, where the Vietnam war originated . . . work there, organize there, strike against the American system at its base."[17]

The scale of the civil rights movement's participation in the Spring Mobilization was considerable. In addition to King, Floyd McKissick, Cleveland Robinson and James Bevel had spoken at the New York rally, SNCC and SCLC had supported the Mobe, and "CORE groups from Baltimore, Cleveland, Ann Arbor, Chicago, Philadelphia, Boston, Long Island and Detroit, as well as all boroughs in New York were among the marchers." CORE had also been involved in the planning of the New York demonstration—"Don Smith, Ron Clark, Jocelyn McKissick and Ruth Turner from the National Office helped out as part-time or volunteer staff. Harlem and Brooklyn CORE organized large contingents of black youth. " The organization had also placed antiwar advertisements in the *New York Times* and *Muhammed Speaks* prior to the march.[18] There was also a heavy black presence at the San Francisco actions. Commentators noted the high profile involvement of so many civil rights organizations and leaders. The *National Guardian* proclaimed that the April 15 actions "represented the broadest involvement so far of the black freedom movement against the war."[19]

On the surface, such developments seemed promising for those who hoped to create a truly multi-racial antiwar movement. But rather than representing the beginning of any "rainbow coalition," the Spring Mobilization was in fact indicative of the rising racial tension that existed between the white and black components of the antiwar forces. The events in Harlem on April 15 offer a glimpse at the early stages of a trend that would eventually result in a more racially separatist peace movement.

On the morning of April 15, at the junction of 135th Street and Lenox Avenue, several hundred African Americans attended a rally arranged by the Black United Action Front as part of the Spring Mobe's official program of events.[20] Stokely Carmichael told the crowd that "black people have been trying to prove to white people in every war what good Americans we've been, only to come back and find racism, but we're not going to Vietnam. We're working for Black Power" in America.[21] The mood of the protesters was one of "strident militancy" as they marched behind Carmichael and Floyd McKissick later that morning to Central Park to join with the main body of antiwar protesters. Marching under their official slogan "U.S. Get Out of Vietnam Now," and shouting "Hell no, we won't go" and "No Vietnamese ever called me nigger," the ranks of the black demonstrators swelled to 1,000. Their chants often linked the war in Vietnam with the struggle for justice and equality at home. One journalist described the scene—"'Fight in Watts!' a chant leader shouted. 'But not in Viet Nam.' 'Fight in New York!' ' . . . but not in Vietnam.'"[22] The Harlemites appeared to be antagonistic towards whites —"small groups of whites tried to join the line of the march. They were turned away." In one amusing incident, at the north edge of central park, "15 white college students greeted the Negro marchers. One of the boys was playing stirring Scottish airs on a bagpipe. Parade leaders made it clear the boys were not welcome." According to one marcher, the anti-white feeling was "directed against the 'hippies' and certain middle-class elements who gave the rally an atmosphere of a picnic." He went on to express resentment at the fact that "most of the whites would talk about 'peace' and then return to comfortable homes," while blacks faced a daily struggle for survival.[23] After tiring of waiting for the main march to leave Central Park, the Harlem protesters set off for the UN by themselves.

The emergence of racial separatist tendencies within the antiwar movement, seen at the Spring Mobilization, would continue and increase during the remainder of 1967. With Black Power ideology holding increasing sway over the civil rights movement, and with emotions running high over urban disorder, cooperation between white and black activists became ever more difficult. Indeed, among black activists there was growing criticism of the peace movement for being unresponsive to black demands and needs.

Racial division manifested itself the following month, at a national planning conference sponsored by the Student Mobilization Committee (SMC or "Student Mobe"). About 600 delegates, the majority from high schools and colleges, attended the event, held May 13–14 at the University of Chicago. They agreed to cooperate in efforts to reach out to adult constituencies, encourage local referenda on the war and support draft resistance.[24] A workshop on black student organizing resulted in the formation of a Black Student Caucus, which argued for a number of radical measures as well as changes in the structure of the peace movement.[25] For example, the Caucus pushed for the SMC to endorse the creation of black draft resistance unions and to offer full support to African American draft resisters.[26] While welcoming discussion on forming a coalition between the peace and civil rights movement, the Caucus felt that it was time to "define exactly what this means." The problem thus far had been that "the relationship has been seen as civil rights forces supplementing peace efforts rather than the coalition of two equally important facets of revolutionary activity." However, if the civil rights movement was expected to "spend time and energy developing creative alternatives to the racist war in Vietnam," the blacks explained, then "the peace movement must be expected to spend equal time seeking creative alternatives to the racist wars here at home." The Caucus suggested, in line with Black Power thinking, that white antiwar activists work to eliminate racism in the white community and leave blacks to organize themselves.[27]

Criticism of the predominantly white peace movement also surfaced at the first national Black Power conference, held in Newark in July. Approximately 1,300 African Americans representing more than forty organizations gathered at the Mount Zion Baptist Church to engage in wide ranging discussions about Black Power and the future of the black struggle. The conference took place in the aftermath of a six-day riot in Newark, which had left 23 people dead.[28]

The conference initially split into fourteen workshops whose aim was to produce a resolution stating the role that the members could contribute towards the goal of attaining Black Power.[29] These resolutions were then to be presented to the body of the conference for ratification on the final day. Numerous resolutions were passed, covering such subjects as the creation of a black militia, the establishment of black universities, the election of more black Senators and Representatives, and cultural and educational exchange programs with African nations. There was also discussion on the creation of a separate black homeland within the United States. Overall, the conference was viewed as a first step in the search for a new route to equality.[30]

The black delegates also voiced their disgruntlement with the antiwar movement. In a speech to the delegates on July 21, CORE's Floyd McKissick argued for the link between Vietnam and black America, a link that he felt the antiwar movement needed to address. The CORE leader explained that "even our friends in the peace movement find it too easy to look thousands of miles away from home and, with much indignation, see the extermination of the Vietnamese. On the other hand, they cannot see ten blocks away, where many Black People are the Walking Dead—dead in mind and spirit, because of lack of hope and lack of chance."[31] Despite this reproach for the peace movement, the conference did urge support for the Mobe's plans for antiwar activity in Washington, D.C. on October 21. A resolution from the floor urged blacks to oppose the "racist" war, support the NLF, and demand an immediate withdrawal of American troops.[32]

Black Power's increasing popularity, and the hostile attitudes towards white America that often accompanied it, sharpened African American criticisms of the white-dominated peace movement and made progressive interracial coalitions more difficult to construct. The National Conference for New Politics (NCNP) convention that was held later that summer at Chicago's luxurious Palmer House Hotel, provides one of the most potent examples of this.

Addressing the opening night rally of the NCNP convention on August 31, 1967, the organization's executive director William F. Pepper informed the several thousand delegates that

Historians may well count your presence here as the most significant gathering of Americans since the founding of our nation. Never before have so many Americans, from so many different living conditions, come from so many diverse sections of the land to dedicate themselves to the rebuilding, indeed to the reclamation of their government and their destinies.

Pepper concluded his remarks by declaring that "it may well be that what you begin here may ultimately result in a new social, economic and political system in the United States.[33]

Outside the auditorium a bongo group was chanting "Kill Whitey."[34] The convention was one of the most ambitious attempts to forge a broad political alliance of antiwar organizations, New Left insurgents, and the radical wing of the civil rights movement in 1960s America. It was planned by the NCNP, a coordinating organization that hoped for a fundamental reconstitution of the American social, economic, and political order.[35]

While the NCNP convention has largely been portrayed as a farcical horror show, a more detailed understanding of the NCNP's doomed attempt to bring together antiwar liberals, New Left radicals, and African American activists, casts light on some of the important problems encountered by the American left during the 1960s.[36] The NCNP, like the wider movement, faced difficulties in establishing black-white cooperation during the Black Power era; and the arguments over to what extent, if at all, radicals would work within the American political system, or cooperate with white liberals, proved debilitating. Moreover, the task of prioritizing issues proved extremely problematic. While it proved possible to organize around a particular demand, such as ending the Vietnam War, the movement was unable to achieve any useful consensus over more broad aims. The NCNP convention confronted each of these problems, but the issue of race proved most divisive. The dramatic role played by race at the convention is illustrative of the complex relationship between black and white radicalism in the 1960s.

On July 11, 1967 the NCNP issued a call for a planning convention to "end the reign of Lyndon Baines Johnson"—many antiwar liberals now felt that defeating Johnson was a moral imperative.[37] The press reported that the convention hoped to set up a political party to run candidates in the 1968 elections—there was talk of a King-Spock ticket even though King had publicly ruled this out in April—but that was only one option under consideration.[38] Running local presidential tickets, a temporary national ticket, or focusing on community organizing were also on the agenda. The invitation to the convention ambitiously proclaimed "we intend to build a different American future . . . to end the destruction of Vietnam . . . to begin the building of 'Mankind' . . . to end poverty, fear and despair at home. . . . We intend to make our government accountable to us."[39] Any democratic group committed to "some form of organizing work in the community" and willing to "conceivably endorse an independent candidate at some time" was eligible to participate.[40] The NCNP invited New Left radicals, antiwar protesters, and militant black activists to "take over" the convention—which they duly did. The proceedings began amidst high hopes, many of the delegates believed that "nothing less than the nation's rebirth was on the agenda."[41] In the aftermath of the convention, however, the optimism had vanished. C. Clark Kissinger, an SDS community organizer who had helped chair the gathering, stated that "it worked out pretty well in the end—no one was killed."[42]

The several thousand delegates representing some 200 different organizations (including SCLC, SNCC, CORE, MFDP, SDS, SANE) who convened in Chicago varied enormously. The convention attracted much of America's "curious left."[43] The various groups also arrived committed to different political strategies. The Socialist Workers Party (SWP) and the Trotskyists favored creating a third party. SDS, disenchanted with electoral politics and its "co-opting" effects, preferred local organizing. The California Delegation (also known as the New Politics Group) favored leaving each state free to have a national ticket if it wanted, while concentrating energies on local community action.[44]

The opening night rally at the Chicago Coliseum did not bode well. After William Pepper's dramatic introduction, co-chairman Julian Bond, introduced by African American performer Ossie Davis as a "black terror in tennis shoes," spoke briefly, left quickly, and took no further part in the convention.[45] The highlight of the evening, Martin Luther King's keynote speech, turned out to be something of a disappointment. According to one report, King "read from a lengthy script which did not deal with a single real issue of the convention."[46] He left shortly thereafter and later complained to an aide that the black nationalists were trying to take over and drive the whites out.[47] Indeed, King—fearful of being linked too closely with New Left radicals—had made it clear that he was "merely a guest speaker" at the rally and had "no relationship to the general policy or strategy" of the NCNP. According to David Garrow, a reluctant King participated in the convention because Martin Peretz, husband of leading SCLC donor Anne Farnsworth, was heavily involved with it.[48]

Several weeks before the convention was due to begin, it had appeared as if the black movement was going to be very poorly represented in Chicago. African Americans were viewed as a key new politics constituency, and the radical civil rights movement was idealized on the left as America's leading revolutionary force. A concentrated effort was therefore made to encourage black participation. In early August civil rights leaders including Julian Bond, Floyd McKissick, and Fannie Lou Hamer signed a letter urging blacks to ally with progressive whites at the convention. The letter stated that "the necessity for cooperation between black militants and white progressives" could not be overemphasized."[49] This hasty effort to add legitimacy to the convention by involving black groups had unforeseen consequences.

The issue of race dominated the convention. Early on, 350 black militants walked out to attend their own conference. Approximately 400 remained and formed a caucus—although there were black delegates, representing other groups, who did not join it. The official plenary session, which began on Friday, was dominated by debate over the role of blacks in the convention. The Black Caucus, meeting in secret, presented the delegates with an ultimatum—they had to accept without alteration a thirteen-point list of resolutions, or the blacks would walk out. They stated that, "we, as black people, believe that the United States system is committed to the practice of genocide, social degradation, to the denial of political and social self-determination of black people, and cannot reform itself. There must be revolutionary change. "[50] The Caucus demanded 50 percent representation on all convention committees, and called on the convention to support all wars of national liberation around the world, black control of black political groups in black communities, making "immediate reparation for the historic, physical, sexual, mental, and economic exploitation of black people," setting up white "civilizing committees" to eliminate white racism, rebuilding the ghettos, support for the Newark Black Power Conference resolutions (which most delegates had not seen) and condemnation of the "imperialist Zionist" six days war.[51] Indeed, the anti-Semitism of many Black militants, whether real or imagined, harmed efforts at constructing interracial coalitions, given the significant Jewish presence in the New Left and antiwar ranks.

On Friday night, "in an orgy of confession about their childhood feelings toward Negroes," the whites debated the ultimatum. After lengthy discussions they voted by a margin of 3–1 to accept the black demands, much to the chagrin of white liberal commentators. Renata Adler declared that the adoption of the thirteen points constituted a version of white paternalism that would shock a South African plantation owner.[52] While countless journalists attacked the decision to accept the ultimatum as a product of paternalism or white guilt, many of the delegates voted for points that they personally disagreed with because they felt that a wider and more important issue was at stake—the issue of black-white unity. A Maryland woman who asked not to be identified said that while she did not agree with the black demands, she felt that they had to make a gesture.[53] The "non-black ad hoc committee to support the resolution of the Black Caucus" explained that trying to change the specifics of the points was "completely missing the point" and urged delegates to "vote with the spirit of it."[54] The ultimatum had been presented as a test of the white delegates' commitment to work with the black movement, and nothing less than an unequivocal endorsement of the thirteen points would have prevented the Black Caucus from walking out. Following the vote, the blacks rejoined the convention. On Saturday evening the plenary voted down the proposal to form a third party, and a proposal to run a third ticket was narrowly defeated by a complicated system of weighted voting by 13,519 to 13,517.[55]

That evening the Black Caucus, which had been meeting in secret with shaven-headed bodyguards at the doors, demanded half the convention votes in addition to 50 percent representation on all the committees. This demand was presented in terms of an "equal voice," even though the blacks would gain effective control of the convention since they would vote in one bloc, while the whites would be split. Numerous speakers declared that such control was right, because the white radicals had no power base outside the convention, whereas the blacks could summon up their "17 million ghetto brothers." Bertram Garskoff of Ann Arbor Citizens for Peace declared that "we are just a little tail on the end of a very powerful black panther. And I want to be on that tail—if they'll let me." Garskoff went on to explain that, once whites had surrendered power, they should "trust the blacks the way you trust children." Perhaps realizing the paternalistic overtones of his words, Garskoff added "now I don't mean to say it like that because these are very sophisticated people and they've taught the whites here a hell of a lot."[56] Arthur Waskow argued that 1,000 liberals were trying to become good radicals by castrating themselves, and rejected the argument that once given the votes the blacks would cooperate.[57]

Finally, when the whites acquiesced in the early hours of Sunday morning by a margin of 2–1, "pandemonium broke loose. The black people broke into hysterical cheering over their victory. . . . [Caucus chairman] Carlos Russell then received the delegates' credentials for 28,498 votes; he seemed moved almost to the point of tears, and almost the entire body were cheering their heads off." One commentator declared that "some sort of unity between black and white, no matter how tenuous, had been achieved. Without this unity, no convention could possibly go forward."[58] William A. Price, writing in the *National Guardian*, declared that "the first major political bond between blacks and whites in 20th Century U.S.—based on equality of partnership—was forged in the grand ballroom of Chicago's Palmer House."[59]

The reaction to events at the convention was predictably unsympathetic. A *New York Times* editorial referred to the "flagrant example of organizational surrender to the blackmail of Negro extremists," while the *Berkeley Barb*'s Marvin Garson claimed that the demagogic debates and speeches supporting the Caucus ultimatums were exercises in masochism, with frequently heard statements of white guilt.[60] Scholarly judgment has often reflected this contemporary criticism. Robert Weisbrot has written that "the politics of emotional catharsis left little room . . . for a workable coalition with even the most serious white activists."[61]

Although black demands for half the convention votes when they constituted only 15–20 percent of the convention delegates seemed profoundly undemocratic, the issue was more complex. In their initial ultimatum the Black Caucus had complained that the NCNP had not "involved Blacks meaningfully in the initiation, planning or operation" of the convention.[62] There was certainly a good deal of truth to this charge. The last-minute effort to involve African American activists in the convention, coupled with a parliamentary structure that failed to take account of Black Power political reality, proved catastrophic.

While most white delegates viewed the convention as a paradigm of democracy, with voting weighed according to the size of "active" group membership, to many blacks "it looked like another manipulated vehicle to win white political power with a little help from the black movement."[63] The Black Caucus accused the NCNP of "political paternalism," and declared that "blacks must define for themselves, the role, if any, they are to play at this convention, and the terms on which they will participate with whites."[64] The black position was that they had to be treated as equals. In theory, "a majority of the whites" could have "bound a majority of the blacks to a given course of action against their will." In hindsight, Arthur Waskow conceded that the blacks had been correct in refusing to "bow to any majority but their own."[65] Concern about being "used" by white radicals (and liberals) was not limited to blacks attending the NCNP convention. In July 1967 Robert F. Williams, the militant black freedom fighter then living in exile in China, had warned that the New Left was "seeking hegemony over the black revolution."[66] Concern over white "co-optation" seriously impeded attempts to build a multiracial movement against the Vietnam War. In January 1968, when one of the first black antiwar groups—the National Black Antiwar Antidraft Union (NBAWADU)—was formed, it was for the purpose of building a "secure black base for antiwar activity to *eliminate the possibilities of being absorbed by the white anti-war movement.*"[67]

Rather than giving in to demands that resulted in the Black Caucus controlling the convention, a more reasonable solution, proposed at the time but lost amid the chaos, was a bicameral approach. Marvin Garson declared that "we simply aren't ready for any organic unity . . . the only true unity must be an alliance giving each wing of the movement a veto over any proposals for joint action in areas of mutual concern, and allowing each wing to formulate and carry out its own programs whenever it feels necessary to do so."[68] Arthur Waskow shared this view, and tried to persuade the convention to adopt it.[69] However, this effort came too late. There were two movements in Chicago—one white, and one black. If this political reality had been acknowledged earlier, then appropriate arrangements might have been possible. That was not the case, and once the black delegates made their demands any attempt by whites to dilute or modify them appeared to be an attempt to control the black movement. By exposing its weaknesses in such a public manner, the NCNP opened itself up to massive criticism, which was at least partly unwarranted and avoidable.

In trying to be too democratic, the NCNP ended up being accused of exploiting the black movement. While there was some truth in this, it is hard to be positive about the acrimonious and bitter debate, fueled by a mixture of guilt, hypocrisy, and radical posturing, that ensued. From the pages of the *Village Voice,* June Greenlief mourned the loss of peaceful integration as a movement ideal. She lambasted the hypocritical nature of the convention, with "whites masquerading as either poor or black, blacks posing as revolutionaries or as arrogant whites, conservatives pretending to be communists, women feigning to be oppressed, and liberals pretending not to be there at all." The scene reminded her of old Communist Party gatherings where members looked for a *Worker* before whom to genuflect, only in 1967 the *Worker* had become the *Black.* David Burner has claimed that the convention is a perfect example of the embryonic political correctness that he argues formed part of the "radical experience" at the end of the 1960s.[70]

When the plenary reconvened following the acceptance of black demands for 50 percent of the convention votes, the Black Caucus was expected to endorse a national third ticket for 1968—which many blacks apparently favored.[71] However, in a "surge of fellow-feeling," the Caucus submitted a proposal that supported an earlier compromise—allowing third tickets where there was local support, but leaving the primary focus on community organizing.[72] Nevertheless, the debates over the black demands had left the whites drained and dispirited. There was a comparatively short debate on tactics for 1968 "and beyond," and peace tickets were only expected in six or seven states. This constituted a clear victory for the white community organizers who feared that a national campaign would detract from their efforts to build a genuinely revolutionary movement at the grass-roots level. It disappointed many delegates from moderate peace groups who had thought that a national third party with black support could hold the balance of power in 1968.[73]

In the short time found to discuss the "New Politics," the delegates did manage to pass resolutions urging immediate withdrawal from Vietnam, supporting draft resistance, the struggle of Mexican-Americans and the poor of Appalachia, and backing Adam Clayton Powell's struggle against congressional excommunication; plans were also made for October's demonstration at the Pentagon. However, most of the convention had been spent arguing about the role of blacks.[74] The remaining substantive problems were left in the hands of a 26-man steering committee, which was to continue to coordinate "New Politics" activities through the NCNP. This new board was split into two sections—one to concentrate on community organizing, the other to promote candidates in elections. The board also had the authority to call another convention in 1968 to consider nominating a third party ticket.[75] Unsurprisingly, no such convention took place. In fact, the NCNP national office closed for good in April 1968, due to severe financial problems caused mainly by the unfavorable publicity that the convention had generated.[76]

At the end of the traumatic weekend some delegates, both black and white, felt that the convention had laid the groundwork for a "new politics" in America—not all believed that the NCNP was necessarily a spent force.[77] Perhaps the greatest achievement of the event was that no major group had walked out—"the coalition did not quite jell at the Palmer House, but it didn't fly apart either. It can be built," wrote Chicago organizer Sidney Lens.[78] Most delegates admitted that the proceedings had been farcical, but the "handout" to the Black Caucus was a symbol, a necessary gesture of goodwill for establishing two wings of the political movement.[79] However, many blacks wondered why they had chosen to ally with a white group that lacked both financial power and popular support.[80] CORE's Roy Innis was blunt: "why should I negotiate with the whites here? They've got nothing to deliver. I'd rather bargain with the power structure."[81]

The problems with the NCNP convention were partly rooted in the internal tension within the organization itself. Lacking a clear program or ideological position, the convention brought together disparate groups from varying ends of the left-of-center political spectrum. Rather than focusing on the one issue that more or less united the delegates, the war in Vietnam, the convention became an amorphous gathering of "the movement." Yet the movement was too heterogeneous and socially diverse, and contained too many differing political perspectives, to agree on a single multi-issue program.[82] For example, it proved impossible for the radical left to deal collectively with the problem of prioritizing issues, as the question of women's liberation at the convention revealed. There were just too many competing agendas.[83] Moreover, the organizers and paymasters of the NCNP wanted something different from many of the delegates. William Pepper had advocated a King-Spock ticket at the Spring Mobilization in April 1967, but many of the delegates favored community organizing. Although the convention has been seen as a failure because attempts to form a political party or run a third ticket did not succeed, the fact that this was not the central aim of most of the participants has frequently been overlooked.

The convention revealed that "the movement" was too large and diverse to organize anything other than massive street demonstrations at the national level. There was not enough area of agreement concerning areas other than Vietnam on which to build a successful multi-issue radical movement. Black-white hostility compounded the differences, but the "unruly diversity of New Left groups stretched the very notion of coalition beyond workable bounds."[84] In 1967 there were two distinct branches of the movement—with separate interests. The white branch was obsessed with Vietnam, American imperialism, and student affairs; while the black branch was concerned with destroying a culture of oppression and creating a new kind of identity for African Americans—

a job that had to be done by blacks. Ironically, there was a need to treat the two wings of the movement as "separate but equal."[85]

The Black Caucus did not want to "run the movement," but did want to have black radicals recognized for what they were: the "most powerful and most radical motive force in the U.S."[86] If the convention had been structured differently then there would have been no need for the resolutions, but as it was, "yes" votes for the Caucus demands were symbols of trust. This point seems to be borne out by the fact that once the decision had been made for blacks and whites to be treated as "equals" in the convention, the Caucus articulated sensible proposals, accepted a compromise political strategy for 1968, and appeared prepared to cooperate. Following the decision to give the Black Caucus 50 percent of the convention votes, the whites were treated with "ostentatious kindness . . . the blacks seemed to remove their fearsome bearded masks of hatred."[87] This reasonableness was partly due to the fact that many of the most militant African Americans had left the convention, but it also reflected the more complex nature of the debate—once some form of equality was achieved, a degree of cooperation was possible. It would, however, be a mistake to over-estimate the willingness for meaningful collaboration. During the convention the Caucus had shown almost no desire to negotiate, stifling dissent even within its own ranks.[88] Black radicals also ignored warnings that many of their demands would damage "the movement." Robert Weisbrot has concluded that the most forceful black critics of the Vietnam War, who had at one point been "ardently courted" by white radicals, had "burned their bridgeheads to the New Left." He concluded that racial animosity caused the "grandly conceived" coalition of black and white radicals to "emerge stillborn."[89]

For those who had hoped for a "grand coalition" of antiwar liberals, radicals, and African Americans, that would precipitate a radical political reconstruction of the United States, the NCNP convention was a cause for despair. One journalist declared that "we know now that there is not thunder, but only static on the left."[90] The convention debates offer an important insight into the state of race relations in late sixties America; and the reluctance of the delegates to engage with the traditional political process is a reflection of the depth of disillusionment that existed among America's political youth, at least on the left. The events that took place at the Palmer House in the summer of 1967 help to show how the radical movement of the 1960s was seriously weakened by racial divisions. The issue of race dominated the delegates' deliberations, ultimately destroyed the nascent coalition, and helped produce a climate in which it proved impossible to consider tactical issues, or, indeed, the wider goals of the movement itself. It is an irony that the white radical movement, which had been largely inspired by the civil rights struggles of the early 1960s, found itself, by 1967, unable to work effectively with its African American counterpart. In many ways the NCNP convention foretold the demise of a New Left that was increasingly alienated from mainstream politics, contemptuous of white liberals, and estranged from, while simultaneously attracted to, Black Power. In terms of interracial cooperation within the peace movement, meanwhile, things were about to get worse.

The March on the Pentagon to Confront the Warmakers, held in the fall of 1967, was one of the most momentous peace protests in American history. On the morning of October 21 more than 100,000 Americans gathered at the Lincoln Memorial for a mass rally protesting against the Vietnam War. Later that afternoon 35,000 marched to the Pentagon to engage in acts of civil disobedience. The demonstration, organized by the Mobe, came to symbolize the essence of sixties protest. The event, immortalized by Norman Mailer in *The Armies of the Night*, was rich with drama. Antiwar activists placed flowers in the barrels of the guns that were being pointed at them, as rumors spread that several soldiers had joined the ranks of the protesters. Meanwhile a grim-faced Robert McNamara was captured on camera as he looked down from his office window at the mob below.[91] The Pentagon action signified the trend in the antiwar movement from protest to resistance.[92] The march was also important in revealing the growing split between black and white anti-war radicals—one of the most important peace demonstrations of the Vietnam era was boycotted by black groups.

    While David Burner has recognized the importance of the Pentagon march in his book, *Making Peace with the 60s*, he draws the wrong lessons from the episode. In his lengthy discussion of Black Power, entitled "Killers of the Dream," Burner fails to discuss any of the reasons for the black movement's decision not to participate in the Pentagon action. Instead, he simply uses it as evidence with which to condemn African American militants for thumbing their noses at the "camaraderie of resistance" by holding "meetings by themselves while confrontations [between troops and white demonstrators] were taking place." More-over, when Burner asks whether Black Power would "accommodate itself to white radicalism?" he reveals the biased premise of his argument.[93]

    In May 1967 the Mobe stated its intention to hold a demonstration in Washington, D.C., on October 21.[94] In August the decision was made to concentrate efforts on the Pentagon. The Mobe's official press release declared that they intended to shut it down—"we will fill the hallways and block the entrances. Thousands of people will disrupt the center of the American war machine. In the name of humanity we will call the warmakers to task."[95] SDS was unhappy with the decision to stage yet another national mass protest. Such actions, they believed, had "no significant effect on American policy in Vietnam." It also ran the risk of deluding "many participants into thinking that the 'democratic' process in America" functioned in a "meaningful way."[96] SDS favored organizing around local actions, draft resistance or issues not specifically tied to the war. The organization urged those members who wished to take part in the demonstration to promote immediate withdrawal as a policy of the antiwar movement. Furthermore, it urged "SDS chapters and the National Mobilization Committee to use the demonstration only as a tool for organizing . . . the march can be best used if it is seen as a tactic to involve people more extensively in the movement."

SDS had long been wary of the Vietnam War as a focus of protest, fearing that it would distract from efforts to build a genuine radical movement in America. Believing Vietnam to be the product of a malignant American system, SDS leaders talked of organizing to stop the "seventh war from now" by forging a radical movement to change America's social, economic and political structures in fundamental ways. Underestimating the potential importance of the antiwar movement to the creation of such a radical movement, in the summer of 1965 SDS had opted to avoid Vietnam as a potential single-issue trap that would stifle the organization's radicalism. Thus, despite planning the first major national antiwar demonstration in April 1965, America's premier New Left organization did not assume a leading role in the peace movement. This deprived the antiwar forces of a powerful, radical voice linking the war abroad with poverty and racism at home. Ultimately, however, SDS was unable to ignore the war, which was responsible for the vast growth in its membership after 1965, and it gradually turned its attentions back to Vietnam.[97]

By October, SDS had become decidedly more enthusiastic about the planned Pentagon action. Writing in *New Left Notes*, Carl Davidson and Mike Spiegal of the SDS national staff urged all members to participate, unless it would harm their local organizing projects. They placed this new policy in the context of the move "from protest to resistance" in the antiwar movement—"the peace and civil rights movements have moved together and transformed themselves. Where we once spoke of civil rights, we now speak of black liberation. Where we once spoke of peace, we now speak of anti-imperialist struggle."[98] SDS had first adopted the strategy of "from protest to resistance" in the winter of 1966, when it committed itself to a national antidraft program and pledged resistance to the American war machine.[99] SDS viewed the attempt to "shut down" the Pentagon as congruent with its own radical antiwar strategy. However, the organization made clear that it still had reservations about periodic mass actions, and preferred to devote its energies to "organizing on the local and regional levels permanent, multi-issue, radical constituencies with a capacity for resistance rather than protest." Nevertheless, the radical nature of the planned Pentagon action helped ensure SDS support.[100]

Some SDS leaders might have argued that the peace and civil rights movements were moving together, but tensions between the white peace movement and black radicals indicated that the opposite was true. The Mobe, which had grown out of the Spring Mobilization Committee, retained the commitment to developing fruitful links with the African American freedom struggle. The September issue of the *Mobilizer* stated clearly that the Mobe was dedicated not just to ending the war, but to fighting racism as well—"we in the American anti-war movement are committed to building a mass movement that can end racism and militarism no matter how long it takes and no matter how deep the sacrifices."[101] In the same issue the Mobe's national coordinator, Cornell mathematics professor Robert Greenblatt, acknowledged that the predominantly white peace movement had been guilty of ignoring black issues—"whether the reasons given were those of principle or political expediency, the effect was the same. While protesting the war in Vietnam, the peace movement was unable to address itself to the problems of the 'Vietnamese' on its own shores." Now the organization was prepared to respond to the demands of the black movement. The Mobe was willing to petition the UN about the American government's "de facto genocidal" policies against its black citizens. It also called for the release of all those arrested during the recent "rebellions"; dropping of "frame up" charges against SNCC leader Rap Brown, who had been indicted for leading a riot in Cambridge, Maryland; support for Muhammed Ali and other draft resisters; and spending the war budget on ending poverty at home.[102]

This newfound anxiousness to relate to the black movement was welcome, but the timing was far from conducive. The increasing attractiveness of Black Power ideology to civil rights groups and ordinary African Americans made it more difficult for black and white radicals to work together closely. The NCNP convention had dramatically highlighted the growing racial tensions that threatened to hamper radical organizing, and critical views of white activists, often long-suppressed, were surfacing more easily and more often in the black freedom movement.[103]

The Mobe continued to try to bring the black freedom struggle more fully into the antiwar fold, but it appeared as though the two movements, at least at the radical end of the spectrum, might diverge. At a Mobe Administrative Committee Meeting on September 30, SNCC's John Wilson, who along with fellow black activist Ivanhoe Donaldson held a senior position in the Mobe, presented a report. Wilson stated that there was a feeling within the black community that "everything black people do must be relevant to the black struggle." A representative meeting of black activists had been held in New York City the previous day, where it had been decided that blacks would participate at the rally at the Lincoln Memorial but would not engage in civil disobedience at the Pentagon. As an alternative they would go to the black community in Washington, D.C., and wage a door-to-door campaign concerning the war in Vietnam and the "neocolonial state" of the nation's capital— whose residents had no voting representation in Congress.[104]

John Wilson and CORE's Omar Ahmed explained the black position in more detail at a meeting of the Mobe's leadership on October 7. They stated that African Americans were "prepared to defend themselves in their own community but not at the Pentagon or the bridges where they might be stranded by the white participants." When asked whether they could "guarantee the participation of blacks at the rally" if it was decided to hold it at the Pentagon, Wilson responded tersely. He was, he said, "tired of being used and was no more responsible for turning out black people than whites were for turning out white people." Relations between black and white members of the Mobe were clearly strained. In a November memorandum to the SNCC Central Committee, Gwendolyn Patton described some of the tensions that had surrounded the October demonstration. She explained how the black community had been split, with some favoring the Pentagon protest as a show of solidarity with the Vietnamese, while others thought that it was pointless and would risk violence against African Americans who would be an "obvious target for harsh treatment." Patton also raised the issue of racial tension when she explained another reason for the separate black action—"many militant blacks coming to Washington—were anti-white and could react to any white person in a way that would cause a fiasco."[105] *Mobilizer News*, the Mobe's official newsletter, explained that "Black people across the nation disagree with the Mobilization's concentrated emphasis on the Pentagon." As an alternative, blacks were urged, "in the interests of Black American unity," to assemble at the Lincoln Memorial under the banner "Black Nation's Viet Conference." After the main rally, they would "then go to the Black community of Washington to discuss the issue of Vietnam and its meaning to Black America and Black American survival."[106] Clearly, Black Power worked to limit African American involvement in white-organized peace activities, but it was by no means the only contributing factor. Counterculturalism also played an important role.

As the baby boomers came of age in the 1960s, American society saw the blossoming of a vibrant youth culture. Through its rock music, advocacy of drugs like marijuana and LSD and celebration of sexual freedom, the counterculture challenged traditional social mores. Based primarily on the nation's college campuses and with important centers in the San Francisco Bay Area and New York's East Village, this movement blended individualist and communitarian values in a quest for authenticity.

The year 1967 represented a high point for the counterculture, with the "summer of love" taking place in San Francisco's bohemian Haight-Ashbury district. Although the counterculture and "hippies" were distinct from the New Left, there was a good deal of overlap and exchange between them. Increasingly, the student protest movement adopted countercultural forms, while attempts were made to "politicize" hippies—most famously by the Yippies, or Youth International Party, founded by activists Jerry Rubin and Abbie Hoffman in January 1968.[107]

The counterculture had begun to permeate the New Left and antiwar movements as early as 1965. During 1965–66, SDS membership trebled to 15,000. Many of the new recruits came from colleges without a history of left-wing activism. Dubbed the "prairie power" contingent, these new members tended to be less intellectual and more interested in casual drug use, sexual freedom, and rock music than were the organization's founding generation. Meanwhile the Vietnam Day Committee, founded in Berkeley in the spring of 1965 by Free Speech Movement veteran Jerry Rubin and mathematics professor Stephen Smale, also betrayed the counterculture's growing influence on popular protest. Described by Charles DeBenedetti as a "strange concoction of radical pacifism, student protest, civil rights activism, leftist politics, and cultural bohemianism peculiar to the Bay Area," the VDC was most famous for its attempts to blockade trains carrying troops bound for Vietnam.[108]

The April 1967 Spring Mobe demonstrations also bore a countercultural imprint, with the San Francisco demonstration described as resembling a "be-in" or countercultural happening.[109] Indeed, the increasing use of culture by the antiwar movement was part of a broader 1960s trend, which saw culture used as a political weapon by civil rights activists and New Left organizers, as well as feminists, homosexuals and peace activists.[110] The counterculture, however, was overwhelmingly a white phenomenon, and African Americans seldom related to it. Indeed, black activists increasingly interpreted countercultural forms of protest as evidence of the white movement's lack of seriousness.

The countercultural elements involved in the Pentagon demonstration were a cause of its unpopularity among African Americans. CORE's Omar Ahmed, a former lieutenant in Malcolm X's Organization of Afro-American Unity, declared that "black people are in no mood for marching to [the Pentagon] and listening to folk singing."[111] Blacks sometimes had good reason to doubt the seriousness, even the sanity, of white peace activists. Jerry Rubin's claim that the Pentagon would be levitated

300 feet in the air where it would take on an orange glow, and vibrate as the demon of war was exorcized, was not popular with black radicals.[112] As Gwen Patton explained, "Black People are not going to go anywhere to *levitate* the Pentagon, okay. We don't find that cute."[113]

Indeed, a wider mistrust of the white radicals who dominated the antiwar movement until 1969 was an important reason behind the black refusal to participate in one of the most symbolic peace actions of the era. The Harlem contingent at the April 15 Spring Mobilization had illustrated the emergence of racial divisions within the peace movement, and the Stop the Draft Week (STDW) activities in Berkeley-Oakland, which took place just before the Pentagon demonstration, also saw separate black and white antiwar activities.

Draft resistance had seemed an area where black-white cooperation would be possible. In February 1967, Stokely Carmichael had welcomed the white radicals' focus on building an antidraft movement. At a May meeting of the Berkeley Anti-Draft Committee, local SNCC worker Terry Cannon had stated that "in antiwar work, SNCC can cooperate most with anti-draft groups, since in this area there is finally an equality of risks shared by Blacks and Whites."[114] However, the feeling that blacks would disproportionately share the danger prompted the tentative interracial antidraft coalition in Berkeley to come apart. In sentiments echoed by African American opponents of the Pentagon action, black organizer Mark Comfort explained that, although the idea of a Stop the Draft Week was popular in East Oakland, African Americans "felt that when the cops attacked, the white kids would run away and leave the blacks fighting the cops."[115] Two members of STDW who were also members of the Maoist Progressive Labor Party claimed that STDW had tried to "use" the black community by staging rallies in Oakland even though they had done no organizing work there, in an attempt to charm the blacks into giving support.[116] In the face of objections from the African American community, which apparently included veiled threats that black youth would attack the whites if protests attracted the police to their community, the planned antidraft rally at Seventeenth Street and Castro in Oakland was abandoned. This was to minimize the risk of police invading the ghetto, which was situated near to the Oakland Induction Center.[117] Such concerns were not uncommon among black activists, who often opposed staging peace demonstrations in black neighborhoods because they feared that it would increase police patrols.[118]

On Tuesday October 17, 3,000 white militants converged on the Center, where they were beaten by the police; about twenty were injured. On Friday, 10,000 demonstrators gathered in the streets around the Induction Center at 6 a.m. to try to shut it down. An hour later the police began their assault; but this time the demonstrators were prepared to fight back.[119] Cannon and Segal argued that these actions had two important consequences. First, white radicals realized that they did not need black help to sustain militant protest. Second, among black militants there emerged "a new empathy toward the white movement and a feeling that white people are finally beginning to talk their language."[120] Similar claims would be made after the Pentagon protests.

On the morning of October 21, 100,000 Americans gathered at the Lincoln Memorial to hear speeches and protest publicly against their nation's foreign policy in Southeast Asia. Most African American demonstrators joined the "Black Nation's Viet Conference" at the rally. This group carried placards that read "Self-Determination for Black America and Vietnam"; "End Armed Occupation of Black American Communities"; "Black People: 23 percent of the GI Dead, 2 percent of the U.S. Bread—WHY?"; and "Black Men: Fight White Racism—Not Vietnamese." At the bottom of each sign was the slogan of the march—STOP THE WAR NOW.[121] CORE's Lincoln Lynch, Dagmar Wilson of the liberal Women Strike for Peace, and David Dellinger of the Mobe all made speeches. So too did John Wilson, who told the crowd that "white people are just beginning to find out what it's like to have grievances and not be able to influence the government. Welcome to the club. "[122]

At 1:30 p.m., under the cover of army helicopters and marching behind a giant banner that read "Support Our GIs, Bring Them Home Now!" tens of thousands of Americans, almost all of them white, walked across the Arlington Memorial Bridge into the north parking lot of the Pentagon.[123] Small groups of demonstrators attempted to break into the building and a few actually succeeded, although they were quickly arrested.[124] Led by Beat poet and countercultural icon Alan Ginsberg and the anarchic-rock group *The Fugs*, an attempt to levitate the Pentagon was made as the crowd chanted "Out, demons, out."[125] The Pentagon remained stubbornly immune to these efforts. As darkness fell and the crowd shrank, several hundred draft cards were burned. Around midnight, with most of the press gone, the government moved to clear the demonstrators away. Many activists were clubbed by U.S. marshals—women apparently bore the brunt of their anger—and overall some 683 people were arrested.[126] Numerous commentators condemned not the beatings meted out to the demonstrators, but the protest itself. David Brinkley called it a "coarse, vulgar episode," while Barry Goldwater condemned what he viewed as a "hate-filled, anti-American, pro-Communist and violent mob uprising."[127]

The willingness of white antiwar activists to risk their safety in opposing the government impressed many black radicals. In a talk at Columbia University, SNCC leader H. Rap Brown said that he considered white radicals to be "brothers in the vanguard of revolution." He emphasized the need for black-white unity and stated that the increasing militancy and revolutionary tactics of white leftists had brought them closer to black militants, since both now faced the problem of extermination. But Brown also expressed disdain with the white counterculture, condemning hippies as "apolitical . . . in a time when we need political people."[128] John Wilson, meanwhile, told a news conference that "this demonstration proved one good thing to white Americans—that this government will whip you, too. During this anti-draft week . . . Black America has gained new respect for the white left. There are going to be dramatic changes in the movement."[129]

Following the March on the Pentagon, SDS decided to work more closely with the Mobe by attending meetings to try and push for policy changes and a more representative organizational structure. One reason for this decision to become more actively involved in the mechanics of the peace movement appears to have grown out of the Pentagon March. Several SDS leaders believed that "black organizations were opening up to the idea of working within the peace movement with white organizations. A restructured Mobilization Committee was seen as a forum where a working alliance based on the mutual respect developed during October 16 to 21 might take place."[130]

In December, Carl Davidson and Greg Calvert criticized past SDS policy regarding the antiwar movement and called for a fundamental change. They explained that the organization had "stood apart from the wheelings and dealings of the various mobilization committees," and sought to separate SDS from the peace movement by "insisting on a program of on-going, multi-issue, local organizing." But, they continued, "the mass of SDS members on the local level, as well as the younger students just entering the movement, were mainly involved in the anti-war programs emanating from the mobilization committees." Davidson and Calvert believed that SDS had influenced the peace movement— "the draft became a major issue at our insistence. And the themes of black liberation and the powerlessness of the poor were woven into the movement rhetoric partially as a result of our pressure." Nevertheless, they concluded that the time had come for "SDS to assume a leadership position within the anti-war movement."[131]

Around the time of the Pentagon demonstration there was evidence that suggested that a genuine peace and civil rights coalition could be assembled. In the fall of 1967 the Michigan State Conference of the NAACP passed a resolution recognizing the cost of the Vietnam War—both in terms of black lives and the undermining of the war on poverty. They went on to call for an unconditional bombing halt and a gradual deescalation of the war.[132] The day after the Pentagon demonstration, the New

York State NAACP voted to oppose the war during a stormy convention. Initially, older NAACP members had blocked attempts to oppose the war because this would have clashed with national policy. But nineteen-year-old Gerald Taylor led the youth contingent in an 18-minute demonstration that forced the issue onto the floor. Ultimately the delegates voted 107–72 to ask the NAACP national board of directors to "use its good offices to urge an immediate termination of hostilities in that war-ravaged land." Their opposition to the war was based upon the disproportionate black casualty rate and the detrimental effect of the conflict on the war on poverty.[133]

Ultimately, however, black and white opposition to the war would diverge. The white peace movement would continue to be accused by black radicals of failing to understand the racist nature of the war. In addition, moderate black opponents of Vietnam would come to share the criticisms of Black Power militants that the peace movement consistently failed to relate to the black freedom struggle in any meaningful way. The use of radical rhetoric and pro-civil rights slogans by the peace movement was not enough to attract black support. The presence of the white counterculture in the peace movement would also help to alienate black critics of the war. Moreover, many of the most likely black supporters of the peace movement—the militants who shared the white radicals' interpretation of both the war and the wider American system—found themselves prevented from cooperating effectively with the white peace movement because of their Black Power ideology.

One consequence of this would be the development of black antiwar organizations. SNCC's Gwendolyn Patton argued for this in the winter of 1967–68. In a memorandum she called for SNCC to develop an anti-war program that was directly related to the black community, and urged the organization to stop reacting to whites. While acknowledging the "unrealized potential" of the white radicals, she warned against the black movement being absorbed by the white movement—"we must build our own movement with power so that we can deal and talk about coalitions on whatever issue."[134]

Patton, a native of Detroit, had become active in the civil rights movement at an early age. When, at age nine, she was refused a seat at the Liggett Drugstore lunch counter during a family visit to Montgomery, Alabama, she overturned a cup of water in protest. At sixteen, following the death of her mother, she moved to Montgomery to be raised by her grandparents—and soon joined the youth arm of the Montgomery Improvement Association. She enlisted with SNCC in 1962 and helped organize Freedom Schools in Macon County, Georgia; participated in the Selma to Montgomery voting rights march; and worked with the

Lowndes County Freedom Organization. A graduate of Tuskegee, she had been student body president in 1965.[135]

Patton, one of SNCC's most active antiwar movement participants, believed that even though there were some whites who were "honest and sincere about the evils of capitalism, imperialism, and racism," blacks needed to take charge because whites did not fully understand the "struggle that goes with defeating those evils."[136] In her position paper, "Why Black People must develop own Anti-War and Anti-Draft Union . . . Heed the Call!" Patton emphasized the communication problems that existed between blacks who had received their education "on the streets" and the "naïve intellectualism" and "deep-seated factionalism" of the whites. While whites tended to oppose the war on moral grounds, for blacks it was a matter of survival—and it was "at this conjecture black militants find it necessary to coerce the Peace Movement to call for certain demands which in fact can have only black implementation. This is one of the greatest contradictions that exists in the total Movement." Patton concluded that "we must separate forces at this time in order to build a stable coalition in the future."[137]

The Bread and Puppet Theater performing at the Lincoln Memorial, October 21, 1967. Copyright © John C. Goodwin.

Rally at the Lincoln Memorial, October 21, 1967. Copyright © John C. Goodwin.

SNCC's John Wilson addresses the October 21, 1967, rally. Copyright © John C. Goodwin.

Marching to the Pentagon, October 21, 1967. Copyright © John C. Goodwin.

Protesters confronting Military Police at the Pentagon, October 21, 1967.
Copyright © John C. Goodwin.

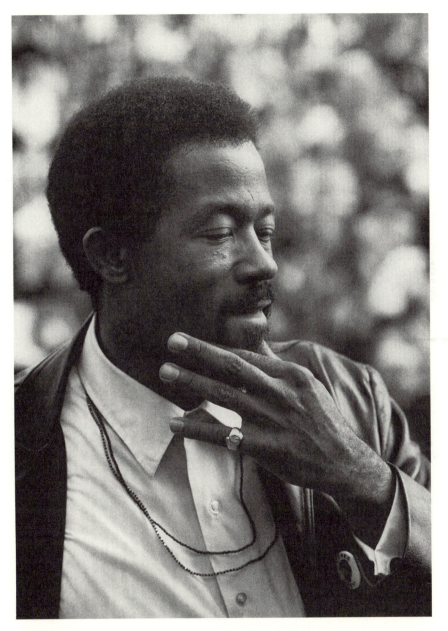

Eldridge Cleaver, Minister of Information for the Black Panther Party and presidential candidate for the Peace and Freedom Party, speaking at American University, October 1968. Library of Congress.

Counter-inauguration protests in Washington, D.C., January 1969. Copyright ©
John C. Goodwin.

Counter-inauguration protests in Washington, D.C., January 1969. Copyright ©
John C. Goodwin.

Coretta Scott King speaking at a CALCAV demonstration, Washington, D.C., February 5, 1969. Copyright © John C. Goodwin.

Vietnam Moratorium protests in New York City, October 15, 1969. Records of *WIN* magazine, Swarthmore College Peace Collection, photograph by Diana Davies.

Vietnam Moratorium protests in Washington, D.C., November 15, 1969.
Copyright © John C. Goodwin.

Chapter 5

Radicalism and Respectability

Actions around racism must be forthcoming if the white anti-war movement expects to have any validity to the black anti-war movement.

—Gwendolyn Patton, 1968

By branching out into the question of racism . . . we will end up in a diffuse fog.

—Bill Rothman, Fifth Avenue Vietnam Peace Parade Committee, 1968

The years between 1968 and 1970 saw some important victories and bitter disappointments for the peace movement. In the spring of 1968, for instance, it seemed that a major breakthrough had been made, as Lyndon Johnson announced a bombing pause and a push for negotiations to resolve the Vietnam conflict. To many Americans, it looked as though the nightmare in Southeast Asia might soon be over. The war, however, would continue for four and a half more years. A few days after Johnson's policy shift, tragedy struck in Memphis as Martin Luther King, Jr., in town to lead a garbage workers' strike, was felled by an assassin's bullet. In response, America's cities erupted in bitter violence—twenty blocks of Chicago burned, while more than 5,000 troops were needed to restore order in the nation's capital.[1] Then, just two months later, Robert Kennedy—standard bearer of American liberalism—was gunned down hours after winning the crucial Democratic primary in California. When the Democratic Party national convention became engulfed in riot and anarchy in August, the country seemed to be teetering on the brink of an abyss.

The mobilization of antiwar dissent within the Democratic Party, followed by Richard Nixon's election and his subsequent escalation of the war, energized the liberal wing of the peace movement. At the same time, more radical antiwar groups continued to struggle with the problems of multi-issuism and attracting black support.

The debate over "multi-issuism"—whether the antiwar movement should concentrate its efforts solely on ending the conflict in Southeast

Asia, or focus on domestic concerns as well—had divided antiwar activists from the time of the earliest protests against America's military involvement in Vietnam. In many ways, the arguments mirrored earlier discussions within black groups about the war. In the mid-1960s, some civil rights activists had warned that opposing Vietnam would divert energy from their primary objective of securing black equality, and also offend white supporters. Similarly, some within the peace movement believed that incorporating additional issues, such as civil rights, would weaken the antiwar struggle and alienate potential middle class support. Between 1968 and 1970, disagreement over multi-issuism would not only become important enough to split the peace movement, it would also have important ramifications for the relationship between black and white antiwar protest.

In the fall of 1965, SDS ideologues Paul Booth and Lee Webb argued that Vietnam was linked to other salient social, economic and political issues. SDS hoped to fashion a broad-based movement that would change American society in fundamental ways. Confident of their abilities, and convinced that they had been presented with a unique historical opportunity, Booth and Webb advocated a United States based on the ideals of participatory democracy. They wrote, "our chance has been the first in a generation to organize a movement to confront America with a vision: a vision of societies both here and abroad where all individuals can participate in the decisions that affect their lives." They placed the war within a broad framework, stating that "Vietnam is not a separate moral or political issue. It is a political issue, as is Mississippi racism, Chicago unemployment, university paternalism . . . that can be dealt with only by attacking the way that decisions are made in America, who makes them, and the purpose of a society." Booth and Webb also argued that the antiwar movement had to adopt a multi-issue approach—"we look with extreme concern on the single issue orientation of the anti-war protest. We think that this single issue politics, perhaps valid in another time is simply an obstacle. . . . We are concerned about all the issues of America and think that the only way to deal with them is together."[2]

In general, those who argued for a multi-issue perspective shared an interpretation of the Vietnam War that emphasized it as a product of the "American System," rather than defining it as the tragic result of a mistaken policy. In his speech at the March on Washington in April 1965, SDS president Paul Potter had stated that a movement needed to be created that understood "Vietnam, in all its horror, as but a symptom of a deeper malaise."[3] In the summer of 1967, in its first pronouncement on the war for nearly a year, SDS declared that Vietnam was "not a mistake of any essentially good government, but the logical result of a government which oppresses people in the U.S. and throughout the world."[4]

Black antiwar radicals also placed the war within a wider context that emphasized other unsavory aspects of the "system." Black Panther Eldridge Cleaver, for instance, argued that "the relationship between the genocide in Vietnam and the smiles of the white man towards black Americans is a direct relationship." Multi-issuism became a key area around which radical black involvement with the antiwar movement would be contested. Civil rights groups, such as SNCC and CORE, opposed the Vietnam War not simply because they thought it was wrong, but because they saw that the conflict was linked to domestic racism and repression. When elements within the peace movement sought to focus solely on ending the war, in an attempt to win support among white America, it alienated black radicals who accused the movement not simply of failing to recognize the important relationship between the war and racism, but of being racist itself. Given the growing appeal of Black Power, the continuing failure of the antiwar movement to embrace an analysis of the war that emphasized racism and adopt a genuinely multi-issue orientation, resulted in the divergence of black and white antiwar protest and the formation of black antiwar organizations.

One of the first important black antiwar groups was founded at the January convention of the Student Mobilization Committee, which gathered more than 900 people representing some 110 colleges and 40 high schools from 25 states.[5] Blacks attending the SMC convention were asked to join a Black Caucus, organized by John Wilson. The SNCC veteran argued that "too long we have allowed for the predominantly white movement with its few 'influential' blacks make decisions for actions when we too are engaged in a struggle for self-determination." He explained that this contradiction could "only be resolved with the development of a black base. We must begin in a collective voice [to] make decisions about our own actions for the coalition."[6] It was from this SMC caucus that the National Black Antiwar Antidraft Union (NBAWADU) emerged.

Over the winter of 1967–1968, SNCC's Gwendolyn Patton had argued for the development of an independent black antiwar base in order to prevent black anti-Vietnam War protest from becoming absorbed by the white peace movement. Black Power ideology stressed that blacks could only work constructively with whites if they did so from a position of strength. The formation of the NBAWADU was a logical outgrowth of this theory. As Patton explained, "black militants are interested in creating a black base that will deal with international affairs. We have come to the conclusion that the reason for chaos when blacks and whites move to coalesce is that black people do not speak from a base of power."[7]

One of the reasons for the formation of the NBAWADU was that black radicals opposed the Vietnam War for different reasons from those of the white movement. The most important difference concerned race—both the role of racism in the war itself, and the relationship between the war and repression in the United States. The predominantly white peace movement had, according to many black critics, failed to emphasize the racist nature of the war, and failed to make antiwar protests relevant to particular black concerns—such as domestic racism and the disproportionate impact of the draft on African Americans. Gwendolyn Patton explained that the NBAWADU was formed "because we desperately needed a secure black base for anti-war activity to eliminate the possibilities of being absorbed by the white anti-war movement whose goals in many instances were not congruent with ours." According to Patton, peace movement activities had been "completely irrelevant to black people" because they "had no significant effect toward changing the lot of black men who were being drafted into the racist genocidal Vietnam war."[8] John Wilson agreed—"in only a few cases have [antiwar actions] reached black people."[9] For the NBAWADU, opposition to Vietnam would be centered on African American concerns.

In Washington, D.C., in the aftermath of Martin Luther King's assassination, the NBAWADU led a march from a local high school to Howard University. A crowd of more than 1,000 cheered their approval as the American flag was lowered and replaced with the Black Nationalist colors.[10] Then, over Easter weekend, an antiwar conference sponsored by the organization was held in New York City. More than 700 black activists attended, to discuss what were seen as two linked themes—the survival of blacks in America, and solidarity with the Vietnamese struggle. There was also some discussion of the planned action at the forthcoming Democratic Party National Convention in Chicago. This was discussed further in a meeting attended by regional NBAWADU chairmen—"participants in this meeting were generally critical of plans to mobilize black people at the convention and contended that black people now had nothing to do with the Democratic party other than its dissolution. There was also a strong undercurrent of concern that black people would be the victims of violence that might occur at the demonstration" (similar concerns had prevented blacks from participating in the 1967 March on the Pentagon). Stokely Carmichael attended the conference, and he voiced criticism of the white left, which he claimed had "used" black people in the past. The former SNCC chairman told the delegates that the black movement was "further differentiated from the white left because the white left is not fighting for its survival . . . they want to save America. We have to burn America down. In order for black people to survive America must be destroyed."[11]

This "differentiation" between black radicals and white leftists resulted partly from the fact that many black radicals continued to doubt the seriousness of their white comrades. Black Power placed strains on the prospects for cooperation between black and white activists. During the student protest at Columbia University in April 1968, for example, black and white demonstrators ended up occupying different buildings.[12] Throughout 1968–1970, black radicals continued to question the depth of their white counterparts' commitment to the cause. Writing from exile in China, Black Power icon Robert F. Williams fired off a passionate attack on white radicals in *The Crusader* in the summer of 1967, which subsequently appeared in the March 1968 edition of *Black Politics: A Journal of Liberation*. Williams accused the New Left, which he described as a "white man's baby born to a black man's wife," of "seeking hegemony over the black revolution," and argued that the oppressed could only trust their fate to themselves. Williams skillfully blended wit and sarcasm with his own brand of revolutionary black nationalism to construct a devastating critique of the white radical movement—a movement that he viewed as racist and reactionary. Indeed, he claimed that the "'new left' carpetbagger fabians" were not "conduits of revolution but the Trojan Horse of counter-revolution."[13] Williams charged that the New Left was unconcerned with the "savage oppression" of African Americans, and called upon black revolutionaries to "denounce and defeat the great new white supremacy conspiracy to capture and subvert the black revolution."[14]

Williams's attack may have been the most acerbic, but other important black leaders shared much of his skepticism, and some of his hyperbole, toward white radicals. Speaking before a crowd of 3,000 at a rally in Berkeley in February 1968, SNCC's James Forman challenged the white radicals—"you who support the NLF, will you support us? You who call yourselves leftists and revolutionaries, what will you do when they seal-off Oakland and Harlem? Will you fight and die for your black brothers? Will you kill a white cop?"[15] The following month, Robert L. Allen, writing in the *Guardian*, explored black militants' distrust of white radicals. Allen wrote that "continuing and far-reaching alliances with the white student movement are viewed with skepticism. In interviews with black student leaders it became clear that this skepticism stems from their concern over whether white radical students are more white and middle-class than they are radical."[16]

While a *Freedomways* editorial condemned the "hustler element among those who call themselves Black Nationalists peddling the illusion that the growing nation-wide movement against the war in Vietnam is none of black folks' concern," skepticism of white radicals within the Black Power movement dogged attempts at forging an interracial antiwar movement.[17]

SDS's implosion during its disastrous 1969 convention—which saw fierce battles between supporters and opponents of the Maoist Progressive

Labor faction—helped to re-enforce black notions of white radicals as unreliable allies. Stew Albert, described by Todd Gitlin as "a bohemian . . . with curly blond locks and a guileless manner," reflected on the New Left's collective madness in the pages of the *Berkeley Barb*.[18] He compared the scenes on the convention floor to "a reactionary newspaper cartoon satirizing the New Left. The PL and anti-PL factions waved fists and red books at each other and drowned out rival speeches by shouting Mao Mao Mao Tse Tung (PL) and Ho Ho Ho Chi Minh (anti-PL)."[19]

Ironically, while the militant black movement was unsure about the effectiveness of white leftists, many white radicals fawned over black radicals, who they romanticized to an extraordinary degree. SDS's Don Newton, for example, argued that Rap Brown, Bobby Seale, James Forman and Stokely Carmichael had no equals in the white movement. Newton claimed that these leaders "clarity of purpose, depth of understanding and devotion to their people were "far beyond the scope of the white movement at this time." He concluded that "it is important that we recognize that there are leaders in America, men who are beginning the fight to destroy the monster in his lair—men who speak for their people, fighting in the streets with guns. The time of the black men has come. Dig it."[20]

Throughout 1968, as black militants voiced criticism over white radicals' failure to respond to black concerns, a number of mainly white peace organizations wrestled with the question of multi-issuism. In early 1968, SNCC's James Forman sent an "open letter" to the Fifth Avenue Peace Parade Committee's antiwar conference, which was scheduled to meet on February 3. The Committee had been founded in New York City in September 1965 in response to a call issued by *Liberation* magazine's David Dellinger (an alumnus of Yale and Oxford whose pacifism had landed him in jail during World War II) and school teacher Norma Becker, to plan local events for the October 15–16 First International Days of Protest antiwar demonstrations. By the end of 1966, more than 150 groups made up the coalition, which was the largest and most important local antiwar group in the United States. A. J. Muste had served as the Committee's first chairman.[21] In his letter, Forman argued that antiwar actions had to be made relevant to issues of racism, both at home and abroad. He declared that "all activities against the United States' genocidal war in Vietnam must be seen as efforts to help oppressed people around the world to obtain self-determination—including black people in the United States . . . this is a point which must be constantly stressed throughout the discussions." As far as Forman was concerned, the antiwar movement had to be based on the principles of "anti-racism, anti-capitalism, and anti-imperialism."[22]

The question whether to broaden the scope of the antiwar movement to encompass imperialism and racism was discussed by the conference delegates. Moderates successfully resisted this, arguing that such a step was too far ahead of grass-roots opinion on the war.[23] The issue was raised again during a June 5 meeting of the Parade Committee's Administrative Committee. Members debated whether the organization should "move programmatically into both the question of war and the racial crisis in America." While some members spoke in favor, Harry Ring, a card-carrying member of the Socialist Workers Party, which advocated a single-issue peace movement, declared that such a move would harm efforts to organize peace demonstrations. On June 12 the topic was debated once more, this time during a full Parade Committee meeting. Ring once again led the opposition to linking the peace movement with the black liberation struggle.[24] At the end of the year the debate over multi-issuism was still unresolved—one member argued that "by branching out into the question of racism or other domestic problems we will end up in a diffuse fog."[25]

Like the Fifth Avenue Peace Parade Committee, the Student Mobilization Committee—one of the largest and most successful antiwar organizations—also grappled with multi-issuism. In the spring of 1968, debates over this boiled over into bitter factionalism. The crisis was provoked at a May meeting of the New York National Staff Working Committee when two members of the Young Socialist Alliance, Sid Stapleton and Kipp Dawson, were voted off their staff positions. It was argued that leftist sectarianism was contributing to major tensions in the SMC office. Gwendolyn Patton recalled that "the constant bickering between the [Communist Party] and SWP made it unbearable for anyone who wanted to work to function in the SMC office. On many occasions I complained about the 'Montagues and Capulets feud.' In all honesty I must admit that most of the problem was provoked by the YSAers."[26] Behind the decision to expel the two staffers lay a broader dispute over the Student Mobe's political orientation, as multi-issue proponents attempted to reduce the influence of the single-issue oriented YSA and SWP members.[27]

The YSA's Pete Camejo supported the single-issue stance. He pointed out that opposition to the Vietnam War was an area on which broad agreement between diverse groups could be achieved, whereas activists differed widely in their analysis of domestic problems such as racism and poverty. Camejo concluded that "to suggest that the SMC be a coalition coordinating antiwar work is simply to be realistic if you want to see mass united actions. Such a position does not mean rejection of importance of other issues such as racism or electoral activity."[28] He believed that adding other issues into the antiwar mix would serve only to increase disagreement and factionalism, thereby making mass coordinated action more difficult. Given the rhetorical excess that plagued much of the radical left in the late 1960s, it is unsurprising to learn that proponents of the single-issue perspective risked being called racists. One activist recalled that the arguments over multi-issuism were "savage," and described the "honky-baiting" of single-issue proponents as "the most powerful single political attack I've ever heard in the radical movements in this country."[29]

There were some within the Student Mobe's leadership who were trying to push the organization in a multi-issue direction. Phyllis Kalb, SMC national coordinator, claimed in the spring of 1968 that "the fight against racism . . . has got to be one of the major directions of the student movement."[30] Gwendolyn Patton was also trying to get the SMC to adopt a multi-issue perspective, and she believed that "actions around racism must be forthcoming if the white anti-war movement expects to have any validity to the black anti-war movement."[31] Patton argued that it was "politically naïve for us to organize activities against the Vietnam War without also organizing against racism in this country which creates wars like Vietnam and wars in our black community."[32]

At a policy meeting in June, the SWP and YSA mobilized to prevent the SMC from adopting a multi-issue perspective and program. They packed the SMC meeting, even signing up the sixty-six-year-old Harry Ring, a member of the SWP's central committee, as a Student Mobe representative. Linda Morse, SMC executive secretary, recalled that the entire first day of the conference was devoted to a discussion about who was allowed to vote—"we never got past that, we never got into any substantive discussions. Period. There were all of these large Trots [laughs] who were pretending to be students." Many of the independent SMC activists formed a Radical Organizing Committee and walked out of the conference. The SMC was now finished as a major antiwar group, and would continue only as a Trotskyist front.[33]

Disagreements over multi-issuism were not restricted to the meeting halls of peace organizations, they also arose on the ground at the local level. As events at Duke University, North Carolina, during early April 1968 showed, the debate over multi-issuism could cut more than one way. Student protest, even when centered on radical demands, did not necessarily embrace opposition to the war. During the Silent Vigil, the largest student demonstration in Duke's history, the mainly white students resisted attempts to broaden the struggle for civil and economic rights for local blacks to include criticism of the Vietnam War.

The Silent Vigil resulted from the assassination of Martin Luther King, Jr., in Memphis on Thursday April 4—which according to a contemporary account created a "mixture of sadness, fear, guilt, and frustration" on campus. The following day a group of 450 students marched to the residence of Duke President Douglas Knight, and some of them began a peaceful occupation of his house. Student leaders presented Knight with four demands. First, that he sign a newspaper advertisement calling for a day of mourning and asking Durham citizens to work for racial equality. Second, that he resign from the segregated Hope Valley Country Club. Third, that the university establish a $1.60 minimum wage for the mostly black nonacademic workers at Duke. Finally, that he recognize the nonacademic employees' right to collective bargaining. Knight refused, and on Sunday the protest moved to the main quadrangle in front of the university chapel. Over 500 students and faculty slept there overnight. The following day the night shift of cafeteria workers voted to strike—they would be joined by the maids and janitors on April 10. By April 9 more than 1,400 had joined the protests and picket lines were springing up all over campus. Eventually the university authorities agreed to phase in wage increases and appoint two committees to undertake an examination of Duke's relationship with its nonacademic employees.[34]

The Duke Vigil drew support from networks of activists and political institutions that had developed and mobilized around the issues of peace, civil rights and economic justice during the previous few years. The increase in student activism was recognized by the *Duke Chronicle*, which characterized the 1967–1968 academic year the Year of the Activist. In the fall of 1967, African American students had staged a sit-in at the office of President Knight demanding that the university introduce a policy of refusing to patronize segregated facilities, and won concessions. In December a small number of New Leftists urged fellow students to support the organization of nonacademic employees (mostly black maids and cafeteria workers) into Union Local 77. Moreover, protests against the war, including teach-ins, were attracting a small but growing following. An important moment for Duke activism came on January 31, 1968, when 250 students protested against Dow Chemical recruitment activities on campus. Student leader David Henderson believed this event was decisive—"a lot of people showed up, which made us feel that we had reached a turning point in being able to mobilize that many people." By the spring of 1968, then, a group of committed New Left activists existed at Duke. Furthermore, all the issues that constituted the central agenda of the Vigil—racism; the university's treatment of its nonacademic employees and their right to collective bargaining; and the right of students to protest had formed the focus of previous organizing activity.[35]

The majority of students participating in the Vigil rejected all attempts to broaden the scope of the protest to include criticism of the war in Vietnam. The prominent antiwar activists Joan Baez and David Harris, in town to speak about the draft resistance movement at Duke, instead joined the Vigil on the quadrangle on the Monday. There, Baez and

Harris attempted to widen the protest to include discussion of Vietnam. As one student recalled, "she appeared at the Vigil and implied that people who were participating . . . were supporting the draft resistance movement." When "someone . . . pointed out that the Vigil had nothing to do with resistance on the draft issue," Baez replied, " 'if you resist on one issue, you have to resist on them all.'—A Number of boos rang out from the group." Another student recalled that "many, I felt a solid majority . . . myself included, shouted her down . . . she was rejected and we got back to the strike issue."[36] Most of the protesters felt that Vietnam was an unwanted intrusion that would deflect attention from the main demands of the protest—economic and political rights for nonacademic workers. David Henderson, who kept a detailed journal of the Vigil, described one antiwar student's reaction to Baez's comments—"[he] was distressed . . . [and] said her appearance almost caused a crisis and a split among supporters of the Duke goals."[37]

Duke's Afro-American society had initially been skeptical about the Vigil. Many doubted that it was militant enough to produce results, and only a handful of blacks participated. Some questioned the extent of white commitment. The initial reaction of black leader Stef McLeod was that "it was a group of white students trying to show briefly their concern." Gradually, however, blacks—both at the university and in the wider community—became impressed by the students' commitment. McLeod eventually declared that "we see the Vigil as a belated . . . yet welcome show of concern by the white people." He particularly appreciated the help that the protests gave to the local unionizing efforts. The willingness of whites to "put their bodies on the line" when they occupied the President's house undoubtedly contributed to this increasingly positive reaction.[38] The Duke Silent Vigil is an example of how many black activists in the late 1960s often demanded evidence of genuine commitment before endorsing white protest. It also reveals the complex interaction between activism, the war and civil rights on a local level.

Away from the militant wing of the antiwar movement's factional infighting, attempts were being made by liberal opponents of the war to channel dissent over the war into the political mainstream. The tentative opposition to LBJ's Vietnam policy within the Democratic Party, which had first emerged in 1965–66, began to gather steam during 1967–68. In the spring of 1967 the United Auto Workers Victor Reuther, Americans for Democratic Action's Joe Rauh, and former Kennedy administration officials John Kenneth Galbraith and Arthur Schlesinger, Jr., had urged a bombing halt and negotiations with the NLF. As discontent with the war grew, liberal opposition to the Vietnam War would play a decisive role in the 1968 presidential election campaign.

With the New Left unable or unwilling to use traditional electoral politics to try and end the war, political activist and charismatic intellectual Allard Lowenstein set about organizing an antiwar insurgency within the Democratic Party—known as the "Dump Johnson movement." Lowenstein's first-choice candidate was Robert Kennedy, junior senator for New York and icon of Democratic Party liberalism. But while Kennedy's heart told him "yes," his head told him "no"—challenging an incumbent president would be tantamount to political suicide. Lowenstein turned instead to Minnesota senator Eugene J. McCarthy, who had been considering a presidential bid for some months.

McCarthy, a one-time novice monk and academic, had been passed over by LBJ for the 1964 vice-presidential nomination in favor of his Minnesotan colleague Hubert Humphrey. McCarthy had never forgotten the snub, and his personal dislike for Johnson played a role in his decision to challenge the president. McCarthy, in many ways a traditional Cold War liberal, had first voiced public opposition to the war in February 1967. On November 30, McCarthy announced his decision to challenge President Johnson in the upcoming presidential primaries.

McCarthy's lackluster campaign seemed headed for humiliating defeat—despite the thousands of young college students who, legend has it, shaved off their beards to knock on doors in the New Hampshire primary on his behalf. With the election looming, McCarthy was trailing badly in the polls. Help, though, was to come from afar. On January 30, the eve of the Vietnamese lunar New Year (Tet), the NLF launched a major offensive throughout the South. Thirty-six provincial capitals and five of the six major cities were attacked, and communist forces briefly occupied the grounds of the American embassy in Saigon. Although in retrospect it was a military defeat for the NLF, at the time Americans viewed it as a major setback. Johnson's claims that victory was around the corner rang particularly hollow, and Tet transformed the presidential contest. On March 12, McCarthy won 42.4 percent of the New Hampshire vote. Although many of his supporters apparently favored stronger military action in Vietnam, it boosted McCarthy's antiwar candidacy and dealt President Johnson a crushing blow. Four days later, Robert Kennedy announced his own entry into the race. With liberal dissent mobilized within the Democratic Party, LBJ knew he was in serious political trouble. Demoralized by the war and domestic opposition to it, worried about his health, and lacking the appetite for a bruising electoral contest, on March 31, 1968, he announced that he would neither seek nor accept his party's nomination as the presidential candidate in the November election. He also announced a partial bombing halt and signaled a willingness to begin negotiations with the North Vietnamese.

With Johnson gone, the fight for the Democratic nomination turned into a three-horse race when vice president Hubert Humphrey, Johnson's favored candidate, entered the contest in late April. Though he was too late to enter the primaries, Humphrey appeared to have a lock on the nomination as, with Johnson's help, he piled up delegates from nonprimary states. His triumph was sealed when, after winning the California primary on June 4, Kennedy was shot dead by an Arab nationalist. Although McCarthy remained in the race, he no longer had the heart to keep on fighting. At the Democratic national convention in Chicago in August, the antiwar camp attempted unsuccessfully to get a "peace plank" into the party platform.

Meanwhile, the area outside the convention center became the site of running battles between Mayor Richard Daley's police and antiwar protesters—including the outrageous Yippies of Abbie Hoffman and Jerry Rubin. The Yippies promised a "festival of life" in the Windy City, and talked of lacing the city's water supply with LSD and running a pig for president. Daley, determined to protect his city from lawless hoodlums, ensured a heavy-handed response. As the television networks beamed pictures of policemen clubbing demonstrators and journalists alike, while proceedings in the convention hall descended into chaos, the Democratic Party appeared to implode. In the November election, despite a late rally in support and a boost from organized labor, Humphrey lost to the Republican nominee, Richard Nixon, by 43.4 percent to 42.7 percent in the popular vote.

While important, the 1968 campaign, with the possible exception of Robert Kennedy, does not constitute an example of coalition between the antiwar and civil rights movements. Eugene McCarthy, for example, received almost no black support and made little effort to get any. Kennedy, by contrast, held huge appeal among blacks. Frequently campaigning in ghettos, Kennedy's campaign held out the enticing prospect of uniting poor blacks and whites in a new politics that would shift the political spectrum leftward. However, many antiwar activists, especially in the radical wing of the movement, rejected all involvement with mainstream politics. Although Tom Hayden, the University of Michigan graduate and New Left icon who had helped write the Port Huron Statement in 1962, wept after Kennedy's assassination, he had called him a "fascist" a few days before. Finally, despite the chaotic scenes at the Democratic convention, the protests outside were a white-only affair. There were almost no blacks among the antiwar protesters, while the vast majority of African Americans, grateful for the progressive civil rights policies of the Johnson administration, cast their ballot for Hubert Humphrey in the November election.[39]

As the antiwar movement regrouped in the aftermath of the tumultuous events of 1968, disputes over multi-issuism remained an open sore. In April 1969 the SWP asked the Cleveland Area Peace Action Council to sponsor a national antiwar conference for the purpose of planning another big national mobilization against the war. The CAPAC had been founded in 1967 and, working closely with the local SMC chapter, it had made Cleveland an important center of antiwar activity. After a period of decline it had revived in 1969 under the leadership of Jerry Gordon, a civil liberties lawyer. Leading antiwar figures Sidney Peck and David Dellinger put aside their fears that the SWP would seek to control the convention and pledged their support. The conference, an invitation-only affair, was held July 4–5 at Case Western Reserve University, Cleveland. After much wrangling, the diplomatic skills of Sidney Lens—a veteran of radical movements who had written for such magazines as the *Progressive* and the *Nation*—helped persuade the conference to support two antiwar demonstrations.[40]

The first, to be held in Chicago, was a protest against the trial of eight activists who had been involved in the demonstrations at the 1968 Democratic Party convention. The Mobe's Dave Dellinger, Rennie Davis, and Tom Hayden; Yippies Jerry Rubin and Abbie Hoffman; two demonstration marshals; and Bobby Seale of the Black Panthers had been indicted by the Nixon Justice Department in March 1969 on charges of conspiring to incite a riot.[41] The second planned action was an antiwar demonstration in Washington, D.C., scheduled for November 15. In other important decisions, the gathering voted to endorse the Vietnam Moratorium and to support the March Against Death. Finally, the renovated antiwar coalition was renamed the New Mobilization Committee to End the War in Vietnam (New Mobe).[42]

Analyzing the Cleveland Conference later that month, the *Guardian* took issue with the minority who had opposed the Chicago action. The Chicago protest, the paper argued, was "in its larger aspects a united project of the antiwar movement, the Black Panthers . . . and SDS. It opens the prospect of bringing the well-known opposition to the war within the black and Latin communities on to the streets in unity with the organized antiwar movement, now predominantly made up of whites." The *Guardian*, which argued consistently for a multi-issue antiwar movement, claimed that "the struggle against the war must not be isolated from that against racism and poverty. To achieve maximum involvement of the mass of people in the U.S. who oppose the war, the Vietnam War and its consequences must be related to problems they confront in their lives." According to the paper, most delegates to the Cleveland gathering had "called for a united movement against the war . . . repression . . .

racism and poverty." This was a position with which they were in hearty agreement.[43]

The New Mobe, like previous antiwar coalitions, hoped to attract black support. In August, Sidney Peck attended a meeting with African American leaders in the San Francisco region. Peck, a sociology professor at Western Reserve in Cleveland, was a former left-wing trade unionist and amateur prize fighter who had cut his political teeth in Minnesota's Farmer-Labor Party. He persuaded the black activist and future congressman Ronald Dellums to help with the November 15 protests. Peck also met with the leadership of the Black Panther Party. He reported back that "Brothers Seale and Hilliard indicated that there would be substantial Black Panther cooperation with the New Mobilization Committee provided that the national actions contained significant demands dealing with the necessity of the anti-war movement to combat incipient fascism in this country."[44]

Despite being connected in the popular (white) imagination with revolutionary violence and hatred of all things Caucasian, the Black Panther Party, founded in Oakland in 1966, was willing to forge alliances with white groups around issues of common interest. During late 1967 and 1968, the BPP had entered into coalition with the California-based Peace and Freedom Party (PFP), a white radical organization that was committed to ending the war in Vietnam and promoting radical social and political change at home. It had run Eldridge Cleaver for president in the 1968 election.

The BPP was a staunch opponent of the war in Vietnam, and the pages of the *Black Panther* frequently contained fierce condemnation of the "Yankee Imperialist" war of "aggression."[45] Point Six of the party's platform demanded that "all black men" be exempted from military service—"we will not fight and kill other people of color in the world who, like black people, are being victimized by the white racist government of America."[46] According to the Panthers, the Vietnam War was "a struggle for liberation; [a] revolutionary war against the largest and most repressive monopoly system in the world—the United States."[47] The BPP did not just oppose the war, it also believed that the antiwar and black liberation movements shared in a common struggle. The party's Minister of Information, Eldridge Cleaver, argued that "those who are primarily concerned with improving the Negro's condition recognize, as do proponents of the liquidation of America's neo-colonial network, that their fight is one and the same."[48] For Cleaver, "the black man's interest" lay "in seeing a free and independent Vietnam, a strong Vietnam which is not the puppet of international white supremacy."[49] The Panthers' opposition to Vietnam seemed to hold out the promise of cooperation with the antiwar movement.

In addition, the BPP was one of the few Black Power groups that was enthusiastic about working with white leftists.[50] On a philosophical level, the Panthers supported attempts to create a left wing interracial coalition. Eldridge Cleaver explained that "it's necessary to pull a lot of people together, black and white." Cleaver believed it important to "build some machinery" so that black and white radicals could work together, in a national coalition, rather than being at "cross purposes," "isolated and alienated from one another."[51] The BPP viewed their alliance with the PFP as representing a "new direction" for black and white radical groups.[52] There was also an element of *realpolitik* to the relationship. Cleaver wanted access to white money and administrative skills to aid the Panther campaign to free Huey Newton from prison, where he was awaiting trial for the murder of Oakland police officer John Frey. The PFP, meanwhile, wanted help in garnering the 66,000 signatures needed to qualify for the state ballot.[53]

A PFP convention was held in March 15–17, 1968, in Richmond, California. Like many leftist gatherings of the decade, the meeting had a distinctive style. The Gorilla Band of the San Francisco Mime Troupe played the "Star Spangled Banner," "punctuated by screams at 'the rockets red glare, the bombs bursting in air.'" During the actual deliberations, "bellowing and booing accompanied each speech until 20 seconds of silence were invoked." *Guardian* columnist Don Newton reported that "the most dramatic aspect of the convention was the surprisingly intense relationship" between the BPP and PFP. Newton explained that the Panthers had been active in the Bay Area, accompanying PFP sound trucks through ghetto areas to help obtain the thousands of signatures needed for the PFP to qualify for the November ballot. In return, the PFP had pledged support to the "Free Huey" campaign. The coalition was, though, specific to the Bay Area. "In Los Angeles, which provided at least a third of PFP's registration, PFP organizers have been warned on pain of death to stay out of Watts and other black areas."[54]

The Richmond gathering had not been devoid of racial tension. There was a fierce debate, for example, over the wording of the "Free Huey" resolution. Delegates initially voted for "Free Huey Newton Now" over "Free Huey Newton by Any Means Necessary" by 227 to 223. Mario Savio declared that "I don't think the revolution in America depends on burning down half of the city of Oakland to free one man." After Bobby Seale reminded the convention that he favored the latter wording—"What's wrong with a gun? What's so damn wrong with a gun?"—the resolution was reconsidered. A compromise of "Free Huey Newton by Any Means Which Will Advance the Black Liberation Movement" was passed by a margin of three to one.[55]

The ghost of the NCNP also hung over the deliberations. Many white delegates feared that demands for 50 percent of the vote from the non-white participants would destroy the PFP. Ultimately, however, the "Black and Brown Caucus," made up of African Americans and Chicanos, settled for a "calm statement" that they would "leave the party if it failed to support self-determination for oppressed minorities." This arrangement was strongly condemned by SNCC's James Forman, who believed it "imperative" that blacks should have "50 percent of all voting power in any relation with whites." The SNCC leader held that the PFP had "skirted this issue by entering into a coalition with the Panthers." Forman lectured the white radicals, explaining that blacks "have suffered from the racism in this country. You have not." Instead of following the NCNP model, the PFP adopted a bicameral approach, whereby the Panthers decided the PFP program for the black community, and the white radicals defined it for the white community.[56] Despite racial tensions, the PFP agreed to run Huey Newton for congress in the 7th congressional district, and Bobby Seale and Kathleen Cleaver for state assembly. The PFP also endorsed the BPP's ten-point program.[57]

Although the PFP attracted respectable levels of support in the Bay Area it lacked strength elsewhere. One exception was New York State, where a branch of the PFP was founded in the spring of 1968. Cornell University professor and Mobe leader, Doug Dowd, had been involved in this effort. He explained that "we saw ourselves as an educational and protest, not electoral, group." By the summer, though, a majority favored entering the electoral arena. One fall weekend, Dowd happened to be in Manhattan visiting his mother, when he noticed that the PFP was holding its state convention. He decided to drop by, and ended up receiving the party's vice-presidential nomination. Dowd's friends convinced him that he had to stand as Cleaver's running mate in the Empire State, despite his personal opposition to electoral politics, to prevent the nomination going to Jerry Rubin, whom Dowd "hated." Ultimately, Cleaver ran with two running mates—Rubin in California, and the reluctant Dowd in New York. The PFP state convention struck Dowd as utterly unreal—it reminded him of a "bunch of little . . . high school kids, playing mayor for a day or convention for a day."[58] The PFP did succeed in qualifying for the ballot in both New York and California. This triumph of leftist organizing, however, was more than matched by George Wallace's American Independent Party.[59] As well as qualifying for the California ballot, Wallace received almost ten million votes nationally, whereas the Peace and Freedom slate was supported by a mere 36,563 Americans. Most of them lived within spitting distance of Berkeley.[60]

The PFP had shown that it was possible for the Panthers to work productively with white radicals, provided that the relationship provided tangible benefits. But during 1969 the New Mobe's reluctance to embrace fully a multi-issue approach to organizing prevented it from winning substantial black support. In mid-August, the New Mobe Steering Committee discussed the question of black support for the antiwar movement. A number of activists worried that the antiwar focus would be eclipsed if the November demonstrations were orientated toward the Panthers' concerns.[61]

The BPP was not the only black group whose demands troubled the New Mobe's leaders. Abe Bloom (chairman of Washington SANE and a leader of the Washington Mobilization Committee) reported on negotiations with the Washington Black United Front (BUF). The BUF had stated that "any national movement that does not relate itself to our particular situation here as a federal colony is of little concern to us." In addition to insisting that the New Mobe give strong support for "D.C. Statehood," the BUF also demanded that participants in the November demonstration be taxed $1, with ten percent of the projected total "being given in advance to the BUF as a sign of commitment to the struggle."[62] The Mobe decided to set up a meeting with the BUF, and promised to make D.C. statehood an issue in its Washington protests. The BUF's demand for an up-front payment of $25,000, made in an August letter, was subsequently proven to have been the work of the ever-meddling FBI—who played on white guilt and interracial tension to try and undermine radical dissent.[63]

In spite of concerns surrounding the authenticity of some of the BUF "leaders," the New Mobe remained anxious to win African American support. In September a proposal was made to invite BUF participation in the Mobe's steering committee and to give any profits from the Washington Action to the black group. Others within the Mobe cautioned against making any financial agreements with the BUF until a "satisfactory political arrangement" was made.[64] Toward the end of 1969 an anonymous memorandum accused the New Mobe's national steering committee of being hijacked by Trotskyists who were opposed to working with blacks. The writer declared—"I have been sickened—on more than one occasion—by the promises made to the Black United Front, promises not kept, promises made with the mouth and not the heart. The attitude of the steering committee toward the BUF was and is a matter of disgrace."[65] At a September steering committee meeting of the Washington Action Committee (part of the New Mobe coalition), an invited representative of the BUF had to leave before he had been given an opportunity to speak. This re-enforced the impression that whites were not committed seriously to facilitating black participation in the peace movement.[66] However, the general attitude within the Mobe's leadership was that the BUF's demands were unacceptable, though they remained willing to support the black movement's political goals.

The BUF episode showed some of the potential pitfalls in trying to assemble a radical coalition. The rise of Black Power militancy, and black radicals' distrust of whites, sometimes led them to make outrageous demands, which guilt-ridden whites were on occasion too eager to appease. These problems arose, in part, from the collapse of the civil rights movement as a coherent national coalition. With Martin Luther King dead, and with groups like SNCC and CORE in serious decline, the peace movement was obliged to negotiate with a series of small, locally based and often unstable black organizations. Dealing with such transient black groups complicated yet further the already difficult task of trying to build interracial antiwar actions.

Perhaps the most important development within the antiwar forces during 1969 was the revival of the peace movement's liberal wing. Although moderate peace groups, such as SANE, Women Strike for Peace, the War Resisters League, and Clergy and Laity Concerned about Vietnam had taken part in many of the antiwar protests of 1965–1968, the radical wing of the peace movement had gradually assumed a dominant position. This radical ascendancy culminated in the March on the Pentagon in 1967 and the protests at the Democratic National Convention in 1968. With the presidential campaigns of Eugene McCarthy and Robert Kennedy, and the election of a Republican to the presidency, liberal peace protest began to grow, aided by many dovish Democrats who now found themselves free to oppose the war.

Antiwar liberals asserted that the radical peace movement had been ineffective and had even harmed the effort to end the war in Vietnam. Tactics such as draft card burnings, revolutionary rhetoric and links with the counterculture had, liberals claimed, alienated the peace movement from mainstream America. The result was an antiwar movement that was even more unpopular than the Vietnam War.[67] Peace movement historian Charles DeBenedetti has argued that the popular identification of antiwar protesters with rowdy students and restless blacks led to them being viewed as "troublemaking deviants." The result was that peace protests were at best irrelevant, and at worst they actually strengthened support for the war by provoking a counter-reaction among middle Americans.[68]

In many ways the public perception that the peace movement was made up primarily of "freaks" was due to media distortion of the radical wing of the movement. The antiwar movement found itself in something of a dilemma regarding the media—they needed coverage to generate publicity and distribute their message, but were unable to control the nature of the coverage. Theodore Otto Windt, Jr., has pointed out that, "lacking the instruments of power" that were available to those who were waging the war, the peace movement had to rely on self-generated publicity. But, by seeking media attention, the peace movement often "created rhetorical forms and committed symbolic acts which . . . seemed at odds with their goals and which often outraged both proponents and opponents of the war.[69]

Jack Newfield complained bitterly that during the two months following the April 1965 SDS antiwar March on Washington, *"Time, Newsweek, The Saturday Evening Post, The New York Times Magazine, Life,* and two television networks all popularized the New Left. They smeared it, they psychoanalyzed it, they exaggerated it, they cartooned it, they made it look like a mélange of beatniks, potheads, and agents of international Communism; *they did everything but explain the failures in the society that called it into being."*[70] Milton Katz noted that "when SANE held its overwhelmingly middle-class, middle-aged, middle-of-the-road march in Washington in November 1965, what appeared on television news and in news photos were Viet Cong flags, interruptions by the tiny American Nazi Party, and the handful of marchers, out of several thousand, who were wearing beards and sandals."[71] Numerous scholars have shown how the media distorted the antiwar movement by focusing excessively on fringe elements at protests; emphasizing violent incidents; underestimating the numbers at demonstrations; framing antiwar stories as "deviant" or "criminal" activities; and giving disproportionate coverage to right wing counter-demonstrations.[72]

By the late 1960s, growing numbers of antiwar activists were calling for a change in the peace movement's tactics in order to make it more effective. Many of these forces came together in the Vietnam Moratorium Committee (VMC), which was founded in the summer of 1969. Originally the idea of Boston envelope manufacturer and peace activist, Jerome Grossman, the VMC was shaped by veterans of Eugene McCarthy's failed 1968 presidential campaign. The likes of Sam Brown, David Hawk, and David Mixner shared veteran peace campaigner I. F. Stone's concerns about the nature of antiwar protest. Stone had, as early as 1965, warned that the New Left's "melange of Maoism and Stalinism with Negro nationalism" would win support on the left only at the expense of "strengthening the widespread mania about a Communist conspiracy."[73] In 1968 he had argued that the radicals' addiction to "revolution" would result in a harmful counterrevolution. In his *Weekly,* Stone wrote that "to play with revolutionary talk and tactics as the New Left is doing, when there is no revolutionary situation, is to act as the provocateurs for an American fascism."[74]

The Moratorium Committee was made up of Americans who were opposed to the Vietnam War but who still believed in working within the two party system. Moreover, the VMC had a single-issue orientation.

Moratorium coordinator Sam Brown, himself a veteran of Freedom Summer, an associate of Allard Lowenstein, and a leader of McCarthy's 1968 campaign, argued that "unrelated issues" weakened the peace movement.[75] The organization also tended toward moderation, which it combined with a keen desire for respectability. This was reflected in its name—"Moratorium" had been chosen rather than the more militant "Strike."[76] Brown understood that potential peace supporters were put off by long hair, campus protest, indeed by "anything which irritates the nerve endings of middle-class values," and that when the "Silent Majority" were pitted against the radicals there could only ever be one winner. For Brown, these "middle Americans" were the key to peace— they held the political "balance of power between continued Nixonian Vietnamization or worse, and an early end to the war."[77] The Moratorium believed that "only a peace movement which reaches Richard Nixon's constituency can stop it." The VMC hoped to move the antiwar movement beyond its student base, and to nurture a new peace leadership composed of "Senators, Congressmen, governors, mayors, businessmen—all the straight people who are willing to make a firm and unequivocal commitment against the war."[78]

The idea behind the Moratorium was to have a national strike against American "business as normal," which would increase by one day every month that the war continued. The VMC hoped to encourage scores of local grass-roots protests throughout the nation. The plan was to initiate a monthly antiwar escalation that would mobilize the broadest possible coalition, and the date of the first protest was set for October 15.[79] By the end of September the Moratorium had received endorsements from numerous liberal figures and institutions. The *New Republic,* the ADA, and the New Democratic Coalition lent their support, as did John Kenneth Galbraith, W. Averill Harriman, and some two dozen Senators—including Charles Goodell, Mark Hatfield, Eugene McCarthy, and George McGovern. Support from organized labor came from the United Auto Workers and the Teamsters. By October, the VMC had a full-time staff of 31, based in an office on the eighth floor of 1029 Vermont Avenue, just four blocks from the White House, as well as 7,500 field organizers.[80]

The October 15 activities involved hundreds of thousands of Americans in antiwar activities, both large and small, throughout the nation. *Life Magazine* described the day as "a display without parallel, the largest expression of public dissent ever seen in this country."[81] A crowd of 100,000 gathered on Boston Common, and up to 250,000 people were involved in various antiwar events in New York City. Thousands more attended demonstrations, teach-ins, memorial services, vigils, or gatherings in Chicago, Philadelphia, Minneapolis and Los Angeles.[82]

Despite its single-issue orientation, the VMC managed to secure African American support from across the political spectrum. Fannie Lou Hamer explained that "with the kind of pain we are undergoing here in Mississippi, to have black and white men dying in Vietnam is a shame and a disgrace. It is essential that we support the Vietnam Moratorium Committee's efforts to end the war." The National Welfare Rights Organization's George Wiley (formerly of CORE) offered support for the VMC, albeit within a multi-issue framework. Wiley declared, "ours is a government that has imposed immense suffering on poor people in Vietnam and poor people in this country. On October 15, we must demonstrate, dramatically and directly, our outrage against these policies and our commitment to change the nation's priorities."[83] Gwendolyn Patton, now national coordinator for the National Association of Black Students, urged African Americans to support the October 15 protests. She asked black students to go into their communities to raise the issue of Vietnam, and to "alert our people about the atrocities this government is committing on the Vietnamese people and the senseless dying of black brothers who really need to be and should be alive to help us fight our struggle for freedom and liberation in this country."[84]

For the first time more moderate black organizations joined the antiwar coalition. The National Urban League's Whitney Young issued a statement supporting the October VMC demonstrations. The Urban League executive director had, during 1967, put aside his concerns about Vietnam to offer a virtual endorsement of the war when he traveled to South Vietnam as part of the official American delegation sent to observe the elections. The year 1968 had seen the Tet offensive, the withdrawal of LBJ from the presidential contest and the triumph of Richard Nixon. Like many other Americans, Whitney Young reevaluated his opinion of the war in light of the continued suffering in Southeast Asia and the seeming inability of America to win. He came to believe that Martin Luther King had been "more right" about the war than he, and, perhaps freed politically now that a Republican occupied the White House, he felt able to express his concerns publicly. Indeed, one of his biographers has argued that Young had little reason to resist those who declared that the war was morally wrong and harmful to African Americans, because President Nixon lacked Johnson's stature in civil rights.[85] There was also pressure from below. In a meeting with Urban League trustees on October 7 Young had spoken of the "terrific pressure" from the "black community," youth, and white liberals for the organization to take a position against the war.[86]

Young's opportunity to express his opposition to Vietnam came after the VMC invited him to speak at the October 15 rally in Washington. Young was unable to accept the invitation, but issued a personal statement supporting the VMC's efforts.[87] Young explained that he had, for some time, been viewing America's "agony in Vietnam with a sense of deepening distress." He went on to declare that he was "totally convinced that this war has an extra dimension for black people that it does not have for many whites. We are suffering doubly. We are dying for something abroad that we do not have at home." Young continued, "I am further convinced that the most effective way for America to win credibility as a democracy in the eyes of the world is through the immediate resolution of its domestic crisis rather than through expansion of its defense capability."[88] Using language that was reminiscent of Martin Luther King's, Young charged that the Vietnam War had "twisted America's soul," before concluding with a demand for the "immediate termination" of the conflict.

Support for the VMC also came from the NAACP. With antiwar feeling rising among the American population, with the emergence of a "respectable" antiwar movement, and with the election of Nixon, peace advocates were able to prosper within the NAACP for the first time. At the Association's 60th Annual Convention, held in Jackson, Mississippi June 30–July 5, antiwar sentiment finally began to flourish. On July 1, at the annual Ministers' Breakfast, Los Angeles clergyman Thomas E. Kilgore, newly elected to the presidency of the American Baptist Convention, told his audience that "our values are inverted . . . we cannot go on killing in Vietnam."[89] Although NAACP delegates passed a resolution reaffirming that the Association was primarily a civil rights organization, they also noted that "billions of dollars are being spent in a cruel, inhuman, and unjust war in Vietnam." They called on the U.S. government to "institute the speediest measures to withdraw American troops from Vietnam and concentrate our wealth and skills on peaceful measures to prosecute our own domestic war on poverty."[90] It was within this context that the NAACP came to offer limited support to the Moratorium. In October, James Blacke, national vice president in charge of youth affairs, agreed to send out a mailing urging full support of the Moratorium. In his capacity as an NAACP official, Blacke also endorsed a statement calling for an immediate cease-fire and "prompt" withdrawal of American soldiers from Vietnam.[91] NAACP activists at the local level supported the VMC too. Bert Harris, president of the Greenwich Village-Chelsea branch, attended the October 15 Moratorium protests along with other branch members.[92]

Although there was a good deal of black support for the Moratorium, interracial tensions continued to torment the peace movement. The *Guardian* noted that while "tens of thousands of blacks," including some BPP leaders, participated in the Moratorium, "the vast majority of the participants were white." Many African Americans still saw the peace movement as irrelevant, even hostile, to black America. The *Guardian* reported that, at a Moratorium rally at Buffalo College, a black speaker had told the students "You don't empathize with the black man. . . . This Moratorium was called because the white man is dying in Vietnam, not the black man."[93] Such problems would persist and deepen.

For example, on Wednesday November 12, the Black Panther Party held a rally in San Francisco, to demand the freeing of all political prisoners—and specifically to generate support for a North Vietnamese offer to free American POWs in return for the release of jailed Panthers. Numerous speakers attacked the white-dominated peace movement and its single-issue orientation. Angela Davis, for example, stated that "we have to talk about what's happening in Vietnam as a symptom of what's happening all over the world." The UCLA professor criticized the single-issue advocates within the peace movement—"they feel it's necessary to tone-down the political content of that movement in order to attract as many people as possible. They think that numbers will be enough." Black Panther minister of education, Masai Hewitt, warned the peace movement that it risked isolating itself from the black community if it continued to ignore the leadership of black people in the antiwar struggle. Hewitt argued that support for the proposed exchange of American POWs for U.S. "political prisoners" was an opportunity for the white antiwar movement to prove itself, and he condemned those peace activists who were afraid to endorse the prisoner exchange, lest it cost them support. Hewitt also joined those demanding that the peace movement take a multi-issue stance.[94]

Peace movement veteran Fred Halstead—a militant union organizer and SWP stalwart who had been raised in an Old Left household—has characterized the period between October 15 and November 15 as one of tension within the antiwar movement.[95] At the Cleveland convention in July it had been decided to hold a mass antiwar demonstration in Washington on November 15—the date of the second Moratorium protests, and also to stage the March Against Death, which was to begin on November 13. Delicate negotiations took place between the Moratorium and the New Mobe regarding cooperation between them. On October 21 the VMC announced that, while it would continue to concentrate its efforts on mobilizing local antiwar constituencies, it would support the New Mobe's actions in Washington and San Francisco. One of the reasons for the VMC's endorsement was a hope that it would be able to exert influence to ensure that the protests would remain peaceful.[96] Sam Brown later explained that "we decided to support the Mobe activities, partly because we thought they clearly intended to have a nonviolent demonstration, and partly because the events were going to happen anyway and would reflect on the whole peace movement."[97]

It was at a meeting of the leadership of the Moratorium and the New Mobe, on the evening of October 20, where a deal had been struck. The New Mobe's leaders agreed to the VMC demand for a senator from each party to be allowed to speak at the November rally. They also offered VMC coordinators positions on the New Mobe's executive committee, and granted the Moratorium ten seats on the steering committee. In return, the VMC agreed to support the nonexclusion of communists and the demand for immediate withdrawal.[98] The agreement was ratified at the next meeting of the New Mobe steering committee, on November 2, in the face of fierce objections. Former SNCC field secretary Phil Hutchings accused the New Mobe chairmen of having made a deal with right wing liberals, and spoke of "bourgeois cooptation." But the sentiment advocated by Western Regional Mobe chairman Terrance Hallinan carried the day, just. Hallinan stated that "we're playing games trying to be ideologically pure while people are dying . . . our task is not to go to meetings we dig but to get peace, and for that we've got to unite with the Moratorium."[99]

The awe-inspiring March Against Death set the tone for the peace demonstrations held over the weekend of November 15. The 36-hour march involved 45,000 people walking in single file from the banks of the Potomac River, at the west end of Arlington Memorial Bridge, to the White House. There, each participant read out the name of an American soldier killed in Vietnam or the name of a Vietnamese village that had been destroyed. The demonstrations on the Saturday were similarly impressive. November 15 was a clear, crisp day in the nation's capital, with temperatures in the thirties. At about 10 A.M., antiwar protesters who had gathered on the Mall began marching up Pennsylvania Avenue toward the Washington Monument. By mid-afternoon there were more than half a million Americans at the rally, making it the largest demonstration in U.S. history. For more than ten minutes the crowd chanted John Lennon's "All we are saying, is give peace a chance."[100]

Like previous antiwar demonstrations, this one was overwhelmingly white, despite the presence of Dick Gregory and Phil Hutchings. Hutchings, who was also a *Guardian* columnist, spoke about the need for the antiwar movement to engage with the oppression of African Americans and other nonwhites. Although the New Mobe had invited the Black Panthers to participate in the Washington demonstration, they had declined. The New Mobe's refusal to adequately support the Panther demands was clearly a source of tension between the two groups. On November 12, the Harlem Branch of the BPP had issued a statement explaining their decision not to participate. Black people, they said "should strongly support the demand for immediate withdrawal of all United States troops from Vietnam and should support the Moratorium actions." However, "Black people should understand that there is no unity of will between black people and the leadership of the New Mobilization because the New Mobilization has either failed to see or does not want to see the importance of black people's just struggle or its direct relationship with the struggle of the Vietnamese people."[101] There were few black faces in the Washington crowd. Seventeen-year-old Gail Morton, a black student at Baltimore's Eastern High School, explained that "the Mobilization really didn't let the black community know about the demonstration."

November 15 also saw the largest ever antiwar demonstration in San Francisco, where between 100,000 and 250,000 people attended a rally in Golden Gate Park. Ralph Abernathy, who had succeeded King as SCLC president, gave an anticapitalist speech. But it was Black Panther David Hilliard who provoked the biggest crowd reaction. The BPP chief-of-staff offended liberals by criticizing the presence of American flags at the demonstration, and he alienated hippies by condemning the use of rock music. Hilliard called on whites to support the Panther's plans for community control of the police, as well as the release of Huey Newton and Bobby Seale in exchange for American prisoners of war. *Guardian* correspondent Patty Lee Parmalee reported that "as Hilliard's anti-fascist, pro-Marxist-Leninist speech became more militant and as he cursed President Nixon, the young, white hippy throng started booing. Hilliard responded angrily: "We will kill Richard Nixon—we will kill any motherfucker that stands in the way of our freedom. We ain't here for no goddam peace because we know that we can't have no peace, because this country was built on war. But if you want peace you've got to fight for it, fight for it, fight for it!' " As angry hippies shouted "peace, peace," Hilliard responded, "Peace, peace, peace . . . at the risk of more suffering for the people of Vietnam, at the risk of more lives being taken in the black community."[102] Parmalee noted the large participation of "third world people" at the San Francisco demonstration—an exception to the "norm" of peace protests. However, she wondered whether nonwhites would "continue to work with the antiwar movement or whether such responses as met Hilliard will discourage the tenuous alliance."

Moratorium protests took place in communities across the nation, including Gainesville, Florida. One of the first antiwar protests by students at the University of Florida had taken place early in 1966, when the Georgia State Legislature refused to seat Julian Bond following his endorsement of SNCC's opposition to the war. A group of thirty demonstrators from the University of Florida, a third of them black, had followed route 301 to the border with Georgia, some twenty miles north of Jacksonville. They took with them signs bearing slogans such as "You are now leaving the American sector," and protested on the state line for

about an hour.[103] On November 15, 1969, 170 people marched from the
University of Florida Plaza of the Americas to the Federal Building
downtown. The marchers carried 39 crosses—representing each Ala-
chua County citizen killed in Southeast Asia. The group held a rally at
the mall across from the Post Office entrance, sang "This Land Is Your
Land," and heard speeches attacking the war. Charles Fulwood, a black
radical, linked Vietnam and domestic repression—"the exploitation of
people is what makes this country bad. I'm talking about the exploitation of the Vietnamese and of people here in the United States."[104]

At the end of 1969 the peace movement faced many of the same problems that had dogged it since the beginning of its crusade against
America's military involvement in Southeast Asia. Political factionalism,
divisions over tactics and goals, and racial tensions all harmed efforts to
build an effective antiwar coalition. The rise of a liberal, single-issue
peace movement, centered on the Vietnam Moratorium Committee, had
won support from moderate black groups such as the NAACP and the
Urban League, although their primary concern remained civil rights,
and some of the largest ever peace demonstrations had been organized.
But the VMC's very existence had highlighted splits within the peace movement. Importantly, the debate over multi-issuism refused to disappear.
Indeed it would cause further major splits among the antiwar forces.

Chapter 6
New Coalitions, Old Problems

Unity cannot be based on air or rhetoric. It must be concrete and reflect the real ties that exist between different sections of the population.

—*NCAWRR Non-White Caucus Position Paper, circa 1971*

The winter and early spring of 1970 was a particularly low period for the antiwar movement. The April antiwar demonstrations, sponsored by the New Mobe and the Vietnam Moratorium Committee, although widespread, were relatively small. Richard Nixon's policy of Vietnamization, leaving the South Vietnamese to do most of the ground fighting while the U.S. increased its bombing campaign, commanded wide public support, and helped to drain the movement's strength. The antiwar coalition was weakened further by internal strains, which threatened to break out into open warfare. The VMC, which had been so spectacularly successful during 1969, ran out of steam and closed its national office on April 19. Divisions between radicals and moderates, meanwhile, seriously compromised the New Mobe's effectiveness.[1]

Ironically, it was Richard Nixon who managed to energize the peace movement, enabling it to overcome its ideological factionalism, albeit temporarily. The president's April 30 announcement that he was sending American ground forces into Cambodia to destroy North Vietnamese supply lines resulted in some of the most impressive antiwar demonstrations in the nation's history. A national student strike took hold almost instantly—after four days over 100 schools were affected. The killing of four students at Kent State on May 4 further outraged the peace movement and the campuses erupted—536 were shut down completely with 51 remaining closed for the remainder of the academic year. Protests were held at 1,350 colleges during May, with almost half the nation's students participating. Domestic antiwar dissent had never been stronger.[2] Even the NAACP's Roy Wilkins was moved to describe the protests against the Cambodian invasion as "legitimate and timely" and declared that the "outpouring of national feeling over Kent State" was good.[3]

Many leading antiwar activists recognized that they had failed to connect meaningfully with other struggles and continued to push for a genuinely multi-issue peace movement. Writing for the *Guardian* in January 1970, Carl Davidson argued that "those with the greatest stake in the victory of the antiwar movement and the defeat of imperialism . . . must not only be the main force in that movement, but make up its leadership as well." The erstwhile SDS intellectual understood that this would not happen "unless the antiwar movement takes up the just demands of these movements, relates them to the war, and struggles to win them as their own."[4] The following month a *Guardian* editorial explained that "Unity is a two-way street. If the antiwar movement is to receive support and leadership from millions of blacks who oppose the war, then the millions of whites who identify with the antiwar movement are going to have to give organized support to blacks in their war against oppression here at home." The paper pointed out that "An antiwar movement which speaks eloquently in one massive voice against the oppression directed toward the Vietnamese . . . but only gives token support to 23 million blacks . . . cannot expect black Americans to enlist in the actions of the antiwar coalitions."[5]

To a considerable degree African Americans were interested in the Vietnam War only insofar as it affected them. The growth of Black Power and rising racial consciousness meant that blacks were reluctant to commit themselves to a white-dominated movement that did not speak to their concerns. Multi-issue advocates within the peace movement certainly believed that America's foreign and domestic problems were intrinsically bound together. But there was also a pragmatic motive at work—they understood that a single-issue approach held a strictly limited appeal for non-white Americans. The internal debate within the peace movement about the wisdom of a multi-issue approach bubbled to the surface in a number of important antiwar organizations during the early months of 1970, and disagreements over this eventually produced a new schism in the antiwar coalition.

The New Mobe Steering Committee had met at Case Western Reserve University December 13–14, 1969. The meeting was dominated by a "radical caucus" that argued for emphasizing local-orientated actions and building radical constituencies around a multi-issue program.[6] The participants voted to protest "war profits, political repression, [and] the draft" in addition to the war. The Mobe also addressed the black struggle, with specific reference to the Black Panther Party. The Mobilization went on record in support of the Panthers, and also "agreed to provide additional support for the Panthers if they take their protest against U.S. repression to the UN as has been indicated." The *Guardian*, which had supported the efforts of the "radical caucus," explained that "unless the antiwar movement engages in acts of solidarity with third-world people and the poor, these people are not going to act in solidarity with the antiwar movement—and for good reason."[7]

At a steering committee meeting in Philadelphia the following month, the organization attempted to map its strategy for the forthcoming spring antiwar protests. The New Mobe hoped that "local antiwar coalitions . . . would link the third world liberation struggle within the U.S. to the war in Vietnam," and the organization declared that one of the primary aims of the spring actions was to "build meaningful unity between the antiwar and third world movements."[8] In February the New Mobe's radical caucus met to discuss tactics. It quickly agreed on the "absolute necessity of including Black and Third World groups, Women's Liberation groups, and Labor groups" in the antiwar actions, but found formulating ways to bring this about tricky. Indeed, the minutes of the meeting explain that it was "the most perplexing and difficult problem discussed."[9]

Not everyone in the New Mobe was happy with the direction in which it was moving, and the Socialist Workers Party led calls for the organization to revert to a single-issue focus. Writing in the *Militant* in December 1969, Harry Ring had argued that multi-issuism would simply deflect attention from the effort to end the war, and warned that there was a "flight from antiwar struggle to diffuse activities around a grab bag of issues in the name of greater 'radicalism'." He believed that those who wished to "derail" the antiwar movement into a "multi-issue morass" were unlikely to succeed.[10] Richard Fernandez, director of Clergy and Laity Concerned, was also worried that multi-issuism would deemphasize the war. Fernandez was "sick and tired of meetings where people who have known each other for a long while feel they have to lecture each other about racism, corporate atrocities, role of women, and other such topics. . . . For me, the war is the issue that has to be dealt with."[11] Tom Wells has concluded that, as a result of internal splits, by early 1970 the New Mobe was "critically ill, riddled by conflict and led by radicals with a tiny constituency."[12]

The Student Mobilization Committee was scarcely doing any better. In February 1970, attempts by radicals to break the SWP's control of the group and transform it into a multi-issue anti-imperialist organization, were successfully thwarted. Carol Lipman, SMC executive secretary explained that while it was important for the peace movement to link up with other struggles, it would be a big mistake "if we lost sight of the relationship that already exists. Immediate total withdrawal is not a white demand." Lipman argued that the SMC's slogan, "Self-Determination for Vietnam and Black America," was "rooted in . . . the reality of a common struggle by the Vietnamese and by the oppressed peoples inside the United States, which must be the basis for encouraging third world participation in the antiwar movement."[13] Radicals, led by the Progressive Labor rump of SDS, accused the SMC of being racist, and sometimes the ideological disagreements became physical.[14] At a May meeting of the SMC steering committee, between 50 and 60 SDS-PL members forced their way in. According to some reports, a "pitched battle" ensued, which resulted in serious injury to SMC activist John McCann.[15]

Within the Cleveland Area Peace Action Council (CAPAC), a radical minority reacted against the leadership of Jerry Gordon and attempted to push the organization in a multi-issue direction. At a meeting on May 21, 1970 the question of black participation in forthcoming peace protests was discussed. Cleo Malone, representing welfare groups, explained that "black people see their problems as being here at home and not in Southeast Asia." The executive committee's Joan Campbell suggested that the four blacks present form a caucus to "seek out other black leaders in the community and ask them how the antiwar movement can join with them to protest the killings" at Jackson State (ten days after the deaths at Kent State, police in Mississippi had opened fire on unarmed black students at Jackson State College, killing two and injuring twelve).[16] When the CAPAC decided to hold an Emergency Antiwar Conference in Cleveland in June, some members objected to its single-issue focus. Louise Peck, for example, complained that the conference was only being called around the war and thus excluded the demands of black people.[17] Ultimately, three members of the nine-person CAPAC executive committee (Dan Elliot, Joan Campbell, and Sidney Peck) resigned in order to form a group that would be "against not only the war, but also against racial and government oppression in the U.S."[18]

On May 22 the New Mobe's steering committee had, at the invitation of the Southern Christian Leadership Conference, convened in the civil rights group's Atlanta headquarters to signify unity between the struggles. Ralph Abernathy, who had succeeded the martyred King as SCLC president, attempted (largely unsuccessfully) to continue King's "campaign against the Vietnam War and his crusade on behalf of the poor." However, the organization, beset by internal divisions and weakened by the loss of its founder, quickly declined.[19] The New Mobe also joined SCLC in a march to commemorate those killed at Kent State and Jackson State. It was hoped that this would be a "first step" on the road to closer cooperation between the antiwar and civil rights movements.

In response to CAPAC's decision to hold a single-issue-oriented conference, the New Mobe's leaders agreed to call for an Emergency Action Conference. The conference, to be held in Milwaukee in late June, was for the purpose of "developing a unifying offensive in the face of the deepening interrelated crises of race, war, and the economy."[20] This seemed to suggest a basis for a "multi-issue alignment of black and antiwar forces."[21] Sidney Peck certainly felt that the possibilities for building a radical, interracial peace movement had never been better. He explained that "in discussions with SCLC persons, it became obvious that it was urgent for forces in the anti-war movement and the Black movement to move together in a much more serious form of cooperation." Peck believed that "the possibilities for a real breakthrough in terms of a more unified political relationship developing between white forces in the anti-war movement and forces in the Black community struggling against repression, racism and poverty, were becoming evident." However, the success of such a relationship clearly depended on "the degree to which the white anti-war movement would struggle with equal concern and energy on the issues of repression, racism and poverty."[22] As the National Welfare Rights Organization put it, "what we want to see is the peace movement's commitment to the poor."[23]

The two rival antiwar conferences held in June 1970 would be very different. The Emergency Action Conference would "express the organic unity of the anti-war movement, the Black movement, and the student strike movement" and focus its efforts on local grass-roots organizing rather than large national demonstrations. The aim of the Emergency National Conference, however, was to plan mass, legal, single-issue demonstrations against the Vietnam War. Indeed, it was "not intended to solve or even necessarily discuss all the problems of our crisis-ridden society."[24] The conferences would also produce two rival antiwar organizations.

The Emergency National Conference, hosted by the CAPAC, met in Cleveland June 19–20. In addition to receiving support from the SWP/YSA, the gathering was endorsed by the SMC and some local black groups, including Cleveland SCLC.[25] Around 1,500 delegates attended.[26] The New Mobe was, however, conspicuous by its absence. According to Abe Weisburd, a steering committee member from New York, this was because the conference organizers excluded the issues of racism and repression—"the entire text of their call says absolutely nothing about racism or black people—absolutely nothing."[27] Rather than attend the gathering to make the case for multi-issuism, the New Mobe leadership voted to boycott the conference.

The organizers of the Emergency National Conference may have advocated a single-issue antiwar movement and rejected calls to incorporate domestic policy concerns such as racism into their program, but they still courted nonwhite support. A pre-convention press release made this clear when it stated that "More than ever before for such a meeting, Third World organizations and individuals are endorsing and planning to attend the conference." The press release pointed out that many of the labor sponsors of the conference were black.[28]

Radicals, however, opposed the convention's single-issue orientation. An article in *New Left Notes* explained that "more and more people are seeing that in order to build an anti-war movement that can win, we must reject liberal politicians and union mis-leaders; that it is necessary to fight racism and male chauvinism and ally with working people, in order to fight against the war."[29] The attempts to persuade the convention of the merits of the multi-issue argument failed, and the National Peace Action Coalition (NPAC), which was founded at the Cleveland convention, was essentially an SWP-front group that would concentrate its energies on building legal, peaceful, demonstrations against the war.[30] As the NPAC's Bob Bresnaham explained, "we believe the single-issue approach of building the biggest coalition around the single demand of immediate and total withdrawal of all U.S. forces from Vietnam and through peaceful and legal mass actions is the best way to build the antiwar movement." When asked about relating the war to nonwhite peoples, he stated that NPAC was "trying to relate to the black community by getting together a group of black leaders who will draw up an appeal calling on black people to turn out."[31]

In many ways the Emergency Action Conference was a direct repudiation of the Cleveland approach to building an antiwar movement.[32] The conference, sponsored by SCLC, the New Mobe, and the NWRO, brought about 800 delegates to Milwaukee on June 26–27. The gathering was designed to "bring together persons active in the black community, the welfare rights struggle, trade unions, and the peace movement."[33] The Black Panther Party was unable to participate directly in the conference because of organizational commitments. Indeed, the BPP explained that its "primary concern" was not Vietnam, but the "question of national salvation and the genocide that is being committed against Black People right here in Babylon." The party did, however, offer its support to the Milwaukee gathering—"we endorse any organization that is against the barbaric and genocidal war that is being waged in Vietnam and Cambodia by the imperialist United States aggressors."[34] In general, the Milwaukee delegates felt that national mass antiwar actions were no longer relevant, and that a combination of civil disobedience and local-level decision making was a more attractive proposition.[35] The attempt to bring together diverse groups and peoples was successful, and a broad representation of interests was assembled. But this very diversity created problems.

Although socialist and veteran pacifist David McReynolds concluded that the conference represented a "good and necessary beginning . . . in the needed effort of creating a new coalition," he also outlined some of the difficulties this brought. While the range of participation had been broad, the "experience of working together or even meeting together was so limited that the first half of the conference was wasted in recriminations."[36] An example of intergroup tension came from Roberto Rios, a Chicano activist. He criticized the conference organizers for placing him last on the program, so that he spoke to a dwindling audience of 100 people. He also attacked the broader peace movement which, he argued, had "hurt us, not helped us. It has been geared mainly to white middle-class youth. I think all minorities feel the same about this."[37]

According to welfare rights activist George Wiley, the peace movement, or at least the portion of it represented at Milwaukee, had "endorsed an attitude of broadening their base on issues. This is to say that, rather than being a single-issue movement of 'End the War,' there was to be a realistic move to embody the goals of the poor and oppressed people of this country and show how the issues of the domestic war are directly related to ending the war in Asia."[38] But, the conference had failed to agree to a definitive action plan, so it arranged a series of regional meetings to discuss strategy over the summer. The eventual result, in September, was the formation of the National Coalition Against War, Racism and Repression (NCAWRR). The NCAWRR was dedicated to building a multi-issue peace movement. The group's leadership explained that it differed significantly from the NPAC "on the importance of bringing other issues into the antiwar movement," and, unlike its rival, it was prepared to advocate mass civil disobedience.

NCAWRR refused to endorse the NPAC-planned antiwar actions for October 31. One coalition member explained that "they felt very strongly against supporting actions not including the issues of war and racism." NCAWRR coordinator William Douthard stated that after traveling "from city to city talking with various black groups," he could report that they were "concerned about the sometimes overt racism and . . . plain old ignorant paternalism of those who have been in the antiwar movement." Douthard explained that if African Americans felt that "the actions planned and the issues we move out on are ones that bring anti-racism and anti-repression struggles on a partnership basis with the antiwar movement, then we will be on our way toward bringing movement people together in a united front."[39] The NCAWRR's fall agenda reflected this strategy—it included support of jailed Panthers and of welfare rights, multi-issue community organizing, and antiwar protests. Despite this, the organization came under attack for not doing enough. In January 1971 a nonwhite caucus claimed that "the reason Blacks, Chicanos, Puerto Ricans, Indians, and Asians have not responded to NCAWRR consistently lies not in our lack of political understanding against the war; we are strongly anti-war. The answer lies in the gap between word and deed in this 'coalition'." The caucus called for the group to give greater attention to racism and related issues.[40]

Other critics derided the NCAWRR as the "coalition against every-thing," and even some of its supporters were somewhat unenthusiastic. Sidney Peck, for example, had consistently argued for a multi-issue peace movement.[41] But he was critical of the NCAWRR, recalling that "it took on such a wide range of stuff that there was no clear focus". Doug Dowd explained how each constituent group pressed its own agenda, with the result that it became almost impossible to hold the coalition together.[42] Indeed, when looking at the NCAWRR one is reminded of some of the problems that the NCNP had faced in 1967—namely, the difficulty of establishing priorities in the midst of competing radical agendas, compounded by the fact that existing organizations often proved unwilling to compromise their goals in order to aid a new coali-tion that did not command strong loyalty.

Meanwhile, the radical remnants of SDS continued to accuse the NPAC of racism. At a December NPAC conference in Chicago, SDS argued that "to build a movement that ignores racism is racist—this racism is what divides the movement!"[43] The NPAC was not ignoring nonwhite people, however. Activist-entertainer Dick Gregory and Cairo, Illinois, civil rights leader Charles Koen had both been invited to address the conference. Moreover, in a keynote speech the black Chicago alder-man A. A. Rayner, Jr., told the delegates that peace efforts could have no relevancy "until you bring peace to the black and brown ghettos."[44] In response, a resolution was passed setting up a Third World Task Force to broaden antiwar activity and urged NPAC to show solidarity with the antiwar struggles of all third world groups.[45]

On January 8–10, 1971 a deeply divided NCAWRR met in Chicago. David Dellinger and Rennie Davis pushed for a program of massive civil disobedience in May, in an attempt to "stop the government." Other ac-tivists feared that such action would quickly escalate into violence. The January conference agreed only on a vague program for the spring, cen-tered on support for a symbolic "People's Peace Treaty." It was also agreed to hold rallies and nonviolent militant protests. By all accounts, it was a "real difficult meeting."[46] The coalition's commitment to a multi-issue approach remained strong, however. At the conference David McReynolds cogently explained that "our movement has become 'multi-issue' not as an artificial way of building a coalition; not because the white peace movement is afraid of being 'race-baited' . . . ; and not because the poor are so desperate for allies that they will settle for a coalition with white liberals and radicals in the peace movement, but because *not one of our interests can be resolved* without tackling a range of problems."[47] The following weekend, representatives of NCAWRR and NPAC met to consider uniting for a mass antiwar demonstration in the spring. The two sides were unable to decide on a date—NPAC had already set its sights on April 24, while NCAWRR preferred May 2—and the meeting failed to reach an agreement. Soon after, NCAWRR was renamed the People's Coalition for Peace and Justice (PCPJ).[48]

Once again it was President Nixon who managed to unite a fractious antiwar movement. The invasion of Laos in February 1971 and the specter of further escalation prompted the PCPJ to abandon its May 2 protest to join with NPAC on April 24.[49] Despite the decision to cooperate, NPAC refused to allow the PCPJ any organizational control over the demonstration. In addition to the jointly sponsored rally, the PCPJ decided to hold a "People's Lobby" in Washington during the period between April 24 and "May Day" (May 3). The lobbyists would debate federal government employees and demand an end to the war, the release of all political prisoners, and a guaranteed family income of $6,500. On April 24 an estimated 500,000 protesters gathered on the ellipse in Washington before marching to the Capitol. Some 200,000 demonstrators also gathered at Polo Field, San Francisco, in the biggest antiwar demonstration ever seen on the West Coast.[50]

Serious attempts had been made to attract African American support for the April 24 demonstrations. In January, NPAC leader Jerry Gordon had written to Roy Wilkins requesting NAACP endorsement of the spring antiwar actions. The NAACP had begun to speak out against the war the previous year and had also gone on record as opposing the Nixon administration. Indeed, at its June 1970 convention NAACP chairman Bishop Stephen Spottswood had launched what the *Guardian* termed a "stunningly brutal" attack on the federal government. Spottswood had declared that "this is the first time since 1920 that the national administration has made it a matter of calculated policy to work against the needs and aspirations of the largest minority of its citizens."[51] Despite these developments, Wilkins refused to give organizational support to the peace movement. Although he wrote to Gordon that "we, too, believe that the war ought to be brought to a rapid close and share your concern about its re-escalation," the NAACP executive director stated that the Association would be unable to officially endorse the antiwar actions. Wilkins explained that this was because the NAACP was concentrating on a membership drive and he feared that antiwar activities would prove a distraction.[52] Wilkins's decision did not, however, prevent NAACP participation in the April 24 rally, which was endorsed by Lonnie King, president of the Atlanta NAACP, Kate Moore of the NAACP national staff, and the Detroit NAACP, among others.[53]

The newly formed Third World Task Force (TWTF) had also been building nonwhite support for the antiwar actions. TWTF had been formed at an NPAC-sponsored conference, held in Chicago on December

2–4, 1970. According to NPAC records, "Third World people at the conference concluded from the discussion that what is needed to get our people in motion against the war is a vehicle that will be organized on a national basis." The TWTF set out to destroy the "distorting concept" that "the antiwar struggle here in America was solely a struggle geared, manned, and related to whites." The TWTF believed that "an independent, Black controlled, Black led antiwar movement" was imperative, and argued that African Americans had to organize antiwar activities based on their own needs and experiences.[54]

In Washington, D.C., on April 3, local black activists staged an independent antiwar demonstration in which about 500 mainly young African Americans participated. In Chicago, in a demonstration organized by the Martin Luther King Memorial Committee (a coalition of antiwar, civil rights, and trade union organizations), about 1,000 marched "against the war and in support of the NWRO demand for a guaranteed $6,500 annual income, end to draft, and release of political prisoners." It is interesting that TWTF was willing to participate in antiwar activities that stressed concerns other than Vietnam even though the NPAC itself held a single-issue perspective. As well as staging memorial events for Martin Luther King in early April—actions that encompassed antiwar, civil rights, and antipoverty concerns—TWTF set about building black support for April 24. They courted the support of local NAACP leaders, black members of Congress, and civil rights activists.[55]

The TWTF efforts appear to have been relatively successful. The Washington Area Peace Action Council newsletter explained that there was "significant representation" from the black community at the April 24 antiwar demonstration. It was estimated that 3,000 African and Asian Americans had joined a TWTF feeder march down Sixteenth Street to Pennsylvania Avenue, where they had linked up with the main demonstration.[56] *Guardian* reports stated that "several people in interviews . . . noted that there appeared to be more working people, black and white, than before."[57] This impression was shared by Nat Russell of the Tucson, Arizona, branch of the NAACP. He attended the demonstration and was impressed by the "large proportion of black faces he saw among those marching down Pennsylvania Avenue."[58]

The massive demonstration in San Francisco also included a large "third world" contingent. This did cause some problems—there were complaints from some nonwhite groups that white middle-class marchers were interested only in ending the war and not in the struggles against racism. There was also some disruption of the rally by nonwhites. At one point Abe Tupia, president of the Mexican-American Political Association, called for Raza (Mexican) and Native Americans to storm the stage. About a dozen did, and expressed anger at the nonmilitant nature of the rally and at being told when and for how long to speak. Tupia declared "we've had enough of having limits placed on us by our white oppressors."[59]

The People's Lobby, which took place in Washington in the week following April 24, staged pray-ins, enacted guerrilla theater on Capitol Hill, nonviolently picketed the Selective Service System, and saw welfare and civil rights groups stage a rally in the Department of Health Education and Welfare auditorium. Then the May Day protests began. Things got "really wild" as police moved to prevent demonstrators from closing the city down. More than 7,000 were arrested on May 3—crammed into city jails and a detention camp that had been constructed on a football field near RFK stadium. Local African Americans brought the mostly white prisoners soup and sandwiches. As one civil rights veteran explained, "we gave them food so that they can put their bodies on the line and disrupt the government . . . anything that does that can help our people."[60] Brad Lyttle, a veteran nonviolent activist, recalled that Washington's black community was amazed by May Day—"I never saw black people so friendly. . . . Everywhere you went, as soon as they found out you were associated with the peace movement, they were just *effusive* in their warmth. They thought it was tremendous . . . here The Man was getting it."[61] Support came from some thirty local black leaders including Mary Treadwell (program director, Youth Pride, Inc.) and John Gibson (chairman, Washington Urban League). The *Guardian* reported that, at a press conference on May 3, Treadwell had linked the antiwar and civil rights protests—"Mrs. Treadwell stated that the militant antiwar demonstrators were being subjected to the same beatings, jailings, and repression meted out to black people when demonstrating for human rights." Treadwell then addressed the limited support that black people had hitherto given to the peace movement—"the antiwar movement had to understand . . . that while black people were aware that the U.S. government was committing genocide against the people of Indochina, as well as against the black people at home, their need to fight everyday for survival prevented their giving undivided attention to ending the war." Treadwell explained that African Americans were supporting the peace movement in increasing numbers, and made clear that much of this support was due to its "multi-issue" nature—"black people . . . were, she said, finding ways to ally themselves more closely to the antiwar movement, and they welcomed the fact that the antiwar forces had moved into active support of the black people's struggles against repression."[62]

Over the next eighteen months a pattern emerged of antiwar protests that involved a visible yet still small black element—often independently organized. But many African Americans remained skeptical of whites' commitment to building an interracial movement that would speak effectively to their concerns, and internal peace movement fissures continued to stymie efforts to construct a broad-based leftist political force. Following the May Day protests, for example, the PCPJ held another conference in Milwaukee. It was agreed to "consult more closely in future with the local coalition in Washington, D.C., so that relations between national demonstrators and the black community in D.C. would be even better than during the Mayday actions." However, the PCPJ's decision to continue to work with the NPAC caused worry among some black and poor supporters, who were concerned that "their needs and interests would be sold out in the eagerness for unity with the single-issue NPAC." This concern was articulated succinctly by Mary Saroka, an antipoverty organizer from Milwaukee, who warned that "if you continue to patronize the poor in national conferences, the poor will set you flat on your intellectual middle-class asses, and the poor will say to hell with your coalition."[63]

The antiwar protests that took place during the late spring and early summer of 1972 provide more evidence of the peace movement's limited success at attracting black participation. In June a group of prominent black Washington politicians, including D.C. congressional delegate Walter Fauntroy and school board chairman Marion Barry, denounced the peace movement as "racist" and demanded that a planned "Ring Around the Capitol" demonstration be canceled. In a statement released on June 16 they "charged that the peace movement has few black leaders, does not emphasize that funds spent in Vietnam should be used for programs in black ghettoes and fails to support black anti-war congressmen."[64] They demanded that antiwar leaders attend a meeting to discuss what the peace movement could do to help black Washingtonians. Peace activists Rennie Davis, David Dellinger, and Sidney Peck met with Marion Barry and other signers of the statement at All Souls Unitarian Church, but the gathering achieved nothing of note. Jerry Gordon was barred from the meeting for refusing to declare publicly that the peace movement was racist, while Walter Fauntroy declined to attend. Indeed, the SCLC veteran disavowed the statement and claimed to have signed it unseen on the advice of Marion Barry.[65] It has been suggested that the "Fauntroy 60" (as the statement's signers were dubbed) acted out of political expediency in an attempt to "keep people quiet . . . and off the streets in exchange for votes in Congress for home rule for D.C."[66] Whatever the motivations, the charges did have a ring of truth to them and, if nothing else, the episode provides further illustration of the often fraught nature of the peace movement's relationship with black America.

African Americans had many reasons to oppose the war, but far fewer reasons to join with the white-dominated peace movement. The numerous antiwar coalitions, even those that adopted a multi-issue perspective, proved to be good on rhetoric but poor on action when it came to black issues. One of the few white antiwar groups that backed up its words with actions—that, in the words of Mary Treadwell, gave "active support" to "black peoples' struggles against repression," was the Vietnam Veterans Against the War (VVAW).[67]

VVAW was formed in June 1967 by twenty-five-year-old Jan Barry, who had dropped out of West Point in 1965 to criticize a war that "made no sense whatsoever," and five other veterans. Although relatively small— the organization claimed 8,000 active members in 1972—VVAW came to have a powerful impact on the American psyche, and it evolved into one of the most outspoken antiwar groups. The veterans' experiences in Vietnam gave them unique credibility, and they were able to convince some of their fellow peace protesters to reach out to soldiers rather than berate them. VVAW was also prepared to engage in acts of civil disobedience, which often led to arrest and trial. Increasingly, the organization became decentralized, and focused on local concerns.[68] One of the most famous actions carried out by the group was the Winter Soldier Investigation, which was held at a Howard Johnson Motor Lodge in Detroit. The hearings, which took place between January 31 and February 3, 1971, examined American war crimes in Vietnam and revealed the often-chilling atrocities that were being committed by the U.S. military.[69]

Like numerous other peace groups, VVAW grappled with race and the links between racism and the Vietnam War. As early as August 1970, VVAW had attempted to win the support of black veterans when it sponsored a vigil at Fort Pierce, Florida, to protest the refusal of an all-white cemetery to bury a black soldier killed in Vietnam.[70] Nevertheless, VVAW membership was overwhelmingly white—the Black Panther Party proved a more popular destination among black veterans, and some African Americans believed the VVAW was paying inadequate attention to racial issues.[71] At the Winter Soldier hearings one black veteran, dressed in a black sweater and wearing sunglasses, told a group of whites that the solitary session dedicated to discussing racism was insufficient. He declared "that's how come you ain't got no black people behind you, because you forget about racism, man. . . . The brothers look at that and they say, 'Why? Why I wanna go down there and get involved in this shit? It ain't for me.'"[72] Perhaps in response to such criticism, the VVAW increasingly linked Vietnam with domestic racism. The organization ultimately developed a multi-issue critique of the war, arguing for a change to the "domestic social, political and economic institutions that have caused and permitted the continuance of the war."[73] Moreover, VVAW became one of the few peace groups to offer tangible support to the

African American freedom struggle. In the summer of 1971 the group began to give "aid and comfort" to the black community of Cairo, Illinois.

Situated at the southern tip of Illinois, at the confluence of the Mississippi and Ohio rivers, the city of Cairo (which had served as a major Union base during the Civil War) had once seemed destined for greatness as a trading and commercial center. But, in the words of one journalist, it was a place where "the wildest of dreams, the limitless possibilities of this land mixed with the bitterest disappointments, the hardest truths."[74] Early visitors to Cairo noted the tendency of its citizens to think in grandiose ways. The Frenchman Jules Rouby wrote in the mid-nineteenth century that "this tiny village gives itself anticipatory airs of a great city . . . it aspires to become some day a giant colossal center of progress, the key of all the commerce of the South, West and Northwest." This was a vision that would remain unfulfilled. Cairo's population reached 15,000 in 1920 but declined thereafter, as one by one the local industries—river freight, cottonseed oil, hardwood manufacturing, and finally gambling and prostitution—folded.[75] By 1960 the population of Cairo was 9,348 and 39 percent black.[76] Almost half the city's residents lived on incomes less than $3,000 a year, and the black unemployment rate of 20 percent was twice that of whites.[77] At the end of the 1960s, to some observers, Charles Dickens's description of the city as "a grave, uncheered by any gleam of promise" seemed appropriate.[78]

Although located in a northern state, Cairo was and is very much a part of the South. The city's Chamber of Commerce waxed lyrical over the city's "Southern-ness," describing it as a community "where catfish still sizzle in frying pans and canebrakes cluster in the river, where dignified old Southern mansions hear the swish of sternwheelers."[79] Culturally and politically Cairo had more in common with Jackson, Mississippi, than Chicago, Illinois, and this was reflected nowhere better than in the racial problems that characterized the city. As black activist Cordell McGoy explained, "the attitudes from the South is here, the mentality of a superiority race, the lack of empowerment of the black community."[80]

In the nineteenth century Cairo had formed part of the underground railroad—and the dockside cellars where, according to local legend, fugitive slaves were hidden, remain. The American novelist Mark Twain celebrated Cairo's association with freedom in *Huckleberry Finn*, when he had Jim excitedly shout—"We's safe, Huck, we's safe. Jump up and crack yo' heels! Dat's de good ole Cairo at las."[81] In the late 1960s Cairo once again became a powerful symbol—this time not of freedom but of racial oppression and the struggle to overcome injustice.

African American progress in Cairo had been slow since the founding of the local NAACP chapter in 1918.[82] There had been some successes—such as gaining equal pay for black teachers and the desegregation of the public schools, but white racism was pervasive. In 1963, for example, the city closed the swimming pool rather than accept integration, and blacks were not welcome in many of the white-owned downtown restaurants. The majority of the city's black population lived either in Pyramid Court, a sprawling public housing project, or in decrepit frame houses unfit for human habitation. Many local stores were reluctant to hire black employees, as were the few factories that had been encouraged to move to Cairo, and African Americans were denied political power by the city's steadfast refusal to introduce an aldermanic form of government.[83] Indeed, the city council was controlled by elderly whites (with an average age of 66), many of whom were wealthy. The city was, in the words of local NAACP president Preston Ewing, Jr., in the hands of "decadent white racists."[84] African Americans remained second class citizens in Cairo, untouched by many of the civil rights gains of the 1960s. As Cairo activist Hattie Kendrick explained to one reporter, the Civil Rights Act "may be on its way, but it hasn't gotten here yet!"[85]

There was, though, a history of civil rights activism in Cairo. In the summer of 1962, for example, SNCC had engaged in a campaign in the city after racial problems had been brought to its attention by two incidents. In early spring, four SNCC workers had been denied service in a local restaurant. Then, on June 22, one of the organization's field secretaries was the victim of a knife attack. Under the auspices of the Cairo Nonviolent Freedom Committee (and its sixteen-year-old leader Charles Koen), activists challenged segregation at the town's restaurants, swimming pool, and bowling alley. In return they suffered brutal beatings and more than forty arrests.[86] SNCC's grass-roots work left a legacy of black activism and leadership in Cairo that would be drawn upon in later years.

On July 15, 1967, Robert L. Hunt, a nineteen-year-old black soldier, was found hanged in the Cairo police station. The authorities claimed that he had committed suicide, but blacks reacted with skepticism. Their suspicions were fueled by the secretive actions of the police in the immediate aftermath of Hunt's death.[87] In response, the African American community staged a series of demonstrations. Three white-owned stores were firebombed and the National Guard was called in—for three days surrounding Pyramid Court. That same month the white community reacted by forming a vigilante group, the Committee of Ten Million, led by Alexander County State's Attorney Peyton Berbling, for the purpose of "protecting our families, our homes, and our property." Nicknamed the "White Hats" after the plastic civil defense helmets they wore, they patrolled the streets with rifles in radio-equipped cars. Many of the 500 or so members were designated deputy sheriffs or deputy coroners. The group was eventually forced to disband by the state government in the summer of 1969, and it reorganized as the United Citizens for Community Action, which was affiliated with the United Citizens' Council of America.

Racial tensions in Cairo were inflamed by a number of incidents that occurred during 1968 and 1969. In January 1968, Larry Potts, pastor of Cairo Baptist Church, clubbed to death a seventy-three-year-old black man whom he accused of trying to rape his wife. A coroner's jury cleared Potts and no trial was held. In June the city decided to discontinue Little League baseball rather than integrate St. Mary's Park. In January 1969, armed, white vigilantes threatened blacks attending a high school basketball game. Then, on March 31, shots were fired at the car of black leader Charles Koen (now a minister). This was followed by a 2½ hour gun battle, with heavy shooting into Pyramid Court—the first of more than 150 similar battles that occurred over the next two years. Cairo's embattled black community responded in April 1969 by forming the United Front—a coalition of civil rights groups, including the local NAACP—under Koen's leadership. The United Front demanded that blacks be hired in downtown stores and that the city government be reformed to give African Americans political power. On April 7 it launched an economic boycott of white-owned stores in Cairo that would continue until 1973.[88]

It was into this increasingly polarized and violent situation, where militant black protest was countered by an odious amalgam of white violence, institutional racism, and political impotence that VVAW arrived in the summer of 1971. The VVAW leadership had first been made aware of the Cairo situation by their Arkansas coordinator Sonny Keys, during a March 1971 steering committee meeting. The following month, VVAW held Operation Dewey Canyon III, a week-long protest in Washington that culminated in 700 veterans throwing their medals over a wire fence that had been erected around the Capitol.[89] During the course of the week, Bobby Morgan, a United Front representative, told many VVAW members about the Cairo protests and the help that was needed; he hoped that the veterans would bring much needed publicity and attention to the Cairo struggle. At a meeting of the VVAW steering committee that in New York City in May, the decision was made to become involved with Cairo at a national and local level.

The result was Lifeline to Cairo—a project headed by executive committee member Scott Moore, Al Hubbard (VVAW's most prominent African American, a veteran of both Korea and Vietnam who had joined the organization in the fall of 1969), and Philadelphia coordinator Jon Birch.[90] Moore explained that Cairo was considered important to the VVAW because "In many ways the black people of Cairo are suffering the same indignities as the Vietnamese people. They are being economically exploited, socially ostracized, and politically denied a say in their destiny. Like the Vietnamese they have finally united against that power structure that has suppressed them and are fighting it." Moore believed that the "racism which we saw in Vietnam and which many of us agree is one of the reasons for war crimes, exists in Cairo, Illinois . . . the government of this country has justified this war by saying that we are fighting for freedom and equality and self-determination [for] the Vietnamese and yet here in our own country people are denied that right and are involved in a struggle to obtain that right; their struggle is our struggle."[91] After placing Cairo within this multi-issue framework, Moore addressed the peace movement's lack of legitimacy regarding its relationship with the black freedom struggle. He acknowledged that the peace movement "has never been able to identify very effectively with the Third World movement because they have not really dealt seriously with the struggle; there has been a lot of liberal talk but no action." Cairo provided a good opportunity to rectify this. Moore argued that the black community was "watching Cairo . . . on a national level very closely. If VVAW relates in a concrete manner to Cairo, this will bring us closer together in solidarity. It will also make easier working and organizing conditions on the local level."

The decision to launch the Cairo project was not universally popular within the organization. In July, for example, there was a "complex reaction" to the Cairo project within the Northern New England VVAW. While a majority agreed that VVAW should broaden its concerns from withdrawal from Vietnam to include wider community issues, many members felt that "being . . . 1200 miles from Cairo and recognizing the problems in our own black community" it would be better to "relate to Cairo through the Black United Front of Boston."[92] They thus argued that Cairo was something that should be dealt with not by the organization at a national level but by individual chapters at their own discretion. The national leadership disagreed, explaining that VVAW aid to Cairo should be a national issue because "what is being done in Cairo is the same as that which is being done in Vietnam and we are against that kind of thing happening."[93] Localized hostility toward Lifeline to Cairo continued to be expressed, however. In the summer of 1971, Scott Moore spent a month traveling across America, meeting chapter coordinators and speaking to members in an effort to assess the state of his organization. He discovered that Cairo "was not received enthusiastically by the coordinators" that he talked to—"they felt it was viable but had their own problems."[94] Despite these doubts, the project continued.

In New York, on August 10, 1971, the first of many VVAW convoys traveled to Cairo. The large trucks carrying food, clothes, and medical supplies were welcomed by a grateful black community who "made their expression of thanks for the efforts of the vets."[95] Brooklyn-born Al Hubbard declared that the episode was one of his organization's "crowning moments."[96] On August 14, three veterans from Harlem, Minneola, and Buffalo traveled to Cairo to work there for several days.[97] Another convoy, organized by the Western Missouri-Kansas VVAW, traveled to Cairo on October 2 with $400 in donated food and clothing, and the veterans remained overnight having "intense raps with blacks who have been in the struggle in that community since its beginnings." As well as engendering a sense of brotherhood and having an educational impact on the veterans, valuable publicity for the United Front was generated.[98] On October 23 the Lawrence, Kansas, chapter of VVAW led another convoy to Cairo. Dressed in "camouflage, fatigue and field jackets," the seven women and twelve men traveled the 419 miles to Cairo, where they delivered $500 in food and $90 in cash that had been raised in a dormitory fast at Ottawa University's Peace Center. The veterans, led by Byron Edmonton, temporary president of the Lawrence chapter, attended a United Front rally and religious service at the St. Columba church. There, they joined in singing "I'm Pressin' On," a "hand-clasping gospel song," contributed to a United Front collection; and heard Preston Ewing, Jr., demand a share of what little Cairo had to offer—before unloading the supplies. They were then treated to a covered-dish dinner prepared by local black women.[99]

Many other convoys were organized by VVAW and, while whites occasionally shot at them, they usually received a warm reception from Cairo's black community.[100] Wayne Pycior, who traveled with a relief convoy in the winter of 1972, recalled how, after they pulled up outside the United Front headquarters at St. Columba church, a "very old black brother came over to the car and clasped my hand. . . . He was near tears. Brokenly, he said, 'Thank you, brother. Thank you for doing this . . . this is wonderful.'"[101]

Sometimes, though, tensions between the white veterans and local blacks emerged. In May 1972 a convoy left Chicago to celebrate the third anniversary of the United Front. VVAW's Jeff Hillier recalled that there were "smiling faces and high expectations, in general lots of happy people eager to head on down to Cairo." After leaving Chicago with a "ten car caravan loaded up with food . . . the good mood stays with us on the way down and the remembrance of the warm welcome and good vibes on the last trip serve to heighten our own eagerness." On arrival in Cairo, however, there was no one to meet them and the veterans were left uninformed about the anniversary activities. Hillier explained that "People milled around, the heat built up and our good mood started to vanish. The feeling started changing into one of a real let-down. No warm greetings from the Black community this time, in fact, their attitude seemed one of disinterest and mistrust. It almost seemed that somehow they didn't even want the food or appreciate the fact that we had come a long way and now were being pushed to the side." Indeed, "By the time the services started we were all very tired and disillusioned so the decision was made to split." Hillier wondered if this sense of let-down was due to VVAW "ego-tripping," before concluding that "whatever the causes, this trip seemed cold and unwelcomed and cast a dark shadow over the good vibes and friendship of the last one."[102]

Charles Koen responded to these concerns, apologizing for any incident which had led to the veterans feeling unappreciated. The civil rights leader made clear his indebtedness to the veterans and pointed out that, in contrast to many other groups, VVAW had backed up its words with deeds. Koen declared that "the United Front and the struggling people of Cairo . . . recognize the consistent support we have received from VVAW. Where other organizations have merely voiced support for the struggle in Cairo, the VVAW from all over the country have supported us materially with food and clothing and bodily support on a continuous basis." The civil rights leader expressed his hope that "this misunderstanding will soon be forgotten and our organizations can continue to struggle for the liberation for all Black, Poor and other Oppressed Peoples in this country."[103] This deterioration in relations proved temporary, and did not prevent further convoys. In November 1972 VVAW scheduled a supply run to coincide with the Thanksgiving holiday. In addition to delivering food, clothes, and medical equipment, the veterans participated in workshops, a march through downtown Cairo, a community dinner, and a rally. VVAW was also presented with a "Frederick Douglass Liberation Award" by the United Front.[104]

VVAW not only developed and articulated an analysis of the Vietnam War that placed the conflict within a radical multi-issue perspective, but it was one of the few peace groups that acted in concrete ways that were congruent with its intellectual and rhetorical stance.[105] Even so, the organization was not immune to the charge of "failure" regarding its relations with the nonwhite movement. At a meeting of the national steering committee, held in Chicago, January 4–8, 1973, the Third World Caucus of VVAW made a report. The caucus, which had been created to build support for the group among nonwhites, stated that "One of the biggest problems in VVAW is that, as yet, our organization has had little success in relation to third world people in general, and third world veterans in particular." The caucus felt that "one of the principal reasons for this has been that most of our efforts have been directed at relating to third world people through our eyes instead of theirs."[106]

This judgment appears harsh when one considers that Lifeline to Cairo was not the only VVAW project designed to help nonwhites. VVAW also offered support to the American Indian Movement (AIM), the protests at Wounded Knee, and the defense of Gary Lawton, a black activist from Riverside, California, who had been indicted for the shooting of two white police officers in April 1971.[107] Despite these efforts, VVAW membership remained overwhelmingly white. Black membership was concentrated in the Harlem chapter, and the slightly larger Chicano membership, estimated at 2 percent of the total, was centered in Texas and California, due largely to the fact that VVAW sponsored a number of Chicano-oriented events there. Andrew E. Hunt, VVAW's historian, has concluded that although the organization never became heterogeneous, most of its members "rejected the insensitivity of many of their New Left predecessors" regarding women, gays, and nonwhites.[108] Despite its problems in relating to the nonwhite movement, VVAW was one of the few radical white groups of the 1960s that was prepared to back up its words with deeds. Lifeline to Cairo was an all-too-rare example of white antiwar radicals and black freedom fighters working together closely.

Between 1970 and 1972 the peace movement had been torn apart by factional infighting centered on disagreements over the merits of a single-issue versus a multi-issue perspective. Two new coalitions were created, and both attempted to attract black support. Apart from a few successes, such as the April 24, 1971 demonstration in Washington, black participation in antiwar protests remained visible but relatively limited. Single-issue antiwar organizations often lacked direct relevance to the black struggle, while multi-issue coalitions faced the intractable problem of trying to accommodate various groups with competing agendas. The peace movement as a whole experienced fraught relations with the black movement. Even VVAW, one of the few peace groups that backed up its strident rhetorical support for black America with tangible action, encountered problems relating to the African American freedom struggle. The collapse of SNCC and the precipitous decline of CORE and SCLC greatly complicated efforts at building an interracial peace movement. The NAACP and NUL might have been able to facilitate such an endeavor, but they remained reluctant to devote their energies to peace activity despite their opposition to the war. The fragmentation of the civil rights movement meant that the peace movement was often forced to negotiate with local leaders of questionable standing. It also meant that an organizational infrastructure capable of mobilizing significant numbers of African Americans no longer existed. It is, then, hardly surprising that a genuine peace and freedom coalition was not established and that even cooperation between the two movements was relatively rare.

Conclusion

Although every major civil rights group would come to oppose the war in Vietnam, they did so at different times and for different reasons. Understanding the reasons behind the contrasting response of black groups to the war helps to sharpen our perceptions of the civil rights movement itself. When, in January 1966, SNCC bitterly denounced the war in Vietnam, they were not merely subscribing to leftist dogma.[1] When Roy Wilkins asked whether it was wrong for people to be patriotic and to support American troops fighting abroad, he was not simply towing the Johnson Administration line.[2] The way in which civil rights groups responded to the war in Vietnam was shaped by a number of factors. Generational considerations had a part to play, with younger activists more likely to dismiss the pragmatic rationale for not opposing the war, for example. However, civil rights workers' experiences in the black freedom struggle had a fundamental impact on how they viewed the conflict in Southeast Asia. It should come as no surprise that SNCC, the group most dedicated to grassroots organizing, was the first to publicly oppose the war in Vietnam.

Activists on the front lines of the black freedom struggle in the early 1960s learned some sobering lessons about white America. They realized that the federal government was not prepared to protect their lives. They discovered that the national media and white northerners took more notice when a white rather than a black activist was killed. They also learned that liberal Democrats were prepared to compromise their principles (and their black allies) for political expediency. The experiences of grassroots activists in the small towns and rural communities of the Deep South helped to transform them into radicals, made them much more critical of the United States, and explains why they were willing to oppose the war in Vietnam. James Forman understood that "five years of struggle had radically changed . . . many people, changed them from idealistic reformers to full-time revolutionaries."[3] The summer of 1964 stands as a turning point in the history of the civil rights movement. The rejection of the Freedom Democratic Party at Atlantic City, coming as it did at the end of a tumultuous summer of activism in Mississippi, marked the point of no return for the activist wing of the movement. The "coalition strategy" of working in partnership with white progressives and the national Democratic Party was discredited in the eyes of many frontline civil rights workers. SNCC's Courtland Cox explained that "from that day on we felt that playing by the rules was not enough, that the power was aligned to maintain itself."[4]

The organizing experience of civil rights activists helped shape their reaction to the war in Vietnam. SNCC's own 1966 antiwar statement contained a reference to "lessons learned" while working for black freedom.[5] Howard Zinn has argued that antiwar sentiment among black civil rights activists in the South came "from the cotton fields, the country roads, the jails of the Deep South, where these young people have spent much of their time." In other words, antiwar sentiment flowed, at least in part, from the organizing experience itself. As Bob Moses put it, "our criticism of Vietnam policy does not come from what we know of Vietnam, but from what we know of America."[6]

The "organizing experience" paradigm not only helps us understand why groups like SNCC, CORE and the MFDP came to oppose the war in Vietnam, it also explains why some in the civil rights movement were reluctant to take a stand. Until 1969, moderate groups like the NAACP and the Urban League refused to take a position on the war, believing that civil rights should remain the sole focus of the black movement. Roy Wilkins and Whitney Young joined Bayard Rustin and A. Philip Randolph in arguing that the future of the black freedom struggle lay in a realignment of the Democratic Party.[7] This "coalition strategy" was best articulated by Rustin, who maintained that an alliance of organized labor, the civil rights movement, religious groups, and white liberals could reshape American politics.[8] Such a strategy made forthright criticism of the Vietnam War impossible.

The unwillingness of the moderate wing of the black movement to oppose the war in Vietnam was the result of a combination of factors. As well as the practical considerations of the coalition strategy, which made it impolitic to criticize a major policy of an important ally, the moderates' response was also shaped by anti-communism, Cold War ideology, and the close personal relationship Roy Wilkins and Whitney Young enjoyed with President Johnson. However, the failure to oppose the war was also influenced by organizing experience.

While the civil rights experiences of SNCC and CORE activists tended to make them disillusioned with white liberals and skeptical of the federal government, for moderates like Roy Wilkins and Whitney Young the opposite was true. The passage of the 1964 Civil Rights Act and 1965 Voting Rights Act, which dismantled the legal framework for segregation and facilitated black enfranchisement, confirmed their belief in the fundamental goodness of America. Likewise, the progressive rhetoric and liberal activism of Lyndon Johnson's Great Society cemented their belief that coalition with liberal Democrats was the only realistic means to secure further gains. The goal of moderates like Wilkins had always been the full participation of black Americans in all areas of national life. With the federal government, for the first time in the nation's history, seemingly dedicated to achieving this goal there was simply nothing to gain, and a good deal to lose, by opposing the war in Vietnam. Indeed, with the vast majority of American blacks supportive of Lyndon Johnson's presidency in the mid-1960s (due to its progressive civil rights and welfare policies) black leaders who attacked LBJ over the war risked alienating their followers.

Acknowledging that the response of civil rights groups to Vietnam was shaped by their differing experiences in the movement is important. It not only adds to our understanding of how and why groups such as SNCC became more radical as the 1960s progressed, but also helps rescue the likes of Whitney Young and Roy Wilkins from a historiography that has too often dismissed black leaders who refused to oppose the war as conservative sell-outs.

Many civil rights historians have viewed the war as a major contributor to the fracture and ultimate collapse of the movement in the late 1960s. Robert Cook, for example, has argued that "the intensification of U.S. military intervention in Southeast Asia . . . contributed further to the decline of the civil rights coalition."[9] However, Vietnam is more useful when used as a lens through which existing movement tensions and divisions are viewed. The constituent elements of the civil rights movement reacted to the war in ways that illustrate their differing conceptions of "freedom," "democracy," and "equality," as well as their distinct experience of the freedom movement itself. The movement had always been a shaky coalition at best: only unity over immediate goals had glued it together. With the primary objectives of the freedom struggle achieved by August 1965, however, that glue would not have been strong enough to prevent fragmentation irrespective of developments in Southeast Asia. Disagreement within the black movement over tactics, aims, nonviolence, the role of whites, and interpretations of American society existed before anyone had heard of napalm or Ho Chi Minh. SNCC and CORE had been heading in the direction of Black Power before LBJ ordered ground troops to Southeast Asia. The range of responses by black leaders and civil rights groups to Vietnam highlighted and sharpened *existing* divisions. Although it did not help matters, the civil rights movement would have disintegrated as a coherent national force by 1968–69 even if there had been no American war in Vietnam.

Despite the prominent opposition to the war by Martin Luther King,

Malcolm X, Muhammed Ali, James Farmer, Floyd McKissick, and Stokely Carmichael; despite African Americans being the "most dovish social group"; and despite the numerous reasons for black Americans to oppose the war in Vietnam, black participation in antiwar activities remained relatively limited throughout the Vietnam era.[10] There were a number of reasons for this. At a basic level, blacks were more interested in focusing their energies on civil rights than opposing the war. Additionally, traveling to Washington or New York to protest the war in a large demonstration was an inherently middle-class activity, requiring money and time off work (although this does not explain the lack of middle-class or local blacks at such gatherings). However, Black Power and the peace movement's failure to relate to African Americans were the most important reasons for the absence of widespread black participation in antiwar agitation.

Black Power was at best a double-edged sword for the peace movement. While black radicals shared the New Left's critique of liberalism and its radical analysis of the war, Black Nationalism complicated the task of constructing an interracial antiwar movement. Black Power brought with it heightened sensitivity to race, cultural distinctiveness, and hostility toward interracial cooperation, all of which made a meaningful peace and freedom coalition less likely. Moreover, the anti-Semitism of some black militants further exacerbated tensions with white antiwar activists, significant numbers of whom were Jewish. At the same time, Black Power presented some white civil rights activists with a handy excuse for moving their attention onto the war. The 1967 convention of the National Conference for New Politics, which imploded amid divisive debates over race, shows how Black Power made attempts at constructing broad-based multiracial alliances treacherous.

Moreover, many Black Power militants became fierce critics of the New Left, which they often viewed with skepticism. Robert F. Williams, for example, claimed that the "carpetbagger fabians" of the New Left were "not conduits of revolution but the Trojan Horse of counter-revolution."[11] Some black radicals feared that the predominantly white peace movement was intent on coopting the black movement, and this fear motivated the formation of black antiwar groups. The National Black Antiwar Antidraft Union, for example, was established "because we desperately needed a secure black base for anti-war activity to eliminate the possibilities of being absorbed by the white anti-war movement."[12]

Association with the counterculture and political factionalism were other reasons why blacks often treated the white peace movement with disdain. The former led many African American activists to doubt the seriousness of their white comrades. At a January 1971 antiwar conference, for example, black participants warned against staging "another series of middle class—white-nude-be in or psychedelic 'cultural experiences'." Those "suffering from hunger, poverty, racism . . . exploitation and police terror," they explained, did not take such actions, seriously.[13] Political factionalism also contributed to the failure of the antiwar movement to attract significant African American support. Throughout the Vietnam era the peace movement was bedeviled by leftist infighting that sapped its morale, drained its energies, and weakened its effectiveness. It also alienated black antiwar activists and discouraged them from cooperating on an organizational level with the peace movement.[14]

Often the political infighting was related to the debate within the antiwar movement over multi-issuism. The arguments over whether the peace movement should concentrate exclusively on ending the conflict in Southeast Asia, or focus on domestic concerns as well, had divided antiwar activists from the time of the earliest protests against America's military involvement in Vietnam. Americans, of course, opposed the war for a variety of reasons. Some were simply upset by what they saw as America's unjust actions and demanded deescalation and negotiations, others were critical of the Cold War in general or even viewed the war as a symptom of a fundamentally corrupt American state. Antiwar activists also had different views on the purpose of the peace movement. Some thought that it should focus on ending the war, while others viewed it as a vehicle for reforming or renewing American society.

The debate over multi-issuism did not just affect the black movement because of the resulting factionalism, it became a key issue around which radical black involvement with the antiwar movement was contested. Black organizations opposed the war not simply because they thought it was wrong, but because they understood that the conflict was linked to domestic racism and repression. When peace groups sought to focus solely on the war in an attempt to nurture broader support amongst white America, rather than build a coalition that also incorporated domestic concerns, it offended black radicals who accused the movement not simply of ignoring the relationship between the war and racism, but of being racist itself. As Gwendolyn Patton explained, "if the Peace Movement does not struggle for decent housing, education, and employment then it may be an anti-imperialist movement, but racist to its core."[15] Many blacks who joined the antiwar movement became "frustrated because the issue of racism was always dropped."[16]

Even peace groups that did adopt a multi-issue perspective often did little more than link the struggles rhetorically. The VVAW was one of the few antiwar organizations that combined a militant critique of the war and American society with tangible action in support of both the peace and freedom movements.[17] Ultimately, the antiwar movement's failure to embrace an analysis of the war that emphasized racism, and to adopt a genuinely multi-issue orientation, resulted in the divergence of black and white antiwar protest and the formation of black antiwar organizations.

It is perhaps unfair to be so hard on white antiwar activists for their failure to construct a broad-based multi-issue movement. The majority of white peace activists were concerned primarily with the war in Vietnam; and while many of them supported civil rights, welfare rights and other progressive policies, they were moved to action by the war in Southeast Asia. The PCPJ's Brad Lyttle explained this in August 1971, when he suggested that "it may be that the [PCPJ] can't be any more than an anti-war group. Most of the people in leadership positions in our coalition *do* feel more concerned about the war than any other issue, regardless of how right or rational this feeling may be."[18]

Moreover, the creation of a "beloved community"-style interracial peace movement after 1965 was never very likely. Activists who tried to construct one were swimming against the tide of history. Given the growth of Black Power, the rage and disillusionment generated by the urban riots, and the New Left's embrace of revolutionary rhetoric and militancy, it is perhaps surprising that the antiwar and civil rights movements were able to work together as closely as they did.[19]

The "dump Johnson" effort has not been explored in any great detail here, not least because several excellent studies already exist.[20] But a case can be made for considering the presidential campaigns of Eugene McCarthy and Robert Kennedy as examples of the coalescing of the civil rights and peace movements—particularly in the case of Kennedy, who, unlike his Minnesotan rival, attracted a good deal of black support.[21] Both candidates also opposed Lyndon Johnson's policies in Vietnam, although neither supported an unconditional American withdrawal. While Kennedy and McCarthy received support from prominent liberal Vietnam dissenters such as Allard Lowenstein, John Kenneth Galbraith, and Arthur Schlesinger, Jr., and from activists within moderate peace groups like CALCAV, the "dump Johnson" effort was not supported by the major radical groups that dominated the antiwar movement until 1969.[22] Tom Hayden, for example, had referred to RFK as a "little fascist" just days before the senator's murder.[23] Despite the arguments of neorevisionists like Ronald Radosh and many a conservative commentator, the Democratic Party was never infiltrated to any meaningful degree by the peace movement and it was certainly never captured by the New Left.[24] It is more sensible and more accurate to view the "dump Johnson" movement as part of an internal battle within the Democratic Party between antiwar liberals, unreconstructed Cold Warriors, and moderates rather than as a fusion of the peace and freedom movements.[25]

The rise of the liberal peace movement in the aftermath of Richard Nixon's 1968 election victory should, perhaps, have heralded wider black participation in the peace movement. Both Whitney Young and the NAACP came out against the war at the same time that a "respectable" peace movement emerged, centered around the Vietnam Moratorium Committee, which black moderates found easier to support. However, while there was support for the Moratorium from a variety of black groups it did not result in sustained widespread black participation in peace activities.

James Earl Ray did not just weaken the black freedom struggle when he shot Martin Luther King in Memphis on April 4, 1968, he also dealt a savage blow to the antiwar movement. During the last six months of his life, while continuing to condemn both the war and the draft, and welcoming the antiwar candidacies of Eugene McCarthy and Robert Kennedy, King appears to have moved away from some of his more strident antiwar activism of 1967.[26] Perhaps this reflected his own concerns about some of the radical elements within the peace movement and his sensitivity toward accusations that he had been neglecting black problems. Adam Fairclough has argued that, "frustrated by his inability to play a unifying role" in the peace movement, King "concluded that the domestic issues of poverty and racism should remain his primary concerns." Hence the September 1967 decision to organize the Poor People's Campaign.[27] Nevertheless, the blossoming of a more moderate peace movement in 1969 would have offered King new opportunities to assert his opposition to the war more effectively. One can only speculate on the role King might have played in Richard Nixon's America, but his ability to mobilize large numbers of activists and to articulate the feelings of millions of black Americans, combined with the esteem in which much of white America held him, might well have resulted in a larger and more diverse antiwar movement.

The years between 1960 and 1972 saw the emergence of two of the most significant social movements in American history—the African American freedom struggle and the movement to end the war in Vietnam. On the surface there were good reasons why they should have cooperated closely: many early opponents of the war were veterans of the civil rights movement; African Americans had powerful reasons to oppose the war in Vietnam; and the two movements shared a similar critique of American society. For a variety of reasons, though, a meaningful coalition was never constructed. Nothing better illustrates this than the fact that at both the March on the Pentagon and the demonstrations at the 1968 Democratic Convention in Chicago, two protests that have come to symbolize the peace movement in the popular imagination, African Americans were conspicuous by their absence.

While the failure of the peace and freedom movements to work together closely does not answer Werner Sombart's famous question, "why is there no Socialism in the United States?" it does help explain both the weakness of the American left and the strength of conservatism in America during the last thirty years.[28] By combining attacks on the anti-war movement, black extremism, liberal excess and countercultural hedonism with their own distinctive individualistic and religious vision of America, conservatives were able to achieve remarkable electoral success in the years after 1968 by appealing to "middle America" while tapping into white working class and ethnic discontent, in the process undermining the New Deal coalition.[29]

It would be a brave or foolish historian who claimed that the apparent victory of the New Right was wholly dependent on the failure of the peace and freedom movements to unite between 1965 and 1972. During the 1960s the American left was weakened in numerous ways—the labor movement was fractured by tensions over race; Black Power made it more difficult to construct interracial coalitions; and the white New Left, in viciously attacking "corporate liberals" and rejecting traditional politics, harmed the Democratic Party (itself deeply split over race and Vietnam) while leaving itself powerless and hopelessly irrelevant. Structural changes in American society and in the economy also aided conservatives. But the failure of the peace and freedom movements to coalesce or work together effectively was symptomatic of an increasingly segmented left.[30] With the forces of progressivism detached and often at odds with each other, the New Right's rise to political ascendancy was made easier.

Notes

Introduction

1. *The Eyes on the Prize Civil Rights Reader: Documents, Speeches, and Firsthand Accounts from the Black Freedom Struggle, 1954–1990,* general editors Clayborne Carson, David J. Garrow, Gerald Gill, Vincent Harding, and Darlene Clark Hine (New York: Penguin, 1991), 440, 452–57.

2. Rhodri Jeffreys-Jones, *Peace Now: American Society and the Ending of the Vietnam War* (New Haven, Conn.: Yale University Press, 1999), 104.

3. See Charles DeBenedetti with Charles Chatfield, *An American Ordeal: The Antiwar Movement of the Vietnam Era* (Syracuse, N.Y.: Syracuse University Press, 1990), 158.

4. Martin Luther King, "A Time to Break Silence," quoted in *The Eyes on the Prize Civil Rights Reader,* 390, 392.

5. Adam Fairclough, *Better Day Coming: Blacks and Equality, 1890–2000* (New York: Penguin, 2002), 133–40, 152–56.

6. Fairclough, *Better Day Coming,* 183–85; Robert Cook, *Sweet Land of Liberty? The African-American Struggle for Civil Rights in the Twentieth Century* (Harlow, Essex: Longman, 1998), 53–56.

7. See James Farmer, *Lay Bare the Heart: An Autobiography of the Civil Rights Movement* (New York: Plume, 1985), 74, 81–85, 175; Tim Tyson, *Radio Free Dixie: Robert F. Williams and the Roots of Black Power* (Chapel Hill: University of North Carolina Press, 1999); Robert Weisbrot, *Freedom Bound: A History of America's Civil Rights Movement* (New York: Plume, 1990), 55.

8. Fairclough, *Better Day Coming,* 22, 46; Farmer, *Lay Bare the Heart,* 193.

9. Fairclough, *Better Day Coming,* 236–38; Jervis Anderson, *Bayard Rustin: Troubles I've Seen. A Biography* (New York: HarperCollins, 1997), 3–17, 153–54.

10. Anderson, *Bayard Rustin,* 236–38.

11. Anderson, *Bayard Rustin,* 193–94; James A. Colaiaco, *Martin Luther King, Jr. Apostle of Militant Nonviolence* (Basingstoke: Macmillan, 1993), 34; Weisbrot, *Freedom Bound,* 56.

12. Robert S. Browne, "The Freedom Movement and the War in Vietnam," in *Vietnam and Black America: An Anthology of Protest and Resistance,* ed. Clyde Taylor (Garden City, N.Y.: Anchor/Doubleday, 1973), 69; editorial, "Close Ranks," *Crisis* 16, 3 (July 1918): 1, quoted in David L. Lewis, *W. E. B. Du Bois: Biography of a Race, 1868–1919* (New York: Henry Holt, 1993), 556.

13. Gerald Horne, *Black and Red: W. E. B. Du Bois and the Afro-American Response to the Cold War, 1944–1963* (Albany: State University of New York Press, 1986), 19. See also Manning Marable, *Race, Reform, and Rebellion: The Second Reconstruction in Black America, 1945–1990* (Basingstoke: Macmillan, 1991).

14. Lewis, *Biography of a Race*, 522; Leon D. Pamphile, "The NAACP and the American Occupation of Haiti," *Phylon* 47, no. 1 (1986): 92, 93, 98.

15. Fairclough, *Better Day Coming*, 111–21.

16. Brenda Gayle Plummer, *Rising Wind: Black America and U.S. Foreign Affairs, 1935–1960* (Chapel Hill: University of North Carolina Press, 1996), 40–51.

17. Mark Naison, *Communists in Harlem During the Depression* (Urbana: University of Illinois Press, 1983), 196–97.

18. Horne, *Black and Red*, 21.

19. Horne, *Black and Red*, 20.

20. See, for example, George Padmore, "The Vietnamese Struggle for Independence," *Crisis* 55, 3 (March 1948): 92.

21. The slogan was popularized by the *Pittsburgh Courier*; see Plummer, *Rising Wind*, 85.

22. Cook, *Sweet Land of Liberty?* 74; Plummer, *Rising Wind*, 102.

23. See Thomas Borstelmann, *The Cold War and the Color Line: American Race Relations in the Global Arena* (Cambridge, Mass.: Harvard University Press, 2001); Mary L. Dudziak, *Cold War Civil Rights: Race and the Image of American Democracy* (Princeton, N.J.: Princeton University Press, 2000); Azza Salama Layton, *International Politics and Civil Rights Policies in the United States, 1941–1960* (New York: Cambridge University Press, 2000); Penny M. Von Eschen, *Race Against Empire: Black Americans and Anticolonialism, 1937–1957* (Ithaca, N.Y.: Cornell University Press, 2001).

24. See Kenneth R. Janken, "From Colonial Liberation to Cold War Liberalism: Walter White, the NAACP, and Foreign Affairs, 1941–1955," *Ethnic and Racial Studies* 21 (November 1998); Plummer, *Rising Wind*, 184, Horne, *Red and Black*, 50–56; Adam Fairclough, "Race and Red-Baiting," in *The Civil Rights Movement*, ed. Jack E. Davis (Malden, Mass.: Blackwell, 2001), 98–100; Cook, *Sweet Land of Liberty?* 95.

25. See, for example, Irving Bernstein, *Promises Kept: John F. Kennedy's New Frontier* (New York: Oxford University Press, 1991), 63; Cook, *Sweet Land of Liberty?* 82–98; Mary L. Dudziak, "Desegregation as a Cold War Imperative," *Stanford Law Review* 41 (1988–89); Dudziak, *Cold War Civil Rights*; Azza Salama Layton, "International Pressure and the U.S. Government's Response to Little Rock," *Arkansas Historical Quarterly* 56, 3 (Autumn 1997): esp. 272.

26. Malcolm X speech at the Ford Auditorium, February 14, 1965, in *February 1965: The Final Speeches*, ed. Steve Clark (New York: Pathfinder, 1992), 85.

27. Paul Robeson, "Ho Chi Minh Is the Toussaint l'Ouverture of Indo-China," *Freedom*, March 1954, reprinted in *Freedomways Reader: Prophets in Their Own Country*, ed. Esther Cooper Jackson (Boulder, Colo.: Westview Press, 2000), 147–49.

28. Malcolm X speech at Corn Hill Methodist Church, Rochester, February 16, 1965 in, *February 1965: The Final Speeches*, 150.

29. Plummer, *Rising Wind*, 305.

30. Plummer, *Rising Wind*, 305.

31. Bernard C. Nalty, *The Vietnam War: The History of America's Conflict in Southeast Asia* (New York: Smithmark, 1996), 19–20; DeBenedetti, *An American Ordeal*, 104.

32. Martin Luther King, "A Time to Break Silence," April 4, 1967, in *A Testament of Hope: The Essential Writings and Speeches of Martin Luther King, Jr.*, ed. James Melvin Washington (San Francisco: HarperSanFrancisco, 1991), 233.

33. Stokely Carmichael, speech in Chicago, July 28, 1966, quoted in Robert W. Mullen, *Blacks and Vietnam* (Washington, D.C.: University Press of America, 1981), 67.

34. See, for example, SNCC Statement on Vietnam War, January 6, 1966, Atlanta, in Massimo Teodori, *The New Left: A Documentary History* (London: Jonathan Cape, 1970), 252.

35. James E. Westheider, *Fighting on Two Fronts: African Americans and the Vietnam War* (New York: New York University Press, 1997), 27.

36. Weisbrot, *Freedom Bound*, 247.

37. Weisbrot, *Freedom Bound*, 247.

38. Westheider, *Fighting on Two Fronts*, 30; Jack D. Foner, *Blacks and the Military in American History: A New Perspective* (New York: Praeger, 1974), 202–13, quoted in Herbert Shapiro, "The Vietnam War and the American Civil Rights Movement," *Journal of Ethnic Studies* 16, 4 (1989): 136.

39. Westheider, *Fighting on Two Fronts*, 24–25.

40. Westheider, *Fighting on Two Fronts*, 28.

41. Westheider, *Fighting on Two Fronts*, 20.

42. Martin Luther King, Jr., "A Testament of Hope," *Playboy*, January 1969 (posthumously published essay), in Washington, *A Testament of Hope*, 317–18.

43. Stokely Carmichael, "At Morgan State," in Taylor, *Vietnam and Black America*, 266.

44. SNCC fieldworker quoted in Howard Zinn, *Vietnam: The Logic of Withdrawal* (Boston: Beacon Press, 1967), 19.

45. King, "A Time to Break Silence," 233.

46. For example, in 1960 only 15 percent of black workers compared with 44 percent of white workers held professional, managerial, clerical, or sales positions. Almost 50 percent of black families lived below the federal poverty line of $3,000 for a family of four, and black median family income was 55 percent that of white families. The rate of unemployment for black adults (10.2 percent) and black teenagers (24.4 percent) was roughly twice that of whites. In 1964 black infant mortality rates were 90 percent higher than white rates. Weisbrot, *Freedom Bound*, 155–58.

47. Maurice Isserman and Michael Kazin, *America Divided: The Civil War of the 1960s* (Oxford: Oxford University Press, 2000), 188.

48. King, "A Time to Break Silence," 232–33.

49. Tom Wells, *The War Within: America's Battle over Vietnam* (Berkeley: University of California Press, 1994), 70; Sidney Verba et al., "Public Opinion and the War in Vietnam," *American Political Science Review* 61 (June 1967): 323–25.

50. S. Washington, "Negro Opinion on Viet Is Shifting: Majority Favor Pull-Out," *Chicago Daily Defender*, April 22–28, 1967, 1.

51. See for example, "Southerners Move Against the War," *Southern Patriot*, May 1972, 1, 7; Anne Braden, "Peace Sentiment Grows," *Southern Patriot*, April 1966, 1, 3; Jack A. Smith, "Anti-War Groups of South Confer," *National Guardian*, April 30, 1966, 1, 4.

52. John Lewis with Michael D'Orso, *Walking with the Wind: A Memoir of the Movement* (New York: Simon and Schuster, 1988), 330.

53. NAACP executive committee meeting, March 8, 65, National Association for the Advancement of Colored People (NAACP) Records, Group III, Box A26, Folder "Minutes, 1964–65," Library of Congress.

54. Editorial, *Crisis* (March 1965): 142.

55. William A. Price, "Freedom Party Rallies Aid for Mississippi Drive," *National Guardian* (New York), May 1, 1965, 6.

Chapter 1. The Organizing Tradition

1. Howard Zinn, *You Can't Be Neutral on a Moving Train: A Personal History of Our Times* (Boston: Beacon Press, 1994), 103.

2. Zinn, *You Can't Be Neutral,* 104.

3. Draft article by Howard Zinn, Winter 1965, 9–10, Howard Zinn Papers, 1956–1994, Box 3, Folder 5, State Historical Society of Wisconsin (SHSW).

4. Robert Cook, *Sweet Land of Liberty? The African-American Struggle for Civil Rights in the Twentieth Century* (Harlow: Longman, 1998), 150, 165–67; Robert Weisbrot, *Freedom Bound: A History of America's Civil Rights Movement* (New York: Plume, 1990), 127.

5. Doug McAdam, *Freedom Summer* (New York: Oxford University Press, 1988), 96.

6. See Cook, *Sweet Land of Liberty?* 156–57; Charles Payne, *I've Got the Light of Freedom: The Organizing Tradition and the Mississippi Freedom Struggle* (Berkeley: University of California Press, 1995), 108–10; and John Lewis with Michael D'Orso, *Walking with the Wind: A Memoir of the Movement* (New York: Simon and Schuster, 1988), 217.

7. John Dittmer, *Local People: The Struggle for Civil Rights in Mississippi* (Urbana: University of Illinois Press, 1994), 245.

8. Howard Zinn, *SNCC: The New Abolitionists* (Boston: Beacon Press, 1964), 194–95.

9. Dittmer, *Local People,* 239.

10. Cook, *Sweet Land of Liberty?* 89–90, 121–22.

11. Zinn draft article, 4.

12. See McAdam, *Freedom Summer,* 128.

13. Letter by Michael Kenney, July 15, 1964, quoted in McAdam, *Freedom Summer,* 97.

14. McAdam, *Freedom Summer,* 127–28.

15. Brian Peterson, "Thoughts About Mississippi" (unpublished), Peterson Papers, SHSW, quoted in McAdam, *Freedom Summer,* 128.

16. Quoted in Ronald Fraser, ed., *1968: A Student Generation in Revolt—An International Oral History* (New York: Pantheon, 1988), 51–52.

17. McAdam, *Freedom Summer,* 128–30.

18. Cook, *Sweet Land of Liberty?* 172–73; Weisbrot, *Freedom Bound,* 116–23.

19. See, for example, Cook, *Sweet Land of Liberty?* 172–73.

20. Dittmer, *Local People,* 302.

21. Author's interview with Courtland Cox, February 4, 2000.

22. In Clayborne Carson, *In Struggle: SNCC and the Black Awakening of the 1960s* (Cambridge, Mass.: Harvard University Press, 1981), 126.

23. Lewis, *Walking with the Wind,* 282.

24. See Carson, *In Struggle,* 42; James Forman, *The Making of Black Revolutionaries* (Washington. D.C.: Open Hand, 1985), 395–96, my emphasis.

25. Carson, *In Struggle,* 134–35.

26. See for example, Robert Dallek, *Flawed Giant: Lyndon Johnson and His Times, 1961–1973* (Oxford: Oxford University Press, 1998).

27. The Fifth Circuit was particularly important for the civil rights movement, which relied on it to overturn racist decisions made in the state courts of the Deep South.

28. Dittmer, *Local People,* 58, 60.

29. "Editorial: Open Letter to President Johnson," *The Movement* 1, 7 (July 1965): 5.

30. Dittmer, *Local People*, 338.

31. June 29, 1965, statement by Victoria Gray, Mississippi Freedom Democratic Party (MFDP) Records, 1962–1971, Reel 2 (Item 2: MFDP Records—General Papers, 1963–1971), SHSW.

32. William A. Price, "NAACP and CORE Reassess Their Goals," *National Guardian* (New York), July 17, 1965, 3.

33. "Open Letter to President Johnson," 5.

34. *Life with Lyndon in the Great Society* 1, 3 (June 3, 1965), 5, SHSW.

35. Zinn draft article, 4.

36. Dittmer, *Local People*, 391–92.

37. *National Guardian*, July 16, 1966, 5.

38. Dittmer, *Local People*, 391–92.

39. *Life with Lyndon in the Great Society* 1, 39 (October 28, 1965), 6.

40. Roy Wilkins, "LBJ and the Negro," *New York Post*, December 2, 1967.

41. Anne Braden, "The SNCC Trends: Challenge to White America," *Southern Patriot*, May 1966, 2.

42. Comments by Mike Thelwell at "The Ongoing Radicalization of SNCC and the Movement," a panel session at "'We Who Believe in Freedom Cannot Rest': Miss Ella J. Baker and the Birth of SNCC," National Conference, April 13–16, 2000, Shaw University, Raleigh, N.C. Transcription and tape of session in author's possession.

43. Statement of George Vlasits, September 25, 1968, SSOC Press Release, David Nolan Papers, 1960–1987, Box 5, Folder 19, SHSW.

44. Tom Wells, *The War Within: America's Battle over Vietnam* (Berkeley: University of California Press, 1994), 96.

45. Howard Zinn, "Should Civil Rights Workers Take a Stand on Vietnam?" *Student Voice*, August 30, 1965, 3.

46. Zinn draft article.

47. SNCC Statement on the War in Vietnam, January 6, 1966, in Massimo Teodori, *The New Left: A Documentary History* (London: Jonathan Cape, 1970), 251.

48. Bernard C. Nalty, *The Vietnam War: The History of America's Conflict in Southeast Asia* (New York, 1996), 19–20; Teodori, *The New Left*, 478; Charles DeBenedetti with Charles Chatfield, *An American Ordeal: The Antiwar Movement of the Vietnam Era* (Syracuse, N.Y.: Syracuse University Press, 1990), 109; Wells, *The War Within*, 24.

49. For good general histories of the New Left, see Maurice Isserman and Michael Kazin, *America Divided: The Civil War of the 1960s* (New York: Oxford University Press, 2000); James Miller, *Democracy Is in the Streets: From Port Huron to the Siege of Chicago* (Cambridge, Mass.: Harvard University Press, 1994); Kirkpatrick Sale, *SDS* (New York: Random House, 1973).

50. See Isserman and Kazin, *America Divided*, 168–69; Miller, *Democracy Is in the Streets*, ch. 10.

51. Wells, *The War Within*, 13–14.

52. Sale, *SDS*, 174.

53. Sale, *SDS*, 177.

54. Sale, *SDS*, 179.

55. Jervis Anderson, *Bayard Rustin: Troubles I've Seen: A Biography* (New York: HarperCollins, 1997), 295.

56. Sale, *SDS*, 179.

57. Ibid., 185–86.

58. Lewis, *Walking with the Wind*, 354.

59. Carson, *In Struggle*, 184–85.

60. Sale, *SDS*, 188–90.

61. SNCC Executive Committee Meeting, Holly Springs, Mississippi, April 12–14, 1965, 31, Student Nonviolent Coordinating Committee (SNCC) Records 1964–1965 (1 folder), SHSW.

62. SDS Press Release, April 14, 1965, Students for a Democratic Society (SDS) Records, 1958–1970, Box 9, Folder 6, SHSW.

63. William A. Price, "A Joining of Forces," *National Guardian*, April 24, 1965, 1.

64. Todd Gitlin, *The Whole World Is Watching: Mass Media in the Making and Unmaking of the New Left* (Berkeley: University of California Press, 1980), 54.

65. David J. Garrow, *Bearing the Cross: Martin Luther King, Jr. and the Southern Christian Leadership Conference* (1986; London: Vintage, 1993), 394.

66. *Face the Nation*, CBS, Sunday, April 25, 1965, Papers of the Congress of Racial Equality, 1944–1968 (microfilm) (CORE), 1944–68, Reel 1, Frame 21, SHSW.

67. Emergency Rally on Vietnam, June 8, 1965, Madison Square Garden, program/leaflet, in SDS Records, Box 8, Folder 14, SHSW; see also reports in the *New York Post* and *New York Herald Tribune* on June 9.

68. News conference, June 30, 1965, Durham, N.C., 3, Meier-Rudwick Collection of Congress of Racial Equality Records, 1943–1969, Box 1, SHSW.

69. "New Directions and CORE Policy," Minutes, National Action Council Meeting, April 10–11, 1965, 4 (April 10), Congress of Racial Equality (CORE) Records, 1941–1967, Series 4, Box 2, NAC, Folder 1: Meetings, Minutes, 1963–1965, SHSW.

70. Brooklyn CORE, National Convention Resolutions, 2, CORE Records, 1941–1967, Series 4, Box 1, NAC, Folder 4: Conventions, 1965, SHSW.

71. August Meier and Elliot Rudwick, *CORE: A Study in the Civil Rights Movement, 1942–1968* (New York: Oxford University Press, 1973), 376.

72. Press release, re: Convention Decisions, Morning Session, July 5, 1965, CORE Records, 1941–1967, Series 4, Box 1, NAC, folder 4: Conventions, 1965, SHSW.

73. Farmer's annual report to the National CORE Convention, Durham, N.C., July 1, 1965, 2, CORE Papers, 1944–1968, A: I: 7 (microfilm), SHSW.

74. There was some legitimacy to this claim. In the summer of 1965, for example, Bayard Rustin was shocked by the negative response among Harlem's blacks to Martin Luther King's Vietnam peace initiative. They wanted King to focus on civil rights. See Adam Fairclough, *To Redeem the Soul of America: The Southern Christian Leadership Conference and Martin Luther King, Jr.* (Athens: University of Georgia Press, 1987), 273.

75. Minutes of 23rd Annual Convention, July 1–5, 1965, Durham, N.C., 32, James Leonard, Jr., and Lula Peterson Farmer Papers, 1908, 1921–1997, Box 2R570, Folder "Records of Professional Activities: Congress of Racial Equality (CORE): Minutes and Reports, 1963–1966," Center for American History, University of Texas at Austin; and "CORE Retreats on Vietnam," *National Guardian*, July 10, 1965, CORE Records, 1941–1967, Series 4, Box 1, NAC, Folder 4: Conventions, 1965, SHSW.

76. Meier and Rudwick, *CORE*, 404.

77. Transcript, James Farmer Oral History Interview II, July 20, 1971, 7–8, by Paige Mulhollan; Internet Copy, Lyndon Baines Johnson Presidential Library, Austin, Texas.

78. Unknown newspaper report, July 31, 1965, Howard Zinn Papers, 1956–1994, Box 3, Folder 5, SHSW.

79. Dittmer, *Local People*, 351.

80. Dittmer, *Local People*, 350.

81. "Negroes and the Draft," *New York Post*, August 29, 65, Roy Wilkins Papers, Box 39, Folder "newspaper clippings 1964–65," Library of Congress.

82. MFDP Press Release, 31 July 1965, Howard Zinn Papers, Box 3, Folder 5, SHSW.

83. Roy Reed, "Freedom Party Head Disavows Plea to Negroes to Dodge Draft," *New York Times*, August 4, 1965, Howard Zinn Papers, Box 3, Folder 5, SHSW; Dittmer, *Local People*, 350–51.

84. Reed, "Freedom Party Head Disavows Plea."

85. The Reminiscences of Edwin King (March 10, October 30, 1988), 137–38, Oral History Collection of Columbia University.

86. Payne, *I've Got the Light of Freedom*, 200.

87. James Bonney (AUP), "Letter's Author Recalls Praise of FDP Leaders," *Greenwood Comment*, August 4, 1965, MFDP Records (microfilm), Reel 2, Item 2: MFDP Records—General Papers, 1963–1971, SHSW.

88. Mississippi Journal, July 1965, Daniel J. Wacker Papers, 1965–1967, 1993, Box 1, Folder 5, SHSW.

89. Howard Zinn Papers, Box 3, Folder 5 (August 3, 1965 interview transcript), SHSW.

90. AFSC Report, September 13, 1965, Zinn Papers, Box 3, Folder 5, SHSW.

91. DeBenedetti, *An American Ordeal*, 120.

92. SDS, Port Huron Statement, Teodori, *The New Left*, 163–72; quoted in Sale, *SDS*, 52.

93. "We Declare Peace: Call for an Assembly of Unrepresented People in Washington, D.C., on August 6 through 9," 1, CORE Papers, 1944–68, Reel 9, Frame 42, SHSW.

94. Walter Tillow, Bob Parris, Francis Mitchell, Courtland Cox, Dona Richards, et al., "An Idea for a Project Based in Washington, D.C. This Summer," *SNCC Staff Newsletter*, July 17, 1965, 1, 2, SHSW.

95. "We Declare Peace . . . ," 1.

96. *Peace and Freedom News* 5, September 20, 1965, 3, SNCC Records (microfilm), Reel 52, Library of Congress; see also author's interview with Frank Emspak, December 9, 1999, 12.

97. DeBenedetti, *An American Ordeal*, 121.

98. Anne Braden, "Issues of Peace Confronts Freedom Movement," *Peace and Freedom News* 4, 2, September 13, 1965, Student Nonviolent Coordinating Committee (SNCC) Records, Reel 58, Library of Congress.

99. Carson, *In Struggle*, 185; Braden, "Issues of Peace Confronts Freedom Movement."

100. Report of the Executive Director for June, July, and August, 1965, September 13, 1965, *Papers of the NAACP: Supplement to Part 1, 1961–1965*, editorial advisor August Meier, edited by Mark Fox (Frederick, Md.: University Publications of America, 1982–1997), Reel 1; memo from Wilkins to Branch and Youth Council Presidents re "Washington, D.C. Jamboree August 6–9, 1965," July 30, 1965, National Association for the Advancement of Colored People (NAACP) Records, Group III, Box A328, Folder "Vietnam War, 1964–65," Library of Congress.

101. Braden, "Issues of Peace Confront Freedom Movement."

102. Jack Newfield, "Some Things Unite Them, Some Things Divide Them," *Village Voice*, August 19, 1965, 3.

103. Sale, *SDS*, 240.

104. DeBenedetti, *An American Ordeal*, 131.

105. NCCEWV Steering Committee Meeting Minutes, Ann Arbor, September 19, 1965, 3, National Coordinating Committee to End the War in Vietnam (NCC) Records, 1964–1967, Series 1, Box 1, Folder 2: Steering Committee, 1965, September 18–20, Ann Arbor Meeting, Notes and Minutes, SHSW.

106. See report of the march in *National Guardian*, December 4, 1965.

107. Garrow, *Bearing the Cross*, 429; William Chapman, "Negotiated Viet Peace Proposed by Dr. King," *Washington Post*, July 3, 1965, A2.

108. Garrow, *Bearing the Cross*, 438–39, 440, 443–46; Peter Ling, *Martin Luther King, Jr.* (London: Routledge, 2002), 258–59.

109. Wells, *The War Within*, 61.

110. Sale, *SDS*, 241.

111. DeBenedetti, *An American Ordeal*, 131; SDS, "Call to March on Washington to End the War in Vietnam, November 27, 1965," NCC Records, Series 1, Box 1, Folder 9: Conferences; 1965, November 25–28 Convention, Position Papers, SHSW.

112. Wells, *The War Within*, 62.

113. Wells, *The War Within*, 62; DeBenedetti, *An American Ordeal*, 132; Sale, *SDS*, 195, 242–44.

114. NCCEWV Steering Committee Meeting Minutes, Ann Arbor, September 19, 1965.

115. DeBenedetti, *An American Ordeal*, 133.

116. DeBenedetti, *An American Ordeal*, 133–34.

117. Wells, *The War Within*, 60.

118. Minutes of a meeting of people from the South, Thursday November 24, 1965, 1, NCC Records, Series 1, Box 1, Folder 7, SHSW.

119. Mel Pine, "The November 25–28 Convention," 1, NCC Records, Series 1, Box 1, Folder 8: National Anti-War Conference 1965—November 25–28, Constitutional Material, SHSW.

120. Emspak interview, December 9, 1999.

Chapter 2. Black Power

1. Charles DeBenedetti with Charles Chatfield, *An American Ordeal: The Antiwar Movement of the Vietnam Era* (Syracuse, N.Y.: Syracuse University Press, 1990), 141.

2. Maurice Isserman and Michael Kazin, *America Divided: The Civil War of the 1960s* (New York: Oxford University Press, 2000), 187–91.

3. DeBenedetti, *An American Ordeal*, 142.

4. Clayborne Carson, *In Struggle: SNCC and the Black Awakening of the 1960s* (Cambridge, Mass.: Harvard University Press, 1981), 183.

5. James Forman, *The Making of Black Revolutionaries* (Washington, D.C.: Open Hand, 1985), 445.

6. SNCC was launching a congressional challenge against the seating of the Mississippi Representative on the grounds of racial discrimination.

7. Howard Zinn, "Should Civil Rights Workers Take a Stand on Vietnam?" *Student Voice*, August 30, 1965, 3. A detailed discussion of this theme can be found in Chapter 1.

8. " . . . One Freedom Worker's Views," *Southern Patriot*, October 1965, 3.

9. Mitchell Zimmerman, "SNCC Should Not Take a Stand on Vietnam," September 1965, in Howard Zinn Papers, 1956–1994, Box 3, Folder 5, State Historical Society of Wisconsin (SHSW). Dona Richards seems to have been

incorrectly cited as the author of this article by Clayborne Carson; see Carson, *In Struggle*, 187, 21–22 for information on Marion Barry.

10. John Lewis with Michael D'Orso, *Walking with the Wind: A Memoir of the Movement* (New York: Simon and Schuster, 1988), 356.

11. SNCC Staff meeting, November 24–29, 1965, Atlanta, 20–23. I am indebted to Professor Clayborne Carson for generously providing me with a copy of these minutes.

12. Cleveland Sellers, *The River of No Return: The Autobiography of a Black Militant and the Life and Death of SNCC* (1973; Jackson, Miss.: University Press of Mississippi, 1990), 149.

13. Carson, *In Struggle*, 188; Cheryl Lynn Greenberg, ed., *A Circle of Trust: Remembering SNCC* (New Brunswick, N.J.: Rutgers University Press, 1998), 161.

14. Carson, *In Struggle*, 155–57.

15. For a detailed study of Sammy Younge, Jr., see James Forman, *Sammy Younge, Jr.: The First Black College Student to Die in the Black Liberation Movement* (1968; Washington, D.C.: Open Hand, 1986).

16. Sellers, *The River of No Return*, 149–50.

17. Author's interview with Julian Bond, May 15, 2001, Cambridge, England.

18. Lewis, *Walking with the Wind*, 358.

19. SNCC statement against the war in Vietnam, January 6, 1966, printed in Forman, *The Making of Black Revolutionaries*, 445–46.

20. SNCC Staff meeting, November 24–29, 1965, 19–26.

21. Carson, *In Struggle*, 257, chapter 13.

22. On the reaction to the statement see, for example, Robert Weisbrot, *Freedom Bound: A History of America's Civil Rights Movement* (New York: Plume, 1990), 191–92.

23. Carson, *In Struggle*, 189; Lewis, *Walking with the Wind*, 360–61.

24. Bond interview.

25. Lewis, *Walking with the Wind*, 361.

26. Lewis, *Walking with the Wind*, 361; "Vietnam Issue Used to Attack Civil Rights," *The Movement* 2, 1 (January 1966): 2.

27. Bond interview.

28. Poll cited in Adam Fairclough, "Martin Luther King Jr. and the War in Vietnam," in *Martin Luther King, Jr. Civil Rights Leader, Theologian, Orator*, ed. David J. Garrow (New York: Carlson, 1989), 317 n. 26.

29. "Vietnam Issue Used to Attack Civil Rights."

30. Lewis, *Walking with the Wind*, 361.

31. Julian Bond, "Memoirs of a Southern Gentleman (part II)," *Ramparts* 5, 8 (February 1967): 56.

32. Bond interview.

33. Information taken from the Finding Aid to the SNCC-Arkansas Project Records, SHSW.

34. Finding Aid; telephone interview with Mitchell Zimmerman, January 18, 2001.

35. Zimmerman telephone interview.

36. William W. Hansen, "The Black Man and the Constitution," letter to *Arkansas Gazette*, December 1, 1965, in SNCC-Arkansas Project Records, 1960–1966, Box 1, Folder 7, SHSW.

37. Report by Mitchell Zimmerman, December 6, 1965, 5, SNCC-Arkansas Project Records, Box 1, Folder 14, SHSW.

38. "Bates Says NAACP Doesn't Advocate Avoiding the Draft," *Arkansas Democrat*, January 12, 1966, SNCC-Arkansas Project Records, Box 3, Folder 17, SHSW.

39. Information taken from the Finding Aid to the SNCC-Arkansas Project Records, SHSW, and SNCC-Arkansas Project, Box 3, Folder 3, SHSW.

40. Finding Aid to the SNCC-Arkansas Project Records.

41. Larry Fugate, "Anti-War Rally Scheduled Here," *Pine Bluff Commercial,* January 12, 1966, SNCC-Arkansas Project Records, Box 3, Folder 12, SHSW.

42. Letter from Vincent O'Connor to Jon Jacobs, January 11, 1966, SNCC-Arkansas Project Records, Box 6, Folder 4, SHSW.

43. Associated Press story—February 11, 1966, SNCC-Arkansas Project Records, Box 3, Folder 17, SHSW.

44. Zimmerman telephone interview.

45. Jimmy Jones, "19 at Little Rock Protest the War With a Short March in the Rain," *Arkansas Gazette,* February 13, 1966, 1, SNCC-Arkansas Project Records, Box 3, Folder 17, SHSW.

46. For a history of SSOC, see Gregg Laurence Michel, "'We'll Take Our Stand': The Southern Student Organizing Committee and the Radicalization of White Southern Students" (Ph.D. dissertation, University of Virginia, 1999).

47. David Nolan, "A Personal History of the Virginia Students' Civil Rights Committee," 1–2, David Nolan Papers, 1960–1987, Box 6, Folder 7, SHSW.

48. "The Story of VSCRC," 1, David Nolan Papers, Box 6, Folder 11, SHSW.

49. William Faulkner, *Go Down, Moses* (New York: Vintage, 1973 edition), 298, 278.

50. J. Harvie Wilkinson III, *Harry Byrd and the Changing Face of Virginia Politics, 1945–1966* (Charlottesville: University Press of Virginia, 1968), 207–8.

51. James W. Ely, Jr., *The Crisis of Conservative Virginia: The Byrd Organization and the Politics of Massive Resistance* (Knoxville: University of Tennessee Press, 1976), 22; Wilkinson, *Harry Byrd,* 11.

52. For an excellent discussion of this, see Richard Kluger, *Simple Justice: The History of* Brown v. Board of Education *and America's Struggle for Equality* (New York: Vintage, 1975), esp. 451–507.

53. Ely, *The Crisis of Conservative Virginia,* 155.

54. Julius Lester, *Search for the New Land: History as Subjective Experience* (New York: Dial Press, 1969), 59; Taylor Branch, *Parting the Waters: America in the King Years, 1954–1963* (New York: Simon and Schuster, 1988), 822

55. David Nolan, "Book Notes—Where We Came From," 3, David Nolan Papers, Box 6, Folder 7, SHSW; "Experiment in Virginia," *Southern Patriot,* September 1965, 1.

56. Nolan, "The Story of VSCRC," 2.

57. VSCRC fund-raising letter, May 10, 1965, David Nolan Papers, Box 6, Folder 8, SHSW.

58. Nolan, "The Story of VSCRC," 2.

59. W. Lester Banks letter to Harry Flood Byrd, August 4, 1957, Papers of the NAACP, Supplement to Part 4, Voting Rights, General Office Files, 1956–1965, Group III, Series A, General Office File, Box A-271, States: Virginia, 1956–1965, Library of Congress.

60. Nolan, "A Personal History," 3; Carson, *In Struggle,* 252.

61. Letter from David Nolan to Bill Wallace (SNCC), June 25, 1965, David Nolan Papers, Box 6, Folder 8, SHSW.

62. VSCRC Fund-raising letter; Nolan, "The Story of VSCRC," 2.

63. "Experiment in Virginia," 1.

64. Letter from Ed Hamlett to Lucy Montgomery, April 7, 1965, David Nolan Papers, Box 6, Folder 8; Nolan, "The Story of VSCRC," 2.

65. "Report to Taconic Foundation on Program Development," March 23, 1966, 1, David Nolan Papers, Box 6, Folder 9, SHSW.

66. Letter from David Nolan to Bill Wallace, June 25, 1965 David Nolan Papers, Box 6, SHSW.

67. "Experiment in Virginia," 2.

68. "Report to Taconic Foundation on Program Development," 1.

69. David Nolan, "Some Problems of Community Organizing in Southside Virginia," September 1965, 1, David Nolan Papers, Box 6, Folder 11, SHSW.

70. Charles Payne, *I've Got the Light of Freedom: The Organizing Tradition and the Mississippi Freedom Struggle* (Berkeley: University of California Press, 1995), 404.

71. "Report to Taconic Foundation on Program Development," 2.

72. "Report to Taconic Foundation on Program Development," 2–3.

73. Minutes, VSCRC Staff Meeting, January 18, 1966, 3; February 13, 1966, 2; March 2, 1966, 2, David Nolan Papers, Box 6, Folder 6, SHSW.

74. David Nolan, "The War in Vietnam," 4, July 26, 1966, David Nolan Papers, Box 6, Folder 15, SHSW.

75. Rives Foster, "Notes on VSCRC," 3, David Nolan Papers, Box 6, Folder 11, SHSW.

76. Minutes, VSCRC Staff Meeting, July 18, 1966, 1, David Nolan Papers, Box 6, Folder 6, SHSW.

77. Nolan, "Some Problems of Community Organizing in Southside Virginia," 1.

78. James Miller, *Democracy Is in the Streets: From Port Huron to the Siege of Chicago* (Cambridge, Mass.: Harvard University Press, 1999), 214.

79. Foster, "Notes on VSCRC," 3, my emphasis.

80. David Nolan, "Book Notes—Finances," 4, David Nolan Papers, Box 6, Folder 7, SHSW.

81. Minutes, VSCRC Staff Meeting, April 25, 1966, 2, David Nolan Papers, Box 6, Folder 6, SHSW.

82. David Nolan Papers, Box 6, Folder 10, SHSW.

83. Letter from David Nolan to "uncle ed" [Ed Hamlett], August 2, 1966, 2, David Nolan Papers, Box 6, Folder 7, SHSW.

84. David Nolan, "Book Notes- Black White Hangups," 1, David Nolan Papers, Box 6, Folder 7, SHSW.

85. Bill Bradley, "Our Southern Projects: A Review" (1965), section 4, Robert Curvin Papers, SHSW.

86. David Nolan, "Book Notes- Black White Hangups," 1; "Book Notes— Where We Came From," 3, David Nolan Papers, Box 6, Folder 7, SHSW.

87. Nolan, "Some Problems of Community Organizing in Southside Virginia."

88. Foster, "Notes on VSCRC," 3.

89. Minutes, VSCRC Staff Meeting, November 22, 1966, 1, David Nolan Papers, Box 6, Folder 6, SHSW.

90. David Nolan, "Book Notes—The Larger Revolution," 2, David Nolan Papers, Box 6, Folder 7, SHSW.

91. David Nolan, "Lack of Direction in VSCRC," 1, 10 July 10, 1966 Staff Memo, David Nolan Papers, Box 6, Folder 11, SHSW. See also Bob Dewart, "Master Plan B," July 21, 1966, David Nolan Papers, Box 6, Folder 11, SHSW.

92. Michael Ferber, "Why I Joined the Resistance," in *Against the Vietnam War: Writings by Activists*, ed. Mary Susannah Robbins (Syracuse, N.Y.: Syracuse University Press, 1999), 113.

93. Stokely Carmichael, "Power and Racism," 3 (my emphasis), originally published as "What We Want," *New York Review of Books*, September 1966; Student Nonviolent Coordinating Committee (SNCC) Records (microfilm edition), Reel 2, Library of Congress.

94. Robert Cook, *Sweet Land of Liberty? The African-American Struggle for Civil Rights in the Twentieth Century* (Harlow: Longman, 1998), 201; David Burner, *Making Peace with the 60s* (Princeton, N.J.: Princeton University Press, 1996), 49–83.

95. John Dittmer, *Local People: The Struggle for Civil Rights in Mississippi* (Urbana: University of Illinois Press, 1994), 396–97.

96. Stokely Carmichael and Charles V. Hamilton, *Black Power: The Politics of Liberation in America* (Harmondsworth: Penguin, 1969), 58, quoted in Cook, *Sweet Land of Liberty*, 201–2.

97. William L. Van Deburg, *New Day in Babylon: The Black Power Movement and American Culture, 1965–1975* (Chicago: University of Chicago Press, 1992), 15.

98. Adam Fairclough, *Race and Democracy: The Civil Rights Struggle in Louisiana, 1915–1972* (Athens: University of Georgia Press, 1995), 412–13; Fairclough has demonstrated that the NAACP's reaction to Black Power was not monolithic but multi-layered, and often involved generational conflicts within the Association. Indeed, according to Fairclough, there was a good deal of "separatist thinking" at the grass-roots level, and "antiwhite, antiestablishment feeling" often permeated the "mental outlook of young NAACP members." See *Race and Democracy*, 434.

99. Van Deburg, *New Day in Babylon*, 11; Dittmer, *Local People*, 397.

100. McKissick quoted in Van Deburg, *New Day in Babylon*, 12.

101. Timothy B. Tyson, *Radio Free Dixie: Robert F. Williams and the Roots of Black Power* (Chapel Hill: University of North Carolina Press, 1999), 308.

102. See Juan Williams, *Thurgood Marshall: American Revolutionary* (New York: Random House, 1998), 154–55, 249; Andrew Manis, *A Fire You Can't Put Out: The Civil Rights Life of Reverend Fred Shuttlesworth* (Tuscaloosa: University of Alabama Press, 1999), 70; and Payne, *I've Got the Light of Freedom*, 44.

103. Kenneth R. Janken, "From Colonial Liberation to Cold War Liberalism: Walter White, the NAACP, and Foreign Affairs, 1941–1955," *Ethnic and Racial Studies* 21 (November 1998): 1077.

104. Carson, *In Struggle*, 101–3. One of Randolph's objectives was to keep out Communists. For a discussion of this see Paula F. Pfeffer, *A. Philip Randolph, Pioneer of the Civil Rights Movement* (Baton Rouge: Louisiana State University Press, 1990), 55–58.

105. Carson, *In Struggle*, 206.

106. Anne Braden, unpublished 1964 article, 1964, Carl and Anne Braden Papers, 1928–1990, Box 62, Folder 4, SHSW.

107. Cook, *Sweet Land of Liberty?* 182–83; Weisbrot, *Freedom Bound*, 244.

108. Cook, *Sweet Land of Liberty?* 187, 202; Weisbrot, *Freedom Bound*, 236–37; John Morton Blum, *Years of Discord: American Politics and Society, 1961–1974* (New York: W.W. Norton, 1991), 264–67. For examples of the Panthers' community activism, see Yohuru Williams, *Black Politics/White Power: Civil Rights, Black Power, and the Black Panthers in New Haven* (New York: Brandywine Press, 2000). A more negative portrayal can be found in Hugh Pearson, *The Shadow of the Panther: Huey Newton and the Price of Black Power in America* (New York: Addison-Wesley, 1994)

109. For the problems with the War on Poverty see Robert Dallek, *Flawed Giant: Lyndon Johnson and His Times, 1961–1973* (New York: Oxford University Press, 1998), 329–34. See also Fairclough, "Martin Luther King, Jr. and the War in Vietnam," 319.

110. See Weisbrot, *Freedom Bound*, 158–61, 182–83, 216–18, 262–75; Blum, *Years of Discord*, 260–64.

111. Dallek, *Flawed Giant*, 339.

112. DeBenedetti, *An American Ordeal*, 158; Burner, *Making Peace with the 60s*, 73.

113. Stokely Carmichael, "At Morgan State," quoted in *Vietnam and Black America: An Anthology of Protest and Resistance*, ed. Clyde Taylor (Garden City, N.Y.: Anchor/Doubleday, 1973), 266–67.

114. "NLF Vietnam," *Black Panther*, August 16, 1969, quoted in *The Black Panther Leaders Speak*, ed. G. Louis Heath (Metuchen, N.J.: Scarecrow Press, 1976), 112.

115. Larry Jones, "Power to the People of Viet Nam," *Black Panther*, July 26, 1969, 16, quoted in Heath, *The Black Panther Leaders Speak*, 111.

116. Eldridge Cleaver, "The Black Man's Stake in Vietnam," extract from *Soul on Ice*, quoted in *Two, Three . . . Many Vietnams: A Radical Reader on the Wars in Southeast Asia and the Conflicts at Home*, ed. Banning Garrett and Katherine Bradley for Ramparts (New York: Canfield Press, 1971), 220.

117. "Support American Negroes' Use of Revolutionary Violence Against Counter-Revolutionary Violence," 19; "Speech by U.S. Negro Leader Robert F. Williams," 24, both in *Peking Review* 9, 33 (August 12, 1966).

118. "Speech by U.S. Negro Leader Robert F. Williams," 26.

119. Carson, *In Struggle*, 175.

120. *New Left Notes*, June 24, 1966, 2.

121. *New Left Notes*, June 24, 1966, 1, 4; The picketing of Luci Baines Johnson's wedding was cited as an example.

122. *SNCC News of the Field*, 1, February 23, 1966, 3, SHSW. At an April meeting of peace and freedom activists in Nashville, concerns had been expressed about the economic pressure to which black antiwar activists were subject to— see *Southern Patriot*, April 1966, 3.

123. Ed Hamlett, "Black Consciousness," *New Left Notes*, May 27, 1966, 7.

124. All information and quotations about the Nashville SCC conference are taken from Anne Braden, "Peace Sentiment Grows," *Southern Patriot*, April 1966, 1, 3, and Jack A. Smith, "Anti-War Groups of South Confer," *National Guardian* (New York), April 30, 1966, 1, 4.

125. *New Left Notes*, July 8, 1966, 1.

126. Bob Ross, "New Politics and Old Problems," *New Left Notes*, May 27, 1966, 5. The article was written in early March.

127. Tom Wells, *The War Within: America's Battle over Vietnam* (Berkeley: University of California Press, 1994), 116.

128. SNCC Central Committee Meeting Minutes, March 4, 1967, Atlanta, 7, SNCC Records (microfilm), Reel 3; Gwendolyn Patton position paper—"Why Black People Must Develop Own Anti-War and Anti-Draft Union . . . Heed the Call!" (end of 1967, early 1968), 2, SNCC Records, reel 58, Library of Congress.

129. Memorandum Re: SMC, from Gwendolyn Patton to SNCC Central Committee, November 6, 1967, 1, SNCC Records, Reel 58, Library of Congress.

130. *Political Activities of the Johnson White House, 1963–1969. Part 1: White House Central and Confidential Files. Series A: Candidates, Campaigns, Elections, and Parties*, ed. Paul L. Kesaris; Guide compiled by Robert E. Lester (Frederick, Md.: University Publications of America, 1987), Reel 27, Frame 1316, University Library, Cambridge University (*Political Activities IA*).

131. Letter from Arthur Waskow to Anne Stadler, January 3, 1967, Arthur I. Waskow Papers, 1958–1977 (unprocessed), Box 1, NCNP Folder 3, SHSW.

132. Memorandum for the Record, July 15, 1967, *Political Activities IA*, Reel 27, Frame 1317.

133. "Don't Mourn for Us . . . Organize . . . The Call of the National Conference

for New Politics" (published program, c. July 1967), *Political Activities IA*, Reel 27, Frame 1328.

134. "Don't Mourn for Us . . . Organize."

135. NCNP Letter, c. June 1966, White House Central Files, Name File, "National Conference L-P," Box 26, Lyndon Baines Johnson Presidential Library, Austin, Texas (LBJ).

136. NCNP Letter; this position contrasts with the advocates of the "Freedom Budget," such as Bayard Rustin, who took the line that America could afford both guns *and* butter.

137. Thomas Powers, *The War at Home: Vietnam and the American People, 1964–1968* (New York: Grossman, 1973), 124.

138. Daryl E. Lembke, "New Left to Test Strength at Oakland Polls," *Los Angeles Times*, June 6, 1966, 3.

139. Serge Lang, *The Scheer Campaign* (New York: Benjamin, 1967), 53.

140. Daryl E. Lembke, "Scheer in Close Race in Oakland," *Los Angeles Times*, June 9, 1966, 3.

141. See Kirkpatrick Sale, *SDS* (New York: Random House, 1973), 277.

142. The Community for New Politics was the organization that carried on the community work after the election.

143. Andrew Kopkind, "Anti-Vietnam Politics: Peace Candidates in Oregon, California," *New Republic*, June 4, 1966, 16.

144. George Kaufmann, "Condemn War and Ghettos," *Berkeley Barb*, 2, 3, January 21, 1966, 1; Finding aid, Carlton Benjamin Goodlett Papers, 1942–1967 (microfilm), SHSW. An interesting aside concerns Goodlett's relationship with the NAACP national staff. In a letter to June Shagaloff on September 21, 1962 Goodlett wrote "Give my regards to Gloster Current. You might even say hello to Roy Wilkins for me. I am continuing to work on a good retirement plan for him (smiles)"—Carlton B. Goodlett Papers, Reel 2, NAACP correspondence, SHSW.

145. Lang, *The Scheer Campaign*, 139–40.

146. For a detailed account of the campaign, see Lang, *The Scheer Campaign*.

147. Many NCNP board members thought that Scheer was too radical.

148. Letter from Don McKelvey to Waskow, September 21, 1966, and Waskow's reply of September 27, Arthur I. Waskow Papers (unprocessed), Box 1, NCNP Folder, SHSW; Paul Booth memo to NCNP Board, June 24, 1966, Donna Allen Papers, 1960–1987, Box 2, Folder 4, memo and reports, 1966–68, SHSW.

149. Simon Casady memo to NCNP board, Donna Allen Papers, Box 2, Folder 4, SHSW.

150. See Chapter 4.

151. August Meier and Elliot Rudwick, *CORE: A Study in the Civil Rights Movement, 1942–1968* (New York: Oxford University Press, 1973), 415.

152. Meier and Rudwick, *Core*; Northeast Regional Conference, April 23, 1966, Philadelphia, Report, 10—Resolutions Committee—Sol Herbert, Robert Curvin Papers, 1965–1969, SHSW.

153. *National Guardian*, July 16, 1966, 5.

154. Letter to James Farmer from Jim Williams, Chairman of Philadelphia CORE, March 8, 1966, James Leonard Farmer, Jr. and Lula Peterson Farmer Papers, 1908, 1921–1997, Center for American History, University of Texas at Austin (Farmer Papers), Series I, Records of Professional Activities, Box 2R566, Folder "CORE: Internal Correspondence, 1965–1970."

155. Letter from James Farmer to Jim Williams, March 24, 1966, Farmer Papers, Box 2R566, Series I, Records of Professional Activities, Folder "CORE: Internal Correspondence, 1965–1970." for an account of the Literacy Program

episode, see James Farmer, *Lay Bare the Heart: An Autobiography of the Civil Rights Movement* (New York: Plume, 1985), 293–305.

156. Weisbrot, *Freedom Bound*, 193; see also "To Fulfill These Rights," Report of the White House Conference, June 1–2, 1966, 158, National Security File—Subject File, Box 5, Folder—"Civil Rights, Vol. 1," LBJ.

157. Dallek, *Flawed Giant*, 222, 225–26.

158. Weisbrot, *Freedom Bound*, 193.

159. "To Fulfill These Rights," Box 29, Folder—Committee I, Panel no. I—"Housing," afternoon session, June 1, 1966, 81, LBJ.

160. "To Fulfill These Rights," Box 29, Folder—Committee I, Panel no. I, "Administration of Justice and Other," afternoon session, June 2, 1966, 20, 37.

161. Cook, *Sweet Land of Liberty?* 245.

162. "Civil Rights Groups Against Viet War," *Southern Patriot*, April 1966, 1.

163. *The Guardian*, April 2, 1966, 3.

164. *The Guardian*, April 2, 1966, 6.

165. *SNCC News of the Field*, 1, February 23, 1966, 4, SHSW.

166. March 1966 MFDP memo: Viet-Nam Pray-in: and Sunflower City Election, Mississippi Freedom Democratic Party (MFDP) Records, Box 1, Folder 15, SHSW.

167. MFDP Records, Box 1, Folder 19, SHSW.

168. *SNCC News of the Field*, 6, March 30, 1966, 3, SHSW.

169. MFDP Records (microfilm), Reel 2, SHSW. "Maximum feasible participation" refers to the call in the War on Poverty legislation for poor people to be involved in the administration of antipoverty programs.

170. Farmer, *Lay Bare the Heart*, 263, letter from George Raymond, Collier for Congress Committee, Canton, Mississippi to Mr. Herb Callender, NCNP, May 1966, New York, Papers of the Congress of Racial Equality, 1944–1968 (microfilm), F: I: 58, SHSW.

171. "FDP Sues to Block Operation of Draft," *Clarion Ledger*, July 12, 1966, MFDP Records, Reel 2, SHSW.

172. SNCC Press Release, October 22, 1966, Howard Zinn Papers (processed), Box 3, Folder 5, SHSW; Forman, *Sammy Younge, Jr.*, 224.

173. See "12 Jailed for Draft Protest," *Southern Patriot*, November 1966, 1, 6; *Atlanta's Black Paper*, compiled by the SNCC Atlanta Project, August 25, 1966.

174. Dick Magidoff, "Anti-War Groups Meet in Cleveland," *New Left Notes*, August 5, 1966, 8.

175. *New York Times*, May 16, 1966, Office Files of Marvin Watson, Box 32, Folder—Vietnam, LBJ.

176. "SCC Meets," *New South Student* 3, 5, May 1966, 8.

Chapter 3. Black Moderates

1. David J. Garrow, *Bearing the Cross: Martin Luther King, Jr. and The Southern Christian Leadership Conference* (1986; London: Vintage, 1993), 552–53.

2. Garrow, *Bearing the Cross*, 540.

3. Garrow, *Bearing the Cross*, 554.

4. Garrow, *Bearing the Cross*, 562.

5. Garrow, *Bearing the Cross*, 553–54.

6. Robert Cook, *Sweet Land of Liberty? The African-American Struggle for Civil Rights in the Twentieth Century* (London: Longman, 1998), 118.

7. Denton L. Watson, "Reassessing the Role of the NAACP in the Civil

Rights Movement," *Historian* 55 (Spring 1993): 453–68; Denton L. Watson, "The Papers of the '101st Senator': Clarence Mitchell Jr. and Civil Rights," *Historian* 63 (Spring/Summer 2002): 623–41.

8. Roy Wilkins with Tom Matthews, *Standing Fast: The Autobiography of Roy Wilkins* (New York: Da Capo, 1994), xi, 19, 45–46, 48–49, 55–56, 104–7, 154–55, 220. See, for example, John Dittmer's account of how the NAACP national leadership helped to blunt the radicalism of the movement in Jackson, Mississippi. John Dittmer, *Local People: The Struggle for Civil Rights in Mississippi* (Urbana: University of Illinois Press, 1994), 160–69; Cook, *Sweet Land of Liberty?* 117–18, 223. For the grass-roots perspective, see especially Charles M. Payne, *I've Got the Light of Freedom: The Organizing Tradition and the Mississippi Freedom Struggle* (Berkeley: University of California Press, 1995).

9. Nancy J. Weiss, *Whitney M. Young, Jr., and the Struggle for Civil Rights* (Princeton, N.J.: Princeton University Press, 1989), xi-xii, 4, 119.

10. Adam Fairclough, *Better Day Coming: Blacks and Equality, 1890–2000* (New York: Viking Penguin, 2001), 236; Peter J. Ling, *Martin Luther King, Jr.* (London: Routledge, 2002), 47–48; Jervis Anderson, *Bayard Rustin: Troubles I've Seen: A Biography* (New York: HarperCollins, 1997), 186–89, 198, 247–64.

11. Cook, *Sweet Land of Liberty?* 201–2, 208.

12. See Manfred Berg, "Guns, Butter, and Civil Rights: The National Association for the Advancement of Colored People and the Vietnam War, 1964–1968," in *Aspects of War in American History,* ed. David K. Adams and Cornelius A. van Minnen (Keele: Keele University Press, 1997), 220.

13. Henry Wallace to John Morsell, January 13, 1966, NAACP Papers, Group IV, Box A86, Folder "Vietnam Correspondence 1966," Library of Congress. Although Manfred Berg's analysis of the NAACP is quite sympathetic, he still accuses the organization of "moral and intellectual hypocrisy" in not opposing the war. See Berg, "Guns, Butter, and Civil Rights," 214.

14. Bayard Rustin, "Dr. King's Painful Dilemma," *New York Amsterdam News,* March 3, 1967, in *Down the Line: The Collected Writings of Bayard Rustin,* intro C. Vann Woodward (Chicago: Quadrangle Books, 1971), 169.

15. Rustin, "Dr. King's Painful Dilemma," 169–70.

16. Tom Wells, *The War Within: America's Battle over Vietnam* (Berkeley: University of California Press, 1994), 196, 212–19, 277.

17. Anderson, *Bayard Rustin: Troubles I've Seen,* 293, 298. Rustin's dedication to the realignment of the Democratic Party played a role in his somewhat conservative stance with regard to the peace movement. It is also widely rumored that Rustin began to work for the CIA.

18. John D'Emilio, "Homophobia and the Trajectory of Postwar American Radicalism: The Career of Bayard Rustin," *Radical History Review* 62 (Spring 1995), 99.

19. D'Emilio, "Homophobia and the Trajectory," 96–98.

20. Roy Wilkins, "Sidetrack," *New York Post,* July 18, 1965, Roy Wilkins Papers, Box 39, Folder "newspaper column clippings, 1964–65," Library of Congress.

21. Garrow, *Bearing the Cross,* 555; Berg, "Guns, Butter, and Civil Rights," 223.

22. Garrow, *Bearing the Cross,* 555.

23. 1 "Dr. King's New Role," *New York Post,* April 15, 1967, Roy Wilkins Papers, Box 39, Folder "newspaper column clippings 1967–69," Library of Congress.

24. "Freedom House Sharply Censures Dr. King for Ties to Red-Tainted Antiwar Move," *Worcester Sunday Telegram,* May 21, 1967, National Association for the Advancement of Colored People (NAACP) Papers, Group IV, Box A86, Folder "Vietnam Correspondence, 1967–68," Library of Congress. King had

recently lent his support to the Spring Mobilization Committee to End the War in Vietnam.

25. Letter from Esther S. Frankel, April 12, 1967, NAACP Papers, Group IV Box A86, folder "Vietnam Correspondence, 1967–68," Library of Congress.

26. Letter from Sidney L. Jackson to the editor of *Life* Magazine, April 20, 1967, NAACP Papers, Group IV Box A86, Folder "Vietnam Correspondence, 1967–68," Library of Congress.

27. Roy Wilkins, "LBJ's Programs Would Aid Negro," *Detroit News*, August 26, 1967, Office Files of Frederick Panzer, Box 331, Folder—Civil Rights 1967–1968, Lyndon Baines Johnson Presidential Library; Austin, Texas (LBJ).

28. Letter from John Morsell to Henry Wallace, January 10, 1966, NAACP Papers, Group IV, Box A86, Folder "Vietnam Correspondence, 1966," Library of Congress.

29. Letter from Roy Wilkins to Joseph Stern, March 17, 1966, NAACP Papers, Group IV, Box A86, Folder "Vietnam Correspondence, 1966," Library of Congress.

30. See Berg, "Guns, Butter, and Civil Rights."

31. "Carmichael Assails Democrats, Liberals," *Washington Post*, January 19, 1967.

32. Wilkins, *Standing Fast*, 321.

33. Joseph Wershba, "Daily Closeup: Herbert Hill, NAACP's Labor Secretary," *New York Post*, December 14, 1959, 49; author's interview with Herbert Hill, May 16, 2000.

34. See Wershba, "Daily Closeup: Herbert Hill"; Paula F. Pfeffer, *A. Philip Randolph, Pioneer of the Civil Rights Movement* (Baton Rouge: Louisiana State University Press, 1990), 226–32; Wilkins, *Standing Fast*, 221.

35. Hill interview.

36. Transcript, Roy Wilkins Oral History Interview I, April 1, 1969, by Thomas H. Baker, Internet Copy, LBJ, 14.

37. Wilkins, *Standing Fast*, 321.

38. Anderson, *Bayard Rustin*, 284.

39. Bayard Rustin, "From Protest to Politics: The Future of the Civil Rights Movement," *Commentary*, February 1965, *Down the Line*, 115.

40. Rustin, "From Protest to Politics, " 119.

41. Cook, *Sweet Land of Liberty?* 181; Berg, "Guns, Butter, and Civil Rights," 225.

42. Weiss, *Whitney M. Young, Jr.*, 158.

43. Anderson, *Bayard Rustin*, 296.

44. Staughton Lynd, "Coalition Politics or Nonviolent Revolution?" *Liberation* (June–July 1965): 18.

45. See Pfeffer, *A. Philip Randolph*, 17–18, 21, 43.

46. See Charles DeBenedetti with Charles Chatfield, *An American Ordeal: The Antiwar Movement of the Vietnam Era* (Syracuse, N.Y.: Syracuse University Press, 1990), 85, 100; Philip S. Foner, *American Labor and the Indochina War: The Growth of Union Opposition* (New York: International Publishers, 1971), 30–32.

47. Pfeffer, *A. Philip Randolph*, 68–73, 192–93.

48. Cook, *Sweet Land of Liberty?* 205.

49. Pfeffer, *A. Philip Randolph*, 149; undated paper, *The Papers of A. Philip Randolph*, ed. John H. Bracey, Jr. and August Meier (microfilm project of University Publications of America, 1990), Reel 32, Speeches and Writings File, Box 41, "Research Notes and Related Material, undated, 196 pp.," Sterling Memorial Library, Yale University (SML). See also Pfeffer, *A. Philip Randolph*, 278.

50. Letter from A. Philip Randolph to Jerome Davis, September 14, 1966, *Papers of A. Philip Randolph*, Reel 2, General Correspondence, Box 2, "A-Y, 1966," SML.

51. 2 Randolph undated paper.

52. Garrow, *Bearing the Cross*, 553; Pfeffer, *A. Philip Randolph*, 278; DeBenedetti, *An American Ordeal*, 108, 110. See letter from Lyndon Johnson to A. Philip Randolph, April 15, 1965, in *Papers of A. Philip Randolph*, Reel 2, General Correspondence, Box 2, "A-W, 1965," SML.

53. Letter from Norman Thomas to A. Philip Randolph, May 20, 1965; telegram, Randolph to Thomas, May 21, 1965, *Papers of A. Philip Randolph*, Reel 2, General Correspondence, Box 2, "A-W, 1965," SML.

54. Randolph undated paper.

55. Jervis Anderson, *A. Philip Randolph: A Biographical Portrait* (New York: Harvest Books, 1972), 331; Anderson, *Bayard Rustin*, 301.

56. Pfeffer, *A. Philip Randolph*, 278.

57. Randolph, undated paper.

58. Report from *New York Times*, August 3, 1965, C16, Howard Zinn Papers, 1956–1994 (processed), Box 3, Folder 5, State Historical Society of Wisconsin (SHSW).

59. Dennis C. Dickerson, *Militant Mediator: Whitney M. Young, Jr.* (Lexington: University Press of Kentucky, 1998), 271–73.

60. Weiss, *Whitney M. Young, Jr.*, 158–59.

61. Dickerson, *Militant Mediator*, 247.

62. Dickerson, *Militant Mediator*, 257.

63. Weiss, *Whitney M. Young, Jr.*, xi; Dickerson, *Militant Mediator*, 270.

64. Transcript, Roy Wilkins Oral History Interview, 14.

65. Wilkins, *Standing Fast*, 307.

66. White House Central File (WHCF) Name File—Roy Wilkins, February 24, 1966, LBJ to Wilkins, LBJ.

67. WHCF Name File—Roy Wilkins, September 5, 1968, LBJ to Wilkins, LBJ.

68. WHCF Name File—Roy Wilkins, January 17, 1969, LBJ to Wilkins, LBJ.

69. Office Files of Lee C. White, box 4, Folder—Civil Rights—List of Organizations and Political Leaders, Memo from George Reedy to LBJ, September 7, 1965, LBJ.

70. Hill interviews, May 16, August 9, 2000.

71. Hill interview, May 16, 2000.

72. "Vietnam Called 'Excuse' for Lag in Rights Fight," *Washington Post*, January 21, 1967, Office Files of Frederick Panzer, Box 331, Folder—Civil Rights 1967–1968, LBJ.

73. *National Urban League Newsletter*—Washington Bureau, 1, 4, June 30, 1967, 3.

74. Minutes, Council of United Civil Rights Leadership, March 23, 1966, New York; copy in possession of author.

75. Letter from Gloster Current to Locksley Edmondson, February 20, 1968, NAACP Records, Group IV, Box C58, Folder "E," Library of Congress.

76. William A. Price, "NAACP and CORE Reassess Their Goals," *National Guardian* (New York), July 17, 1965, 3.

77. Hill interview, May 16, 2000.

78. Henry Wallace to John Morsell, January 13, 1966, NAACP Papers, Group IV, Box A86, folder "Vietnam Correspondence 1966," Library of Congress.

79. Henry Wallace to John Morsell, January 17, 1966, NAACP Papers, Group IV, Box A86, Folder "Vietnam Correspondence 1966," Library of Congress.

80. Memorandum from Gloster Current to Roy Wilkins, May 1, 1967, 14, NAACP Papers, Group IV, Box C24, Folder "Greenwich Village-Chelsea, N.Y., 1966–67," Library of Congress.

81. See Cook, *Sweet Land of Liberty?*, 206; and "Use Black Power, Says NAACP

Head," *Yakima Herald,* July 13, 1966, NAACP Papers, Group IV, Box A11, Folder "Board of Directors, Tanner, Jack E, 1966–68," Library of Congress.

82. Memorandum from Roy Wilkins to Gloster Current, March 3, 1966, Roy Wilkins Papers, Box 7, "General Correspondence 1966," Library of Congress.

83. NAACP board meeting, November 13, 1950, quoted in Gerald Horne, *Black and Red: W. E. B. Du Bois and the Afro-American Response to the Cold War, 1944–1963* (Albany: State University of New York Press, 1986), 129.

84. Quoted in "NAACP Stand on Colonialism and U.S. Foreign Policy," *Crisis* 62 , 1 (January 1955): 25.

85. Eric Burner, *And Gently He Shall Lead Them: Robert Parris Moses and Civil Rights in Mississippi* (New York: New York University Press, 1994), 139.

86. Berg, "Guns, Butter, and Civil Rights," 215.

87. NAACP Records, Group III, Box A328, Folder "Vietnam War, 1964–65," Library of Congress.

88. Memo from Gloster Current to NAACP staff, April 22, 1965, NAACP Records, Group III Box A328, Folder "Vietnam War, 1964–65," Library of Congress. See also Berg, "Guns, Butter, and Civil Rights," 215.

89. James Farmer, *Lay Bare the Heart: An Autobiography of the Civil Rights Movement* (New York: Plume, 1985), 189; Obituary—Anjali Sekhar, *Detroit News,* July 6, 1997; Hill interview, August 9, 2000.

90. Letter from Gloster Current to Locksley Edmondson, February 20, 1968, NAACP Records, Group IV, Box C58, Folder "E," Library of Congress.

91. Hill interview, August 9, 2000.

92. Memo from Gloster Current to Roy Wilkins, John Morsell, Clarence Mitchell, and Henry Moon, May 14, 1965, NAACP Papers, Group III, Box A20, Folder "1965 Resolutions," Library of Congress.

93. Memo from Current to Wilkins, Stephen Spottswood, John Morsell, Clarence Mitchell, and Henry Moon, April 14, 1966, NAACP Papers, Group IV, Box A87, Folder "Vietnam NAACP 1966–67," Library of Congress.

94. Memo from Current to Spottswood, Mitchell, Moon, Morsell, et al., April 16, 1967, 4, NAACP Papers, Group IV, Box A87, Folder "Vietnam NAACP 1966–67," Library of Congress.

95. Memo from Current to all staff members, June 21, 1967, NAACP Papers, Group IV, Box C24, Folder "Greenwich Village-Chelsea, N.Y., 1966–67," Library of Congress.

96. Wilkins, "Sidetrack," my emphasis.

97. "SNCC's Foreign Policy," *New York Post,* January 16, 1966, Roy Wilkins Papers, Box 39, Folder "newspaper column clippings 1966," Library of Congress.

98. Telephone conversation between Roy Wilkins and Lyndon Johnson, August 15, 1964, 9:50 a.m., Recordings of Conversations and Meetings, Recordings of Telephone Conversations—White House Series, Tape WH6408.21, #4940 & #4941, LBJ.

99. Hill interview, May 16, 2000.

100. Berg, "Guns, Butter, and Civil Rights," 221.

101. Berg, "Guns, Butter, and Civil Rights," 215.

102. Flint, Michigan, Resolution, April 10, 1965, NAACP Records, Group III, Box A328, Folder "Vietnam War, 1964–65," Library of Congress.

103. Hill interview, May 16, 2000.

104. "NAACP Convention: Some Members Complain About 'Restrictions'," *The Movement,* August 1965), 6.

105. "NAACP Convention: Some Members Complain."

106. Hill interview, May 16, 2000.

107. For a detailed account of this campaign, see Serge Lang, *The Scheer Campaign* (New York: W.A. Benjamin, 1967); George Kaufmann, "Condemn War and Ghettos," *Berkeley Barb* 2, 3, January 21, 1966, 1; Finding aid, Carlton B. Goodlett Papers, 1942–1967, SHSW.

108. See Roberts campaign material, National Coordinating Committee to End the War in Vietnam Records, 1964–1967, Series 1, Box 4, Folder "Peace Candidates, 1966," SHSW.

109. Robert Dallek, *Flawed Giant: Lyndon Johnson and His times, 1961–1973* (Oxford: Oxford University Press, 1998), 307–11.

110. *The New Virginia* (VSCRC newsletter), 1, March 1966, SNCC Records, Reel 44, Library of Congress..

111. *Advance*, 6, 4 (April 1966), 1, NAACP Papers, Group IV, Box J7, Folder "Printed Matter NAACP by States, New York—NYC—Greenwich Village, 1966–67," Library of Congress.

112. Ed Preets, "President's Corner," *Advance* 6, 5 (May 1966), 2, NAACP Papers, Group IV, Box J7, Folder "Printed Matter NAACP by States, New York—NYC—Greenwich Village, 1966–67," Library of Congress.

113. NAACP Papers, Group IV, Box A87, Folder "Vietnam NAACP 1966–67," Library of Congress; Berg, "Guns, Butter, and Civil Rights," 221.

114. "Many Challenge War, Draft," *Southern Patriot*, February 1967, 8.

115. *Long Island CORE News*, November 1967, 1–2, SHSW.

116. Letter from Current to Lucile Rose and Donald R. Lee, May 22, 1967, NAACP Papers Group IV Box C24 folder "Greenwich Village-Chelsea, N.Y., 1966–67," Library of Congress.

117. Berg, "Guns, Butter, and Civil Rights," 224–25.

118. John Hammond with Irving Townsend, *On Record: An Autobiography* (New York: Ridge Press, 1977), 374–75.

119. Memo from Current to Dr. John Morsell, October 10, 1967—copy of resolution on Vietnam adopted by Michigan State Conference, NAACP Papers, Group IV, Box A87, Folder "Vietnam NAACP 1966–67," Library of Congress.

120. DuVernay had refused to be a "black mercenary for white imperialism"; see "Many Challenge War, Draft," 8.

121. Adam Fairclough, *Race and Democracy: The Civil Rights Struggle in Louisiana, 1915–1972* (Athens: University of Georgia Press, 1995), 417; *NAACP News*, February 1967, NAACP Papers, Group IV, Box J11, Folder "Printed Matter—West Coast Regional Office Newsletters, 1966-April, 1967," Library of Congress.

122. See Payne, *I've Got the Light of Freedom*, 360–61; Dittmer, *Local People*, 178.

123. *MFDP Newsletter*, 2, 6 (c. February 1968), SHSW.

124. Press Release, Mississippi State Conference of the NAACP, April 22, 1968, NAACP Papers, Group VI, Box C190, Library of Congress.

125. John Morsell to Henry Wallace, January 10, 1966, NAACP Papers, Group IV, Box A86, Folder "Vietnam Correspondence 1966"; Morsell to Sheldon Gutman, April 18, 1967, NAACP Papers, Group IV, Box A86, Folder "Vietnam Correspondence, 1967–68," Library of Congress.

126. "Use Black Power, Says NAACP Head," *Yakima Herald*, July 13, 1966, 2, NAACP Papers, Group IV, Box A11, Folder "Board of Directors, Tanner, Jack E 1966–68," Library of Congress.

127. See letter from William B. Hixon, Jr., to *New York Times*, dated April 10, 1967, reprinted in *Dr. Martin Luther King, Dr. John C. Bennett, Dr. Henry Steele*

Commager, Rabbi Abraham Heschel Speak on the War in Vietnam—with an Introduction by Dr. Reinhold Neibuhr, 29, in *Records of the Southern Christian Leadership Conference, 1954–1970, Part 4: Records of the Program Department* (microfilm edition), editorial adviser Cynthia Lewis (Lanham, Md.: University Publications of America, 1995), Reel 26, Series VII, Records of the Peace Education Project, 1966–1967 cont., Box 176, Folder 8 "Vietnam Summer, 1967–1968," Library of Congress.

128. See Hixon letter.

129. Quoted in "NAACP Stand on Colonialism and U.S. Foreign Policy," 25.

130. See Berg, "Guns, Butter and Civil Rights," 220.

131. Roy Wilkins, "Negroes and the Draft," *New York Post*, August 20, 1965, Roy Wilkins Papers, Box 39, Folder "Newspaper Column Clippings 1964–65," Library of Congress.

132. See Berg, "Guns, Butter, and Civil Rights," 216; Roy Reed, "U.S. Study Asked on Draft Evasion," *New York Times*, August 3, 1965, Howard Zinn Papers (processed), Box 3, Folder 5, SHSW.

133. Letter from John Morsell to Henry Wallace, January 10, 1966, 1–2, NAACP Papers, Group IV, Box A86, Folder "Vietnam Correspondence 1966," Library of Congress.

134. Telegram from Roy Wilkins to LBJ, January 13, 1966, WHCF Name File—Roy Wilkins, LBJ. See also Berg, "Guns, Butter and Vietnam," 220, my emphasis.

135. "Wilkins Raps King's Civil Rights Policy," *Worcester Sunday Telegram*, April 19, 1967, NAACP Papers, Group IV Box A86, Folder "Vietnam Correspondence, 1967–68," Library of Congress.

136. David Nolan, "Domestic Effects of the War in Vietnam," July 1967, David Nolan Papers, 1960–1987, Box 6, Folder 16, SHSW.

137. NAACP Papers, Group VI, Box C190, Folder "Current, Gloster B. Memorandum," Library of Congress.

138. Dickerson, *Militant Mediator*, 270, 271–73.

139. Dickerson, *Militant Mediator*, 273–74.

140. Weiss, *Whitney M. Young, Jr.*, 161.

141. Weiss, *Whitney M. Young, Jr.*, 162. LBJ was referring to the recent appointment of Thurgood Marshall to the U.S. Supreme Court.

142. Andrew Young, *An Easy Burden: The Civil Rights Movement and the Transformation of America* (New York: HarperCollins, 1996), 431.

143. Young, *An Easy Burden*, 431; Weiss, *Whitney M. Young, Jr.*, 168.

144. Weiss, *Whitney M. Young, Jr.*, 162.

145. Dickerson, *Militant Mediator*, 278–79.

146. Memo from Jim Jones to LBJ, September 6 1967, subject: Meeting with Vietnam Election Observers in the Cabinet Room (meeting lasted from 11:09 a.m. to 12:05 p.m.), 3, Diary Backup, Box 75, LBJ.

147. Memo from Jones to LBJ, 4, LBJ.

148. For example, after Young returned from observing the elections, the Johnson administration tried to involve him in efforts to justify the war. He was sent a speech written by a presidential aide to help him gain a "better understanding of the Government's position and the steps that led to our present involvement in Vietnam"; see Dickerson, *Militant Mediator*, 280.

149. Statement by John Wilson in Bratislava, Czechoslovakia, Conference between Vietnamese and Americans (summer/August 1967), 4, SNCC Records (microfilm edition), Reel 23, Library of Congress.

Chapter 4. Racial Tensions

1. See Fred Halstead, *Out Now! A Participant's Account of the American Movement Against the Vietnam War* (New York: Monad Press, 1978), 284; Robert Randolph, "65,000 at S.F. rally Against Vietnam War," *National Guardian,* April 22, 1967, 3.

2. See Charles DeBenedetti with Charles Chatfield, *An American Ordeal: The Antiwar Movement of the Vietnam Era* (Syracuse, N.Y.: Syracuse University Press, 1990), 175–76; David J. Garrow, *Bearing the Cross: Martin Luther King, Jr., and the Southern Christian Leadership Conference* (1986; London: Vintage, 1993), 556–57; Halstead, *Out Now!* 281–86; Tom Wells, *The War Within: America's Battle over Vietnam* (Berkeley: University of California Press, 1994), 133–34.

3. Garrow, *Bearing the Cross,* 556–57; Wells, *The War Within,* 133–34.

4. See Wells, *The War Within,* 100, 105, 123–24, 126, 219. For a history of the Weather Underground, see Ron Jacobs, *The Way the Wind Blew: A History of the Weather Underground* (London: Verso, 1997).

5. Spring Mobilization Committee Press Release, November 1966, in National Mobilization Committee to End the War in Vietnam (Mobe) Records Series III—"History," Box 4, Folder "History 1966," Swarthmore College Peace Collection (Swarthmore).

6. Spring Mobilization Committee Mailing, James Leonard Jr. and Lula Peterson Farmer Papers, 1908, 1921–1997, Box 2R608, Folder—Vietnam, 1968, Center for American History, University of Texas at Austin.

7. Jack A. Smith, "Hope Held for a Wider Peace Movement," *National Guardian* (New York), 4 February 1967, 13.

8. S. Washington, "Should We Stay in Asia? How Negroes Feel," *Chicago Daily Defender,* April 1–7, 1967, 1; Garrow, *Bearing the Cross,* 562.

9. *Mobilizer,* 1, 2, February 6, 1967 1, State Historical Society of Wisconsin (SHSW).

10. Smith, "Hope Held for a Wider Peace Movement," 13.

11. "An Aide to Dr. King Appointed to Head New Antiwar Group," *New York Times,* January 28, 1967, reprinted in a Mobe flyer, February 1967, Mobe Records Series III—History, Box 4, Folder "History—January 1967," Swarthmore.

12. Smith, "Hope Held for a Wider Peace Movement," 13.

13. Student Mobilization Committee to End the War in Vietnam (SMC) Records, 1966–1973, Box 11, Folder 11, SHSW.

14. Wells, *The War Within,* 116.

15. Stanley Levison to Rachel DuBois, March 1, 1967, *The Martin Luther King, Jr., FBI File Part II: The King-Levison File,* ed. David J. Garrow, Guide compiled by Martin Schipper (Frederick, Md.: University Publications of America, 1987), University of Leeds, UK (hereafter *King-Levison FBI*), Reel 6, Frame 802; Garrow, *Bearing the Cross,* 556.

16. Garrow, *Bearing the Cross,* 557; Carmichael speech at the Spring Mobilization, April 15, 1967, 6. See DeBenedetti, *An American Ordeal,* 158.

17. Carmichael Spring Mobilization speech, 5. The draft was an area of specific concern to black antiwar radicals.

18. "CORE and Vietnam," Papers of the Congress of Racial Equality, 1944–1968 (microfilm; hereafter CORE Papers 1944–1968), E: III: 76—CORE-lator (n.d.), SHSW.

19. *National Guardian,* April 22, 1967, 1. Such black antiwar participation must be put in some context—at the end of April 4,000 Harlemites (twice the number who protested the war) attended a rally in support of three top African

American policemen and blacks serving in Vietnam. Organized by the United Block Association—an anti-poverty agency—the parade was led by Lieut. Colonel John D. Silvera, who stated that the rally was "Harlem's loud and clear answer to those who would impugn the patriotism of black people as a group"; see *New York Amsterdam News*, April 29, 1967, 3.

20. See flyer, "Hear Stokely Carmichael," Mobe Records, Series III—History, Box 4, Folder "History—April 1967," Swarthmore. Percy Gilmer of Brooklyn CORE was also the Greater New York area coordinator for black communities in the Spring Mobilization. He worked with the Black United Action Front in Harlem to help solidify black support for the April demonstrations, and was aided by Mobe officials Paul Brooks and Paul Boutelle as well as Omar Ahmed (chairman of East River CORE); see "Black Americans Take the Lead in War Protest," Mobe Press Release, 3, Mobe Records, Series IV—Projects, Box 6, Folder "April 15 (1967) Mass Rally—Releases, Swarthmore.

21. Robert L. Allen, "Harlem Marchers Jolt Times Sq. in Detour," *National Guardian*, April 22, 1967, 4.

22. John Molleson, "Chant of Harlem: Burn, Baby, Burn," *New York Times*, April 16, 1967, Mobe Records Series VI—News clippings, Box 10, Folder "April 15 March (1967) Reports—New York," Swarthmore.

23. Robert L. Allen, "Anti-War Sentiment Among Negroes on the Rise," *National Guardian*, May 6, 1967, 7.

24. DeBenedetti, *An American Ordeal*, 180.

25. Letter from Kipp Dawson to Stokely Carmichael, May 4, 1967, SMC Records, Box 6, Folder 9—Georgia, 1967–, SHSW.

26. "Anti-War Students Mobilized at U of C," *Chicago Seed*, 1, 3, May–June 1967, 14.

27. 3 Black Student Caucus, SMC, May 14, 1967, Madison Committee to End the War in Vietnam Records, 1965–1971, Box 2, Folder 4, SHSW.

28. Robert Weisbrot, *Freedom Bound: A History of America's Civil Rights Movement* (New York: Plume, 1990), 263. For information on the conference, see L. H. Stanton, "The Black Power Conference—A View from Inside," 27 July 27, 1967, *Congress of Racial Equality (CORE) Papers Part 3: Scholarship, Educational and Defense Fund for Racial Equality, 1960–1976, Series B: Leadership Development Files*, associate editor Randolph Brown; Guide compiled by Dale Reynolds, microfilm edition (Frederick, Md.: University Publications of America, 1984) (hereafter Core Papers), Reel 9, Frame 00053; University Library, University of Cambridge; Robert C. Maynard, "New Wall Rising Between the Races?" *Washington Post Outlook*, section B, Sunday July 30, 1967, CORE Papers Part 3 Series B, reel 9, frame 00059; Martin Arnold, "Newark Meeting on Black Power Attended by 400," *New York Times*, July 21, 1967, 34; Thomas A. Johnson, "McKissick Holds End of Violence Iis Up to Whites," *New York Times*, July 22, 1967, 11; Floyd McKissick speech, "Genocide USA: A Blueprint for Black Survival,"July 21, 1967, Newark Black Power Conference, CORE Papers 1944–1968, A: II: 46, SHSW; and "Black Power Manifesto and Resolutions," adopted at the Newark Black Power Conference, CORE Papers Part 3 Series B, Reel 9.

29. Johnson, "McKissick Holds End of Violence Is Up to Whites," 11.

30. Carol A. Moere, "Report of the National Conference on Black Power," 1–2, CORE Papers Part 3 Series B, Reel 9, Frames 00010–11; Maynard, "New Wall Rising Between the Races?"; "Black Power Manifesto and Resolutions," adopted at the Newark Black Power Conference, CORE Papers Part 3, Series B, Reel 9.

31. McKissick speech, "Genocide USA"; "Black Power Manifesto and Resolutions."

32. 4 "Black Power Manifesto and Resolutions."

33. William F. Pepper, "NCNP Convention Address," 4–6, National Conference for New Politics (NCNP) Records, 1966–1968, SHSW.

34. Walter Goodman, "When Black Power Runs the New Left," *New York Times Magazine*, September 24, 1967, 28.

35. "Don't Mourn for Us . . . Organize . . . The Call of the National Conference for New Politics" (published program), *Political Activities of the Johnson White House, 1963–1969. Part 1: White House Central and Confidential Files. Series A: Candidates, Campaigns, Elections, and Parties*, ed. Paul L. Kesaris; Guide compiled by Robert E. Lester (Frederick, Md.: University Publications of America, c.1987), Reel 27, Frame 1328, University Library, University of Cambridge (hereafter *Political Activities I A*)

36. See, for example, Andrew Ridgeway, "Freak-Out in Chicago: The National Conference of New Politics," *New Republic*, September 16, 1967. Robert Cook refers to the convention as a "fiasco"; see Robert Cook, *Sweet Land of Liberty? The African-American Struggle for Civil Rights in the Twentieth Century* (Harlow: Longman, 1998), 210.

37. *Political Activities I A*, Reel 27, 1316.

38. See Garrow, *Bearing the Cross*, 557–59.

39. "Third Parties: First Things First" (editorial), *Newsweek*, September 11, 1967, 15; "Call to Convention," WHCF, name file, "National Conference, L-P," Box 26, Lyndon Baines Johnson Presidential Library; Austin, Texas (LBJ).

40. Goodman, "When Black Power Runs the New Left," 28.

41. NCNP press release (for release September 4, 1967), "press" file, NCNP Records (unprocessed), Box 1, SHSW; William F. Pepper, *Orders to Kill: The Truth Behind the Murder of Martin Luther King* (New York: Carroll and Graf, 1995), 8.

42. "Symposium: Chicago's 'Black Caucus'," *Ramparts* 6, 4, November 1967, 101, 113.

43. Andrew Kopkind, "They'd Rather Be Left," *New York Review of Books*, September 28, 1967, 3.

44. Renata Adler, "Letter from the Palmer House," *New Yorker*, September 23, 1967, 58.

45. Adler, "Letter from the Palmer House," 68. Indeed, Julian Bond's commitment was less than total. In a letter to Arthur Waskow on May 25, 1967, he apologized for missing yet another board meeting, and declared himself to be "probably the most non-chairing chairman in organizational history." Letter from Bond to Waskow, May 25, 1967, Arthur I. Waskow Papers, 1958–1977 (unprocessed), Box 3, NCNP Folder 2, SHSW.

46. Frank Speltz, "Never Come Near (Electoral) Politics," *Washington Free Press*, September 23, 1967, 11.

47. Martin Luther King to Stanley Levison, September 1, 1967, *King-Levison FBI*, Reel 7, 563.

48. Conversation between Stanley Levison and Andrew Young, July 10, 1967, *King-Levison FBI*, Reel 7, Frame 399, and Garrow, *Bearing the Cross*, 713 n. 49.

49. NCNP News Release, "Black Activists Urged to Attend New Politics Convention," 10 August 1967, NCNP Records, SHSW.

50. Ridgeway, "Freak-Out in Chicago," 10.

51. Ridgeway, "Freak-Out in Chicago," 10. The Israel resolution was amended and toned down in the dying hours of the convention.

52. Adler, "Letter from the Palmer House," 80, 57.

53. Richard Blumenthal, "New Politics at Chicago," *The Nation*, September 25, 1967, 274.

54. "Support the Resolution of the Black Caucus," NCNP Records, SHSW.

55. Thomas Powers, *The War at Home: Vietnam and the American People, 1964–1968* (New York: Grossman, 1973), 267.

56. Blumenthal, "New Politics at Chicago."

57. Goodman, "When Black Power Runs the New Left,"125; Blumenthal, "New Politics at Chicago."

58. Karl E. Klare, "New Politics No More?" *Westside News*, September 14, 1967.

59. William A. Price, "New Politics of Black and White," *National Guardian* 19, 49, September 9, 1967.

60. *New York Times*, September 4, 1967, 20; Garson, "The Whites: A Clown Show," 9.

61. Weisbrot, *Freedom Bound*, 256.

62. Andrew Kopkind, "An Exchange on 'Racism,' " *New York Review of Books*, December 7, 1967, 37; Ridgeway, "Freak-Out in Chicago,"10; Black Caucus Notice, NCNP Records, SHSW.

63. Arthur I. Waskow, "Notes on Chicago.""Notes on Chicago," September 19, 1967, NCNP Records (unprocessed additions), Box 2, NCNP 1967 Convention Folder, SHSW.

64. Black Caucus Notice, NCNP Records, SHSW.

65. Waskow, "Notes on Chicago."

66. Robert F. Williams, "The New Left: Old Ideas in a New Front," *Crusader*, July 1967, reprinted in *Black Politics: A Journal of Liberation* 1, 3 (March 1968): 18.

67. SMC Records, Box 1, Folder 1: Minutes, 1967–1972, Student Mobilization Committee Position Papers, Gwen Patton, SHSW, my emphasis.

68. Marvin Garson, "The Whites: A Clown Show, part II," *Berkeley Barb*, September 22–28, 1967, 8.

69. Arthur I. Waskow, Letter to the Editor, *New York Review of Books*, November 23, 1967. See also Sidney Lens, "The New Politics Convention: Confusion and Promise," *New Politics* 6, 1 (Winter 1967):12.

70. 5 June Greenlief, "Static on the Left: Politics of Masquerade," *Village Voice*, October 12, 1967, 5; David Burner, *Making Peace with the 60s* (Princeton, N.J.: Princeton University Press, 1996), 166.

71. Lens, "The New Politics Convention: Confusion and Promise," 5.

72. Adler, "Letter from the Palmer House," 87.

73. Blumenthal, "New Politics at Chicago," 275.

74. Ridgeway, "Freak-Out in Chicago," 12.

75. D. J. R. Bruckner, "Board to Promote New Politics Candidates in Elections Named," *Los Angeles Times*, September 5, 1967, 2.

76. April 10, 1968, memo from William F. Pepper to NCNP board, April 10, 1968, Donna Allen Papers, Box 2 Folder 4, SHSW. The organization was about $20,000 in debt.

77. Contrast, for example, the thoughts of C. Clark Kissinger and Todd Gitlin with Peter Weiss, Maurice Zeitlin, Carlos Russell, and Carlton B. Goodlett in "Symposium: Chicago's 'Black Caucus'," *Ramparts* 6, 4, November 1967, 99–114; the editorial in the *Nation*, September 25, 1967, 261, felt that the NCNP would find a way to participate effectively in political campaigns. The Peace and Freedom Party—formed partially as a result of the NCNP convention—can be counted as a small success and continuation of the New Politics movement.

78. Sidney Lens, "Some Thoughts on the NCNP Conference," Paul Booth Papers, 1956–1970, Box 1, Folder 13, SHSW.

79. Ridgeway, "Freak Out in Chicago," 12.

80. Blumenthal, "New Politics at Chicago," 275.

81. Weisbrot, *Freedom Bound*, 256.

82. Halstead, *Out Now!* 320.

83. 6 The convention offers an insight into both the problems involved in trying to decide which issues to place importance on and the sexism that pervaded the New Left. Sara Evans has explained how the refusal of the convention to take the issue of women's liberation seriously helped spawn the feminist movement. See Sara Evans, *Personal Politics: The Roots of Women's Liberation in the Civil Rights Movement and the New Left* (New York: Vintage Books, 1980), 197–99.

84. Weisbrot, *Freedom Bound*, 256.

85. Writing in the *Village Voice*, September 28, 1967, 9–10, Nat Hentoff wrote that "the Chicago Conference was extremely useful because what happened there showed with bizarre clarity that organic unity can't be wished or traded into being."

86. Kopkind, "An Exchange on 'Racism,'" 38.

87. Blumenthal, "New Politics at Chicago," 275.

88. When James Bevel proposed speaking against the resolution condemning the "imperialist Zionist war" some black militants threatened to kill him—see Fairclough, *To Redeem the Soul of America*, 344.

89. Weisbrot, *Freedom Bound*, 256.

90. Greenlief, "Static on the Left," 18.

91. Wells, *The War Within*, 197; Norman Mailer, *The Armies of the Night: History as a Novel, the Novel as History* (1968; New York: Plume, 1994).

92. David Dellinger quoted in James Miller, *Democracy Is in the Streets: From Port Huron to the Siege of Chicago* (Cambridge, Mass.: Harvard University Press, 1994), 281.

93. Burner, *Making Peace with the 60s*, 73.

94. Wells, *The War Within*, 174.

95. National Mobilization Committee to End the War in Vietnam, press statement for release at Overseas Press Club, New York, August 28, 1967, quoted in Halstead, *Out Now!* 315.

96. "Anti-War Activities," *New Left Notes*, July 10, 1967, 3.

97. See Kirkpatrick Sale, *SDS* (New York: Random House, 1973), 213–15.

98. Carl Davidson and Mike Spiegal, "SDS and Oct. 21st: Repression and Resistance," *New Left Notes*, October 9, 1967, 3.

99. Sale, *SDS*, 315.

100. Davidson and Spiegal, "SDS and Oct. 21st," 3.

101. *Mobilizer* 2, 1, September 1, 1967, 1, 7, SHSW.

102. Robert Greenblatt, "Where We're At," *Mobilizer* 2, 1, September 1, 1967, 1, 4, 7; Clayborne Carson, *In Struggle: SNCC and the Black Awakening of the 1960s* (Cambridge, Mass.: Harvard University Press, 1981), 255–57.

103. See, for example, Sol Stern, "America's Black Guerrillas," *Ramparts* 6, 2, September 1967, 27.

104. National Mobilization Committee—Administrative Committee Meeting Minutes, New York, Saturday September 30, 1967, 4, Sidney M. Peck Papers, 1946–1988, Box 2, Folder 2, SHSW.

105. Memo from Gwen Patton to SNCC Central Committee, November 6, 1967. RE: SMC, 2, *Records of the Student Nonviolent Coordinating Committee* (microfilm; Lanham, Md.: University Publications of America), Reel 58 (hereafter SNCC Records), Library of Congress.

106. "Message to Black People," *Mobilizer News*, October 16, 1967, 4, Donna Allen Papers, Box 5, Folder 10, SHSW.

107. Maurice Isserman and Michael Kazin, *America Divided: The Civil War of the 1960s* (New York: Oxford University Press, 2000), 147–64; DeBenedetti, *An*

American Ordeal, 115, 223. For a general history of the counterculture, see Theodore Roszak, *The Making of a Counter Culture* (New York: Anchor Books, 1969).

108. DeBenedetti, *An American Ordeal*, 115, 135; Isserman and Kazin, *America Divided*, 171.

109. DeBenedetti, *An American Ordeal*, 115.

110. See, for example, Bradford Martin, "Politics as Art, Art as Politics: The Freedom Singers, the Living Theatre, and Public Performance," in *Long Time Gone: Sixties America Then and Now*, ed. Alexander Bloom (Oxford: Oxford University Press, 2001), 159–88.

111. "Leaders Divided on Aims of March," *Washington Post*, October 20, 1967, 17; Minutes—Mobe Administrative Committee Meeting, August 26, 1967, 4, Mobe Records, Series I—Organization, Box 1, Folder "Minutes, Administrative Committee," Swarthmore.

112. Burner, *Making Peace with the 60s*, 206.

113. Wells, *The War Within*, 180.

114. Interview with Stokely Carmichael, *The Movement*, vol. 3 no. 2 (Feb 1967),5; "Black-White Anti-Drafters on Upswing," *Berkeley Barb* vol. 4 no. 21 (26 May–1 June 1967),10.

115. Terry Cannon and Jeff Segal (Stop the Draft Week Steering Committee Members), "Stop the Draft Week," *The Movement* 3, 11, November 1967), 5.

116. *The Movement*, 4, 1 (January 1968), 3.

117. Cannon and Segal, "Stop the Draft Week," 5; "Blacks Drop Out of Stop Draft Week Action," *Berkeley Barb*, October 13–20, 1967, 3.

118. See Minutes—National Mobilization Committee to End the War in Vietnam Steering Committee Meeting, December 14, 1968, 3, National Mobilization Committee to End the War in Vietnam (Mobe) Records, Series I—Organization, Box 1, Folder "Steering Committee Minutes," Swarthmore.

119. 8 Wells, *The War Within*, 191–94.

120. Cannon and Segal, "Stop the Draft Week," 5.

121. *Mobilizer News: To End the War in Vietnam*, October 16, 1967 (published by National Mobilization Committee to End the War in Vietnam), 3, Madison Committee to End the War in Vietnam Records, 1965–1971, Box 1, Folder 6, SHSW.

122. Mailer, *The Armies of the Night*, 100.

123. DeBenedetti, *An American Ordeal*, 197.

124. Wells, *The War Within*, 196.

125. Mailer, *The Armies of the Night*, 125.

126. Wells, *The War Within*, 202–3.

127. DeBenedetti, *An American Ordeal*, 198.

128. Marc Steiner, "Brown Raps with White Left," *New Left Notes*, November 27, 1967, 2.

129. Thorne Dreyer (LNS), "Washington," *Chicago Seed* 1, 10, November 3–24, 1967, 3.

130. Jeff Shero, " . . . And More Particularly, the SDS Relationship to the Mobilization," *New Left Notes*, November 20, 1967, 3.

131. Carl Davidson and Greg Calvert, NIC, "The International Days of Resistance or 10 Days to Shake the Empire," *New Left Notes*, December 4, 1967, 1–3.

132. Quoted in a memo from Gloster Current to Dr. John Morsell, October 10, 1967, National Association for the Advancement of Colored People (NAACP) Papers, Group IV, Box A87, Folder "Vietnam NAACP 1966–67," Library of Congress.

133. See Thomas A. Johnson, "State's NAACP Opposes the War and New Charter," *New York Times*, October 23, 1967; Carolyn Dixon, "NAACP Youths Rough,"

New York Amsterdam News, October 28, 1967; *Advance* 6, 27, November 1967), 4, NAACP Papers, Group IV Box J7, Folder "Printed Matter NAACP by States, New York—NYC—Greenwich Village, 1966–67," Library of Congress.

134. Memorandum from Gwen Patton to SNCC Central Committee, November 6, 1967. RE: SMC, 3–4, SNCC Records, Reel 58, Library of Congress.

135. See http://www.trenholmtech.cc.al.us/library/Archives percent 20web/Gwen_ Patton.htm, 12/17/03; Patton's entry at www.crmvet.org, 12/17/03. Further information taken from "Movement Biography of Gwendolyn M. Patton" and "Curriculum Vita," copies in possession of author.

136. Memorandum from Gwen Patton to SNCC Central Committee, November 6, 1967. RE: SMC,3–4, SNCC Records, Reel 58, Library of Congress.

137. Gwen Patton, "Why Black People Must Develop Own Anti-War and Anti-Draft Union . . . Heed the Call!" (end 1967, early 1968), 2, 3, 5, SNCC Records, Reel 58, Library of Congress.

Chapter 5. Radicalism and Respectability

1. William H. Chafe, *The Unfinished Journey: America Since World War II,* 2nd ed. (New York: Oxford University Press, 1991), 367.

2. Paul Booth and Lee Webb, "The Antiwar Movement: From Protest to Radical Politics" (published by SDS-Chicago for the Thanksgiving 1965 end-the-war activities in D.C.), 3–5, State Historical Society of Wisconsin (SHSW).

3. Potter's speech in Massimo Teodori, *The New Left: A Documentary History* (London: Jonathan Cape, 1970), 248.

4. Kirkpatrick Sale, *SDS* (New York: Random House, 1973), 363.

5. Fred Halstead, *Out Now! A Participant's Account of the American Movement Against the Vietnam War* (New York: Monad Press, 1978), 373.

6. Madison Committee to End the War in Vietnam Records, 1965–1971, Box 2, Folder 7, SHSW.

7. Gwen Patton, "Black Militants and the War," *Student Mobilizer* 2, 1, January 1, 1968, 2.

8. Student Mobilization Committee to End the War in Vietnam (SMC) Records, 1966–1973, Box 1, Folder 1: Minutes, 1967–1972, Student Mobilization Committee Position Papers, Gwen Patton, SHSW.

9. John Wilson, "Liberation Forum: Black People and the war," *Guardian* (New York), February 24, 1968, 16.

10. Mike Marqusee, *Redemption Song: Muhammad Ali and the Spirit of the Sixties* (London: Verso, 1999), 241. In an unpublished 1972 essay Gwendolyn Patton, former national secretary of the NBAWADU, gave a brief outline of the organization's history—"There were strong regional bases in Boston, Detroit, Washington, D.C., Atlanta, New Orleans, Nashville, Tuskegee Institute, San Francisco, Los Angeles as well as in New York State. There was a newsletter and a series of pamphlets entitled: 'Hell No!' There were international trips by NBAWADU representatives to Prague, Tokyo and Korea. There was a mailing list of over 3,000 members. NBAWADU had great potential, but due to internal conflicts in SNCC . . . and this writer's hospitalization, who was then the national secretary of the organization, the organization lasted less than a year." See Gwen Patton, "Essay on the Peace Movement," 14, Gwendolyn Patton Papers, copy in possession of author.

11. Robert L. Allen, "Black Survival Linked to War," *Guardian,* April 20, 1968, 4.

12. See Maurice Isserman and Michael Kazin, *America Divided: The Civil War of the 1960s* (New York: Oxford University Press, 2000), 228–29.

13. Robert F. Williams, "The New Left: Old Ideas in a New Front," *Crusader*, 1967, *Black Politics: A Journal of Liberation* 1, 3 (March 1968): 19, 18, 17.

14. Williams, "The New Left," 19. Williams's biographer, Timothy Tyson, advised me to treat this source with caution. Certainly it was not unknown for the FBI to attempt to foment division between black and white radicals, and it is possible that "Old Ideas in a New Front" was written by someone other than Williams. However, in a 1966 speech Williams made similar points when he referred to "bourgeois minded so-called socialists" in America and asserted that "We Afro-American revolutionaries have discovered that some so-called socialists, we thought to be our comrades and class brothers, have joined the international Ku Klux Klan fraternity for white supremacy world domination." See "Speech by U.S. Negro Leader Robert Williams," *Peking Review* 9, 33, August 12, 1966, 26, 24. Either way, the editors of *Black Politics*, a self-styled "journal of liberation," felt that publishing it would aid the black liberation struggle, while Williams was not the only black radical to argue that the white left was trying to manipulate the black revolution.

15. "Forman, Spock in Fighting Stance for Peace, Rights," *Berkeley Barb* 6, 6, February 9–15, 1968), 3.

16. Robert L. Allen, "Black Campuses Today," *Guardian*, March 9, 1968, 6. See also "Leroi Jones: Part One," *Guardian*, March 23, 1968, 3.

17. "Gunning Down the Vietnamese" (editorial), *Freedomways* 9, 4 fourth quarter, Fall 1969, 296–97. Such an editorial line is, perhaps, unsurprising given the journal's closeness to the Communist Party—which consistently advocated building interracial alliances.

18. Todd Gitlin, *The Sixties: Years of Hope, Days of Rage* (New York: Bantam Books, 1987), 211.

19. Stew Albert, "Refugee's View of SDS Madness," *Berkeley Barb* 8, 26, June 27–July 3, 1969, 7.

20. Don Newton, "Black Power," *Southern California Regional Newsletter* 1, 3, 11, Students for a Democratic Society (SDS) Records, Box 37, Folder 1 "California: Los Angeles, 1965–1968," SHSW.

21. Details taken from finding aid, Fifth Avenue Peace Parade Committee, SHSW. See also Charles DeBenedetti with Charles Chatfield, *An American Ordeal: The Antiwar Movement of the Vietnam Era* (Syracuse, N.Y.: Syracuse University Press, 1990), 24–25.

22. "An Open Letter from James Forman to the New York Anti-War Conference of the Fifth Avenue Vietnam Peace Parade Committee, 3rd February 1968," *New Left Notes*, March 4, 1968, 2, 8.

23. Stanley Aronowitz, "On the Left: Absence of Strategy," *National Guardian*, February 10, 1968, 7.

24. Fifth Avenue Vietnam Peace Parade Committee, Administrative Committee Meeting Minutes, June 5, 1968, Fifth Avenue Vietnam Peace Parade Committee Records, 1965–1971 (Fifth Avenue Records), Box 1, Folder 1, SHSW.

25. Parade Committee Meeting, December 9, 1968, 2, Fifth Avenue Records, Box 1, Folder 1, SHSW.

26. Open Letter from Gwen Patton, June 18, 1968, 3, Gwendolyn Patton Papers. Copy in possession of author.

27. Pete Camejo (YSA), "Student Mobilization Pre-Convention Crisis," *Berkeley Barb*, 6, 22, May, 31, 1968, SMC Records, Box 1, Folder 1, SHSW.

28. Camejo, "Student Mobilization Pre-Convention Crisis."

29. Tom Wells, *The War Within: America's Battle over Vietnam* (Berkeley: University of California Press, 1994), 273–74.

30. Student Mobilization Committee Position Papers, SMC Records, Box 1, Folder 1: Minutes, 1967–1972, SHSW.

31. Open Letter from Gwen Patton, 2.

32. Student Mobilization Committee Position Papers, SMC Records, Box 1, Folder 1: Minutes, 1967–1972, SHSW.

33. Wells, *The War Within*, 275–76; for a more detailed discussion of these events—albeit from an SWP perspective—see Halstead, *Out Now!* 392–404.

34. See Theodore David Segal, "'A New Genesis': The 'Silent Vigil' at Duke University, April 5th–12th, 1968," History Honors Thesis, Duke University, April 23, 1977; William King, "The Vigil That Changed Duke," *Dialogue* (Duke University), December 19, 1997.

35. Segal, "A New Genesis," 8–11; William E. King, "The Year Duke Turned Activist," *Dialogue*, October 24, 1997.

36. Segal, "A New Genesis," 68–69.

37. David M. Henderson, "A Journal of the Duke Vigil" (1968), Duke Vigil, 1968 Collection, 1968, 158, Duke University Archives.

38. "You Have Wrought a Revolution," Special Report on the Duke Silent Vigil April 5–11, 1968, *Duke Chronicle*, Duke Vigil, 1968 Collection, 1968; David Pace, "Vigil Ignites Hopes for Blacks," *Duke Chronicle*, April 29, 1968, 6–7, Duke University Archives.

39. See DeBenedetti, *An American Ordeal*, 200–202, 209–15, 220–28; Wells, *The War Within*, 120–21, 223–27, 249–50; Chafe, *The Unfinished Journey*, chap. 12; Gitlin, *The Sixties*, 310. My thinking on Eugene McCarthy's 1968 campaign has been shaped in important ways by the work of Dominic Sandbrook. See Dominic Sandbrook, *Eugene McCarthy: The Rise and Fall of Postwar American Liberalism* (New York: Knopf, 2004). For the Kennedy campaign, see Jack Newfield, *Robert Kennedy: A Memoir* (London: Jonathan Cape, 1969), esp. 82, 253, 268.

40. See Sidney Lens, *Unrepentant Radical: An American Activist's Account of Five Turbulent Decades* (Boston: Beacon Press, 1980).

41. DeBenedetti, *An American Ordeal*, 246.

42. Wells, *The War Within*, 331–34.

43. "Antiwar Upsurge and Unity," *Guardian*, July 19, 1969, 12.

44. Lens, *Unrepentant Radical*, 311, 313; Sidney M. Peck Papers, 1946–1988, Box 2, Folder 10, SHSW.

45. "NLF Vietnam," *Black Panther*, August 16, 1969, quoted in G. Louis Heath, ed., *The Black Panther Leaders Speak* (Metuchen, N.J.: Scarecrow Press, 1976), 112.

46. BPP Platform in Teodori, *The New Left*, 283.

47. Larry Jones, "Power to the People of Viet Nam," *Black Panther*, July 26, 1969, 16, quoted in Heath, ed., *The Black Panther Leaders Speak*, 111.

48. Eldridge Cleaver, *Soul on Ice* (New York: Dell Ramparts, 1968), 111, 117.

49. Eldridge Cleaver, "The Black Man's Stake in Vietnam" (extract from *Soul on Ice*) quoted in Banning Garrett and Katherine Barkley, eds. for Ramparts, *Two, Three . . . Many Vietnams: A Radical Reader on the Wars in Southeast Asia and the Conflicts at Home*, (New York: Canfield Press, 1971), 220.

50. The Panthers' attitude toward white radicals was not shared by former SNCC chairman Stokely Carmichael, who opposed the BPP alliance with the PFP. At a February 1968 rally in Oakland, at which the merger of SNCC and the BPP was announced, the new Black Panther Prime Minister declared that Communism and Socialism were irrelevant to blacks. "It's not a question of right or left, it's a question of black," he stated. This ran counter to the Panthers'

growing critique of capitalism, attraction toward Marxism, and support for the white left. It was no surprise that the BPP-SNCC merger lasted a matter of months. See Allen J. Matusow, *The Unraveling of America: A History of Liberalism in the 1960s* (New York: Harper and Row, 1984), 370; Clayborne Carson, *In Struggle: SNCC and the Black Awakening of the 1960s* (Cambridge, Mass.: Harvard University Press, 1981), 279–80.

51. "Playboy Interview: Eldridge Cleaver," reprinted in Cleaver, *Eldridge Cleaver: Post-Prison Writings and Speeches*, ed. Robert Scheer (New York: Vintage, 1969), 201.

52. "Explains Why Blacks Joined PFP," *Berkeley Barb*, January 5–11, 1968,3.

53. Matusow, *The Unraveling of America*, 371.

54. "How It Went Down: Convention in Expert Hands," *Berkeley Barb* 6, 1, March 22–28, 1968, 5; Don Newton, "Black-White Coalition in California," *Guardian*, March 30, 1968, 3.

55. "How It Went Down," 5.

56. James Forman, *The Making of Black Revolutionaries* (Washington, D.C.: Open Hand, 1985), 525–26; Matusow, *The Unraveling of America*, 371.

57. Newton, "Black-White Coalition in California," 3; "How It Went Down," 9.

58. Doug Dowd, *Blues for America: A Critique, a Lament, and Some Memories* (New York: Monthly Review Press, 1997), 156–57; Wells, *The War Within*, 264.

59. See Dan T. Carter, *The Politics of Rage: George Wallace, the Origins of the New Conservatism, and the Transformation of American Politics* (Baton Rouge: Louisiana State University Press, 1995), 310–16.

60. http://www.usahistory.com/stats/presstat/1968.htm.

61. New Mobe Steering Committee Meeting Minutes, August 17–18, 1969, Philadelphia, 2, Sidney M. Peck Papers, Box 2, Folder 10, SHSW.

62. New Mobe Steering Committee Minutes, 1.

63. See Halstead, *Out Now!* 484–86. While the effectiveness of the FBI's COINTELPRO program is debatable, it is clear that the Bureau made extensive use of misinformation and informants as part of its systematic campaign against the New Left, antiwar, and militant black movements. See, for example, James Kirkpatrick Davis, *Assault on the Left: The FBI and the Sixties Antiwar Movement* (Westport, Conn.: Praeger, 1997).

64. New Mobe Steering Committee Minutes, September 14, 1969, D.C., 2–3, Sidney M. Peck Papers, Box 2, Folder 10, SHSW.

65. Anonymous Memorandum, Sidney M. Peck Papers, Box 2, Folder 10, SHSW.

66. Washington Action Committee Steering Committee Meeting Minutes, September 27, 1969, Sidney M. Peck Papers, Box 2, Folder 11, SHSW.

67. John E. Mueller, *War, Presidents and Public Opinion* (New York: Wiley, 1973). See also Charles DeBenedetti, "Lyndon Johnson and the Antiwar Opposition," in *The Johnson Years*, vol. 2, *Vietnam, the Environment, and Science*, ed. Robert A. Divine (Lawrence: University of Kansas Press, 1987), 27.

68. DeBenedetti, "Lyndon Johnson and the Antiwar Opposition," 27. See also William R. Berkowitz, "The Impact of Anti-Vietnam Demonstrations upon National Public Opinion and Military Indicators," *Social Science Research* 2, 1 (March 1973); E. M. Schreiber, "Anti-War Demonstrations and American Public Opinion on the War in Vietnam," *British Journal of Sociology* 27 (June 1976); Robert E. Lane and Michael Lerner, "Why Hard-Hats Hate Hairs," *Psychology Today* (November 1970).

69. Theodore Otto Windt, Jr., "The Diatribe: Last Resort For Protest," *Quarterly Journal of Speech* 58, 1 (February 1972): 1.

70. Jack Newfield, *A Prophetic Minority: The American New Left* (London: Blond, 1967), 22.

71. Milton S. Katz, "Peace Liberals and Vietnam: SANE and the Politics of "Responsible" Protest," *Peace and Change* 9 (Summer 1983); 21.

72. See Nathan Blumberg, "Misreporting the Peace Movement," *Columbia Journalism Review* 9 (Winter 1970–1971); Herbert Gans, *Deciding What's News: A Study of CBS Evening News, NBC Nightly News, Newsweek and Time* (London: Constable, 1980); Todd Gitlin, *The Whole World Is Watching: Mass Media in the Making and Unmaking of the New Left* (Berkeley: University of California Press, 1980); Melvin Small, *Covering Dissent: The Media and the Anti-Vietnam War Movement* (New Brunswick, N.J.: Rutgers University Press, 1994).

73. *I. F. Stone's Weekly*, June 28, 1965, 1, quoted in David Cochran, "I. F. Stone and the New Left: Protesting U.S. Policy in Vietnam," *Historian* 53, 3 (Spring 1991): 517.

74. *I. F. Stone's Weekly*, September 9, 1968,3, quoted in Cochran, "I. F. Stone and the New Left," 518.

75. DeBenedetti, *An American Ordeal*, 249; Sam Brown, "The Politics of Peace," *Washington Monthly* 2 (August 1970): 24.

76. Francine du Plessix Gray, "A Reporter at Large: The Moratorium and the New Mobe," *New Yorker*, January 3, 1970; Brown, "The Politics of Peace," 35.

77. Brown, "The Politics of Peace," 26, 44.

78. Brown, "The Politics of Peace," 25, 45.

79. DeBenedetti, *An American Ordeal*, 249–50.

80. 10 DeBenedetti, 253; Gray, "A Reporter at Large," 34.

81. Quoted in Davis, *Assault on the Left*, 154.

82. DeBenedetti, *An American Ordeal*, 255–56.

83. Vietnam Moratorium Committee Press Release, September 30, 1969 (Washington, D.C.), SHSW.

84. Letter from Gwendolyn Patton, National Coordinator, National Association Black Students, September 30, 1969, Vietnam Moratorium Committee (VMC) Records, 1969–1970, Box 4, Folder 6, SHSW.

85. Dennis C. Dickerson, *Militant Mediator: Whitney M. Young, Jr.* (Lexington: University Press of Kentucky, 1998), 282.

86. Dickerson, *Militant Mediator*, 281.

87. Nancy J. Weiss, *Whitney M. Young, Jr., and the Struggle for Civil Rights* (Princeton, N.J.: Princeton University Press, 1989), 194.

88. National Urban League press release 13 October 13, 1969, VMC Records, Box 4, Folder 6; "Statement by Whitney M. Young, Jr., on Vietnam," 2, SHSW.

89. NAACP Annual Report, 1969, 147, SHSW.

90. NAACP Annual Report, 155.

91. "National Youth Leaders Endorse Moratorium," press release, October 11, 1969, VMC Records, Box 4, Folder 6, SHSW.

92. *Advance* 7, 50 (October 1969), NAACP Records, Group VI, Box C174, Folder "Branch Development, Newsletters, New York 1969," Greenwich Village-Chelsea Branch, 4—"President's Corner," Library of Congress.

93. *Guardian*, October 25, 1969, 4.

94. "Moratorium Rally to Free Panthers, POWs," *Berkeley Barb* 9, 19 (November 14–20, 1969), 5.

95. Halstead, *Out Now!* 491, 732–33.

96. Wells, *The War Within*, 390; DeBenedetti, *An American Ordeal*, 260.

97. Brown, "The Politics of Peace," 36.

98. Gray, "A Reporter at Large," 38.

99. Gray, "A Reporter at Large," 39.

100. DeBenedetti, *An American Ordeal*, 261–63; Wells, *The War Within*, 390–93.

101. *Guardian*, November 22, 1969, 4, 16.

102. Patty Lee Parmalee, "West Coast Peace March Biggest Yet," *Guardian*, November 22, 1969, 5.

103. Marshall B. Jones, "Berkeley of the South: A History of the Student Movement at the University of Florida, 1963–1968," 1, University of Florida Archives, University of Florida-Gainesville.

104. Ed Pavelka, "Bit of Washington Seen in Gainesville," *Gainesville Sun*, November 15, 1969, University of Florida Archives, Vertical File, Folder "Student Protest Groups," University of Florida-Gainesville.

Chapter 6. New Coalitions, Old Problems

1. Tom Wells, *The War Within: America's Battle Over Vietnam* (Berkeley: University of California Press, 1994), 403, 405, 409.

2. Wells, *The War Within*, 419–29.

3. "Death Is White," *New York Post*, May 16, 1970, Roy Wilkins Papers, Box 40, Folder "Newspaper Column Clippings, 1970–71," Library of Congress. Wilkins did wonder why whites seemed much more concerned over the Kent State shootings than over the killing of two unarmed black students at Jackson State College, Mississippi, ten days later.

4. Carl Davidson, "From the New Left," *Guardian* (New York), January 10, 1970, 7.

5. "Viewpoint," *The Guardian*, February 7, 1970, 10.

6. Fred Halstead, *Out Now! A Participant's Account of the American Movement Against the Vietnam War* (New York: Monad Press, 1978), 525–26.

7. "Mobilization Committee Plans New Offensive," *Guardian*, December 27, 1969, 3, 8.

8. Carl Davidson, "Mobe Plans Set for April 15," *Guardian*, 24 January 1970, 6.

9. "Report on a Meeting of the Radical Caucus of the New Mobe," February 28, 1970; "Strategies and Problems of Building Toward the April Actions," Arthur I. Waskow Papers, 1958–1977 (unprocessed), Box 2, "Mobe" Folder, State Historical Society of Wisconsin (SHSW).

10. Harry Ring, "Move to Derail Mobe into Multi-Issue Morass," *The Militant*, December 26, 1969, in Arthur I. Waskow Papers (Unprocessed), Box 2, Mobe Folder (3), SHSW.

11. Memo from Dick Fernandez (director, CALCAV) to Trudy Young, re: New Mobilization, April 24, 1970, Arthur I. Waskow Papers (unprocessed), Box 2, Mobe Folder (4), SHSW.

12. Wells, *The War Within*, 403.

13. "Antiwar View by SMC leader," *Guardian*, February 7, 1970, 9.

14. See, for example, SDS flyer, "Link the Anti-War Movement with the Fight Against Racism!" December 1970 NPAC conference in Chicago, National Peace Action Coalition (NPAC) Records (microfilm), Reel 4, SHSW.

15. Summary of Student Mobilization Committee National Steering Committee Meeting, May 23, 1970, Student Mobilization Committee to End the War in Vietnam (SMC) Records, 1966–1973, Box 1, Folder 1: Minutes, 1967–72, SHSW.

16. CAPAC Meeting, May 21, 1970, 2, Cleveland Area Peace Action Coalition (CAPAC) Records, 1966–1973 (microfilm), Reel 1, SHSW; Wells, *The War Within*, 426.

17. CAPAC Coordinating Committee Meeting Minutes, May 24, 1970, 2, CAPAC Records, Reel 1, SHSW.

18. Charles Lally, "Politics of Dissent: Inside the Cleveland Peace Movement," *West Side Sun News*, June 18, 1970, CAPAC Records, Reel 2, SHSW.

19. For a discussion of the SCLC after King, see Adam Fairclough, *To Redeem the Soul of America: The Southern Christian Leadership Conference and Martin Luther King, Jr.* (Athens: University of Georgia Press, 1987), 385–405.

20. Wells, *The War Within*, 451. The Emergency Action Conference was also known as the Strategy Action Conference.

21. Charles DeBenedetti with Charles Chatfield, *An American Ordeal: The Antiwar Movement of the Vietnam Era* (Syracuse, N.Y.: Syracuse University Press, 1990), 281.

22. Sidney Peck, memo on Cleveland Anti-War Conference, 3, NPAC Records, Reel 3, SHSW.

23. Letter from Bill Braggs, Public Relations, to NWRO executive board, field chapters, and coalition groups, George A. Wiley Papers, 1949–1975, Box 32, Folder 3, SHSW.

24. Sidney Peck memo on Cleveland Anti-War Conference, 7; Carl Davidson, "Antiwar Movement Dividing," *Guardian*, June 13, 1970, 3.

25. Davidson, "Antiwar Movement Dividing," 3.

26. DeBenedetti, *An American Ordeal*, 281.

27. Davidson, "Antiwar Movement Dividing," 3.

28. CAPAC press release/information sheet, June 18, 1970, 3, CAPAC Records, Reel 1, SHSW.

29. "Cleveland—SDS Wins Anti-Racist Anti-War Support," *New Left Notes*, July 6, 1970, 5.

30. Wells, *The War Within*, 451.

31. Carl Davidson, "Antiwar Groups Gird for October," *Guardian*, 26 September 26, 1970, 4.

32. DeBenedetti, *An American Ordeal*, 281.

33. David McReynolds, "The Cleveland and Milwaukee Conferences," n.d., Sidney M. Peck Papers, Box 4, Folder 7, SHSW.

34. Black Panther Party Press Release (n.d.), Madison Committee to End the War in Vietnam Records, 1965–1971, Box 2, Folder 17, SHSW. The party was organizing a "Revolutionary People's Constitutional Convention," which it planned for the autumn of 1970.

35. Carl Davidson, "New Mobe Undecided on Program," *Guardian*, July 4, 1970, 3, 17.

36. David McReynolds, "The Cleveland and Milwaukee Conferences," n.d., Sidney M. Peck Papers, Box 4, Folder 7, SHSW.

37. Davidson, "New Mobe Undecided on Program," 3, 17.

38. Letter from Bill Braggs, Public Relations, to NWRO Executive Board, Field Chapters and Coalition Groups, September 29, 1970, George Wiley Papers, Box 32, Folder 3, SHSW.

39. Davidson, "Antiwar Groups Gird for October," 4.

40. Non-White Caucus Position Paper, NCAWRR Conference, Chicago, January 8–10, 1971, 3, People's Coalition for Peace and Justice (PCPJ) Records, Box 4, Folder "PCPJ Coordinating Committee," Swarthmore College Peace Collection (Swarthmore).

41. Sidney M. Peck, "Further Notes on the Strategy and Tactics of the Antiwar Movement," *WIN*, September 15, 1970, 4, CAPAC Records, Reel 1, SHSW.

42. Wells, *The War Within*, 461.

43. SDS flyer, "Link the Anti-War Movement with the Fight Against Racism!"

44. Sam Washington, "Peace Delegates Weigh New Action on War," *Chicago Sun-Times*, December 5, 1970, NPAC Records, Reel 7, SHSW.

45. Chris Lahey, "Washington Peace March Set," *South End* (Wayne State University, Detroit), 61, 67, December 8, 1970, NPAC Records, Reel 4, SHSW.

46. Quote from Sidney Peck in Wells, *The War Within*, 472.

47. Carl Zietlow and Brian Yaffee, PCPJ Training Manual for Nonviolent Direct Action, chaps. 1, 2, Sidney M. Peck Papers, Box 3, Folder 3, SHSW.

48. Much of the information for the last two paragraphs is taken from Wells, *The War Within*, 471–73.

49. Carl Davidson, "Spring Offensive Now United," *National Guardian*, March 6, 1971, 3.

50. Wells, *The War Within*, 478–80, 496–98.

51. "NAACP Sternly Critical of Nixon Administration," *Guardian*, July 11, 1970, 4.

52. Letter from Jerry Gordon to Roy Wilkins, January 22, 1971; Wilkins reply, February 1, NPAC Records, Reel 4, SHSW.

53. "Preliminary Endorsers of the April 24th March on Washington, D.C. and San Francisco for the Immediate Withdrawal of All U.S. Forces from South East Asia," George Wiley Papers, Box 32, Folder 3, SHSW.

54. "Black Moratorium," n.d., 1, 2, NPAC Records, Reel 10, SHSW.

55. TWTF press releases, n.d. and March 26, 1971, "Rep. Parren Mitchell to Speak at Third World Press Conference," NPAC Records, Reel 10, SHSW.

56. Washington Area PAC Newsletter, n.d., NPAC Records, Reel 5, SHSW.

57. *Guardian*, May 5, 1971, 3.

58. Nat Russell on Peace," June 1971 newsletter, NAACP Tucson Branch, NAACP Papers, Group VI, Box C175, Folder "Branch Department, Newsletters, Arizona 1971," Library of Congress.

59. Nick Benton, "Peace March," *Berkeley Barb*, 12, 16 April 30-May 6, 1971, 2.

60. Wells, *The War Within*, 504.

61. Wells, *The War Within*, 504.

62. Abe Weisburd, "Solidarity: D.C. Blacks Back Mayday," *Guardian*, May 19, 1971, 5.

63. Patty Lee Parmalee, "People's Coalition Plans New Actions," *National Guardian*, July 7, 1971, 4.

64. "Joan Baez Leads Hill Protest," *Evening Star*, June 23, 1972, Sidney M. Peck Papers, Box 21, Folder 6, SHSW.

65. "Joan Baez Leads Hill Protest"; Halstead, *Out Now!* 681–84.

66. Julius Hobson in Halstead, *Out Now!* 682.

67. Weisburd, "Solidarity."

68. Wells, *The War Within*, 139–41; Steven R. Weisman, "Militancy of Antiwar Veterans Is Rising," *New York Times*, July 16, 1972, 30.

69. Wells, *The War Within*, 473–74. The Winter Soldier Investigations were named after Thomas Paine's remark about "Summer soldiers and sunshine patriots"—see Weisman, "Militancy of Antiwar Veterans Is Rising."

70. VVAW was not the only veterans' group to give support to blacks. During April 1971, the University of Florida Veterans for Peace showed solidarity with the black students expelled by University of Florida President Stephen O'Connell by bivouacking on the lawn outside his residence. See "Racial Crisis at UF," *Hogarm* (UF Vets for Peace newsletter) 1, July 1971, 1, Vietnam Veterans Against the War (VVAW) Records, 1967–1992, Box 12, Folder 5, SHSW.

71. Andrew E. Hunt, *The Turning: A History of Vietnam Veterans Against the War* (New York: London: New York University Press, 1999), 133. In September 1969

the Black Panther Party made a direct appeal to Vietnam Veterans to join the party "in order to wage a stronger struggle against this racist-pig government, we the people and the Black Panther Party need the continued support from brothers who have served in the fascist military machine," see "GIs and Revolution," *Black Panther*, September 27, 1969 quoted in G. Louis Heath, ed., *The Black Panther Leaders Speak* (Metuchen, N.J.: Scarecrow Press, 1976), 39.

72. Ibid., 134.

73. Weisman, "Militancy of Antiwar Veterans Is Rising."

74. J. Anthony Hopkins, "Bad Day at Cairo, Ill.," *New York Times Magazine*, February 21, 1971, 78.

75. Hopkins, "Bad Day at Cairo," 82.

76. Preston Ewing, Jr., *Let My People Go: Cairo, Illinois, 1967–1973: Civil Rights Photographs*, ed. Jan Peterson Roddy (Carbondale: Southern Illinois University Press, 1996), xxi.

77. Hopkins, "Bad Day at Cairo," 82. In 1969, while annual family income in Cairo was $3,031, black family income was $1,643. Statistics compiled by the U.S. Civil Rights Commission Regional Office, quoted in letter from Sydney Finley to Gloster Current, April 7, 1969, NAACP Records, Group VI, Box C31, Folder "Field Staff, Field Secretaries and directors, Illinois, Finley, Sydney, Correspondence Jan-Sept 1969," Library of Congress.

78. Hopkins, "Bad Day at Cairo," 78.

79. Hopkins, "Bad Day at Cairo," 82.

80. *Let My People Go*, 3.

81. Quoted in Hopkins, "Bad Day at Cairo," 79.

82. Ewing, *Let My People Go*, ix.

83. See Ewing, *Let My People Go*, ix, xv–xvii; Hopkins, "Bad Day at Cairo," 82–83.

84. Kathy McKinney, "There Ain't No Love Downtown," 5, and Pat Gade, "Cairo: Let My People Go," 23, in *On the Battlefield: Cairo, Illinois* (prepared by Concerned Community Coalition of Bloomington-Normal and Community for Social Action, c. 1970), pamphlet collection, SHSW.

85. Ewing, *Let My People Go*, 3.

86. See John Lewis with Michael D'Orso, *Walking with the Wind: A Memoir of the Movement* (New York: Simon and Schuster, 1988), 190–92; James Forman, *The Making of Black Revolutionaries* (Washington. D.C.: Open Hand, 1985), 273.

87. See Ewing, *Let My People Go*, 10.

88. Ewing, *Let My People Go*, xvi, xxi–xxiii; Hopkins, "Bad Day at Cairo," 83.

89. Wells, *The War Within*, 492–96.

90. Scott Moore, "Lifeline to Cairo," *The 1st Casualty* (VVAW newspaper) 1, 1, August 1971, 1, 3, SHSW; Hunt, *The Turning*, 125–26, 132; Gerald Nicosia, *Home to War: A History of the Vietnam Veterans' Movement* (New York: Crown, 2001), 50–51.

91. Moore, "Lifeline to Cairo," 3.

92. Northern New England VVAW Meeting Minutes, July 7, 1971, VVAW Records, Box 12, Folder 6, SHSW.

93. Staff meeting minutes, July 20, 1971, 1, VVAW Records, Box 8, Folder 2, SHSW.

94. Scott Moore, "A Report to the Executive Committee of VVAW Concerning a Month's Trip to the Field and Other Observations," VVAW Records, Box 8, Folder 2, SHSW; Hunt, *The Turning*, 126.

95. "Vets Against the War Aid Cairo Blacks," in "Cairo News: Coverage of Southern Illinois," *East St. Louis Monitor*, August 19, 1971, 6.

96. Nicosia, *Home to War*, 213.

97. VVAW New York State Newsletter, August 30, 1971, VVAW Records, Box 12, Folder 7, SHSW; VVAW Staff Meeting Minutes, August 17, 1971, 1, VVAW Records, Box 8, Folder 2, SHSW.

98. *Veterans Voice*, c. November 1971, 6, VVAW Records, Box 12, Folder 6, SHSW.

99. *Veterans Voice*, "Kansas Vets Support Cairo Blacks," in "Cairo News: Coverage of Southern Illinois," 6.

100. Nicosia, *Home to War*, 214.

101. Wayne Pycior, "Cairo," *Veterans Voice* 1, 5, March 22, 1972, 2, VVAW Records, Box 12, Folder 6, SHSW.

102. Jeff Hillier, "Cairo," Chicago VVAW Newsletter, May 1972, VVAW Records, Box 12, Folder 5, SHSW.

103. Letter from Charles Koen to Bart Savage, Coordinator, Northern Illinois and Iowa and our VVAW Brothers and Sisters, in "More from the United Front," Chicago VVAW Newsletter—*Vet Cong*, September 1972, VVAW Records, Box 12, Folder 5, SHSW.

104. "Truckin' Back to Cairo," VVAW National Newsletter, November 6, 1972, 2, VVAW Records, Box 11, Folder 8, SHSW.

105. Indicative of VVAW's multi-issue, radical analysis of the war in Vietnam is the fact that one of its nine objectives was to change the "domestic social, political and economic institutions that have caused and permitted the continuance of the war"; see Weisman, "Militancy of Antiwar Veterans Is Rising."

106. Minutes of the National Steering Committee Meeting—Chicago, Ill., January 4–8, 1973, 9, VVAW Records, Box 12, Folder 7, SHSW.

107. Cincinnati, Ohio, VVAW Newsletter, March 10, 1973, 2; March 25, 1973, 3, VVAW Records, Box 12, Folder 9, SHSW.

108. Hunt, *The Turning*, 136–37.

Conclusion

1. SNCC Statement on the Vietnam War, January 6, 1966, in Massimo Teodori, *The New Left: A Documentary History* (London: Jonathan Cape, 1970), 251–52.

2. "Wilkins Raps King's Civil Rights Policy," *Worcester Sunday Telegram*, April 19, 1967, National Association for the Advancement of Colored People (NAACP) Papers, Group IV, Box A86, folder "Vietnam Correspondence, 1967–68," Library of Congress.

3. James Forman, *The Making of Black Revolutionaries* (Washington. D.C.: Open Hand, 1985), 395–96.

4. Author's interview with Courtland Cox, February 4, 2000.

5. SNCC Statement on the Vietnam War, 251.

6. Howard Zinn, unpublished article, winter 1965, Howard Zinn Papers, Box 3, Folder 5, State Historical Society of Wisconsin (SHSW).

7. Bayard Rustin, "From Protest to Politics: The Future of the Civil Rights Movement," *Commentary*, February 1965, in *Down the Line: The Collected Writings of Bayard Rustin*, intro. C. Vann Woodward (Chicago: Quadrangle Books, 1971), 115.

8. Rustin, "From Protest to Politics," 119.

9. Robert Cook, *Sweet Land of Liberty? The African-American Struggle for Civil Rights in the Twentieth Century* (Harlow, Essex: Longman, 1998), 176. See also Manfred Berg, "Guns, Butter, and Civil Rights: The National Association for the

Advancement of Colored People and the Vietnam War, 1964–1968," in *Aspects of War in American History*, ed. David K. Adams and Cornelius A. van Minnen (Keele: Keele University Press, 1997), 213–14; Benjamin T. Harrison, "Impact of the Vietnam War on the Civil Rights Movement in the Midsixties," *Studies in Conflict and Terrorism* 19, 3 (1996).

10. Tom Wells, *The War Within: America's Battle over Vietnam* (Berkeley: University of California Press, 1994), 70.

11. Robert F. Williams, "The New Left: Old Ideas in a New Front," *Black Politics: A Journal of Liberation* 1, 3 (March 1968): 17.

12. Student Mobilization Committee to End the War in Vietnam (SMC) Records, 1966–1973, Box 1, Folder 1: Minutes, 1967–1972, Student Mobilization Committee Position Papers, Gwen Patton, SHSW.

13. Non-White Caucus Position Paper, NCAWRR Conference, Chicago, January 8–10, 1971, 3, People's Coalition for Peace and Justice (PCPJ) Records, Box 4, Folder "PCPJ Coordinating Committee," Swarthmore College Peace Collection (Swarthmore). See also William Leach, "Perspective—White Left: Serious or Not?" *Chicago Seed* 3, 6 (c. February 69), 19; Amiri Baraka (LeRoi Jones), "Jimi Hendrix and the Need for a Black Value System," fall 1970, Amiri Baraka Papers, Box 22, Moorland Spingarn Research Center, Howard University. I am grateful to Joe Street for bringing this material to my attention.

14. See, for example, Mel Pine, "The November 25–28 Convention," 1, National Coordinating Committee to End the War in Vietnam Records, 1964–1967, Series 1, Box 1, Folder 8: National Anti-War Conference 1965—November 25–28; Constitutional Material, SHSW and SNCC Central Committee Meeting Minutes, March 4, 1967, Atlanta, 7., Student Nonviolent Coordinating Committee (SNCC) Records (microfilm), Reel 3; Gwendolyn Patton position paper—"Why Black People must develop own Anti-War and Anti-Draft Union . . . Heed the Call!" (end of 1967, early 1968), 2, SNCC Records, Reel 58, Library of Congress.

15. Gwen Patton, essay on the peace movement (unpublished, 1972), 22, Gwendolyn Patton Papers, in possession of author.

16. Patton essay, 13.

17. See September 29, 1970 letter from Bill Braggs, Public Relations, to NWRO Executive Board, Field Chapters and Coalition Groups, George A. Wiley Papers, 1949–1975, Box 32, Folder 3, SHSW. To give PCPJ credit, in February 1971 Braggs wrote to the PCPJ's Brad Lyttle thanking him for a recent check for $1,000, which, he said, "represents a first step toward a true commitment by the Coalition to help poor people." See letter from Bill Braggs to Brad Lyttle, February 19, 1971, PCPJ Records, Box 3, Folder "Coordinating Committee," Swarthmore. On March 6, 1971 the PCPJ's David Dellinger joined an SCLC-NWRO sponsored march of 1,500 in Las Vegas protesting the cutting off of welfare payments. See *Movin' Together* (PCPJ), March 19, 1971, 3, Sidney M. Peck Papers, Box 3, Folder 1, SHSW.

18. Brad Lyttle, "Memo: NPAC Negotiations," August 12, 1971, 3., PCPJ Records, Box 3, Folder "Coordinating Committee," Swarthmore.

19. I am grateful to the anonymous reader for comments made along these lines.

20. See, for example, Arthur M. Schlesinger, Jr., *Robert Kennedy and His Times* (London: Deutsch, 1978); William H. Chafe, *Never Stop Running: Allard Lowenstein and the Struggle to Save American Liberalism* (New York: Basic Books, 1993).

21. John Morton Blum, *Years of Discord: American Politics and Society, 1961–1974* (New York: Norton, 1991), 302–3.

22. Blum, *Years of Discord*, 289–90; Wells, *The War Within*, 120–22, 226–27.

23. See Peter Collier and David Horowitz, *Destructive Generation: Second Thoughts About the 60s* (1989; New York: Free Press Paperbacks, 1996), 270.

24. See, for example, Ronald Radosh, *Divided They Fell: The Demise of the Democratic Party, 1964–1996* (New York: Free Press, 1996).

25. I am grateful to Dominic Sandbrook for helping me clarify my thinking on this subject. See Dominic Sandbrook, *Eugene McCarthy: The Rise and Fall of Postwar American Liberalism* (New York: Knopf, 2004).

26. See David J. Garrow, *Bearing the Cross: Martin Luther King, Jr., and the Southern Christian Leadership Conference* (New York: William Morrow, 1986), 592.

27. Adam Fairclough, "Martin Luther King, Jr. and the War in Vietnam," *Phylon* 45, 1 (1984): 34, 36.

28. Sombart was a German sociologist. See Eric Foner, "Why Is There No Socialism in the United States?" *History Workshop* 17 (Spring 1984): 57.

29. For the rise of the New Right, see Mary C. Brennan, *Turning Right in the Sixties: The Conservative Capture of the GOP* (Chapel Hill: University of North Carolina Press, 1995); Dan T. Carter, *The Politics of Rage: George Wallace, the Origins of the New Conservatism, and the Transformation of American Politics* (Baton Rouge: Louisiana State University Press, 2000); Godfrey Hodgson, *The World Turned Right Side Up: A History of the Conservative Ascendancy in America* (Boston: Houghton Mifflin, 1996); Rebecca E. Klatch, *A Generation Divided: The New Left, the New Right, and the 1960s* (Berkeley: University of California Press, 1999).

30. The role that "identity politics" has played in the segmentation of the American Left is the subject of fierce controversy. While scholars such as Todd Gitlin and Michael Tomasky blame "identity politics" for undermining a class-based universalist Left, they have been subjected to severe counter-attacks by Robin D. G. Kelley, Jesse Lemisch, and Martin Duberman among others. See Todd Gitlin, *The Twilight of Common Dreams: Why America Is Wracked by Culture Wars* (New York: Metropolitan Books, 1995); Michael Tomasky, *Left for Dead: The Life, Death, and Possible Resurrection of Progressive Politics in America* (New York: Free Press, 1996), Robin D. G. Kelley, "Identity Politics and Class Struggle," *New Politics* n.s. 6, 2 (winter 1997): 84–96; Jesse Lemisch, "Angry White Men on the Left," *New Politics* n.s. 6, 2 (winter 1997): 97–104.

Bibliography

Archival Collections—United Kingdom

CAMBRIDGE UNIVERSITY

Civil Rights During the Johnson Administration: 1963–1969. Part 5: Records of the National Advisory Commission on Civil Disorders (Kerner Commission). A collection from the holdings of the Lyndon Baines Johnson Library, Austin, Texas. Editor Steven F. Lawson, project coordinated and guide compiled by Robert E. Lester. Frederick, Md.: University Publications of America, c.1984–1987.

Congress of Racial Equality (CORE) Papers. Part 1: Western Regional Office, 1962–1965. Associate editor Randolph Brown, guide compiled by Dale Reynolds. Frederick, Md.: University Publications of America, 1984.

Congress of Racial Equality (CORE) Papers. Part 3: Scholarship, Educational, and Defense Fund for Racial Equality, 1960–1976. Series B: Leadership Development Files. Associate editor Randolph Brown, guide compiled by Dale Reynolds. Frederick, Md.: University Publications of America, 1984.

Papers of the NAACP: Supplement to Part 1, 1961–1965. Editorial advisor August Meier, edited by Mark Fox. Frederick, Md.: University Publications of America, 1982–1997.

Papers of the NAACP: Part 20—White Resistance and Reprisals, 1956–1965, Editorial advisor August Meier, edited by Mark Fox. Frederick, Md.: University Publications of America, 1982–1997.

Political Activities of the Johnson White House, 1963–1969. Part 1: White House Central and Confidential Files, Series A: Candidates, Campaigns, Elections, and Parties. Editor Paul L. Kesaris, guide compiled by Robert E. Lester. Frederick, Md.: University Publications of America, c.1987)

Political Activities of the Johnson White House, 1963–1969. Part 2: White House Aides, Series A: Office Files of Marvin Watson. Project coordinator Paul L. Kesaris, guide compiled by Robert Lester. Frederick, Md.: University Publications of America, c.1987.

UNIVERSITY OF LEEDS

The Martin Luther King, Jr., FBI File Part II: The King-Levison File. Edited by David J. Garrow, guide compiled by Martin P. Schipper. Frederick, Md.: University Publications of America, 1987.

University of Sheffield

The Bayard Rustin Papers. Introduction by John H. Bracey and August Meier, guide compiled by Nanette Dobrosky. Frederick, Md.: University Publications of America, 1988.

Archival Collections—United States

Center for American History, University of Texas at Austin

James Leonard Farmer, Jr. and Lula Peterson Farmer Papers, 1908, 1921–1997.

Duke University, Durham, North Carolina

Special Collections Department, William R. Perkins Library

Boyte Family Papers
Papers of Milo Guthrie
J. B. Matthews Papers

University Archives

Duke Vigil Collection, 1968
Duke Chronicle

Library of Congress, Washington, D.C.

National Association for the Advancement of Colored People Records
Records of the Southern Christian Leadership Conference. Editorial adviser Cynthia P. Lewis. Microfilm project of University Publications of America, 1995.
Records of the Student Nonviolent Coordinating Committee. Microfilm project of University Publications of America.
Roy Wilkins Papers

Lyndon Baines Johnson Presidential Library, Austin, Texas

Manuscript Collections

Cabinet Papers
Ceil Bellinger Papers
Ramsey Clark Papers
Confidential Name File
Records of the Democratic National Committee, Series I
Diary Backup
To Fulfill These Rights
Robert Hardesty Papers
National Security File—Intelligence File
National Security File Subject File
Office Files of Harry McPherson
Office Files of Fred Panzer
Files of Marvin Watson
Office Files of Lee C. White
White House Central Files (WHCF)
WHCF—GEN PL—ST 24
WHCF Confidential File

WHCF Name File
WHCF Peace

Oral histories
Clifford Alexander
Ramsey Clark
David Dellinger
Charles Evers
James Farmer
Aaron Henry
Thurgood Marshall
Harry McPherson
Clarence Mitchell
A. Philip Randolph
Joe Rauh
John P. Roche
Bayard Rustin
Benjamin Spock
Sterling Tucker
Roy Wilkins
Andrew Young
Whitney M. Young, Jr.

Recordings of Telephone Conversations—White House Series
LBJ and Roy Wilkins, August 15, 1964, tape WH6408.21 [citation # 4940 &
    4941]
LBJ and Richard Daley, August 17, 1964, tape WH6408.25 [citation # 4978, 4979
    & 4980]

STATE HISTORICAL SOCIETY OF WISCONSIN, MADISON

Manuscript Collections
Donna Allen Papers, 1960–1987
Paul Booth Papers, 1956–1970
Carl and Anne Braden Papers, 1928–1990
Chicago Committee to End the War in Vietnam Records, 1965
Cleveland Area Peace Action Coalition Records (microfilm), 1966–1973
Congress of Racial Equality Records, 1941–1967
Papers of the Congress of Racial Equality, 1944–1968 (microfilm)
Congress of Racial Equality, Berkeley Chapter (Calif.) Records, 1953–1967
Congress of Racial Equality, Monroe Chapter (La.) Records, 1961–1966
Congress of Racial Equality, Western Regional Office Records, 1948–1967
Robert Curvin Papers, 1965–1969
FBI File: Student Nonviolent Coordinating Committee (microfilm)
Todd Gitlin and Nanci Hollander Papers, 1961–1970
Carlton Benjamin Goodlet Papers (microfilm), 1942–1967
Fannie Lou Hamer Papers, 1964–1967
Fifth Avenue Vietnam Peace Parade Committee Records, 1965–1971
Alicia Kaplow Papers, 1964–1968
Staughton Lynd Papers, 1938–1997

Madison Area Peace Action Council Records, 1969–1973
Madison Citizens for a Vote on Vietnam Records, 1967–1968
Madison Committee to End the War in Vietnam Records, 1965–1971
Scott L. McNeil Papers
Meier-Rudwick Collection of Congress of Racial Equality Records, 1943–1969
Mississippi Freedom Democratic Party Records, 1962–1971
National Conference for New Politics Records, 1966–1968
National Coordinating Committee to End the War in Vietnam Records, 1964–1967
National Peace Action Coalition Records (microfilm), 1970–1973
New Mobilization Committee to End the War in Vietnam Records, 1969–1970
David Nolan Papers, 1960–1987
Sidney M. Peck Papers, 1946–1988
Mendy Samstein Papers, 1963–1966
Social Action Vertical File
Students for a Democratic Society Records, 1958–1970
Student Mobilization Committee to End the War in Vietnam Records, 1966–1973
Student Nonviolent Coordinating Committee (SNCC) Records, 1964–1965
SNCC—Arkansas Project Records, 1960–1966
SNCC—Vine City Project Records, 1960–1967
Robert Vernon Papers, 1960–1994
Veterans for Peace in Vietnam (New York) Records, 1965–1972
Vietnam Moratorium Committee Records, 1969–1970
Vietnam Veterans Against the War Records, 1967–1992
Daniel J. Wacker Papers, 1965–1967, 1993
Arthur I. Waskow Papers, 1958–1977
Lee D. Webb Papers, 1955–1968
Lynn Wells Papers, 1967–1975
Hank Werner Papers
George A. Wiley Papers, 1949–1975
Howard Zinn Papers, 1956–1994

Pamphlets and Miscellaneous Publications

Action Bulletin (Chicago: Student Mobilization Committee), 1B–3B (March 1969)
Anti-Warrior (Washington, D.C.: Student Mobilization Committee), September–October 1969
Atlanta's Black Paper (Atlanta: SNCC), August 25, 1966
Arkansas Voice (Little Rock, Ark.: SNCC), May–October 1965, June 1966
Berkeley Monitor (Berkeley, Calif.: Community for New Politics), July 1966–April 1969
Black Power: SNCC Speaks for Itself, a Collection of Interviews and Statements. Ann Arbor, Mich.: SNCC Radical Education Project, 1967.
Bond, Julian. *Black Candidates: Southern Campaign Experiences.* Atlanta: Southern Regional Council, 1969.
Coalition News (Berkeley, Calif.: Community for New Politics for the Berkeley Coalition), vol. 3, no. 5.
Communiqué for New Politics and Left-Out News (Berkeley, Calif.: Community for New Politics), vol. 1, no. 1–vol. 3, no. 7.
Community Project Bulletin of the Vietnam Day Committee (Berkeley, Calif.), no. 1.
CORElator (Cleveland, Ohio: CORE), 1945–1967.

Genocide in Mississippi (Atlanta: SNCC, 1964) Ellin (Joseph and Nancy) Freedom Summer Collection, University of Southern Mississippi, McCain Library and Archives.

Interchange (New York: National Conference for New Politics), February 1965, November 1966, January 1967, June 1967.

Life with Lyndon in the Great Society (San Francisco: J. Minnis), June–November 1965.

Long Island CORE News (Hempstead: Long Island CORE), May–December 1967, June 1968.

Los Angeles CORElator (Los Angeles: Los Angeles CORE), vol. 1 no. 5, 1961.

Miscellaneous Publications (New York: Spring Mobilization Committee)

Miscellaneous Publications (New York: Vietnam Moratorium Committee)

Mobilizer (New York: Spring Mobilization Committee to End the War in Vietnam), December 1966–October 1968.

National Action Bulletin (Chicago: Student Mobilization Committee), October–December 1968, March 1969.

National SMC Newsletter (New York: Student Mobilization Committee), 4, 30 September 1970.

NCC Worklist (Madison, Wis.: National Coordinating Committee to End the War in Vietnam), February–April, August–November 1966.

National Urban League—Report (New York), 1963–1964/5, 1967–1968.

Newsletter—National Urban League Washington Bureau (Washington, D.C.), 1967–1969.

New Politics News (New York: National Conference for New Politics), May–November 1967.

New Politics News—Convention Issue (Chicago, 1968), nos. 1–4.

Students for a Democratic Society. *Huey Newton Talks to the Movement.* (San Francisco: SDS and the Movement, 1968).

Peace and Freedom News (newsletter of NCCEWV).

Peace Times (Washington, D.C.: Vietnam Moratorium Committee), March–April 1970.

Press Release (Washington, D.C.: Vietnam Moratorium Committee), September 1969–April 1970.

SANE World, August 1963-February 1970

SCLC Newsletter (Atlanta), April/May, October/November 1965, January/February 1966.

SCLC—Summary of the 9th Annual Convention (Birmingham, Ala., 1965).

Newsletter (Nashville, Tenn.: Southern Student Organizing Committee), December 1964–May 1965.

SNCC—News of the Field (Atlanta), February-May 1966.

SNCC Newsletter (Atlanta), June-July, September-October 1967.

SNCC Staff Newsletter (Atlanta), 17 July 1965.

Student Mobilizer—Wallposter Edition (New York: Student Mobilization Committee), January–November 1969.

VDC News (Berkeley, Calif.: Vietnam Day Committee), June 1965, November 1966-May 1967.

Vietnam (Berkeley, Calif.: Vietnam Day Committee), 1966.

Vietnam News Service (New York: NCCEWV), October, November 1966.

Newspapers

Berkeley Barb, 1965–1972

Black Politics, 1968–1969

Chicago Seed, 1967–1971
East St. Louis Monitor, 1965–1973
Freedomways, 1961–1972
Great Speckled Bird (Atlanta) (March 15, 1968–March 10, 1969; March 1969–July 1970; July 27, 1970–end December 1970)
National Guardian (New York; *The Guardian* after February 20, 1968), October 1965–December 1971
New Left Notes (microfilm-SDS), 1966–1972
Los Angeles Free Press, 1964–1972
The Movement (SNCC—California), 1965–1970
New South Student (microfilm—Southern Student Organizing Committee), 1965–1969
New Mobilizer (microfilm—New Mobilization Committee), 1969–1970
Radish/Protean Radish, 1968, 1969
Ramparts, 1965–1970
Southern Patriot, 1965–1972
Student Mobilizer (microfilm—Student Mobilization Committee), 1967–1972
Student Voice (SNCC—Atlanta), 1960–1965
Village Voice

Oral Histories

Ellice Fatoullah interview, 1967

Swarthmore College, Swarthmore, Pennsylvania, McCabe Library—Swarthmore College Peace Collection

National Mobilization Committee to End the War in Vietnam Records
People's Coalition for Peace and Justice Records

Trenholm State Technical College, Montgomery, Alabama

Gwendolyn Patton Papers. (copy in possession of author)

University of Florida, Gainesville

University Archives

Clipping File
Manuscript Collections—Kenneth A. Megill Papers, 1967–1973
Presidential Collections, Series P12, Office of the President, Stephen C. O'Connell, Administrative Policy Records, 1967–1973
Vertical File

University Library

Florida Alligator

University of North Carolina, Chapel Hill, North Carolina Collection—Clipping File

Lynn Wells Papers
Southern Oral History Program Interviews: Pamela Parker Allen, Julian Bond, Anne Queen, Hugh Stevens
Daily Tar Heel

Yale University

Sterling Memorial Library

Modern Times (publication of the American Independent Movement, New Haven, Conn.), May 1970–February 1973.

Papers of A. Philip Randolph, edited by John H. Bracey, Jr. and August Meier. Microfilm project of University Publications of America, 1990.

Seeley Mudd Library

AIM: The Bulletin of the American Independent Movement (published by the Independent Political Action Committee: New Haven, Conn.), April 1966–July 1969.

Newspapers

Chicago Defender (City Edition)—July 14, 1945–April 29, 1966
Chicago Daily Defender—April 30, 1966–February 15, 1973
New York Times, 1965–1973

Interviews with Author

Julian Bond, Cambridge, England, May 15, 2001
Gloria Clark, January 2001
Courtland Cox, Washington, D.C., February 4, 2000
Frank Emspak, Madison, Wisconsin, December 9, 1999
Herbert Hill, Madison, Wisconsin, May 16 and August 9, 2000
Maurice Zeitlin, January 15, 2000
Mitchell Zimmerman, January 18, 2001
Howard Zinn, April 24, 2000
"The Ongoing Radicalization of SNCC and the Movement," panel session, April 14, 2000 at "We Who Believe in Freedom Cannot Rest: Miss Ella J. Baker and the Birth of SNCC," National Conference, 13–16 April 2000, Shaw University, Raleigh, N.C. Transcription and tape in author's possession.

Published Primary Sources

Carson, Clayborne, David J. Garrow, Gerald Gill, Vincent Harding, and Darlene Clark Hine, eds. *The Eyes on the Prize Civil Rights Reader: Documents, Speeches, and Firsthand Accounts from the Black Freedom Struggle, 1954–1990.* New York: Penguin, 1991.

Cleaver, Eldridge. *Eldridge Cleaver: Post-Prison Writings and Speeches.* Ed. Robert Scheer. New York: Vintage, 1969.

Gallup, George H. *The Gallup Poll: Public Opinion 1935–71.* Vol. 3, *1959–71.* New York: Random House, 1972.

Heath, G. Louis, ed. *The Black Panther Leaders Speak: Huey P. Newton, Bobby Seale, Eldridge Cleaver, and Company Speak Out Through the Black Panther Party's Official Newspaper.* Metuchen, N.J.: Scarecrow Press, 1976.

Jackson, Esther Cooper, ed. *Freedomways Reader: Prophets in Their Own Country.* Boulder, Colo.: Westview Press, 2000.

King, Martin Luther, Jr. *A Testament of Hope: The Essential Writings and Speeches of Martin Luther King, Jr.* Ed. James Melvin Washington. San Francisco: HarperSanFrancisco, 1991.

Levy, Peter B., ed. *Let Freedom Ring: A Documentary History of the Modern Civil Rights Movement.* New York: Praeger, 1992.

Menashe, Louis and Ronald Radosh, eds. *Teach-ins: U.S.A.: Reports, Opinions, Documents.* New York: Praeger, 1967.

Osofsky, Gilbert. *The Burden of Race: A Documentary History of Negro-White Relations in America.* New York: Harper and Row, 1967.

Rustin, Bayard, *Down the Line: The Collected Writings of Bayard Rustin.* Introduction by C. Vann Woodward. Chicago: Quadrangle Books, 1971.

Skolnick, Jerome. *The Politics of Protest: Violent Aspects of Protest and Confrontation.* Staff Report to the National Commission on the Causes and Prevention of Violence. Washington, D.C.: U.S. Government Printing Office, 1969.

Taylor, Clyde, ed. *Vietnam and Black America: An Anthology of Protest and Resistance.* Garden City, N.Y.: Anchor/Doubleday, 1973.

Teodori, Massimo. *The New Left: A Documentary History.* London: Jonathan Cape, 1970.

Terry, Wallace. *Bloods: An Oral History of the Vietnam War by Black Veterans.* New York: Random House, 1984.

Webb, Lee and Paul Booth. *The Anti-War Movement: From Protest to Radical Politics.* Chicago: SDS, 1965.

Secondary Sources

AUTOBIOGRAPHIES AND ORAL TESTIMONY

Cleaver, Eldridge. *Soul on Ice.* New York: Dell, 1970.

Dellinger, David. *From Yale to Jail: The Life Story of a Moral Dissenter.* New York: Pantheon, 1993.

Farmer, James. *Lay Bare the Heart: An Autobiography of the Civil Rights Movement.* New York: Plume, 1985.

Finn, James. *Protest: Pacifism and Politics: Some Passionate Views on War and Nonviolence.* New York: Random House, 1967.

Forman, James. *The Making of Black Revolutionaries.* Washington, D.C.: Open Hand, 1985.

———. *United States 1967: High Tide of Black Resistance.* Chicago: SDS, 1969. Reprinted in *High Tide of Black Resistance and Other Essays.* Seattle: Open Hand, 1994.

Fraser, Ronald, ed. *1968: A Student Generation in Revolt: An International Oral History.* New York: Pantheon, 1988.

Greenberg, Cheryl Lynn, ed. *A Circle of Trust: Remembering SNCC.* New Brunswick, N.J.: Rutgers University Press, 1998.

Gregory, Dick with Sheila P. Moses. *Callus on My Soul: A Memoir.* Atlanta: Longstreet Press, 2000.

Hammond, John with Irving Townsend. *On Record: An Autobiography.* New York: Ridge Press, 1977.

Hayden, Tom. *Reunion: A Memoir.* London: Hamish Hamilton, c.1988. (Uncorrected proof copy.)

Hampton, Henry and Steve Fayar with Sarah Flynn. *Voices of Freedom: An Oral History of the Civil Rights Movement from the 1950s Through the 1980s.* New York: Bantam, 1990.

Johnson, Lyndon Baines. *The Vantage Point: Perspectives of the Presidency, 1963–1969.* London: Weidenfeld and Nicolson, 1971.

King, Coretta Scott. *My Life with Martin Luther King, Jr.* London: Hodder and Stoughton, 1969.

Lens, Sidney. *Unrepentant Radical: An American Activist's Account of Five Turbulent Decades.* Boston: Beacon Press, 1980.

Lester, Julius. *Search for the New Land: History as Subjective Experience.* New York: Dial Press, 1969.

Lewis, John with Michael D'Orso. *Walking with the Wind: A Memoir of the Movement.* New York: Simon and Schuster, 1988.

McDermott, John. *Thoughts on the Movement* (SDS pamphlet). Reprinted in Priscilla Long, comp., *The New Left: A Collection of Essays.* Boston: P. Sargent, 1969.

Sellers, Cleveland with Robert Terrell. *The River of No Return: The Autobiography of a Black Militant and the Life and Death of SNCC.* 1973. Jackson: University Press of Mississippi, 1990.

Wilkins, Roger. *A Man's Life: An Autobiography.* New York: Simon and Schuster, 1982.

Wilkins, Roy with Tom Matthews. *Standing Fast: The Autobiography of Roy Wilkins.* 1984. New York: Da Capo Press, 1994.

Young, Andrew. *An Easy Burden: The Civil Rights Movement and the Transformation of America.* New York: HarperCollins, 1996.

Malcolm X. *February 1965: The Final Speeches.* Ed. Steve Clark. New York: Pathfinder, 1992.

———. *Malcolm X: Speeches at Harvard.* Ed. Archie Epps. New York: Paragon House, 1991.

Malcolm X with Alex Haley. *The Autobiography of Malcolm X.* 1965. Harmondsworth: Penguin, 1980.

Books

Anderson, Jervis. *A. Philip Randolph: A Biographical Portrait.* New York: Harvest Books, 1972.

———. *Bayard Rustin: Troubles I've Seen: A Biography.* New York: HarperCollins, 1997.

Anderson, Terry H. *The Movement and the Sixties.* New York: Oxford University Press, 1995.

Ansbro, John J. *Martin Luther King, Jr.: The Making of a Mind.* Maryknoll, N.Y: Orbis Books, 1982.

Aptheker, Herbert. *Dr. Martin Luther King, Vietnam, and Civil Rights.* New York: New Outlook, 1967.

Bacciocco, Edward J., Jr. *The New Left in America: Reform to Revolution, 1956 to 1970.* Stanford, Calif.: Hoover Institution Press, 1974.

Bernhard, Virginia, Betty Brandon, Elizabeth Fox-Genovese, Theda Perdue, and Elizabeth H. Turner, eds. *Hidden Histories of Women in the New South.* Columbia: University of Missouri Press, 1994.

Bernstein, Irving. *Guns or Butter: The Presidency of Lyndon Johnson.* New York: Oxford University Press, 1996.

———. *Promises Kept: John F. Kennedy's New Frontier.* New York: Oxford University Press, 1991.

Blum, John Morton. *Years of Discord: American Politics and Society, 1961–1974.* New York: Norton, 1991.

Borstelmann, Thomas. *The Cold War and the Color Line: American Race Relations in the Global Arena.* Cambridge, Mass.: Harvard University Press, 2001.

Branch, Taylor. *Parting the Waters: America in the King Years, 1954–63.* New York: Simon and Schuster, 1988.

Breines, Wini. *Community and Organization in the New Left, 1962–1969.* New York: Praeger, 1982.

Brennan, Mary C. *Turning Right in the Sixties: The Conservative Capture of the Gop.* Chapel Hill: University of North Carolina Press, 1995.

Brinkley, Alan. *Liberalism and Its Discontents.* Cambridge, Mass.: Harvard University Press, 1998.

Buhle, Paul. *History and the New Left: Madison, Wisconsin, 1950–1970.* Philadelphia: Temple University Press, 1990.

Burner, David. *Making Peace with the 60s.* Princeton, N.J.: Princeton University Press, 1996.

Burner, Eric. *And Gently He Shall Lead Them: Robert Parris Moses and Civil Rights in Mississippi.* New York: New York University Press, 1994.

Butwin, Miriam and Pat Pirmantgen. *Protest II.* Minneapolis: Lerner, 1972.

Capps, Walter, ed. *The Vietnam Reader.* New York: Routledge, 1991.

Carmichael, Stokely and Charles V. Hamilton. *Black Power: The Politics of Liberation in America.* Harmondsworth; Penguin, 1969.

Carson, Clayborne. *In Struggle: SNCC and the Black Awakening of the 1960s.* Cambridge, Mass.: Harvard University Press, 1981.

Carter, Dan T. *The Politics of Rage: George Wallace, the Origins of the New Conservatism, and the Transformation of American Politics.* Baton Rouge: Louisiana State University Press, 1995.

Chafe, William H. *Never Stop Running: Allard Lowenstein and the Struggle to Save American Liberalism.* New York: Basic Books, 1993.

———. *The Unfinished Journey: America Since World War II.* 2nd ed. New York: Oxford University Press, 1991.

Clark, Kenneth B., Julian Bond, and Richard G. Hatcher. *The Black Man in American Politics, Three Views.* Washington, D.C.: Metropolitan Applied Research Center, for the Institute of Elected Black Officials, 1969.

Colaiaco, James A. *Martin Luther King, Jr.: Apostle of Militant Nonviolence.* Basingstoke: Macmillan, 1993.

Collier, Peter and David Horowitz. *Destructive Generation: Second Thoughts About the 60s.* 1989. New York: Free Press Paperbacks, 1996.

Cook, Robert. *Sweet Land of Liberty? The African-American Struggle for Civil Rights in the Twentieth Century.* Harlow: Longman, 1998.

Cooper, Chester L. *The Lost Crusade: America in Vietnam.* New York: Dodd, Mead, 1970.

Dailey, Jane, Glenda Gilmore, and Bryant Simon, eds. *Jumpin' Jim Crow: Southern Politics from Civil War to Civil Rights.* Princeton, N.J.: Princeton University Press, 2000.

Dallek, Robert. *Flawed Giant: Lyndon Johnson and His Times, 1961–1973.* Oxford: Oxford University Press, 1998.

Davis, Jack E., ed. *The Civil Rights Movement.* Malden, Mass.: Blackwell, 2001.

Davis, James Kirkpatrick. *Assault on the Left: The FBI and the Sixties Antiwar Movement.* Westport, Conn.: Praeger, 1997.

DeBenedetti, Charles. *An American Ordeal: The Antiwar Movement of the Vietnam Era.* Charles Chatfield, assisting author. Syracuse, N.Y.: Syracuse University Press, 1990.

Dickerson, Dennis C. *Militant Mediator: Whitney M. Young, Jr.* Lexington: University Press of Kentucky, 1998.

Diggins, John Patrick. *The Rise and Fall of the American Left.* New York: Norton, 1992.

Dittmer, John. *Local People: The Struggle for Civil Rights in Mississippi.* Urbana: University of Illinois Press, 1994.

Divine, Robert A. *Blowing on the Wind: The Nuclear Test Ban Debate 1954–1960.* New York: Oxford University Press, 1978.

———, ed. *The Johnson Years.* Vol. 1, *Foreign Policy, the Great Society, and the White House.* Lawrence: University Press of Kansas, 1987.

———, ed. *The Johnson Years.* Vol. 3, *LBJ at Home and Abroad.* Lawrence: University Press of Kansas, 1994.

Dowd, Doug. *Blues for America: A Critique, a Lament, and Some Memories.* New York: Monthly Review Press, 1997.

Dudziak, Mary L. *Cold War Civil Rights: Race and the Image of American Democracy.* Princeton, N.J.: Princeton University Press, 2000.

Ely, James W., Jr. *The Crisis of Conservative Virginia: The Byrd Organization and the Politics of Massive Resistance.* Knoxville: University of Tennessee Press, 1976.

Eskew, Glen T. *But for Birmingham: The Local and National Movements in the Civil Rights Struggle.* Chapel Hill: University of North Carolina Press, 1997.

Ewing, Preston, Jr. *Let My People Go: Cairo, Illinois 1967–1973: Civil Rights Photographs.* Ed. Jan Peterson Roddy. Carbondale: Southern Illinois University Press, 1996.

Evans, Sara. *Personal Politics: The Roots of Women's Liberation in the Civil Rights Movement and the New Left.* New York: Vintage Books, 1980.

Fairclough, Adam. *Better Day Coming: Blacks and Equality, 1890–2000.* New York: Penguin, 2002.

———. *Race and Democracy: The Civil Rights Struggle in Louisiana, 1915–1972.* Athens: University of Georgia Press, 1995.

———. *To Redeem the Soul of America: The Southern Christian Leadership Conference and Martin Luther King, Jr.* Athens: University of Georgia Press, 1987.

Farrell, James J. *The Spirit of the Sixties: The Making of Postwar Radicalism.* New York: Routledge, 1997.

Faulkner, William. *Go Down, Moses.* New York: Vintage, 1973.

Fisher, Randall M. *Rhetoric and American Democracy: Black Protest Through Vietnam Dissent.* Lanham, Md.: University Press of America, 1985.

Foner, Jack D. *Blacks and the Military in American History: A New Perspective.* New York: Praeger, 1974.

Foner, Philip S. *American Labor and the Indo-China War: The Growth of Union Opposition.* New York: International Publishers, 1971.

Forman, James. *Sammy Younge, Jr.: The First Black College Student to Die in the Black Liberation Movement.* 1968. Washington, D.C.: Open Hand, 1986.

Fredrickson, George M. *Black Liberation: A Comparative History of Black Ideologies in the United States and South Africa.* New York: Oxford University Press, 1995.

Friedland, Michael B. *Lift Up Your Voice like a Trumpet: White Clergy and the Civil Rights and Antiwar Movements, 1954–1973.* Chapel Hill: University of North Carolina Press, 1998.

Gans, Herbert J. *Deciding What's News: A Study of CBS Evening News, NBC Nightly News, Newsweek, and Time.* London: Constable, 1980.

Garfinkle, Adam. *Telltale Hearts: The Origins and Impact of the Vietnam Antiwar Movement.* New York: St. Martin's Griffin, 1997.

Garrett, Banning and Katherine Barkley, eds. for Ramparts. *Two, Three . . . Many Vietnams: A Radical Reader on the Wars in Southeast Asia and the Conflicts at Home.* San Francisco: Canfield, 1971.

Garrow, David J. *Bearing the Cross: Martin Luther King, Jr., and the Southern Christian Leadership Conference.* 1986. London: Vintage, 1993.

Gitlin, Todd. *The Whole World Is Watching: Mass Media in the Making and Unmaking of the New Left*. Berkeley: University of California Press, 1980.

————. *The Sixties: Years of Hope, Days of Rage*. New York: Bantam Books, 1987.

————. *The Twilight of Common Dreams: Why America Is Wracked by Culture Wars*. New York: Metropolitan Books, 1995.

Guthman, Edwin. *We Band of Brothers*. New York: Harper and Row, 1971.

Hall, Mitchell K. *Because of Their Faith: CALCAV and Religious Opposition to the Vietnam War*. New York: Columbia University Press, 1990.

Hallin, Daniel C. *The "Uncensored War": The Media and Vietnam*. New York: Oxford University Press, 1986.

Halstead, Fred, *Out Now! A Participant's Account of the American Movement Against the Vietnam War*. New York: Monad Press, 1978.

Heale, M. J. *McCarthy's Americans: Red Scare Politics in State and Nation, 1935–1965*. London: Macmillan, 1998.

Hero, Alfred O., Jr. *American Religious Groups View Foreign Policy: Trends in Rank-and-File Opinion, 1937–1969*. Durham, N.C.: Duke University Press, 1973.

Hodgson, Godfrey. *The World Turned Right Side Up: A History of the Conservative Ascendancy in America*. Boston: Houghton Mifflin, 1996.

Hoffman, Abbie and Daniel Simon, eds. *The Best of Abbie Hoffman*. New York: Four Walls Eight Windows, 1989.

Horne, Gerald. *Black and Red: W. E. B. Du Bois and the Afro-American Response to the Cold War, 1944–1963*. Albany: State University of New York Press, 1986.

Hunt, Andrew E. *The Turning: A History of Vietnam Veterans Against the War*. New York: New York University Press, 1999.

Isserman, Maurice and Michael Kazin. *America Divided: The Civil War of the 1960s*. Oxford: Oxford University Press, 2000.

Jacobs, Ron. *The Way the Wind Blew: A History of the Weather Underground*. London: Verso, 1997.

Jeffreys-Jones, Rhodri. *Peace Now! American Society and the Ending of the Vietnam War*. New Haven, Conn.: Yale University Press, 1999.

King, Martin Luther, Jr., *Chaos or Community?* London: Holder and Stoughton, 1967.

Klatch, Rebecca E. *A Generation Divided: The New Left, the New Right, and the 1960s*. Berkeley: University of California Press, 1999.

Kluger, Richard. *Simple Justice: The History of* Brown v. Board of Education *and America's Struggle for Equality*. New York: Vintage, 1975.

Kopkind, Andrew. *America: The Mixed Curse*. Harmondsworth: Penguin, 1969.

Krenn, Michael L., ed. *Race and U.S. Foreign Policy During the Cold War*. New York: Garland, 1998.

————, ed. *The African American Voice in U.S. Foreign Policy Since World War II*. New York: Garland, 1998.

Lang, Serge. *The Scheer Campaign*. New York: W.A. Benjamin, 1967.

Lasch, Christopher. *The Agony of the American Left: One Hundred Years of Radicalism*.1969. Harmondsworth: Penguin,1973.

Lawson, Steven and Charles Payne. *Debating the Civil Rights Movement, 1945–1968*. New York: Rowan and Littlefield, 1998.

Layton, Azza Salama. *International Politics and Civil Rights Policies in the United States, 1941–1960*. New York: Cambridge University Press, 2000.

Levy, David W. *The Debate over Vietnam*. Baltimore: John Hopkins University Press, 1991.

Lewis, David L. *W. E. B. Du Bois: Biography of a Race, 1868–1919*. New York: Henry Holt, 1993.

Liberatore, Paul. *The Road to Hell: The True Story of George Jackson, Stephen Bingham, and the San Quentin Massacre.* New York: Atlantic Monthly Press, 1996.

Ling, Peter. *Martin Luther King, Jr.* London: Routledge, 2002.

Lipset, Seymour Martin. *Rebellion in the University.* Boston: Little, Brown, 1971.

Lynn, Susan. *Progressive Women in Conservative Times: Racial Justice, Peace, and Feminism, 1945 to the 1960s.* New Brunswick, N.J.: Rutgers University Press, 1992.

Lyttle, Bradford, *The Chicago Anti-Vietnam War Movement.* Chicago: Midwest Pacifist Center, 1988.

Mailer, Norman, *The Armies of the Night: History as a Novel, the Novel as History.* 1968. New York: Plume, 1994.

———. *Miami and the Siege of Chicago: An Informal History of the Republican and Democratic Conventions of 1968.* New York: Signet, 1968.

Manis, Andrew. *A Fire You Can't Put Out: The Civil Rights Life of Reverend Fred Shuttlesworth.* Tuscaloosa: University of Alabama Press, 1999.

Marable, Manning. *Race, Reform, and Rebellion: The Second Reconstruction in Black America, 1945–1990.* Basingstoke: Macmillan, 1991.

Marqusee, Mike. *Redemption Song: Muhammad Ali and the Spirit of the Sixties.* New York: Verso, 1999.

Matusow, Allen J. *The Unraveling of America: A History of Liberalism in the 1960s.* New York: Harper and Row, 1984.

McAdam, Doug. *Freedom Summer.* New York: Oxford University Press, 1988.

Meier, August and Elliot Rudwick. *CORE: A Study in the Civil Rights Movement, 1942–1968.* New York: Oxford University Press, 1973.

Miller, James. *Democracy Is in the Streets: From Port Huron to the Siege of Chicago.* Cambridge, Mass.: Harvard University Press, 1994.

Mueller, John E. *War, Presidents, and Public Opinion.* New York: John Wiley, 1973.

Mullen, Robert W. *Blacks in America's Wars: The Shift in Attitudes from the Revolutionary War to Vietnam.* New York: Monad/Pathfinder, 1973.

———. *Blacks and Vietnam.* Washington, D.C.: University Press of America, 1981.

Naison, Mark. *Communists in Harlem During the Depression.* Urbana: University of Illinois Press, 1983.

Nalty, Bernard C. *The Vietnam War: The History of America's Conflict in Southeast Asia.* New York: Smithmark, 1996.

Newfield, Jack. *A Prophetic Minority: The American New Left.* London: Blond, 1967.

———. *Robert Kennedy: A Memoir.* London: Jonathan Cape, 1969.

Nicosia, Gerald. *Home to War: A History of the Vietnam Veterans' Movement.* New York: Crown, 2001.

Parris, Guichard and Lester Brooks. *Blacks in the City: A History of the National Urban League.* Boston: Little, Brown, 1971.

Payne, Charles M. *I've Got the Light of Freedom: The Organizing Tradition and the Mississippi Freedom Struggle.* Berkeley: University of California Press, 1995.

Pearson, Hugh. *The Shadow of the Panther: Huey Newton and the Price of Black Power in America.* New York: Addison-Wesley, 1994.

Peck, Abe. *Uncovering the Sixties: The Life and Times of the Underground Press.* New York: Pantheon, 1985.

Pepper, William F. *Orders to Kill: The Truth Behind the Murder of Martin Luther King.* New York: Carroll and Graf, 1996.

Pfeffer, Paula F. *A. Philip Randolph, Pioneer of the Civil Rights Movement.* Baton Rouge: Louisiana State University Press, 1990.

Plummer, Brenda Gayle. *Rising Wind: Black Americans and U.S. Foreign Affairs, 1935–1960.* Chapel Hill: University of North Carolina Press, 1996.

Powers, Thomas, *The War at Home: Vietnam and the American People, 1964–1968*. New York: Grossman, 1973.

Radosh, Ronald. *Divided They Fell: The Demise of the Democratic Party, 1964–1996*. New York: Free Press, 1996.

Raskin, Jonah. *For the Hell of It: The Life and Times of Abbie Hoffman*. Foreword by Eric Foner. Berkeley: University of California Press, 1996.

Robbins, Mary Susannah, ed. *Against the Vietnam War: Writings by Activists*. Syracuse, N.Y.: Syracuse University Press, 1999.

Rossinow, Doug. *The Politics of Authenticity: Liberalism, Christianity, and the New Left in America*. New York: Columbia University Press, 1998.

Sale, Kirkpatrick. *SDS*. New York: Random House, 1973.

Sandbrook, Dominic. *Eugene McCarthy: The Rise and Fall of Postwar American Liberalism*. New York: Knopf, 2004.

Sayres, Sohnya, Anders Sephanson, Stanley Aronowitz, and Fredric Jameson, eds. *The 60s Without Apology*. Minneapolis: University of Minnesota Press, 1985.

Schlesinger, Arthur M., Jr. *Robert Kennedy and His Times*. London: Andre Deutsch, 1978.

Schudson, Michael. *Discovering The News: A Social History of American Newspapers*. New York: Basic Books, 1978.

Seale, Bobby. *Seize the Time: The Story of the Black Panther Party and Huey P. Newton*. New York: Random House, 1970.

Small, Melvin. *Covering Dissent: The Media and the Anti-Vietnam War Movement*. New Brunswick, N.J.: Rutgers University Press, 1994.

———. *Johnson, Nixon, and the Doves*. New Brunswick, N.J.: Rutgers University Press, 1988.

Thompson, Hunter S. *Fear and Loathing: On the Campaign Trail '72*. 1973. London: Flamingo, 1994.

———. *The Great Shark Hunt: Strange Tales from a Strange Time*. Gonzo Papers 1. 1979. New York: Ballantine, 1992.

Tomasky, Michael. *Left for Dead: The Life, Death, and Possible Resurrection of Progressive Politics in America*. New York: Free Press, 1996.

Tyson, Timothy B. *Radio Free Dixie: Robert F. Williams and the Roots of Black Power*. Chapel Hill: University of North Carolina Press, 1999.

Unger, Irwin with the assistance of Debi Unger. *The Movement: A History of the American New Left, 1959–1972*. New York: Dodd, Mead, 1974.

Urquhart, Brian. *Ralph Bunche: An American Life*. New York: W.W. Norton, 1993.

Van Deburg, William L. *New Day in Babylon: The Black Power Movement and American Culture, 1965–1975*. Chicago: University of Chicago Press, 1992.

Ward, Brian and Tony Badger, eds. *The Making of Martin Luther King and the Civil Rights Movement*. London: Macmillan, 1996.

Wells, Tom. *The War Within: America's Battle over Vietnam*. Berkeley: University of California Press, 1994.

Weisbrot, Robert. *Freedom Bound: A History of America's Civil Rights Movement*. New York: Plume, 1990.

Weiss, Nancy J. *Whitney M. Young, Jr., and the Struggle for Civil Rights*. Princeton, N.J.: Princeton University Press, 1989.

Westheider, James E. *Fighting on Two Fronts: African Americans and the Vietnam War*. New York: New York University Press, 1997.

Williams, Juan. *Thurgood Marshall: American Revolutionary*. New York: Random House, 1998.

Williams, Robert F. *Negroes with Guns*. 1962. Detroit: Wayne State University Press, 1998.

Williams, Yohuru. *Black Politics/White Power: Civil Rights, Black Power, and the Black Panthers in New Haven.* New York: Brandywine Press, 2000.

Wilkinson, J. Harvie. *Harry Byrd and the Changing Face of Virginia Politics, 1945–1966.* Charlottesville: University Press of Virginia, 1967.

Wittner, Lawrence S. *Rebels Against War: The American Peace Movement, 1941–1960.* New York: Columbia University Press, 1969.

Wofford, Harris, *Of Kennedys and Kings: Making Sense of the Sixties.* Pittsburgh: University of Pittsburgh Press, 1992.

Zaroulis, Nancy and Gerald Sullivan. *Who Spoke Up? American Protest Against the War in Vietnam, 1963–1975.* Garden City, N.Y.: Doubleday, 1984.

Zinn, Howard. *A People's History of the United States: From 1492 to the Present.* London: Longman, 1996.

———. *Postwar America: 1945–1971.* Indianapolis: Bobbs-Merrill, 1973.

———. *SNCC: The New Abolitionists.* Boston: Beacon Press, 1964.

———. *Vietnam: The Logic of Withdrawal.* Boston: Beacon Press, 1967.

———. *You Can't Be Neutral on a Moving Train: A Personal History of Our Times.* Boston: Beacon Press, 1994.

Articles and Essays

Adler, Renata. "Letter from the Palmer House." *New Yorker,* September 23, 1967.

Berg, Manfred. "Guns, Butter, and Civil Rights: The National Association for the Advancement of Colored People and the Vietnam War, 1964–1968." In *Aspects of War in American History,* ed. David K. Adams and Cornelius A. van Minnen. Keele: Keele University Press, 1997.

Berkowitz, William R. "The Impact of Anti-Vietnam Demonstrations upon National Public Opinion and Military Indicators." *Social Science Research* 2, 1 (March 1973).

Blumberg, Nathan, "Misreporting the Peace Movement." *Columbia Journalism Review* 9 (Winter 1970–71).

Blumenthal, Richard. "New Politics at Chicago." *The Nation,* September 25, 1967.

Brown, Sam. "The Defeat of the Antiwar Movement." In *The Vietnam Legacy: The War, American Society and the Future of American Foreign Policy,* ed. Anthony Lake. New York: New York University Press, 1976.

———. "The Politics of Peace." *Washington Monthly* 2 (August 1970).

Browne, Robert S. "The Freedom Movement and the War in Vietnam." In *Vietnam and Black America: An Anthology of Protest and Resistance,* ed. Clyde Taylor. Garden City, N.Y.: Anchor/Doubleday, 1973.

Cheng, Charles W. "The Cold War: Its Impact on the Black Liberation Struggle Within the United States." *Freedomways: A Quarterly Review of the Freedom Movement* 13, 3 (third-fourth quarter 1973).

Cochrane, David. "I. F. Stone and the New Left: Protesting U.S. Policy in Vietnam." *Historian* 53, 1 (Spring 1991).

Converse, Philip E., Warren E. Miller, Jerrold G. Rusk, and Arthur C. Wolfe. "Continuity and Change in American Politics: Parties and Issues in the 1968 Election." *American Political Science Review* 63, 4 (December 1969).

Converse, Philip E. and Howard Schuman. "'Silent Majorities' and the Vietnam War." *Scientific American* 222, 6 (June 1970).

Darby, Henry E. and Margaret N. Rowley. "King on Vietnam and Beyond." In *Martin Luther King, Jr.: Civil Rights Leader, Theologian, Orator,* ed. David J. Garrow, vol. 1. Brooklyn, N.Y.: Carlson, 1989.

DeBenedetti, Charles. "Lyndon Johnson and the Antiwar Opposition." In *The Johnson Years*, ed. Robert A. Divine. Vol. 2, *Vietnam, the Environment, and Science.* Lawrence: University of Kansas Press, 1987.

De Groot, Gerard J. "The Limits of Moral Protest and Participatory Democracy: The Vietnam Day Committee." *Pacific Historical Review* 64 (February 1995).

D'Emilio, John. "Homophobia and the Trajectory of Postwar American Radicalism: The Career of Bayard Rustin." *Radical History Review* 62 (Spring 1995).

Drachkovitch, Milorad M. "Radicalization and Fragmentation of the New Left in the United States." In *The New Left in the United States of America, Britain, the Federal Republic of Germany: Interdoc Conference.* The Hague: International Documentation and Information Centre, 1972 (?).

Dudziak, Mary L. "Desegregation as a Cold War Imperative." *Stanford Law Review* 41 (November 1988).

Ellis, Mark. "W. E. B. Du Bois and the Formation of Black Opinion in World War I: A Commentary on "The Damnable Dilemma'." *Journal of American History* 81, 4 (March 1995).

Erskine, Hazel, "The Polls: Freedom of Speech." *Public Opinion Quarterly* 34, 3 (Fall 1970).

Fairclough, Adam. "Martin Luther King, Jr. and the War in Vietnam. *Phylon* 45, 1 (1984). Reprinted in *Martin Luther King, Jr.: Civil Rights Leader, Theologian, Orator*, ed. David J. Garrow, vol. 2. Brooklyn, N.Y.: Carlson, 1989.

———. "Race and Red-Baiting." In *The Civil Rights Movement*, ed. Jack E. Davis. Malden, Mass.: Blackwell, 2001.

Ferber, Michael. "Why I Joined the Resistance." In *Against the Vietnam War: Writings by Activists*, ed. Mary Susannah Roberts. Syracuse, N.Y.: Syracuse University Press, 1999.

Foner, Eric. "Why Is There No Socialism in the United States?" *History Workshop* 17 (Spring 1984).

Garrow, David J. "The King We Should Remember." *Focus* 14 (January 1986).

Garver, Paul and George Abbott White. "What Was Old, What Was New? The New Left and American Exceptionalism." *Journal of American Studies* 22 (April 1988).

Geltman, Emanuel and Stanley Plastrik. "The Politics of Coalition." *Dissent* 13, 1 (January–February 1966).

Gerassi, John. "SANE, Civil Rights and Politics." *Liberation* 11 (July 1966).

Gill, Gerald Robert. "Afro-American Opposition to the United States Wars of the Twentieth Century: Dissent, Discontent and Disinterest." PhD. dissertation, Howard University, 1985.

Goodman, Walter. "When Black Power Runs the New Left." *New York Times Magazine*, September 24, 1967.

Gray, Francine du Plessix. "A Reporter at Large: The Moratorium and the New Mobe." *New Yorker*, January 3, 1970.

Greenlief, June. "Static on the Left: Politics of Masquerade." *Village Voice*, October 12, 1967.

"Gunning Down the Vietnamese." Editorial. *Freedomways: A Quarterly Review of the Freedom Movement* 9, 4, (fourth quarter, Fall 1969).

Gustainis, J. Justin and Dan F. Hahn. "While the Whole World Watched: Rhetorical Failures of Antiwar Protest." In Gustainis, *American Rhetoric and the Vietnam War.* Westport, Conn.: Praeger, 1993.

Hahn, Harlan. "Correlates of Public Sentiments About War: Local Referenda on the Vietnam Issue." *American Political Science Review* 64, 4 (December 1970).

Haines, Herbert H.. "Black Radicalization and the Funding of Civil Rights: 1957–1970." *Social Problems* 32, 1 (October 1984).

Halberstam, David. "When 'Civil Rights' and 'Peace' Join Forces." In *Martin Luther King, Jr.: A Profile*, ed. C. Eric Lincoln. New York: Noonday Press, 1984. Originally published as "The Second Coming of Martin Luther King." *Harper's Magazine*, August 1967.

Hall, Simon. "On the Tail of the Panther: Black Power and the 1967 Convention of the National Conference for New Politics." *Journal of American Studies* 37, 1 (2003).

———. "The Response of the Moderate Wing of the Civil Rights Movement to the War in Vietnam." *Historical Journal* 46, 3 (2003).

Hanberry, Jane Morley, "The Duke Vigil: A Culmination of Issues, 1966–1968." History 196C, Duke University, April 19, 1976.

Harding, Vincent. "Re-Calling the Inconvenient Hero: Reflections on the Last Years of Martin Luther King, Jr." In *Martin Luther King, Jr.: Civil Rights Leader, Theologian, Orator*, ed. David J. Garrow, vol. 2. Brooklyn, N.Y.: Carlson, 1989.

Harrison, Benjamin T. "Impact of the Vietnam War on the Civil Rights Movement in the Midsixties." *Studies in Conflict and Terrorism* 19, 3 (1996).

Hayden, Tom. "The Politics of 'The Movement'." *Dissent* 13, 1 (January–February 1966).

Henderson, Erol A. "The Lumpenproletariat as Vanguard? The Black Panther Party, Social Transformation, and Pearson's Analysis of Newton." *Journal of Black Studies* 28 (November 1997).

Hentoff, Nat, "Them and Us: Are Peace Protests Self-Therapy?" In *The Age of Protest*, ed. Walt Anderson. Pacific Palisades, Calif.: Goodyear, 1969.

Hijiya, James A. "The Free Speech Movement and the Heroic Moment." *Journal of American Studies* 22 (April 1988).

Hopkins, J. Anthony. "Bad Day at Cairo, Ill." *New York Times Magazine*, February 21, 1971.

Horne, Gerald. "Who Lost the Cold War? Africans and African Americans." *Diplomatic History* 20, 4 (Fall 1996).

Janken, Kenneth R. "From Colonial Liberation to Cold War Liberalism: Walter White, the NAACP, and Foreign Affairs, 1941–1955." *Ethnic and Racial Studies* 21 (November 1998).

Jordan, William. "'The Damnable Dilemma': African-American Accommodation and Protest During World War I." *Journal of American History* 81, 4 (March 1995).

Jurma, William E. "Moderate Movement Leadership and the Vietnam Moratorium Committee." *Quarterly Journal of Speech* 68, 3 (August 1982).

Katz, Milton S. "Peace Liberals and Vietnam: SANE and the Politics of 'Responsible' Protest." *Peace and Change* 9 (Summer 1983).

Kelley, Robin D. G. "Identity Politics and Class Struggle." *New Politics* n.s. 6, 2 (Winter 1997).

King, William E. "The Year Duke Turned Activist." *Dialogue*, 24 October 1997.

Kopkind, Andrew. "Anti-Vietnam Politics: Peace Candidates in Oregon, California." *New Republic*, June 4, 1966.

———. "An Exchange on 'Racism'." *New York Review of Books*, December 7, 1967.

———. "They'd Rather Be Left." *New York Review of Books*, September 28, 1967.

Lane, Robert E. and Michael Lerner. "Why Hard-Hats Hate Hairs." *Psychology Today*, November 1970.

Layton, Azza Salama. "International Pressure and the U.S. Government's Response to Little Rock." *Arkansas Historical Quarterly* 56, 3 (Autumn 1997).

Laville, Helen and Scott Lucas. "The American Way: Edith Sampson, the NAACP, and African American Identity in the Cold War." *Diplomatic History* 20, 4 (Fall 1996).

Lemisch, Jesse. "Angry White Men on the Left." *New Politics* n.s. 6, 2 (Winter 1997).

Levy, Peter B. "Blacks and the Vietnam War." In *The African American Voice in U.S. Foreign Policy since World War II*, ed. Michael L. Krenn. New York: Garland, 1998.

Lynd, Staughton. "Coalition Politics or Nonviolent Revolution?" *Liberation* June–July 1965).

Martin, Bradford. "Politics as Art, Art as Politics: The Freedom Singers, the Living Theatre, and Public Performance." In *Long Time Gone: Sixties America Then and Now*, ed. Alexander Bloom. Oxford: Oxford University Press, 2001. 159–88.

McReynolds, David. "Tendencies in the Peace Movement." *New Politics* 6, 2 (Spring 1967).

Meier, August and John H. Bracey, Jr. "The NAACP as a Reform Movement, 1909–1965: 'To Reach the Conscience of America'." *Journal of Southern History* 59, 1 (February 1993).

Michel, Gregg Laurence. "'We'll Take Our Stand': The Southern Student Organizing Committee and the Radicalization of White Southern Students." Ph.D. dissertation, University of Virginia, 1999.

"NAACP Stand on Colonialism and U.S. Foreign Policy." *Crisis* 62, 1 (January 1955).

Newfield, Jack. "Some Things Unite Them, Some Things Divide Them." *Village Voice*, August 19, 1965.

Padmore, George. "The Vietnamese Struggle for Independence." *Crisis* 55, 3 (March 1948).

Page, Benjamin I. and Richard A. Brody. "Policy Voting and the Electoral Process: The Vietnam War Issue." *American Political Science Review* 66, 3 (September 1972).

Pamphile, Leon D. "The NAACP and the American Occupation of Haiti." *Phylon* 47, 1 (1986).

Ridgeway, Andrew. "Freak-Out in Chicago: The National Conference of New Politics." *New Republic*, September 16, 1967.

Robeson, Paul. "Ho Chi Minh Is the Toussaint l'Ouverture of Indo-China." *Freedom*, March 1954. Reprinted in *Freedomways Reader: Prophets in Their Own Country*, ed. Esther Cooper Jackson. Boulder, Colo.: Westview Press, 2000.

Roark, James L. "American Black Leaders: The Response to Colonialism and the Cold War." *African Historical Studies* 4, 2 (1971).

Roche, John P. "The Impact of Dissent on Foreign Policy: Past and Future." In Anthony Lake, ed., *The Vietnam Legacy: The War, American Society, and the Future of American Foreign Policy*. New York: New York University Press, 1976.

Rosenberg, Jonathen Seth. "How Far the Promised Land? World Affairs and the American Civil Rights Movement from the First World War to Vietnam." Ph.D. dissertation, Harvard University, 1997.

Rossinow, Doug. "The New Left in the Counterculture: Hypotheses and Evidence." *Radical History Review* 67 (Winter 1997).

Roszak, Theodore. *The Making of a Counter Culture*. New York: Anchor Books, 1969.

"A Round Table: Martin Luther King, Jr." *Journal of American History* 74, 2 (September 1987): 436–81.

Rowan, Carl T. "The Consequences of Decision." In C. Eric Lincoln, *Martin Luther King, Jr.: A Profile*. New York: Noonday Press, 1984.

Rustin, Bayard. "Dr. King's Painful Dilemma." *New York Amsterdam News*, March 3, 1967. Reprinted in *Down the Line: The Collected Writings of Bayard Rustin*. Introduction by C. Vann Woodward. Chicago: Quadrangle Books, 1971.

———. "From Protest to Politics: The Future of the Civil Rights Movement." In *Down the Line: The Collected Writings of Bayard Rustin*. Introduction by C. Vann Woodward. Chicago: Quadrangle Books, 1971.

Schreiber, E. M. "Anti-War Demonstrations and American Public Opinion on the War in Vietnam." *British Journal of Sociology* 27 (June 1976).

Schuman, Howard. "Two Sources of Antiwar Sentiment in America." *American Journal of Sociology* 78, 3 (November 1972).

Segal, Theodore David. " 'A New Genesis': The 'Silent Vigil' at Duke University, April 5th–12th, 1968." History Honors Thesis, Duke University, April 23, 1977.

Shapiro, Herbert. "The Vietnam War and the American Civil Rights Movement." *Journal of Ethnic Studies* 16, 4 (1989).

"Third Parties: First Things First." Editorial, *Newsweek*, September 11, 1967.

"Third Parties: Black Power." Editorial, *Newsweek*, September 18, 1967.

Tyson, Timothy B. "Robert F. Williams, 'Black Power' and the Roots of the African American Freedom Struggle." *Journal of American History* (September 1998).

Verba, Sidney, Richard A. Brody, Edwin B. Parker, Norman H. Nie, Nelson W. Polsby, Paul Ekman, and Gordon S. Black. "Public Opinion and the War in Vietnam." *American Political Science Review* 61, 2 (June 1967).

Wheeler, Tim. "Remembering Dr. Martin Luther King: 'We Must Get on the Side of Revolution'." *People's Weekly World*, January 18, 1997. Viewed on http://www.hartford-hwp.com/cp-usa/archives97/97–01–18–3.html.

Wilkins, Roger. "What Africa Means to Blacks." *Foreign Policy* 15 (Summer 1974).

Windt, Theodore Otto, Jr. "The Diatribe: Last Resort for Protest." *Quarterly Journal of Speech* 58, 1 (February 1972).

Worthy, William, "Our Disgrace in Indo-China." *Crisis* 61, 2 (February 1954).

———. "Of Global Bondage." *Crisis* 61, 8 (October 1954).

Watson, Denton L. "Reassessing the Role of the NAACP in the Civil Rights Movement." *Historian* 55 (Spring 1993).

Woods, Randall Bennett. "Dixies' Dove: J. William Fulbright, the Vietnam War, and the American South." *Journal of Southern History* 60 (August 1994).

Woodward, C. Vann. "What Happened to the Civil Rights Movement?" *Harper's Magazine*, January 1967.

Young, Whitney M., Jr. "When the Negroes in Vietnam Come Home." *Harper's Magazine*, June 1967.

Yuill, Kevin L. "The 1966 White House Conference on Civil Rights." *Historical Journal*, 41, 1 (March 1998).

Zinn, Howard. "Should Civil Rights Workers Take a Stand on Vietnam?" *Student Voice*, August 30, 1965.

Index

Acknowledgments

During the writing of this book I have received aid and comfort from an assortment of individuals and institutions. These lengthy acknowledgments should be taken as evidence not merely of my own self-indulgence, but also of my considerable good fortune.

This project would not have been possible without the financial support of the Arts and Humanities Research Board, for which I am thankful. Further vital contributions came from the Lyndon Baines Johnson Presidential Library (a Moody Research Grant), the Sara Norton Fund (Cambridge University), and Sidney Sussex College. The incredible generosity of Joseph Carrere and Alison Barbour Fox enabled me to spend the spring semester of 2002 carrying out additional research and writing as a Fox International Fellow at Yale University.

The roots of this project are to be found in Sheffield, South Yorkshire. As an undergraduate newly liberated from the horrors of computer science, I began to acquire an interest in American history while listening to the captivating lectures of Richard Carwardine and Patrick Renshaw (the computer science lecturers never sang!). I became fascinated by the civil rights movement as a student on Robert Cook's excellent special subject, and was ensnared permanently when taking the MA in American History. While Richard and Robert helped me to appreciate the finer points of the historian's craft, Eithne Middleton and Peter Webster provided me with the rent-free housing that made everything else possible. Of the other MA students at Sheffield, Joe Street and Andy Lee deserve special mention for their camaraderie. Others who helped to make the year fun include Emma Barker, Sean Kelly, Graham Macklin, the irrepressible Kevin Watson (more of him later), and Chris Williams.

Like all who have studied American History at Cambridge University in the recent past I owe a great deal to Tony Badger, who has helped build a vibrant and thriving community of Americanists there. Tony encouraged me to write when I did not want to, and offered guidance and criticism without ever being overbearing. He also put me in touch with some of his many contacts in the United States. Through his careful stewardship of the Graduate Workshop, John Thompson helped me to clarify my thoughts, hone my arguments, and develop the confidence to defend my work from the outrageous attacks of my contemporaries. Two of those contemporaries, Andrew Preston and Dominic Sandbrook, were always prepared to engage me in constructive debate and, along with Nathaniel Millett, helped to make the Maypole a great place to watch football. Devin Fergus, François Furstenburg, and Adam Smith offered good advice and good company. Niall Johnson, David Lambert, Matthew Mayer, and Torsten Riotte helped me to come through difficult times with my sanity broadly intact, and I am glad to be able to count them as friends.

The help given to me by staff at various libraries in England—especially the University Libraries of Cambridge, Leeds, the LSE, Sheffield, UCL, and the Newspaper Division of the British Library— is also gratefully acknowledged.

I had the pleasure of spending the 1999–2000 academic year in the United States, where the bulk of the archival research was done. Initially, Liza Millett and Lee Lewis, along with Nat, treated me to some traditional New Jersey hospitality (!) and helped me come to terms with my first, tentative foray in the land of the free.

In Madison, Wisconsin, I was fortunate to meet a large number of people who were helpful beyond the call of duty. Stan Kutler was generous with his time, his advice, and his wallet, and I thank him for going out of his way to support me. Tim Tyson bought me lunch, implored me to drink more, and introduced me to the Harmony Bar, all the time offering wise counsel. He was not obliged to do any of these things but did them anyway, and I am truly grateful. The State Historical Society of Wisconsin is a magnificent institution and its staff were always helpful— but Dee Grimsrud deserves a special mention. Thorsten Wagner and Simon Wendt offered a European perspective when it was needed. Marisa, Catherine, and the many Jennys were lots of fun. Tony Gaughan, Matt O'Brien, John Cornelius, Eric Daniels, and Ted Frantz humored me, drank with me, and, Tony excepted, played soccer with me. Andy could well be the best barman in the whole damned state, and was certainly the best the Silver Dollar ever had. Eric Tadsen immortalized me in the pages of the *Isthmus* and Brian and Laura showed me a proper Thanksgiving. Ben Zarwell drove me around in his van, invited me to lecture to his class, and was generally a top guy. But the topmost were Jordi Getman-Eraso and Patrick Michelson. Always sociable and unwavering in their generosity, they helped make that year in Wisconsin a magnificent experience. I used to joke that this project would be completed despite them. I have come to realize that, in many ways, it was completed *because* of them.

On my trips around America I have enjoyed frequent good fortune. The LBJ Library in Austin, Texas, is so well run that it is only fair to thank the whole staff for their efforts. Dom Sandbrook helped make the time when the library was shut fun. Nat put me up in Florida, gave me good barbecue and liquor, and took me drag racing. Jenn Palmer was hospitable and kind, just as she had been in Cambridge. At the University of Florida Archives, Bruce Chappell was very helpful. When my train to Raleigh, North Carolina, arrived three hours late, Albert Allen III gave me a ride to Durham even though I'd never met him before, thereby proving that Southern hospitality is more than a cliché. The staff of the Duke and UNC Libraries were more than accommodating, while Steve Niven and Brian Ward provided the liquid refreshment that a hard afternoon's researching made absolutely necessary. The archivists in the Library of Congress Manuscript Reading Room responded to my persistent requests with good grace, while Patricia Sullivan bought me dinner and offered me the benefit of her expertise on the NAACP. Louis and Sally Michelson offered a warm welcome in Paducah, Kentucky, and also introduced me to Gladman Humbles, who shared his thoughts on the civil rights movement with me. When I popped over the border to Cairo, Illinois, Patrick tracked down Preston Ewing, Jr., who gave of his time and helped inspire me to write about that fascinating community.

When I returned to America in the spring of 2002, the Preston household (newly augmented by baby Rosie) proved extremely welcoming, and I am grateful to Andrew and Fran for their friendship. All those involved with the Fox program helped make my time at Yale enjoyable, while the staff of Sterling Memorial Library and the archivists at the Swarthmore College Peace Collection were very cooperative. When I visited Montreal for some light relief, Matt Mayer and Blanca were generous hosts.

Kevin Watson deserves a paragraph in his own right. Fittingly for a former actor, he has not restricted himself to just one role. He has been a fellow graduate student and roommate at Sheffield, a displaced Englishman in Wisconsin, and an expert van driver. He has put me up, and put up with me, on occasions too numerous to list even in these protracted acknowledgments. He has helped me through troubled times, made moving house relatively painless, and always been as good a friend as one could want. His own experiences while researching his dissertation on American Primitive Methodism would make an entertaining novel (I firmly believe that too few historians have had to dress up as the king of Jericho in order to gain access to invaluable archives!). While in Wisconsin, I showed him the joys of life in the Mad City and he introduced me to the delights of the small-town Middle West—which include Loren and Arlene Farrey, Steve Calvert, Dean Connors and his bookshop in Mineral Point, Mineral Point itself, Benton, and New Diggings. One of Kevin's historical talks followed by an English tea in a Primitive Methodist church was an experience that I will never forget, no matter how hard I try.

The opportunity to meet some of the people who appear in this book was a particularly enjoyable part of my research, and I am especially grateful to all those who agreed to be interviewed by me. Julian Bond, Courtland Cox, Frank Emspak, and Herbert Hill answered my questions patiently, provided me with valuable information, and helped history come alive. At the April 2000 SNCC conference at Shaw University (expertly organized by Charles Payne), Ivanhoe Donaldson shared some of his experiences with me, while Gloria Clark, Maurice Zeitlin, Mitchell Zimmerman, and Howard Zinn all agreed to telephone interviews. Anne Braden allowed me access to the Braden Papers, Clayborne Carson sent me some important documents on SNCC, and Gwendolyn Patton sent me a copy of her personal archive. Sue Ingledew, Sue Bernard, and their team did a marvelous job of transcribing my tapes.

While I was teaching at Sheffield during the autumn semester of 2001–2002, Hugh Wilford gave sound advice and Robert Cook read chapters and offered encouragement, prescient criticism, and helpful suggestions in equal measure. Colleagues at Sidney Sussex College, Cambridge, and the School of History, University of Leeds, have also been supportive in various ways, while the students who took my Civil rights class in 2003–4 deserve the mention that they asked for! Adam Fairclough gave me useful advice on how to improve the manuscript, especially with respect to Chapter 3.

The staff at the Library of Congress Prints and Photographs Division helpfully supplied four of the photographs that appear in this book. Diana Davies kindly granted permission for the use of her pictures, copies of which were provided by Mary Beth Sigado and Wendy E. Chmielewski of the Swarthmore College Peace Collection. The rest of the photographs were taken by John C. Goodwin. He took time out of his busy schedule to find relevant images and allowed me to use them, and I appreciate his generosity. The University of Pennsylvania Press not only agreed to publish this book, but also sought to make the process as painless as possible. Insightful criticisms from Glenda Gilmore, Maurice Isserman, and Michael Kazin helped to make the book better, while Ellie Goldberg, my editor, Peter Agree, and Alison Anderson answered numerous queries, allayed my fears, and got the job done.

Over the last few years I have had many reasons to be thankful for my friends. In Sheffield, Rick and Tal were (and are) great. Back in

Cheltenham, John Canning, Joe Dodd, Clay, Stuart McGlashan, Chris Ralls, Dan Read, Nigel Sutcliffe, and Paul Thornton were always around when I needed them. Tom Riley offered various dodgy second-hand cars as tempting distractions. Nick E, who's never heard of Cheltenham, is awesome. Over the last dozen years or so, Olive Davies has always urged me to think, to argue, and to be true to myself. An author herself, she generously gave of her time to proof-read an early version of the entire manuscript, for which I am most thankful.

My greatest debt is to my family. My grandparents have constantly supported me and have always been interested in what I have been doing. Angela and Dave have also given valuable encouragement. My sister, Emma, has put up with my teasing with her usual noisy complaints while remaining fantastic. Ian has put me in my place by beating me at squash. My parents, Brian and Marilyn, have not just kept me supplied with hard cash and hot dinners, shifted boxes of books around, and offered lifts to airports (although they have frequently done all of these), but by giving me their love and support they have helped to make everything that I have done possible, and I thank them wholeheartedly.